The Great War and the Death of God

The Great War and the Death of God

Cultural Breakdown, Retreat from Reason, and Rise of Neo-Darwinian Materialism in the Aftermath of World War I

Charles A. O'Connor III

Washington, DC

Library of Congress Control Number: 2014932389
ISBN 978-0-9899169-9-8 paperback

P.O. Box 27420, Washington, DC, 30028-7420
info@newacademia.com - www.newacademia.com

Cover Art. Christopher R. W. Nevinson, *A Bursting Shell*, 1915, Tate Gal-
lery, London, Great Britain.
© Copyright Tate Gallery, London.
Photo Credit: © Tate, London 2013 /Art Resource, NY.

To John F. Haught
for his thirty years of inspirational mentoring

Contents

Illustrations

Cover Art. Christopher R. W. Nevinson, *A Bursting Shell*, 1915.

Preface

I first encountered neo-Darwinian materialism – the view that existence is just mindless matter controlled by blind evolutionary processes – when returning to graduate school in the 1980s. Georgetown University offered a multidisciplinary masters degree in Liberal Studies and I wanted to address some of the "big questions" about life, overlooked in my active Washington D.C. law practice. During the first class of a course entitled "A World in Process," Professor John F. Haught, a lay Catholic theologian, began reading from *Chance and Necessity* by French biochemist Jacques Monod (1910-1976), winner of the Nobel Prize in 1965 for his discoveries in genetics. Monod maintained that science is the only reliable source of objective knowledge; that human beings are just chemical machines, basically just physics and chemistry; and that nature is the product of a mindless evolutionary process, lacking any meaning or purpose. For Monod, the idea of God or transcendent design is just an animist projection of nature's indifferent processes, and humanity is all alone in cosmic darkness. "Do you agree," Haught asked, "and if not, how do you answer Monod?" Now, there was a challenge!

Great scientists, like Monod, with unquestioned brilliance in their respective fields, can be an intimidating group, especially for nonscientists like myself. As a Harvard English major in the early 1960s, I remember being mesmerized by George Wald who taught the basic biology course and later won the Nobel Prize. Pacing back and forth before an amphitheater full of spellbound undergraduates, Wald unraveled nature's molecular mysteries and rhapsodized about nature's handiwork with the authority and charisma of a biblical prophet. The great scientific discoveries about nature and the cosmos since my college days have continued to be awe-inspiring. Scientists have now decoded the human genome, identifying approximately 20,000-25,000 genes and determining the sequences of the 3 billion chemical base pairs that comprise human DNA. They have recently confirmed the existence of the Higgs boson, the so-called "God particle," which contributes mass to subatomic particles and perhaps to the whole universe. And they have extrapolated back into deep time by dating the origin of the universe as almost 13.8 billion years ago. But, after ten years of practicing environmental law, I had found that even the most gifted scientists can advance opinions that overreach their scientific findings.

From the early 1970s, I began cross-examining a broad array of prominent scientists who testified with great assurance about the human and environmental effects of chemicals. It was alarming to observe, however, that many of them advocated (often politically correct) positions that far exceeded their supporting data. This courtroom experience throughout my forty years in private practice made me wary of overbroad scientific claims. Great scientists, it seems, are also susceptible to great hubris. Could this also be the case with those scientists declaring truth of a mindless materialist cosmology having no transcendent purpose? So it was that I approached neo-Darwinian materialism with a healthy skepticism, reinforced upon reading works by some of its impressive critics, like the Harvard philosopher Alfred North Whitehead, not to mention Haught himself.

Some three decades later, while winding down my law practice, I learned that Georgetown was offering a doctorate in liberal studies, and I saw an exciting intellectual challenge for life after law practice. This time my study focused on the cultural impact of World War I–that four-year and four-month cataclysm which most intellectual and cultural historians consider the major turning point in modern Western civilization. I wanted to know how and why the war had affected our civilization. Curiously, as I started to come to grips with Western culture from the Enlightenment through the modern era, materialism kept cropping up, both before and after the war. Could there be a connection between the war, I wondered, and the increasing prominence of neo-Darwinian materialism in the twentieth century? Had the war contributed to the modern secular conviction that science is the only reliable source of truth and that reality is just mindless and purposeless matter? Had the war finally proven the truth of Nietzsche's prewar declaration that God was dead? These questions were fascinating and as yet apparently unexplored. They begged for an answer. All the monotheistic religions teach and depend upon a purposeful and meaningful universe. Indeed, their conviction about the trustworthiness of our world forms the traditional basis for most of our value systems. Have modern scientific developments rendered the Abrahamic faiths and their value systems obsolete and no longer intellectually defensible? Materialism's most outspoken proponents loudly respond to this question with an unequivocal "yes."

The Great War's contribution to the twentieth-century rise of neo-Darwinian materialism is a largely untold tale. Juxtaposing themes from *War Horse* and *Downton Abbey* with those from books such as *The God Delusion* and *Darwin's Dangerous Idea* may seem incongruous, yet I found the relationship not just coincidental but profound. In the aftermath of World War I, Western civilization, facing the prospect of total collapse, searched desperately for sustaining new values, and human reason experienced an unprecedented loss of confidence. Onto this shattered cultural wasteland, materialism rose up, claiming the evidentiary support of objective science, and ever since has stood like a metaphysical colossus over the modern Western consciousness. During the three centuries leading up to the Great War, Western culture had actively engaged with and effectively marginalized this materialist worldview. But after the war, theology, philosophy, literature, and art stopped pondering the nature of reality. Neo-Darwinian materialism promptly filled the resulting cultural vacuum and soon dominated the secular intellectual establishment. Its influential proponents are highly credentialed, irrepressibly outspoken, and aggressively committed to what has been styled the New Atheism. But their claims about the nature of reality have overreached their science. The modern rise of neo-Darwinian materialism to Western cultural supremacy is an unacknowledged and unfortunate legacy of the Great War that deserves telling, and the war's centenary provides an ideal forum.

Acknowledgments

No book of nonfiction with such broad multidisciplinary scope, especially a first endeavor like this, could hope for a responsive readership without considerable academic and critical input. This book is no exception. I have benefited tremendously from the teaching and guidance of numerous professors in the Liberal Studies Program at Georgetown University: John F. Haught grounded me in evolutionary thought and the materialist worldview, Terrence P. Reynolds in Enlightenment philosophy and theology, Francis J. Ambrosio in modern and postmodern philosophy, Michael J. Collins in modern American and world literature, and Percy North in avant-garde Western art. Furthermore, they all offered encouragement and constructive advice on my doctoral thesis, which gave rise to this book. I have also benefited enormously from the substantive and critical input on the thesis from Charles E. Yonkers and Michael Brennan, and on the manuscript for this book from Bernard J. Casey, Charles A. O'Connor IV, and my editor and indexer, Patricia O'Connor of Epiclesis Consulting. In addition, Anne Ridder labored over the thesis citations, and Mark W. Plaeger over the formatting and artwork. Most importantly, my wife Susan F. Plaeger reviewed every draft and offered invaluable advice on the book's content, structure, and wording. For their constructive input and support I remain eternally grateful and hope that the final product lives up to their expectations.

1

Introduction

O judgment! Thou art fled to brutish beasts,
And men have lost their reason!
  — William Shakespeare, *Julius Caesar* (1599)[1]

The modern scientific movement developed in the early seventeenth century confident that the world was divinely created and supervised, and, therefore, ordered and intelligible. This stable, meaningful, and purposeful worldview was the legacy of medieval rationalism and theology. Over the following three centuries, Newtonian physics provided empirical evidence; philosophy and theology provided rational assurance; and literature and art provided aesthetic reinforcement of this teleological worldview. From the Enlightenment to the First World War, this widely accepted conception of reality withstood the religious skepticism of David Hume, the deification of humanity by the Young Hegelians, and the evolutionary theory of Charles Darwin. And then ... Armageddon.

The First World War (1914-18), the Great War as it became known, struck with a vengeance and produced the axial event in modern Western civilization. The war exploded the nineteenth-century myth of unbounded progress, impugned long-standing Enlightenment confidence in human reason, and ended European bourgeois civilization.[2] On August 3, 1914, the eve of Britain's declaration of war against Germany, British Foreign Secretary Sir Edward Grey foresaw the impending destruction of Western civilization: "The lamps are going out all over Europe. We shall not see them lit again in our time."[3] By the war's end, after more than four years of unprecedented human carnage, Grey's dire prophecy appeared to have come true. In *Outline of History* (1920), H. G.

Wells declared that war had altered the world's fixed ideas in a manner "unparalleled in all history."[4] In *England after War* (1923), C.F.G. Masterman called the war "the greatest singular catastrophe which has tormented mankind since the fall of Rome," and worried "whether civilization as we understood it will endure."[5]

The war shook the very foundations of Western civilization, caused an unprecedented revolution in European thought, and cast humanity adrift on a threatening sea of uncertainty. Before the war, the West truly had ruled the world, producing most of its economic output, controlling most of its population and land mass, and developing most of its vibrant culture. Then, in a cataclysmic four-year war, the West devoured itself and sacrificed its young. By the Battle of the Marne after the first month of combat, the war had already cost one million casualties. On a single day, July 1, 1916, when Britain launched the Battle of the Somme, its army suffered 60,000 casualties, including 20,000 dead. This obscene single-day human toll would exceed by six-fold the casualties and by eight-fold the deaths among the Allies on D-Day during World War II, the world's largest amphibious invasion. The major combatant nations in the First World War experienced a casualty rate of about 50 percent and lost a generation of young men. By war's end the grim toll was 15.4 million wounded and 9.45 million dead—averaging 6000 deaths per day over 1500 days.

The war destroyed four Imperial Dynasties (the Habsburgs, the Hohenzollerns, the Romanoffs, and the Ottomans) and caused massive labor, economic, and political strife throughout postwar Europe. It disenfranchised sizable ethnic minorities within the newly created European nations and spawned a virulent indifference to human life. Russia plunged into a barbaric civil war that caused 1.5 million deaths and 6 million total casualties. The Turks perpetrated a genocide that killed one million Armenians.

After a full century of war, we have become somewhat desensitized to such monstrous human casualties. But consider the impact on Europeans, including its leading artists and intellectuals, who greeted war in 1914 with a naïve and near-universal enthusiasm. They found the gruesome butcher's bill in 1918 a hideous embarrassment and unimaginable catastrophe. Cultural disillusionment quickly took hold. Postwar writing and art imagined the war in terms of betrayal, loss, and alienation. The civilian and military leaders had deceived and betrayed the returning soldiers; war dead had become sacrifices rather than heroes. In Ezra Pound's words, young men had died "For an old bitch gone of the teeth, / For a botched civilization." Truly, the Great War changed Western reality.

World War I and the Ascent of Materialism

The war's effect on Western culture and its intellectual elites was profound. In his comprehensive study of the subject, American historian Roland N. Stromberg concluded: "The Western world would never quite recover from the shock; the mind's distrust of itself, of thought and expression and reason, was a permanent legacy, a legacy of skepticism and nihilism and cynicism found in all intellectual circles—one is tempted to say—ever since."[6] Those intellectuals, artists, and writers who endured and survived the war retreated from their prewar cultural heritage and worldview. They distrusted human reason, abandoned metaphysical inquiry, and began to doubt the transcendent. Instead of reengaging the eternal questions about the nature of reality and restoring meaning and purpose to the fractured postwar world, Western culture defaulted. A modern scientific worldview filled the cultural vacuum and came to dominate the shattered postwar landscape.

In his 1925 Harvard lectures, Alfred North Whitehead (1861-1947) labeled this worldview "scientific materialism" and described its deep roots in Western thought.[7] Epistemically, its proponents maintain that the scientific method is the only reliable source of truth about reality, a belief system often called scientism. Metaphysically, they maintain that ultimate reality is merely mindless matter observing physical and natural laws without meaning or purpose. For scientific materialists, this worldview is not a matter of belief but of scientific truth. Consequently, continued belief in a purposeful world, a providential God, or a transcendent power is intellectually indefensible self-delusion. Scientific materialism constituted a paradigm shift in the Western worldview.

For three centuries leading up to the war, Western culture had actively engaged with and effectively marginalized epistemic scientism and metaphysical materialism. But after the First World

War, theology, philosophy, literature, and art disengaged from metaphysical inquiry. Western culture turned inward, focusing on humanity's post-traumatic stress and abandoning its historic curiosity about fundamental reality. Scientific materialism promptly filled the void. It emerged like Phoenix from the ashes of the Great War to become the reigning metaphysic of the twentieth century to the present.[8] This newly emergent reality was impersonal, remorseless, and indifferent, and God was dead. This godless cosmology is the largely unrecognized legacy of the Great War. Scientific materialism still dominates the Western consciousness and spans the Western academic disciplines. Its modern proponents are highly credentialed and irrepressibly outspoken, and the academic and popular presses abound with prominent examples.

World renowned English physicist Stephen Hawking, recently retired from the position at Cambridge University once held by Sir Isaac Newton, declares that complex gravitational forces alone caused the Big Bang, creating the world out of nothing and eliminating the need for "intervention of some supernatural being or God."[9] French biochemist and Nobel laureate Jacques Monod asserts that macromolecules emerged from the pre-biotic soup by chance and produced DNA, the chemical machinery solely responsible for "the origin and descent of the whole biosphere."[10] English zoologist Richard Dawkins credits Darwinian evolution entirely for nature's complexity and creativity and for the emergence of human life and mind, adding that "Darwin made it possible to be an intellectually fulfilled atheist."[11] Basing his materialist worldview on science's acceptance of DNA-based reproduction and Darwinian evolution, American philosopher Daniel C. Dennett dismisses the Judeo-Christian God as a demonstrable illusion—"*that* God is, like Santa Claus, a myth of childhood, not anything a sane, undeluded adult could literally believe in. *That* God must either be turned into a symbol for something less concrete or abandoned altogether." [12]

The death-of-God theme, of course, did not originate in the post-World War I era. Three decades before World War I, Friedrich Nietzsche (1844-1900) had famously proclaimed, "God is dead."[13] But Nietzsche sensed that he had come too soon; Western civilization was not yet ready to receive his momentous critique. Furthermore, Nietzsche's message had a cultural rather than a scientific basis. According to Nietzsche, Christianity and its value system had eroded over the centuries due to its inherent contradictions and had left humanity "straying as through an infinite nothing."[14] Consequently, prewar Christian thinkers construed, even embraced, Nietzsche's message as a call for spiritual renewal.[15] It was only after the war that existential philosophers focused upon Nietzsche's Will to Power, the powerful "drive for distinction," as the ultimate motivating force of all reality, a law of necessity in the impersonal world of fate.[16] Thus, Nietzsche's impersonal and godless metaphysics took hold only in the post-World War I era, complementing and reinforcing the rise of scientific materialism.

The most striking feature of scientific materialism's godless cosmology is its claim of scientific truth. Religion rests upon the fundamental conviction that reality is ultimately trustworthy and transcendently meaningful, despite its empirically inaccessible mystery.[17] For monotheism, exemplified by Judaism, Christianity, and Islam, God is the deepest ground for this ultimate trust in reality and in life's meaningfulness.[18] "Religion can get on with any sort of astronomy, geology, biology, physics," writes Princeton philosopher W. T. Stace, "but it cannot get on with a purposeless and meaningless universe."[19] Consequently, materialism's claim of scientific truth for its worldview poses a profound challenge to theism, to religion, and to their ethical value systems. It calls into question the rational justification and intellectual integrity of a purposeful and meaningful worldview; it substitutes a remorselessly indifferent alternative reality, devoid of absolute truths, ethics, and values; and it leaves humanity alone in cosmic darkness.

Materialism, Scientism, and the Development of Modern Science

Materialism. Metaphysical materialism and epistemological scientism have a long, incremental history preceding their postwar rise to prominence, which warrants preliminary examination. In 1925, Whitehead defined scientific materialism as "the fixed scientific cosmology which presupposes the ultimate fact of an irreducible brute matter, or material, spread throughout space in a flux of configurations. In itself such material is senseless, valueless, purposeless."[20] Scientific materialism (or, simply, materialism) rules out the nonphysical in reality, and reduces all phenomena to their biological and chemical components. Materialism is sometimes clothed in different terminology, such as "scientific naturalism" and "naturalism," intended to recognize nature's emergent phenomena manifested in human life and intelligence.[21] But scientific naturalists, like scientific materialists, consider that these emergent processes of nature, such as life and mind, are wholly explicable in terms of their antecedent physical components.[22] At bottom, they are just physics and chemistry—mindless, valueless, senseless physical "stuff," the chance products of Darwinian evolution. For materialists, all non-naturalistic or theological explanations for these emergent phenomena are groundless, objectionable, and inadmissible.

This view of reality—impersonal, remorseless, and indifferent—is as old as Western civilization. The Greek philosopher Democritus (460-370 B.C.E.), for example, reduced reality to indestructible atoms of matter existing in space or "the void." Yet Whitehead considered the Athenian tragedians, rather than the Greek philosophers, to be the actual fathers of materialism.[23] For the classical Greek tragedians, Necessity (*Ananke*) and Fate (*Moira*)—the determinist world that could not have been otherwise—gave order to reality and even ruled the Olympian gods.[24] There is a crucial difference, however, between the ancient and the modern materialists. The early Greeks accepted the impersonal world of Necessity as a matter of belief; today's materialists proffer it as scientific truth. Modern science, they claim, has demystified existence and explained why there is something rather than nothing and what that something is, namely, mindless matter.

In early nineteenth-century Germany, the materialistic view of nature began to gain prominence as scientific developments in atomic theory, chemistry, and energy indicated the persistence of matter and the constancy of energy.[25] Support for materialism continued to grow in the second half of the nineteenth century with publication of Charles Darwin's *On the Origin of Species* (1859). Ernst Haeckel, for example, used Darwin's evolutionary theory in *Riddle of the Universe* (1899) to argue that life ascended from nonliving carbon compounds due to spontaneous generation and that matter alone constitutes fundamental reality (the so-called monism of matter).[26] Yet Darwin's great advocate Thomas Henry Huxley

(1825-1895) denied that he was a materialist, except when debating his religious opponents; instead, he claimed to be an agnostic, a term which he coined.[27] Furthermore, Yale intellectual historian Franklin L. Baumer cautions against exaggerating materialism's prewar impact. The idea of nature as mechanism was more central to nineteenth-century scientific thought than nature as essentially inert matter. Mechanism also resonated with the industrial age and its interest in machines. It reflected humanity's perceived control over nature and benign view of technology as its beneficial servant.[28] Only after the First World War, when reductionist thinking took hold, did materialism reach its zenith to become the reigning metaphysic of the twentieth century.[29]

Scientism. The history of modern materialism, however, is incomplete without consideration of scientism, its epistemological backbone. American philosopher John Wellmuth defined scientism as "the belief that science, in the modern sense of that term, and the scientific method as described by modern scientists, afford the only reliable natural means of acquiring such knowledge as may be available about whatever is real."[30] English philosopher Bertrand Russell (1872-1970) exemplifies this point of view: "I cannot admit any method of arriving at truth except that of science" and "what science cannot discover, mankind cannot know."[31] This epistemological axiom holds that the various natural sciences, such as physics, chemistry, and biology, reveal the entire field of available and authoritative knowledge about reality, and, further, that the scientific method constitutes the only reliable means of broadening and deepening accurate knowledge.

Scientism shadowed the developments of modern science almost from its origins in the early seventeenth century, with scientists such as Galileo (1564-1642) and Francis Bacon (1561-1624).[32] These pioneering scientists began to study the causes and consequences of observable phenomena rather than to reason philosophically about the nature of things. They asked *how* things happen rather than *why* they happen.[33] They disregarded Aristotle's "final cause" or the *purpose* of phenomena, such as why there is universe, why we exist, and why we search for meaning and truth. Instead, they focused on Aristotle's other three causes (material, formal, and efficient) and questioned how our universe functions and how we human beings function. René Descartes (1596-1650) doubted the products of his senses and even his own existence, but eventually found certitude in his very act of thinking (*cogito ergo sum*). Upon resolving his doubt, Descartes, fatefully, divided reality into mind and matter (thinking and extended substances). Consequently, just as modern science was launching its historic inquiry into the physics and mechanics of nature, Descartes effectively ejected mind from nature.

John Locke (1632-1704) probed the process of human thought, Descartes's *cogito*. He considered the mind an essentially passive substance: ideas originate in sensations, and sensations have either primary qualities (measurable attributes, e.g., shape, motion, solidity, and length) or secondary qualities (subjective attributes, e.g., color, sound, smell, taste). The new mechanistic world of science gave priority to sensation's primary qualities, the measurable characteristics of matter, and ignored sensation's secondary qualities, the subjective characteristics, as scientifically irrelevant. By assuming that these two qualities — the objective and the subjective — were fundamentally different and unrelated, Locke bifurcated the ordinary human experience of nature. Life itself became a dull, colorless, quantitative affair; size, shape, and mass supplanted the beauty, smell, and redness of the rose.

Locke's dissociation of primary and secondary qualities, according to American philosopher William Barrett, planted the seeds of scientism by implying "that the world of physics, the world of material science, gives us the real and basic truth, over against our human world."[34] Furthermore, it separates the observer's mind from the material world. "This primary fact of self-consciousness somehow becomes dubious. Sensations seem such clear and distinct, hard and fast, objective data that the consciousness, or mind, by comparison, begins to look like a fleeting or unwarranted ghost."[35] In short, the mind became unreal, matter became concrete reality, and science became the source of the "really real." Scientism was on its way. Science readily accepted Descartes's dualism between mind and matter, and narrowly focused on Locke's primary qualities — the measurable aspects of matter, such as mass, force, and velocity. For materialists, these measurable aspects of matter became the whole of reality, and science became the sole means of access.

The scientist's inquiring mind, for materialists, seemed irrelevant. Mind was no longer an intrinsic part of nature; it was explainable basically as brain matter, neuronal physics and chemistry. Scientism and materialism had become bedfellows.

The Elements of Inductive and Critical Reasoning

To assess the materialist worldview, Western culture obviously needed to address the philosophic limits of the scientific method, on the one hand, and to advance an alternative worldview consistent with developments in science, on the other. How should culture undertake this formidable task? From the Enlightenment to World War I, both rationalism and empiricism had vied for preeminence as cosmic diagnosticians and interpreters. By definition, rationalism is "the philosophic view that emphasizes the ability of human reason to grasp fundamental truths about the world without the aid of sense impressions"; and empiricism is the philosophic view "that experience is the source of all knowledge, thereby denying that human beings possess inborn knowledge or that they can derive knowledge through the exercise of reason alone." [36] In practice, these two different philosophic viewpoints encroached upon one another even during the period of medieval scholasticism. Whereas St. Anselm (1033-1109) undertook his famous ontological argument for the existence of God entirely within the mind, St. Thomas Aquinas (1225-1274) based his five proofs of the existence of God on a rational understanding of objects within our ordinary experience.[37]

Nature's Order. Rationalism has fallen out of vogue, however, as too remote from the empirical world, especially in light of the new science. Nevertheless, as Whitehead emphasized, medieval rationalism and theology provided the scientific movement of the Enlightenment with the necessary assurance of an ordered and intelligible world and the rational justification for the use of inductive reasoning.[38] Centuries ago David Hume (1711- 1776) had called into question the assumed order of the medieval worldview underlying the inductive reasoning of Enlightenment science. As Hume pointed out, an inductive inference assumes that what we have examined and found to be true will hold true for what we have not examined. The validity of this assumption, Hume notes, depends entirely on the presumed uniformity of nature.[39] Observing that the sun always has arisen in the east does not mean that it will inevitably do so tomorrow. The sun could explode or the Earth could exit its orbit. Although good empirical evidence supports the assumption that nature's past is a reliable guide to its future, it does not prove that assumption. A non-uniform universe is conceivable. This makes Hume's important point that inductive reasoning is not scientifically provable. Inductive reasoning cannot *prove* that nature is uniform without begging the question because it assumes this very premise. It rests upon a fundamental faith in the basic uniformity and intrinsic order of nature. Significantly, medieval rationalism and theology gave Enlightenment science its underlying faith in nature's inherent intelligibility.

Ever since the Enlightenment, of course, science has relied upon inductive reasoning with truly remarkable success. As Whitehead pointed out, however, "induction presupposes metaphysics." Unless you have justified science's underlying philosophical premise that the universe is intelligibly ordered—that the past affords some knowledge of the future, that the cause discloses information about the effect, and that observed connections are not simply arbitrary—"you have made nonsense of induction."[40] Materialists have largely ignored Hume's philosophical mountain.[41] They simply adopted inductive reasoning without rationalizing their instinctive reliance upon nature's fundamental order and intelligibility. Indeed, they use induction illogically to justify their metaphysical conception of the universe as basically mindless—only meaningless, valueless, and senseless physical "stuff" observing indifferent physical and natural laws. As American physicist and theologian Ian Barbour noted, the inductive method, for materialists, was "on its way to becoming an account of the world; a *method* was being turned into a *metaphysic*."[42]

Metaphysical Reductionism. Materialism contains a further methodological flaw; it turns scientific reduction into metaphysical reductionism. Following standard investigative procedure, scientists routinely seek to identify the chemical and physical constituents of some body or organism. Materialists mistakenly assume that the constituents, once identified, constitute the full explanation of the object or entity, whether it is a plant cell, the human mind, or the cosmos. Whitehead identifies this metaphysical error as the Fallacy of Misplaced Concreteness.[43] The materialists have mistaken science's abstract logical reductions for the real world; they have mistaken reductive materialism for ultimate reality. Philosophy, for Whitehead, should serve as "the critic of abstractions." Instead, he says, materialists have "foisted onto philosophy the task of accepting them as the most concrete rendering of fact."[44] The abstractions by which scientific method organizes its research have become a conception of the universe.

Materialists assume that the increasing hierarchies of life—from plants, to animals, to man—are entirely explainable by their most basic constituents. This viewpoint seems myopic. We cannot hope to understand the Mona Lisa's enigmatic smile solely by studying Leonardo's brushstrokes, oil pigments, and poplar panel. Nor can the reader understand the meaning and purpose of this book solely by examining its words, sentence structure, and grammatical usage. As Georgetown theologian John F. Haught explains, "reductionism is just an unproved and unprovable belief that the *only* valid way to understand things as complex as life and mind is to specify their chemical and physical constituents."[45] Although science properly focuses on Locke's primary qualities such as mass, force, and velocity, these measurable aspects of matter are only abstract logical constructions; they are not concrete reality as we observe it.

In the search for truth about reality, Whitehead urges that "we should have in our minds some conception of a wider field of abstraction, a more concrete analysis, which shall stand nearer to the complete concreteness of our intuitive experience."[46] The search requires "dispassionate observation by means of the bodily senses" and comparison of "the various schemes of abstraction which are well-founded in our various types of experience."[47] Thus, sound metaphysical inquiry should take into account a broader empirical observation of the world than just the theoretic and reductive observations of science. Rather, it requires application of critical reasoning to a broad empiricism, which considers the rich and subjective world as we experience it, not just the abstract and objective world as science presents it to us.

Critical Intelligence. Critical reasoning, what Haught calls *critical intelligence*, involves four distinct acts: (1) being attentive to some aspect of experience, (2) being intelligent about understanding that experience, (3) being critical in judging that experience, and (4) being responsible in decision-making about it. In seeking to apprehend the truth of reality, critical intelligence should proceed through humanity's five fields of meaning: (1) *affectivity*, the subjective feeling or mood that stimulates rather than stifles the desire to know, (2) *inter-subjectivity*, the reality of other people's subjectivity that is lost to the world of scientific objectification, (3) *narrativity*, the historical or mythical stories that support our sense of reality, like the Enlightenment trust in the scientific method, (4) *beauty*, the aesthetic experience that historically has aligned beauty and truth from Plato to Keats, and (5) *theory*, the impersonal knowing of subject-object detachment in empirical science.[48]

The true test of a worldview, then, is how well it stands up to scrutiny by one's critical intelligence considering input from a wide experience of existence, or, in Whitehead's characterization, from a broad empiricism. Are the proponents of the worldview being attentive, intelligent, critical, and responsible in assessing the whole of experience? Are the proponents adequately weighing the primal evidence of subjective awareness, interpersonal relationships, aesthetic responses, and historical narratives, as well as objective evidence of theoretic science? Or, are the proponents limiting their critical intelligence solely to theoretic meaning—inferences drawn from objective science—and overlooking the broader empirical evidence available from other means of accessing nature? Finally, are the proponents advancing a worldview consistent with the confidence they place in their minds to pursue the truth about reality? These are the questions to be asked of proponents of any worldview, including materialism.

The Legacy of War on Western Culture, Reason, and Materialism

Materialism's long prewar latency and precipitous postwar ascendancy is a revealing story of cultural breakdown, lost faith in human reason, and anguish over cosmic indifference. Materialism emerged gradually with the burgeoning confidence in science and the scientific method during the Enlightenment, but remained overshadowed by humanity's deeply rooted belief in the divine governance of nature. Prewar philosophy, theology, literature, and art engaged materialist claims by arguing for a broader kind of cognition than merely scientific analysis and for a broader conception of nature than simple mechanism. Thus, Western culture preserved its confident worldview through three centuries until the catastrophe of World War I. To restore meaning and purpose in the shattered postwar world, Western culture needed to reengage the eternal questions about the nature of reality in light of modern scientific advances. In response to a traumatic war, however, theology, philosophy, literature, and art defaulted. They retreated from metaphysical concerns, accepted the dominance of science, and searched for new meaning in a seemingly meaningless universe.

This book tells this multidisciplinary story: How the First World War left Western culture in disarray and helped overturn the dominant centuries-old worldview; how the leading postwar figures in theology, philosophy, literature, and art abandoned metaphysical concerns, and focused instead on an alienated, anxious, and adrift humanity; and how the war overturned the cultural landscape such that it became the natural breeding ground for a long-latent and newly emergent materialist worldview. Materialists offered a spiritually floundering and increasingly secularist society the scientific assurance that their worldview alone was credible, and Western intellectual elites offered no resistance. These elites stood by, unable or unwilling to challenge scientism and materialism, and their passivity ultimately gave rise to materialism's latest manifestation, the very strident New Atheism, which appeared at the turn of the twenty-first century.

The post-World War I rise of materialism is itself a significant development in intellectual history, but it has grave implications for the traditional monotheistic religions and their value system. They rely and depend upon a meaningful and purposeful reality, which materialism has pointedly questioned in light of modern scientific developments. Have these developments left any intellectual room for belief in God? Is the idea of a providential God illusory in light of Darwinian evolution? Yet materialism also raises serious inherent questions about its own justification and internal consistency. Is the mind merely the chance byproduct of a mindless evolutionary process, and if so, can we trust such a mind? What justifies the confidence of materialists in their minds to arrive at truth, and is such confidence consistent with their worldview? Are materialists correct in reducing the human mind solely to brain matter or does the mind have intrinsic reality? Finally, is materialism a science or a philosophy, a scientific truth or a metaphysical belief? This book tells the story of materialism's rise in the post-World War I era, suggests possible answers to all these questions, and concludes by assessing the merits of materialism's claims about reality and the death of God.

2

God, Science, and Reason
in Enlightenment Culture

The year's at the spring,
And day's at the morn;
Mornings at seven;
The hillside's dew-pearl'd;
The lark's on the wing;
The snail's on the thorn;
God's in his heaven –
All's right with the world!
    —Robert Browning, *Pippa's Song* (1841)[1]

Sweet is the lore which Nature brings;
Our meddling intellect
Mis-shapes the beauteous forms of things: –
We murder to dissect.
    —William Wordsworth, *The Tables Turned* (1789)[2]

From the Enlightenment to World War I, scientism and material-ism shadowed the impressive advances in science and technology. Throughout these three centuries, however, philosophy, theol-ogy, and the arts actively addressed questions about the nature of reality, leaving scientism and materialism as just two voices in a vibrant cultural conversation. In the seventeenth century, science emerged amid widespread belief in a divinely created and directed cosmos. René Descartes divided mind from matter after concluding that God, as Infinite Substance, exists and supports them both. In the eighteenth century, when David Hume questioned the limits of reason to understand reality and to prove God's existence, Im-manuel Kant countered with a new epistemology, providing a new foundation for empirical science and for belief in God as a postulate of practical reason and the moral law.

The nineteenth century was more chaotic, with numerous dis-united modes of thought competing to be heard in a civilization increasingly confident about the promise of science and technol-ogy. Yet Georg Hegel relegated science to a niche within history's dialectical unfolding of God, as Absolute Spirit, and the Romantics rejected scientism as an inadequate explanation of the universe. The Romantics also enlarged man's cognitive capability beyond science's narrow analytical mode of thought; they recognized na-ture as a living organism rather than a dead machine. They found "faith in honest doubt" and spiritual assurance in nature. In the sec-ond half of the nineteenth century, Charles Darwin's theory of evo-lution posed an unprecedented challenge to a providential God, purporting to explain all of life, humanity included, as the product of chance mutations, endless time, and natural selection. Even as it led Darwin and many of his followers to agnosticism, theology and philosophy undertook to harmonize evolutionary theory with Christian dogma and divine governance. This chapter tells that three-century story of Western cultural engagement.

The Seventeenth Century and God's Machine

The pioneering scientist Francis Bacon (1561-1624) was intent on freeing natural philosophy (science) to observe and interpret nature unencumbered by medieval scholastic philosophy and revealed theological truths. He adopted the materialism of Democritus and introduced the inductive method for deriving laws of general ap-plicability from observation of particular aspects of nature.[3] Bacon's methodology, however, was pure induction without the use of a working hypothesis to guide his inquiry or selection of facts. Con-sequently his innovative methodology was not yet fully equivalent to the modern scientific method.[4] Nevertheless, Bacon successfully liberated scientific investigation of the natural world from the thrall of medieval scholastic thought. In separating rationalist thoughts about God from the scientific inquiry into nature, however, Bacon had no doubt that God was the author of both.[5]

The father of modern philosophy, René Descartes (1596-1650), undertook an ontological proof of God's existence as a product of pure thought, just as Anselm had done in the eleventh century.[6] Before undertaking his proof, however, Descartes first had to resolve his radical doubt about his own existence. Furthermore, he could not start, as Aquinas had done, with the facts of experience because those facts also remained in doubt. Descartes found his sought-after assurance in his very act of thinking (his *Cogito*), which he could not doubt. Then he proceeded with his ontological proof. He contemplated his consuming idea of an infinite, omnipotent, and perfect Being and determined that it had to originate with God rather than his own imperfect self.[7] Furthermore, such a God would not deceive him about the surrounding world of his senses. Thus, God provided ultimate assurance of all reality. Descartes thereupon divided reality into thinking and extended substances, mind and matter, with God (Infinite Substance) supporting both. In this new Cartesian world, scientists could confidently study nature simply as matter without further concern for Aristotelian metaphysics and theological proofs. Yet, metaphysics, theology, and science all remained deeply inter-connected because God, as Creator of the universe, inspired them all.[8]

The empiricist John Locke (1632-1704) remained a confident Christian throughout his life, finding proof of God's existence in reason and the Bible. In *An Essay Concerning Human Understanding* (1690), Locke reduced theology to certain fundamental truths and accepted scriptural revelation as above, but never contrary, to reason: *"Reason must be our last judge and guide in everything."*[9] Thus, the scientific movement of the seventeenth century, represented by Bacon, Descartes, and Locke, raised no serious question about the existence of God, although it spurred much disagreement about God's nature. The disagreement centered on whether God was an absentee Creator who left the world on its own after setting it in motion, or a providential Creator who remained omnipresent.[10] Yet the seventeenth-century mind considered God immutable and, as Baumer points out, "God's immutability guaranteed the dependability of nature (thought of as God's works) and therefore scientific certainty."[11] Far from being hostile to faith, therefore, scientists of the seventeenth century considered science virtually a religious calling.[12]

Isaac Newton (1642-1727) dominated this divinely ordained universe as the apogee of the scientific revolution. His pronouncements in physics, astronomy, mathematics, and optics became dogma during his life and throughout the next century and a half. In his *Principia* (1687), Newton produced a system of three laws based upon his concepts of velocity and acceleration affecting mass, inertia, and force. First, motion will continue in a straight line absent some countervailing force; second, the force acting on it affects motion's rate of change; and third, two bodies experience an equal and opposite action and reaction.[13] Newton maintained that these principles governed not only the natural world but also the entire universe, controlling the orbits of the planets around the sun and the moon around the earth. So famous and compelling were Newton's achievements, even in his own lifetime, that his younger contemporary Alexander Pope (1688-1744) prepared a famous couplet intended as Newton's epitaph:

> Nature and nature's laws lay hid in night;
> God said, "Let Newton be!" And all was light.

Newton explained scientifically how the universe remained stable and orderly, and provided empirical evidence to complement Descartes's rational proof of a providential Creator.[14]

By the end of the seventeenth century, therefore, reason and sense perception seemed fully aligned in two different schools of thought, identified as rationalism and empiricism. Descartes had resolved his radical philosophical doubt about the potentially deceptive world of the senses, and enabled empirical science to study nature with rationalist assurance of nature's essential intelligibility. Thereafter, each school of thought—rationalism and empiricism—cooperated in the production of knowledge about reality under reason's authoritative direction. Reason remained the final arbiter of conflicts over their respective claims of empirical truth and religious-moral truth. Developments in the eighteenth century, however, perturbed this initial detente between the two schools.

The Eighteenth Century and the Rationalism-Empiricism Debate

During the eighteenth century, rationalism and empiricism drifted apart and developed in isolation from one another. Each fastened upon separate aspects of the dual Cartesian reality—mind and matter—which eventually exposed the weaknesses in the Cartesian system.[15] Empiricists took a path based upon Locke's assertion that all knowledge proceeds from sense experience. Rationalists once again became suspicious of the senses, and empiricists began to question the mind's ability alone to develop reliable knowledge of reality.[16] Then David Hume (1711-1776) shook the common foundation of both schools of thought by questioning the objective validity of *causation*, the idea underlying the rationalist proofs of God and the empiricist faith in inductive reasoning.[17]

Hume's Critique. Hume contended that the idea of causation, like all ideas, must come from a sense impression, but causation per se, he noted, is not an observable quality of objects. Rather, causation is a mere habit of association based upon the contiguous relationship, constant repetition, and temporal order of objects (B repeatedly following A). Observing one billiard ball's striking another billiard ball that subsequently moves does not disclose causation, just the billiard ball's motion after the strike. If Hume is correct that causation lacks any observable impression or necessary connection, then, as Whitehead points out, cause and effect become *"entirely arbitrary* connections."[18] Furthermore, without rational assurance of causation, the validity of science itself is called into question. Then, as Barrett elaborates on Whitehead's point, "the whole edifice of science—that stunning edifice of the New Science, of which Hume's contemporaries stood in awe—becomes merely a highly formal expression of human habit."[19] This sense of matter's arbitrary connections is characteristic of the materialist view of reality.

Hume also contended that *substance* has neither existence nor meaning since no one has any impression of substance per se. The five senses merely convey a collection of the object's qualities, not its essential substance. Finally, Hume denied that individuals can have any idea of *self* since they have no single impression invariably identified with themselves. Rather, the self is just a collection of different impressions received over time. It is from our memory of this bundle of different prior sense impressions that we infer continuous identity.[20]

In short, Hume challenged both Cartesian rationalism and Lockean empiricism as reliable bases for knowledge of reality. Furthermore, Hume detached both the acts of thinking and experiencing from the individual self—thoughts and sensations became disembodied. As Barrett observes, Hume has succumbed to "the philosopher's temptation to take a purely spectator view of the mind, forgetting that he himself is a participant. He stands outside the self and looks for it as some kind of sensory datum, forgetting that he himself has launched the search and is involved in it throughout."[21] Materialists perpetuate Hume's metaphysical oversight by discounting their own subjectivity and critical intelligence as if they were not intrinsic parts of reality.

Armed with this epistemology, Hume took aim at so-called "religious philosophers" to show that their proof of God based upon the order in nature is contrary to reason.[22] We can infer no more about a cause than its effect, he argues. Ten ounces raised on the scale proves only that the counterbalancing weight is more than ten ounces; it proves nothing else about the characteristics of that weight.[23] Consequently, any God or gods responsible for the existence and order of the universe possess only "that precise degree of power, intelligence, and benevolence, which appears in their workmanship"; any further attributes accorded to God are pure speculation.[24] Pointing to evil and disorder in the universe, Hume also argued that the rationalist inference about God as a perfect being who providentially guides the universe, rewards good, and punishes evil is a palpably unjustified idea. It lacks support in human experience.[25] At the end of *An Inquiry Concerning Human Understanding* (1748), Hume concluded that theological and metaphysical positions that contain no quantitative and numerical facts are "nothing but sophistry and illusion."[26]

Although Hume's skepticism came down just as hard on empiricism as on rationalism, science remained indifferent to his critique. Whitehead attributes science's indifference to its instinctive faith in the order of things and its fundamental anti-rationalism.[27] Instead, the rationalist Immanuel Kant (1724-1804) picked up Hume's gauntlet to defend both schools of thought. On behalf of rationalism, Kant argued that philosophic knowledge requires some *a priori* judgments beyond empirical generalizations from sense experience; on behalf of empiricism, he argued that innate ideas which lack supporting sense experience are vacuous.[28] While the mind actively shapes our perceptions of phenomena, mental constructs that ignore experience lack genuine value.

Kant's Rebuttal. Kant addressed Hume's critique by developing a new theory of knowledge, his self-styled "Copernican revolution" in epistemology, which challenged both rationalist metaphysics and empirical science as credible means to address transcendental questions about God and reality. Whereas Hume and Locke considered the mind a passive receptor of external stimuli (a *tabula rasa*), Kant maintained that the mind is an active, albeit limited, cognitive faculty. The mind actively shapes the material of sensory experience (*phenomena*) using conceptual forms, or synthetic *a priori* categories, like substance and causation. The concept of causation, for example, underlies the inductive method; it enables science to predict future results based upon past experience. Although *a priori* categories help shape our knowledge of *phenomena*, they do not enable us to analyze *noumena*, which Kant calls *things-in-themselves* or essential reality. For Kant, the mind lacks the experiential and cognitive capacity for such metaphysical analysis.[29]

In Kant's new epistemology, however, reason can produce "transcendental ideas" with important "regulative" value in guiding human conduct.[30] Reason can elucidate and direct moral conduct because ethics is a matter of practical rather than conceptual understanding.[31] For Kant, the moral law is not the product of empirical experience or pure reason, or of church mandates or divine law. Rather, the moral law arises from practical human reason as a legislative principle, which Kant calls the *categorical imperative*.[32] Whereas belief in God previously provided the grounds for the traditional morality, Kant now maintains the exact converse: "it is reason, by means of its moral principles, that can first produce the concept of God," and it is "trust in the promise of the moral law" that constitutes religion.[33] Thus, Kant's categorical imperative does not prove God's existence; rather, it provides the moral grounds for postulates of God's existence and the soul's immortality.

Kant explains how the human mind actually works to accumulate, categorize, and organize the sense impressions and thereby refutes the empiricist idea that the mind is a *tabula rasa*, a blank slate on which sensations imprint ideas. Picturing the mind simply as responsive to bundles of sense impressions, Hume overlooks the mind's active and creative function. Thus, Kant's epistemology, by comparison to Hume's, is more detailed and (one might conclude) more empirical. Reason, Kant insists:

has insight into that only, which she herself produces on her own plan, and that she must move forward with the principles of her judgments, according to fixed law, and compel nature to answer questions, but not let herself be led by nature, as it were in leading strings, because otherwise accidental observations, made on no previously fixed plan, will never converge towards a necessary law, which is the only thing that reason seeks and requires.[34]

In short, the scientific mind is not passive but active; science and technology "put nature to the rack," in Francis Bacon's famous metaphor, and compel nature to provide answers to its questions.

By emphasizing that the mind actively organizes our understanding of nature, Kant implicitly questions the materialist idea that the mind is just the product of matter. Rather, the mind creatively shapes our understanding of the material world, the world of phenomena; in a loose sense, it creates the phenomenal world, just as God created the noumenal world. Kant insists, moreover, that scientific concepts about nature and scientific technology for investigating nature are just mental constructs, analytical tools, used to probe the phenomenal world of nature; they cannot elucidate the noumenal world of essential reality. How ironic that materialism, which depends upon the scientific mind for its understanding of nature, has accorded the mind no intrinsic reality. For materialists, as Barrett explains, "the mind becomes, in one way or another, merely the passive plaything of material forces. The offspring turns against its parent. We forget what we should have learned from Kant: that the imprint of mind is everywhere on the body of this science, and without the founding power of mind it would not exist."[35]

By characterizing the mind as an aggregation of atomistic sense impressions, Hume divorces the mind from any wider concrete context, just as materialists do today. Kant, by contrast, places the human mind in its cosmic setting—the moral individual resides within the human community, seeking meaning as part of a larger whole. In accordance with the categorical imperative, Kant maintains that everyone should "act only on the maxim whereby thou canst at the same time will that it should become a universal law," and should "treat humanity, whether in thine own person or that of another, in every case as an end withal, never as a means."[36] In other words, dutiful action must constitute a universal standard (not an exception to that standard); it must recognize and honor another's moral autonomy (the right to make his or her own moral decisions); and it must satisfy the objective test of fairness and justice.[37] Thus, for Kant, moral duty is an aspect of man's overall ethical being and has significance within the larger universe. Inevitably, our convictions about the universe—whether it is meaningful and purposeful or mindless and indifferent—shape our morality. Clearly, the Kantian cosmos is not indifferent to man's ethical struggles.[38]

Kant even addresses man's sense of beauty from the perspective of a moral person because the moral person is drawn to cosmic beauty and wonder: "Two things fill the mind with ever new and increasing admiration and awe, the oftener and more steadily we reflect upon them, the starry heavens above me and the moral law within me."[39] In other words, the individual drawn to the beauty of nature, the divinely inspired universe, is likely to be a moral person. Here again, Kant is not attempting to use the aesthetic response to nature as a theological argument from cosmic design. Concepts of God and essential reality, for Kant, transcend the bounds of finite human thought. But, even though metaphysics lies beyond reason's capability, the aesthetic response to the universe is a valuable mode of human cognition, which points to the individual's cosmic setting. Thus, Kant gave critical intelligence a central place and an active role in the search for meaning. In addition, he employed a wide empiricism that found cosmic meaning in individual subjectivity, ethical conduct, and aesthetic sensibility. As a result, Kant embraced and harmonized science, reason, morality, and aesthetics—all essential elements of his fundamentally purposeful, meaningful, and divinely inspired world.

Hegel's Dialectic. Kant's successor Georg Hegel (1770-1831) transformed Kant's moral philosophy into metaphysical idealism, the dialectical march of all history toward truth. Hegel called it an *aufgehoben* in philosophic thought, connoting both replacement and preservation at a higher level.[40] Theologian Stephen D. Crites described it as "a philosophy of reconciliation in which nature and history, religion, politics, and culture are integrated in a single vision of the truth."[41] Hegel found Kant's position concerning the noumenal world inherently contradictory. How can you know something exists and yet consider it unknowable? To the contrary, asserted Hegel, the human mind *can* know the thing-in-itself. Furthermore, Kant's mental categories such as cause and effect have objective, independent being; reality itself is rational and the rational is real. Indeed, everything in the world is a product of mind, for Hegel, and all aspects of human thought, science included, are the unfolding of Absolute Spirit (God).[42] He rejected the materialist idea that reality consists of different configurations of indestructible atomistic matter and, instead, maintained that reality is the dynamic and organic interrelationship of nature, human reason, and the Absolute—all connected in Thought itself.[43]

In his historical dialectic, Hegel envisioned the human mind passing through stages of art, religion, and philosophy toward the ultimate contemplation of Absolute Spirit. Humanity's aesthetic sense generates a feeling of the Absolute as beauty. This aesthetic response leads in turn to religious thought, which pictures or represents the Absolute as spirit. Finally, religious thought turns to philosophical thought, which transcends the representational to become pure thought and worship of the Absolute.[44] Thus, history becomes an irreducible category of reality, governed by reason and proceeding teleologically toward fulfillment in God. Hegel's worldview, moreover, takes into account humanity's various means of accessing existence—the subjective search for meaning, the interpersonal (ethical) concern for humanity's general welfare, the aesthetic appreciation of the Absolute as beauty, and the historical sense of participating in the dynamic unfolding of thought.

Hegel's idealistic world of progressive change, however, remained largely divorced from nature and materialism, although he explicitly rejected the latter. Instead, Hegel swallowed up ideas like scientism and materialism within the triadic movement of his historical dialectic of thesis, antithesis, and synthesis. Consequently, Whitehead properly faulted philosophic idealists like Hegel for having rendered "the world of nature [as] just one of the ideas somehow differentiating the unity of the Absolute" and for having "conspicuously failed to connect, in any organic fashion, the fact of nature with their idealistic philosophies."[45] Basically, Hegel failed to recast a conception of nature to comport with his overall conception of reality. Instead, he simply absorbed ideas like scientism and materialism within his overarching metaphysics. Nevertheless, Hegel did provide a compelling, non-materialistic worldview, and Hegelian thought remained the reigning philosophy at Oxford through the turn of the twentieth century.[46]

The Nineteenth Century, Cultural Anarchy, and God

Matthew Arnold (1822-1888) characterized the nineteenth century as a period of "anarchy," and Yale intellectual historian Franklin L. Baumer agreed that anarchy "*was* one of the principal and most significant developments in nineteenth-century thought."[47] In his essay "Literature and Science" (1882), Arnold identified scientific specialization and fragmentation of knowledge as the primary centrifugal force in the nineteenth century. He urged study of the humanities as the appropriate antidote to synthesize Western thought and "to relate the results of modern science to our need for conduct, our need for beauty."[48] Baumer attributed the era's disunity and crisis to four complex and competing styles or worlds of thought: the Romantic Movement, the New Enlightenment, the Evolutionary World, and the *Fin de Siècle*.[49] Despite the cultural anarchy and increasing hegemony of science, however, scientism and materialism still faced significant opposition from nineteenth-century men of letters all over Europe.[50]

The century opened with the powerful Romantic Movement. The Romantics re-examined basic philosophical questions using an enlarged cognitive capability beyond rational-empirical thought and describing nature as an organism rather than a mechanism. The second world of thought, the New Enlightenment, overlapped Romanticism until mid-century and consisted of the following groups: English utilitarians, like John Stuart Mill (1806-1873) who sought to imitate the French *philosophes* with their criticism of religion and their optimism about history and human nature; French positivists, like Auguste Comte (1798-1857) who attempted to answer all questions scientifically and to deify humanity; German Young Hegelians, like Ludwig Feuerbach (1804-1872) who criticized Hegel for elevating thought over human experience and for overlooking hu-

manity's self-alienation; and finally artistic realists, like the painter Gustave Courbet (1819-1877) and the novelist Charles Dickens
(1812-1870) who portrayed concrete individuals in the real world
as these artists actually observed it.[51] The most optimistic style of
the nineteenth century thought, the New Enlightenment, rejected
metaphysics and religion, embraced scientism, though not necessarily materialism, and, by contrast with Romanticism, considered
science to be man's primary means and hope for an ordered and
better world.[52]

Darwinian Evolution, the third world of thought, was effectively a second phase of the New Enlightenment, picturing nature
as a mindless mechanism and generating an age of agnosticism.
Darwinism, according to Baumer, contributed to the heightened
disunity of the fourth world of thought, the *Fin de Siècle* period. Yet,
before World War I, Nietzschean doubts about God and positivist characterizations about mechanistic nature never overcame the
Enlightenment assumptions about the divinely ordered world.[53]
With respect to scientism and materialism, the worlds of Romanticism and Darwinian Evolution are most important and are addressed separately below. But before reaching them, however, the
nineteenth-century crisis of faith, which arose quite independently
of materialism, warrants separate discussion.

The Crisis of Faith. Throughout the nineteenth century, religious
faith came under attack from within and without, and Hegelianism provided the primary point of contention. Søren Kierkegaard
(1813-1855), a Danish Christian writer, sought to unmask and defeat all forms of rational theology, both the moral idealism of Kant
and the rational idealism of Hegel, and to awaken belief in a more
authentic Christianity. Hegel had found concordance between religion and philosophy: Christ's death and resurrection began the
dialectical process by which Absolute Spirit expresses itself in history. Thereafter, human reason alone could discover the ultimate
truths reposing in the dialectical process.[54] Kierkegaard disputed
both of Hegel's contentions.

Kierkegaard contended that the mind is incapable of objectively
proving the existence of God from Christ's miraculous works, from
the universe's apparent order, or from self-knowledge.[55] Rather, it
requires "a leap of faith." Indeed, Kierkegaard argued that Hegel's

dialectical method for determining the past and prophesying the future is a foolish tautology. History results from freely acting causes, he said, not from necessity.[56] Furthermore, Christian revelation focuses on the moment of Incarnation when God became man. For Kierkegaard, this revelation is an Absolute Paradox beyond rational proofs; it is a matter of faith and personal experience of the divine. Therefore, the Hegelian project of speculative idealism — ascertaining ultimate truth by applying reason to history's dialectical processes — is both logically flawed and fundamentally incompatible with Christian orthodoxy.[57] Instead, Kierkegaard challenged the individual to become a "knight of faith," to place himself or herself "in an absolute relation to the absolute," and to recognize that genuine "Christianity is the absurd, held fast in the passion of the infinite."[58] Kierkegaard's influence remained negligible outside of Denmark until after World War I, when his writings profoundly affected Karl Barth and the Crisis Theologians.[59]

Ludwig Feuerbach (1804-1872), a student and critic of Hegel, believed that Hegel's religious speculations about God revealed humanity's own self-alienation.[60] In *The Essence of Christianity* (1841), Feuerbach contended that Hegel's speculative idealism elevated thought over human experience, tied philosophy excessively to theology, and overlooked the psychological nature of human self-alienation. Standing Hegel's speculative idealism on its head, Feuerbach argued that humanity's thoughts about God effectively reveal its own nature and self-knowledge.[61] Religion must be understood anthropologically, admonished Feuerbach, making his case for a new religion focused, not on God, but on humankind's own alienated self. For Feuerbach, Christianity basically represented humanity's self-consciousness at work; it disclosed humanity's unconscious hopes and fears and its awareness of personal finitude. God was essentially humanity's projection of its idealized self, a product of human self-estrangement, which was sapping humanity's creative energies. By becoming aware of Christianity's true nature and rejecting it for a human religion, human beings can recognize their own ideals and their true selves.[62] Thus, Feuerbach, and the other "left-wing" or "young" Hegelians, divinized humanity and humanized religion, freeing humankind of its "pathologic" interest in theology and metaphysics.

Hegel's thought spurred not only anti-Christian movements like the Young Hegelians, but also Christian reform movements like the "right-wing" or "center" Hegelians (neo-Hegelians, in Britain). These reform movements considered Hegel's speculative idealism the appropriate tool for restructuring Christianity to bring it into alignment with modern experience.[63] Thus, at the one end of these reform movements within Christianity stood the right-wing or neo-Hegelians, who embraced Hegel's thought, and at the other end stood Kierkegaard, who rejected it as a misguided distraction from pursuit of the Christian ideal. All these movements, however, from Kierkegaard to the right-wing, center, and left-wing Hegelians, concerned the nature and meaning of Christianity; they did not concern the nature of the cosmos or metaphysical issues. Instead, they centered on Christianity and the human condition.

Honest Doubt. The questioning and consequent erosion of faith extended beyond philosophy to the world of letters. In his poem "Dover Beach" (1851), Matthew Arnold described his isolation, loneliness, and despair over the receding Sea of Faith, which he hears "Retreating, to the breath / Of the night-wind, down the vast edges drear / And naked shingles of the world."[64] His final stanza is a desperate portrait of the human condition:

> Ah, love, let us be true
> To one another! for the world, which seems
> To lie before us like a land of dreams,
> So various, so beautiful, so new,
> Hath really neither joy, nor love, nor light,
> No certitude, nor peace, nor help for pain;
> And we are here as on the darkling plain
> Swept with confused alarms of struggle and flight,
> Where ignorant armies clash by night.[65]

In his crisis of faith, Arnold found himself "wandering between two worlds, the one dead, / The other powerless to be born."[66]

In *In Memoriam A.H.H.* (1850), composed over a period of 16 years, Alfred, Lord Tennyson (1809-1892) laments the death of his closest friend and sister's fiancé Arthur Hallam at the age of twenty-two. *In Memoriam* expresses Tennyson's religious doubts and the doubts of his age. The poem begins in solid faith:

Strong Son of God, immortal Love,
Who we, that have not seen thy face,
By faith, and faith alone, embrace,
Believing where we cannot prove.[67]

But at midpoint the poet descends into dark despair, like "An infant crying in the night," questioning the apparently wanton loss of life in a world where God and Nature seem at strife and Nature is "red in tooth and claw."[68] Tennyson tries to regain that initial faith:

I stretch lame hands of faith, and grope,
And gather dust and chaff, and call
To what I feel is Lord of all,
And faintly trust the larger hope.[69]

Toward the poem's end, however, Tennyson comes to accept his spiritual struggle and reaffirm his faith:

There lives more faith in honest doubt,
Believe me, than in half the creeds.[70]

Spiritual tension was not limited to the lay poets, but extended to religious poets as well. In his early poetry, the Jesuit priest Gerard Manley Hopkins (1844-1889) celebrates spiritual intensity in "The Windhover" (1877), divine providence in "God's Grandeur" (1877), and divine inner presence in "Felix Randal" (1880).[71] But in his late poems (the "terrible sonnets"), Hopkins experiences his dark night of the soul, a solipsistic despair of knowing anything but himself. In "I Wake and Feel the Fell of Dark, Not Day" (1885), Hopkins sees his entire life as a bitter nightmare ("I am gall, I am heartbroken"), his desperate cries to God as unanswered "dead letters," his troubled flesh as cursed, and his spirit as "lost." His priestly vocation seems over and wasted ("God's most deep decree / Bitter would have me taste: my taste was me"), and his creative spirit seems dulled and soured ("Selfyeast of spirit a dull dough sours").[72] Ultimately, Hopkins' romantic focus on his own creative imagination left him feeling alone, isolated, and estranged from the world that previously had revealed God's grandeur.

At the opposite extreme is the godless, materialist world of Thomas Hardy (1840-1928).[73] In his novels, Hardy's characters suffer at the whim of an indifferent universe that manipulates their lives and thwarts their aspirations. Similarly, in his poems like "Hap" (1866), Hardy asserts that chance rules the universe—not a vengeful God whom we could stoically endure, but "[c]rass Casualty" and "dicing Time," which kill both our joys and hopes. Unlike Hopkins, Hardy finds no romantic inspiration in nature; even the thrush's caroling offers no "blessed Hope."[74] In "Channel Firing" (1914), written presciently just four months before the outbreak of World War I, Hardy depicts an ironic God, speaking to skeletons in a church graveyard. Aroused from the dead by naval gunnery practice in the channel, the skeletons confuse the gunfire for the trumpets heralding judgment day. God assures them that the world has not changed, men are no better, and nations still gird for bloody war: "The world is as it used to be: / All nations striving strong to make / Red war yet redder."[75]

Hardy and the Young Hegelians notwithstanding, God was still in his heaven for most cultural elites, though all was not well in chaotic nineteenth-century Europe. Except for the unusual and limited exceptions like Hardy, however, the cause of spiritual doubt and anguish about Christianity that persisted throughout the century was mostly personal or least anthropocentric, rather than materialist or cosmological in origin. The disunited and anarchic world of nineteenth-century thought constituted a spiritual crisis arising from "honest doubt." But Western culture, beginning with Romanticism, kept scientism and materialism in check throughout the century and until World War I.

The Romantic Revolt against Scientism and the Newtonian Machine

Scientism grew rapidly during the Victorian era, especially between the 1820s and 1880s, according to Baumer. It attempted "to answer all questions scientifically, to turn everything possible into a science, including in some respects even the humanities, and to apply the principles of science to the world of action."[76] Auguste Comte (1798-1857) embodied this trend by developing a scientifically oriented philosophy, called *positivism*. Positivism intended to reform philosophy and society by studying the observable facts and formulating the scientific laws that govern relations among them.[77] Comte's scientism, however, was neither reductionist nor materialist since he did not attempt to explain all phenomena in terms of biology and chemistry.[78] Positivist knowledge, for Comte, constitutes the third and ideal stage in the historical evolution of the human mind. The two prior, developmental stages were theological and metaphysical. In the positivist stage, scientists begin to ask the "how" rather than the "why" questions.[79] In this last stage, Comte thought positivism would transform society by bringing about an intellectual, social, and ethical ideal which raised humanity to the status of God, the so-called Great Being.[80]

During the first half of the nineteenth century, the Romantics forcefully responded to positivism and to the scientific conception of nature as mechanism.[81] They had clear answers to the leading questions about how the mind comes to understand the world and what makes up that world.[82] The Romantics rejected empirical science as too crabbed a viewpoint and broadened man's cognitive engagement with the world to encompass the full range of human experience. They also rejected science's mechanistic model as a myopic and devalued conception of the world. Instead, the Romantics gave full rein to every aspect of human nature—rational, emotional, and unconscious alike—and they considered nature as organic rather than mechanistic. Nature possessed intrinsic aesthetic and spiritual value and was no mere machine. Theology and poetry led the Romantic revolt.

Schleiermacher and Blake. Friedrich Schleiermacher (1768-1834) set Protestant theology on an entirely new foundation based upon personal experience. He redefined religion as a personal response and surrender to the immensity of the Universe. In his *Second Speech, The Nature Of Religion* (1799), Schleiermacher separated religion from metaphysics and ethics and from scientific knowledge and theories about God's relationship to man. Instead, Schleiermacher called religion both an *active* quest and feeling for the Infinite within the world itself and also a *passive* surrender to the whole of existence.[83] For Schleiermacher, "true science is complete vision; true practice is culture and art self-produced; true religion is sense and taste for the Infinite."[84] Both the intuition and feeling for the "unity and difference of religion, science and art," according to Schleiermacher, required that "you must know how to listen to yourselves before your own consciousness."[85]

For Schleiermacher, human life has three interrelated faculties—perception, activity, and feeling—and religion resides in the sphere of conscious feeling.[86] Indeed, he equated religion to feeling and piety. Piety is "the result of the operation of God in you by means of the operation of the world upon you"; it consists "purely of sensations and the influence of all that lives and moves around, which accompanies them and conditions them."[87] Since mankind is part of the universe, moreover, "the religious man must first, in love, and through love, have found humanity" because love for humanity is necessary to receive the life of the World-Spirit.[88] This sense of oneness with all humanity, says Schleiermacher, engenders an "unaffected humility," an intuition of "fellowship with others," and an experience whereby a "single nature embraces all human nature."[89]

Schleiermacher's revolutionary theology redirected the Enlightenment focus away from rational proofs of God's existence and its empiricist rebuttals, away from debate over the authenticity of miracles and the importance of ecclesiastical dogma and ritual, and away from Kantian concern for duty and its derivative postulates about God and immortality. Instead, religion points toward a personal response to the mystery of Creation. It consists of the pious individual's aesthetic feeling about the Universe. In "Auguries of Innocence" (c. 1803), the Romantic poet William Blake (1757-1827) beautifully captures Schleiermacher's sentiment:

> To see a world in a grain of sand
> And a heaven in a wildflower,
> Hold infinity in the palm of your hand
> And eternity in an hour.[90]

In addition to being a personal response and surrender to God's Creation, religion, for Schleiermacher, also entailed fostering such piety in others. He emphasized the fellowship of knowledge and feeling, contemplation and intuition, self-consciousness and human empathy. Significantly, he distinguished the religious sensibility from "the pure impulse to know."[91] Thus, reason, for Schleiermacher, is not limited to the theoretic understanding of science but takes into account subjective feeling, aesthetics, and interpersonal involvements. As a result, Schleiermacher perceived reality as alive with meaning, purpose, and spirituality—a God-given wonder. His revolutionary theology dominated liberal Protestantism until Karl Barth led the rebellion of Crisis theologians after World War I.[92]

Romantics, like Schleiermacher and Blake, reacted against an epistemology that limited human knowledge to inductive generalization from measurable sense experience and against a science-based metaphysic of the universe as merely a giant machine. For Blake, Isaac Newton symbolized such narrow scientific theorizing, which mechanized reality and demeaned human life. In his watercolor print *Newton* (1795), Blake pictures Newton sitting in the center on an algae-covered rock outcropping, at the bottom of the sea (Figure 1). Newton turns his back to nature's beautiful flora and fauna, while bending over, looking down, and drawing with a compass upon a scroll. He apparently is trying to fathom the whole of reality solely by means of instrumental measurement and induc-

Figure 1. William Blake, *Newton* (1795), Tate Gallery, London.
Photo Credit: Tate, London/Art Resource, NY

tive reasoning. In *Newton*, Blake graphically rejects this narrow empirical approach to reality.

In his poem *Jerusalem* (1804), Blake targets Locke as well as Newton and makes the same points about scientism and mechanism explicitly:

> I turn my eyes to the Schools & Universities of Europe
> And there behold the Loom of Locke whose Woof rages dire
> Washd by the Water-wheels of Newton, black the cloth
> In heavy wreathes folds over every Nation; cruel Works
> Of many Wheels I view, wheel without wheel, with cogs
>   tyrannic
> Moving by compulsion each other: not as those in Eden: which
> Wheel within Wheel in freedom revolve in harmony &
>   peace.[93]

Rejecting epistemological scientism and mechanistic nature, Romantics like Blake reached for the Infinite and had a penchant for synthesis. They wanted "to put the world together again if they could," writes Baumer, "to join subject and object, the ideal and the real, spirit and matter, after a century, as they believed, of putting asunder. Individuals, they felt, merely particularized a greater Whole, Spirit, or Universe."[94]

Wordsworth and Shelley. Whitehead credited the Romantic poets, especially William Wordsworth (1770-1850), Percy Bysshe Shelley (1792-1822), and Alfred, Lord Tennyson (1809-1892), for perceiving nature as it impresses itself upon human consciousness.[95] They looked upon nature not as scientific abstractions but as concrete forms, not as mechanism but as organism. In "The Tables Turned" (1798), Wordsworth admonishes, "Enough of Science and of Art"; "Let Nature be your Teacher":

> Sweet is the lore which Nature brings;
> Our meddling intellect
> Mis-shapes the beauteous forms of things: —
> We murder to dissect.[96]

Wordsworth claimed that "all good poetry is the spontaneous

overflow of powerful feelings," and in *Tintern Abbey* (1798), he expresses his powerful feelings about nature and nature's God:

And I have felt
A presence that disturbs me with the joy
Of elevated thoughts; a sense sublime
Of something far more deeply interfused,
Whose dwelling is the light of setting suns,
And the round ocean and the living air,
And the blue sky, and in the mind of man:
A motion and a spirit, that impels
All thinking things, all objects of all thought,
And rolls through all things.[97]

Nature was "all in all" to Wordsworth. He was "[a] worshiper of nature," which "never did betray / The heart that loved her."[98] As Whitehead observed, Wordsworth "always grasps the whole of nature as involved in the tonality of the particular instance," and he "expresses the concrete facts of our apprehension, facts which are distorted in the scientific analysis."[99]

Whereas Wordsworth found God in nature and distrusted science, Shelley was a religious skeptic who delighted in science. Despite his conviction that genuine knowledge only results from reasoning based upon sense-experience, Shelley had an abiding appreciation of nature's secondary qualities and organismic character.[100] As exemplified in *Mont Blanc* (1817), Shelley reversed Wordsworth's poetic approach. First, Shelley poses philosophic questions about mind's relationship to matter and about the nature and source of causation. Then he seeks answers to these philosophic questions by observing nature. In *Mont Blanc*, he searches for those answers while viewing the Alpine mountain scene in southeastern France from a bridge over the Arve River:

The everlasting universe of things
Flows through the mind, and rolls its rapid waves,
Now dark—now glittering—now reflecting gloom –
Now lending splendour, where from secret springs
The source of human thought its tribute brings

Of waters, — with a sound but half its own.
Such as a feeble brook will often assume
In the wild words, among the mountains lone,
Where waterfalls around it leap for ever,
Where words and winds contend, and a vast river
Over its rocks ceaselessly bursts and raves.[101]

Shelley's inquiring mind sought answers in "the clear universe of things around" but found causation to be a power "remote, serene, and inaccessible." In effect, Shelley is acknowledging that Kant's noumenal world lies beyond the mind's finite capability.[102]

In his "Ode to the West Wind" (1820), Shelley calls the wind, "breath of Autumn's being." The west wind drives dead leaves, "like ghosts from an enchanter fleeing," which become the "winged seeds" for rebirth in spring: "O Wind," he asks, "If Winter comes, can Spring be far behind?"[103] Thus, Shelley, like Wordsworth, emphasized inherent change and endurance of nature. Most importantly, as Whitehead points out, these two poets bear "witness to the discord between the aesthetic intuitions of mankind and the mechanism of science" and to the fact "that nature cannot be divorced from its aesthetic values."[104] Thus, as Whitehead observes, "the nature-poetry of the romantic revival was a protest on behalf of the organic view of nature, and also a protest against the exclusion of value from the essence of matter-of-fact."[105]

In their reaction to the world of nature, the Romantics valued human consciousness as an intrinsic part of reality and applied reason across its various fields of meaning. For Schleiermacher, this included his deep feelings toward the wonder of creation and the brotherhood of man. For Wordsworth and Shelley, it involved an aesthetic response to the beauty of nature and to the unique place of humanity in the cosmos. In effect, the Romantics rejected Hume's spectator view of human consciousness, which disassociated the individual's own conscious self from his or her sense impressions. Even Kant failed to fully grasp the conscious self which accompanies thought since he considered the unknowable thing-in-itself to include the individual self.[106] By contrast, the Romantics considered human consciousness accessible and important; it was the centerpiece of their worldview, which pulsated with meaning, value, and purpose.

Darwinian Evolution, Christian Theology, and Vitalism

Before Charles Darwin (1809-1882) published his seminal work, *On the Origin of Species* (1859), the Newtonian view of nature as ordered and static dominated Enlightenment thought. It fit neatly with the religious view of God as Designer, made famous in *Natural Theology* (1802) by William Paley, who analogized God to the Divine Watchmaker: "There cannot be design without a designer."[107] During the nineteenth century, even before Darwin, this alliance between theology and science over nature's design began to erode. In 1795, the geologist James Hutton deduced that the earth had existed an indefinitely long time and implicitly questioned the biblical account of creation. In 1830-33, Charles Lyell theorized that the earth developed gradually over eons of time rather than through upheavals. And in 1844, the amateur naturalist Robert Chambers introduced the idea of evolutionary transformation as the product of God's natural laws rather than God's direct involvement.[108]

These scientific developments paved the way for Darwin's theory of evolution, which he based upon his study on the geographically isolated Galapagos Islands during his five-year voyage (1831-36) aboard the *Beagle.* Darwin theorized that random variations produced fourteen different species of finches on the Islands from a single common ancestor because these variations enabled greater survival potential of the offspring.[109] "This preservation of favorable variation and the rejection of injurious variations," wrote Darwin, "I call Natural Selection."[110] While *Origin of Species* did not address human evolution, Darwin's *Descent of Man* (1871) did so explicitly: "Man the wonder and glory of the Universe proceeded [from Old World monkeys]."[111]

During his studies at Cambridge Darwin "hardly ever admired a book more than Paley 's *Natural Theology,*" but he subsequently concluded that "the old argument of design in nature, as given by Paley, which formerly seemed to me so conclusive, fails now that the law of natural selection has been discovered."[112] Darwin's theory contradicted the belief (advanced by Carolus Linnaeus in 1737) that species had remained unchanged since creation, and indirectly called into question the idea of a superintending providence, albeit without entirely ruling out the possibility of an original Creator.[113] Darwin originally had intended to enter the clergy after Cambridge but gradually drifted toward science and became a reluctant agnostic as his views on evolution solidified. Yet he allowed the possibility of a remote God as a First Cause and even maintained that one could be "an ardent Theist & an evolutionist."[114]

The Theological Response. The nineteenth-century reaction to Darwin among believers and nonbelievers alike was swift, vocal, and persistent. If survival of the fittest among random variations over an indefinite duration of time accounts for the diversity of species, including humankind, then the Genesis account is erroneous. The idea of humanity's unique creation in God's likeness no longer seemed tenable. Darwinian evolution undermined not only the theological argument based upon design, it also called into question the monotheistic belief in humanity's fall from grace and need for redemption. If humankind descended from a dumb animal rather than angelic perfection, and if nature and humanity evolved over millennia from natural selection of chance variations, then the idea of divine providence seemed indefensible, or at least unnecessary.

In the legendary 1860 Oxford Union debate, the evangelical Bishop Samuel Wilberforce opposed the Darwinian apologist Thomas Henry Huxley. In a rhetorical appeal to Victorian womanhood, Wilberforce asked if Huxley was willing to trace his descent from apes on his grandmother's side. Huxley replied that he would prefer an ape for a grandfather than a man of Wilberforce's station who used his influence "for the mere purpose of introducing ridicule into a grave scientific discussion."[115] Conservative theologians challenged Darwinian evolution as an unproven scientific hypothesis that denies humanity's uniqueness and God's providence. Chief among them was the American Presbyterian and Princeton theologian Charles Hodge (1797-1878) who considered Darwin's theory atheistic because chance mutations and natural selection denied God's design of creation and implied God's detachment from nature.[116]

Yet many progressive Christian theologians, including the Anglican theologian Charles Kingsley and the Catholic Cardinal John Henry Newman, accepted the significance of Darwin's findings, while others actively embraced evolutionary thought. The Oxford theological tutor Aubrey Moore (1848-1890) hailed Darwin for his great service to Christianity by overthrowing the belief in separate creation and the argument based upon design. The Congregation-alist theologian Lyman Abbott (1835-1922) became an influential American apologist for evolutionary theism.[117] Because such liberal Christian theologians accommodated their theology to Darwinian evolution, the late nineteenth-century press reported that the debate between Darwinism and theology was over.[118]

The Philosophical Response. One influential philosopher in particular engaged the issue of evolution directly. In his *Introduction to Metaphysics* (1903) and *Creative Evolution* (1907), Henri Bergson (1859-1941) addressed both scientism and evolutionary theory by distinguishing between analytical and intuitive thought, between static and dynamic reality, and between indifferent natural laws and nature's vital impulse.[119] Bergson challenged the adequacy of science's analytical mode of thought because it looks at facts in isolation (looking around the object). Instead, he advocated the need for the mind's intuitive mode of thought, which enters into and appreciates an organism (looking within the object). Bergson considered analysis and intuition two profoundly different but complementary ways of knowing. Asserting "that *theory of knowledge* and *theory of life* seem to us inseparable," Bergson argued that theoretic analysis is static and piecemeal and that scientific reasoning reduces an object to its elements and destroys its essence.[120] Intuition, by contrast, is insightful and holistic and recognizes the object's dynamic and continuous character. Whereas science abstracts the distinct and static parts of an object and reduces the object to its elements, intuition recognizes its continuous, striving, and living existence. For this reason, Bergson contended that analytical reasoning will never uncover the true *self.* That investigation requires an intuitive grasping of the full range of sensations, emotions, and thoughts, which interact over time within the individual.

Although Bergson, like Descartes, began with the conscious mind, he differed from the rationalists by emphasizing the mind's instinctual aspect. He differed from the empiricists by allocating scientific thought only to the static world of inert matter and mechanism. Life and consciousness, however, are not susceptible to scientific analysis, which destroys them and misperceives their essence. They are accessible only through intuition, which apprehends their ongoing process, their continuous becoming, which

Bergson labeled, *duration*. Applying the intuitive mode of thought and the dynamic character of life to his evaluation of Darwinian evolution, Bergson found Darwin's account of nature's transition from lower to higher states incomplete. In addition, he perceived a vital impulse (*élan vital*) that impels all organisms—from vegetation, arthropods, and vertebrates to humankind—toward higher and more complex states of existence. Furthermore, for Bergson, this vital impulse, this creative drive manifested in all of nature, "is of God, if it is not God himself."[121]

To grasp nature's vital impulse requires intuition. The reductive abstractions and analytical reasoning of science overlook nature's vital impulse, dynamic character, and irreversible creativity. Whereas consciousness in animals is habitual and automatic, "with man," writes Bergson, "consciousness breaks the chain. In man, and man alone, it sets itself free."[122] Having broken the evolutionary chain, human consciousness can constructively affect ongoing evolution, thereby opening and enriching humanity's future. In short, Bergson brought a new perspective to Darwin's seemingly mindless evolutionary process. He perceived something more at work in evolution than merely natural selection. This was the vital impulse underlying an inherently creative evolutionary process, which was proceeded toward higher states of complexity, including the new creative force of human consciousness. Thus, we enter Bergson's world of duration, vitality, and novelty.

Fin de Siècle Christian Theology

Protestantism. The dominant voice in nineteenth-century Protestant theology was Friedrich Schleiermacher who sought to establish religion on an entirely new foundation in personal experience. For Schleiermacher, religion was not theory or practice but piety, a personal response and surrender to the immensity of the Universe, "the result of the operation of God in you by means of the operation of the world upon you."[123] He considered history the best source of revelation about God, grace the individual's "intuition and feeling" from worldly participation "through action and culture," and personal experience the basis for theological language and doctrines.[124] At the turn of the twentieth century, liberal Protestant theology retained Schleiermacher's anthropocentric and historical focus, which it coupled with the ethical message of the Gospel.

Adolf von Harnack (1851-1930) conveyed this liberal Protestant perspective in his famous lecture series (1899-1900) and later book by entitled, *What is Christianity?* (1901).[125] Like Schleiermacher, Harnack asserted that the essence of Christianity lies in its personal meaning rather than in any ecclesiastical dogma.[126] But Harnack also asserted that the individual must assess Christ's character in determining what is essential and permanently valid. This assessment, according to Harnack, would reveal that Christ remained focused "upon *man*" and emphasized both divine and brotherly love.[127] Although Schleiermacher and Harnack assumed man's inherent capacity to access God, Harnack's theology differed from Schleiermacher's in that it centered on the Gospel and Christ's message of divine and brotherly love rather than on the mystery of Creation and individual piety.[128]

The German theologian Heintz Zahrnt characterized Harnack's *What Is Christianity?* as

> a great intellectual event, the highest expression and perfect manifestation of the age of bourgeois idealism, an age which was inspired by an optimistic faith in the human mind and progress in history, and believed it could unite God and the world, religion and culture, faith and intellect, divine righteousness and earthly authority, throne and altar in a natural and almost unbroken harmony, and which therefore looked forward with confidence to the future.[129]

This symbiotic relationship between church and state, religion and history, led Harnack, upon the outbreak of World War I in August 1914 to draft the "Manifesto of the Intellectuals" for the German Kaiser in support of the German war effort. In response to the Manifesto, Karl Barth led a generational revolt of so-called Crisis or Dialectical theologians, convinced that Protestant theology no longer could speak about God as it had in the past.

Catholicism. Between 1880 and 1910, Catholicism faced an institutional crisis as the result of the Modernist Movement, which had with two intellectual strains that originated in France. First, the "Philosophy of Action," led by Maurice Blondel and Lucien Laberthonnière, advocated the role of will and action in gaining religious knowledge and the need for Catholic biblical study to catch up with Protestant scholarship. A long-time philosophy professor, Blondel (1861-1949) advocated a new Christian philosophy based upon man's "immanent" source of spiritual activity, drawing upon human consciousness and experience that strives for the transcendent and supernatural.[130] Second, the "Modernist Movement," led principally by Alfred Loisy, George Tyrrell, Édouard Le Roy, and Blondel, advocated change in Catholic thought to bring it current with modern intellectual and social developments.[131] A biblical scholar and Catholic priest, Alfred Loisy (1857-1940), developed a historical-critical apologetic in *The Gospel and the Church* (1902), which sought "to adapt the Catholic religion to the intellectual, moral and social needs of the present time."[132] For Loisy, the Church and the Gospel are interdependent, and the Church must change with the times because its doctrines are spiritual aids rather than inflexible rules: "Reason never ceases to put questions to faith, and traditional formulations are submitted to a constant work of interpretation." The Church's mission, according to Loisy, is to serve as "an educator, rather than a domineering mistress: she instructs rather than directs, and he who obeys her only does so according to his conscience, and in order to obey God."[133]

Though their views often differed, the Modernists agreed that the Church was unreceptive to the intellectual problems and spiritual needs of its members. They challenged scholasticism as an outdated apologetics inconsistent with history, evolution, and modern culture. And they advocated a new conception and further development of dogma, confident that the Church would survive historical-critical analysis. In 1907, however, Pope Pius X issued a catalog of 65 Modernist errors and embargoed further historical study of Scripture and tradition. Pope Pius X followed this catalog with his encyclical, *Pascendi Gregis,* which labeled Modernism's central tenets heretical "agnosticism" and "vital immanence," and effectively established Thomism as fundamental to Catholic theology. Hence, even before World War I, the Catholic Church had taken firm steps to stifle further engagement with modern scientific developments affecting settled theological matters.[134] But the war produced a new Catholic voice for the compatibility of science and religion, Pierre Teilhard de Chardin.

In 1911, four years after these Papal edicts, Teilhard entered the priesthood and enrolled at the Paris Museum of Natural History as a doctoral student in paleontology, recently made a separate discipline within geology. Before he could complete his tertianship for full admission as a Jesuit, however, the war broke out and Teilhard received orders to report for duty in the French Army. While serving at the front as a stretcher bearer and subsequently chaplain, Teilhard developed his views on the compatibility of science and religion and on the war as the inevitable disunity that will occur within the long cosmic evolutionary process. Consequently, as discussed in Chapter 4, World War I became a theological turning point for Teilhard just as it had for Barth, inspiring both men to develop new theological views that challenged the current positions of their respective Christian denominations.

Prewar Culture and Materialism in Summary

Even this brief survey of Enlightenment thought through the nineteen-century reveals a pervasive, persistent, and powerful cultural engagement with the claims of scientism and materialism. Cartesian rationalism assured the reliability of sense experience and the divine supervision of nature. When Descartes's rationalism faltered before Hume's critique, Kant introduced a revolutionary epistemology and moral idealism that restored faith in God and immortality. When science reduced nature to a Newtonian machine, the Romantics revealed nature's organic, aesthetic, and spiritual content. Even Darwinian evolution, which apparently supported a mindless and indifferent worldview, drew a brisk response from progressive theology and vitalist philosophy. Bergson led a strong anti-scientism movement in *fin de siècle* Europe. It resisted the mechanistic model as merely a tool of analysis rather than a source of truth, and rejected the conception of nature as deterministic and reductionist.[135] Intuition integrated the human psyche and pointed a way toward truth that was the product of deep introspection, more penetrating than either rationalist speculation or scientific analysis.

For three centuries, including the chaotic nineteenth century, therefore, a vibrant culture kept scientism and materialism in check. Romanticism and Vitalism advocated a broader epistemology than scientism, which takes account of human feelings, aesthetics, interpersonal involvements, and narratives about humanity's place in the world. These movements employed a wider empiricism than objective science that pictured a universe laden with aesthetic value, meaning, and purpose. Thus, despite the appearance of Darwinian evolution, Western culture preserved a meaningful, purposeful, and God-centered universe, even as that culture became frayed, decadent, and ultimately incapable of forestalling a disastrous war. The Great War summarily ended this engagement, which freed materialism to enter the postwar cultural vacuum largely unchallenged.

3

The Great War and Cultural Breakdown

Things fall apart; the center cannot hold;
Mere anarchy is loosed upon the world,
The blood-dimmed tide is loosed, and everywhere
The ceremony of innocence is drowned;
The best lack all conviction, while the worst
Are full of passionate intensity.
　　—William Butler Yeats, "The Second Coming" (1920)[1]

By definition, *civilization* is a relatively high level of cultural and technological development, and *culture* is excellence in the arts, humanities, and sciences.[2] Thus, culture is both an attribute and by-product of civilization, and prewar Europe abounded in both—an unprecedented level of civilization and cultural excellence. Civilization requires sufficient material prosperity to provide leisure for cultural development, and bourgeois European society certainly had this in abundance. But, more important, says English art historian Kenneth Clark, is "confidence in the society in which one lives, belief in its philosophy, belief in its laws, and confidence in one's own mental powers."[3] All great civilizations, says Clark, have "a weight of energy" and "a sense of permanence" behind them, but however solid and complex they may appear, are rather fragile. Like Greece and Rome, they can collapse from exhaustion and lost confidence.[4] World War I proved Western civilization's fragility, and prewar culture forewarned of it.

The First World War shattered confidence in Western civilization, introduced an unnerving sense of impermanence, and created a grave mistrust of man's mental powers. American cultural and literary historian Paul Fussell called the war a "hideous embarrassment" to the century-old Meliorist Myth of inevitable progress.[5] For

William Barrett, it exposed a "sense of weakness and dereliction before the whirlwind that man is able to unleash but not to control"; it also caused an existential alienation in Western man who found himself "a stranger to God, to nature, and to the gigantic social apparatus that supplies his material wants."[6] The war opened an enormous chasm into which Western civilization collapsed. Furthermore, prewar culture –"the best that has been thought and known"[7]—seemed to anticipate its coming fall from greatness.

Fin de Siècle Civilization and Culture

"What an extraordinary episode in the economic progress of man that age was which came to an end in August 1914!" exclaimed English economist John Maynard Keynes in *The Economic Consequences of the Peace* (1919).[8] English historian Niall Ferguson recited the evidence supporting Keynes's remark: the world economy grew "faster between 1870 and 1913 than in any previous period"; and Europeans could buy the world's wares, invest in international securities, and travel the globe, in "unprecedented freedom and peace."[9] In addition, central banks voluntarily valued national currencies under the international gold standard, which produced long-run price stability. Goods, capital, and labor enjoyed international mobility barely equaled even today, and unparalleled political globalization supported this remarkable economic progress. European empires spread over most of the world's land surface and populations, dissolved traditional professional barriers within Europe, and enabled remarkable assimilation of diverse ethnicities.[10]

As the world's biggest empire, Britain seemed poised to contain the geographic spread of any continental crisis and to ensure continued *Pax Britannica*, especially considering Queen Victoria's genealogical intertwining of Europe's aristocratic elite.[11] The Russian Czar Nicholas II and the German Kaiser Wilhelm II were cousins and addressed each other as "Nicky" and "Willy."[12] Great Power diplomacy had limited or prevented European wars since the Congress of Vienna following Napoleon's defeat in 1815. Furthermore, as Ferguson notes, these wars "were nearly all remarkable for their limited geographical extent, short duration, and low casualties," including the six-month Franco-Prussian war (1870-71).[13] The European economies, moreover, were inextricably intertwined. As Polish financier Ivan Block and English journalist Norman Angell widely publicized, a European war would be ruinous for victors and vanquished alike.[14]

Beneath the geopolitical and economic power of the European empires, however, unrest simmered. Ireland percolated ominously in political revolt; suffragettes protested violently for women's rights; trade unions threatened a general strike in the British Isles; the Socialist International planned the destruction of world capitalism; and anarchists assassinated several dozen European political leaders.[15] In addition, nineteenth-century industrialization had drawn a large percentage of the rural population into dramatically enlarged cities, and urbanization had destroyed the social integration and group solidarity of previously tight-knit rural communities. Furthermore, capitalism proved indifferent to human cares, customs, and values.[16] German sociologist Max Weber pointed to the disenchantment and lost sense of wholeness that resulted from the "iron cage" of modern bureaucratized society. French sociologist Emile Durkheim gave a new label to this condition of personal isolation, anonymity, and alienation found in modern urban life—he called it "anomie."[17]

An even darker side of *fin de siècle* civilization was social Darwinism, which promoted "racial hygiene" and attacked "miscegenation," especially with so-called "alien" races, like the Jews.[18] For thirteen years (1897-1910), the Viennese continuously reelected Karl Lueger as Mayor on an anti-Semitic platform.[19] Lueger's mayoralty overlapped France's notorious Dreyfus Affair (1894-1906). In 1894, the Jewish army officer Captain Alfred Dreyfus was wrongfully convicted of treason for allegedly spying for Germany, and was exonerated only in 1906 after serving years of imprisonment on Devil's Island. The Dreyfus affair, in Barbara Tuchman's words, produced a "sudden and malign bloom of anti-Semitism in France."[20] In short, the urban, capitalist, and technological forces that produced nineteenth-century bourgeois prosperity also tore apart social relations, unleashed political violence, and exposed latent unrest and racial prejudice throughout Europe.

Fin de siècle culture was every bit as creative, chaotic, and precarious as the civilization that produced it. In art, Braque and Picasso

Figure 2. Pablo Picasso, *Les Demoiselles d'Avignon*, 1907, The Museum of Modern Art, New York, NY.
© Estate of Pablo Picasso/Artists Rights Society (ARS), New York.
Digital Image © The Museum of Modern Art/Licensed by SCALA/Art Resource, NY.

found reality in geometric forms (Cubism), Léger in industrial machines, German Expressionists in inner emotional states, and Italian Futurists in action and violence. In 1907, Pablo Picasso (1881-1973) painted the groundbreaking work, *Les Demoiselles d'Avignon*, which injected the pagan world of ritual masks and African art into the Renaissance tradition of structural order and monumental nudes (Figure 2). Planes and arcs dissect the five female anatomies, flouting traditional depictions of bulk by fracturing mass and solidity; color becomes abstract and expressive; and jagged unpredictable patterns and planes animate the pictorial surface—all disregarding pictorial representation of external reality.[21]

In music, Debussy, Elgar, Mahler, Ravel, Schoenberg, Strauss, and Stravinsky impressed European audiences with their widely different styles.[22] In 1908, Sergei Diaghilev brought the Russian Ballet to Paris with its stars, Anna Pavlova and Vaslov Nijinsky, and

in 1913, Diaghilev premiered Stravinsky's groundbreaking ballet
Le Sacre du Printemps (*The Rite of Spring*) choreographed by Nijinsky. The ballet depicts a ritual victim in pagan Russia dancing to
her death while Stravinsky's avant-garde music pulsates with almost total dissonance, constantly shifting meters, and percussive
violence. Pierre Monteux conducted, Camille Saint-Saens walked
out, Maurice Ravel cried "Genius!" and the entire theater rioted.[23]
European culture was not only wildly creative but also internationally appreciated. The French loved Wagner even more than the
Germans; the English loved the Russian novel and ballet; and Ni-
etzscheanism spread throughout the continent "a 'new culture' of
radical individualism and the supremacy of art."[24]

In his celebrated 1909 Manifesto, published on the front page
of the Paris newspaper *Le Figaro,* Filippo Tommaso Marinetti
(1876-1944), the Italian poet and flamboyant founder of Futurism,
declared the end to Italy's reactionary reliance on its classical and
Renaissance past, and inspired a new artistic sensibility among Italian painters.[25] Marinetti's Manifesto advocated the creation of a for-
ward-looking and dynamic society, poetics, and art that garnered
support throughout Europe:

> We will glorify war—the only true hygiene of the
> world—militarism, patriotism, destructive gesture of the
> anarchist. ... We shall sing the love of danger, the advent
> of energy, boldness. We declare that the world's splendor
> has been enriched by a new beauty: the beauty of speed.
> A racing automobile, its hood adorned with great pipes
> like snakes with explosive breath ... a roaring automobile,
> which seems to run like a machine-gun, is more beautiful
> than the Victory of Samothrace.[26]

Marinetti extolled violence as the source of all creativity, and glorified war against capitalism, bourgeois society, and European civilization.[27]

The cultural critiques of Western civilization focused on bourgeois indifference, corruption, and depravity and also on individual loneliness and lost community. In *Heart of Darkness* (1902),
Joseph Conrad (1857-1924) exposes the compromised idealism, un-

restrained greed, and brutal inhumanity of European colonialism in Africa. "To tear treasure out of the bowels of the land was their desire, with no more moral purpose at the back of it than there is in burglars breaking into a safe," declares Conrad's narrator Charlie Marlow; it was "just robbery with violence, aggravated murder on a great scale."[28] In *Lord Jim* (1900), Conrad emphasizes the importance of preserving and protecting community. His laconic narrator and alter ego Marlow reflects upon Jim's cowardly abandonment of helpless passengers shipboard on the *Patna*: "the real significance of Jim's crime is in its breach of faith with mankind"; "in our hearts we trust for our salvation in the men that surround us."[29] In *The Love Song of J. Alfred Prufrock* (1911), T.S. Eliot portrays the human toll of bourgeois capitalism in loneliness and boredom. Prufrock walks "through certain half-deserted streets, / The muttering retreats / Of restless nights in one-night cheap hotels / And sawdust restaurants with oyster shells," preparing "a face to meet the faces that you meet," and measuring out his life "with coffee spoons."[30]

In *The Street* (1913) Ludwig Kirchner (1880-1938) dramatically displays the restless, dehumanized emptiness, the clandestine, disturbed sexuality, and the widespread moral hypocrisy of bourgeois life in prewar Berlin (Figure 3). Two strikingly attired ladies wearing tight-fitting coats with fur collars and hats with feathers are followed by equally well-dressed businessmen in black coats and hats. The man to the right, ostensibly viewing merchandise in the display window, is assessing the women's reflection on the window just outside the picture frame and making a discrete overture with his phallic walking stick. The women nonchalantly stride ahead with hands and V-shaped fur coats discreetly yet suggestively pointing to their pubic area. Kirchner employs garish colors and bold hatchings plus an extremely foreshortened perspective to thrust this furtive commercial enterprise at the viewer.[31]

In achingly poignant symphonic music Gustav Mahler (1860-1911) expresses his wildly vacillating states of angst and exhilaration, grief and resignation, love and loneliness from grappling with life's most profound questions. As he said famously, "The Symphony must be like the world; it must embrace everything." His Symphony No. 5 (1902) evokes the progressive emotional states of the

Figure 3. Ernst Ludwig Kirchner, *The Street*, 1913, The Museum of Modern Art, New York, NY.
Digital Image © The Museum of Modern Art/Licensed by SCALA/Art Resource, NY.

grieving process following the death of a loved one—from despair, grief, and resignation to reaffirmation of life. His Symphony No. 9 (1910) intones an intense premonition and ultimate acceptance of his own coming death from a fatal heart condition. Yet despite his brilliance as a composer and recognition as a preeminent conductor, Mahler felt alienated, lonely, and isolated in anti-Semitic Austria, even as a converted Catholic and celebrated music director of the Vienna Opera: "I am thrice homeless, as a Bohemian in Austria, as an Austrian among Germans, as a Jew throughout the world, everywhere an intruder, never welcomed."[32] In August 1914, nationalism became the surrogate for the lost sense of community felt among Europeans, and war became the antidote for the various ills perceived within European society.

The Shock, Euphoria, and History of War

Despite this undercurrent of social and cultural unrest, the First World War took most Europeans completely by surprise.[33] George Bernard Shaw wrote: "only the professional diplomats and a very few amateurs whose hobby is foreign policy even knew the guns were loaded."[34] On June 28, 1914, in Sarajevo, a young Bosnian Serb named Gavrilo Princip assassinated Archduke Franz Ferdinand, the Habsburg heir to the Austro-Hungarian throne, and his wife Sophie. On July 23, less than a month after the assassination, Austria-Hungary gave Serbia a written ultimatum and demanded an immediate reply. Unsatisfied with Serbia's prompt and mostly compliant reply, Austria-Hungary declared war on Serbia the day after its receipt. In a largely political gesture Russia mobilized in support of Serbia, and Germany reacted by demanding Russia's immediate demobilization. When Russia refused, Germany declared war on Russia on August 1. In accordance with its pre-existing Schlieffen plan designed to avoid a potentially unsustainable two-front war, Germany needed a quick victory over France, Russia's ally in the West. So, before turning its forces East to fight Russia, Germany planned to attack France and encircle the French Army by proceeding through neutral Belgium. When Belgium refused Germany's request for permission to enter its territory, Germany invaded anyway and, on August 3, declared war on France. In response to Germany's violation of Belgian neutrality, Britain declared war on Germany on August 4.[35] Thirty-seven days after the terrorist attack in Sarajevo, Europe was at war.

The precipitous declarations of war came with little justification except Austria's desire to protect its fragile Empire, Germany's belief in speed as essential to military success, and Europe's entangling national alliances.[36] In his recent study of the origins of World War I, English historian Christopher Clark concludes that the war was caused, not just by "the belligerence and imperialist paranoia of Austrian and German policy-makers," but by a common imperialist paranoia among all the major players: "The crisis that brought war in 1914 was the fruit of a shared political culture." There was no "smoking gun" or a malevolent conspiracy among a few powerful individuals because all the major players were complicit in the tragedy. "The protagonists of 1914 were sleepwalkers, watchful but unseeing, haunted by dreams, yet blind to the reality of the horror they were about to bring into the world."[37]

Although war appeared seemingly from nowhere, Europeans greeted it with almost unanimous enthusiasm. With the announcement of war, "August Madness" erupted, with enormous supportive crowds gathering in the major capitals of Europe—Paris, London, St. Petersburg, Vienna, and Berlin.[38] The Irish joined the British Army to protect Belgium, the women's movement volunteered to aid the war effort, the Socialist International became nationalistic and raised no opposition, and the artists and intellectuals throughout Europe, young and old alike, embraced the war.[39] "Among the elite of each country," observed French musicologist and writer Romain Rolland at the start of war, "there is not one who does not proclaim and is not convinced that the cause of his people is the cause of God, the cause of liberty, and of human progress."[40] Europe's leading theologians, philosophers, poets, historians, sociologists, psychologists, and scientists gladly joined this martial chorus for various idealistic reasons: self-identity and self-understanding, recovery of lost community, and relief from anomie, materialism, corruption, and inhumanity within bourgeois capitalist society.[41]

Philosophers Henri Bergson and Max Scheler, novelist Thomas Mann and poet Rainer Maria Rilke, psychologists Sigmund Freud and Émile Durkheim, musicians Igor Stravinsky and Alexander Scriabin all supported the war.[42] For Max Scheler, it was a war against capitalism; for G. K. Chesterton, it was a war against England's crimes and antidemocratic class-ridden society; and for Edmund Gosse, writer, critic, and Librarian for the House of Lords, it was a "sovereign disinfectant" to purge England's self-indulgence and luxuriousness.[43] With a few prominent exceptions, Albert Einstein, Bertrand Russell, and the Bloomsbury group among them, there were virtually no conscientious objectors to the war.[44] "I discovered to my amazement," remarked Bertrand Russell, "that average men and women were delighted by the prospect of war."[45]

According to American historian Roland N. Stromberg, "the war spirit of 1914 was a new concoction" because it did not emphasize traditional martial themes of necessity, duty, or justice, but rallied behind novel ideas of "renewal, adventure, apocalypse."[46]

The August Madness grew out of "a powerful thirst for identity, community, purpose," says Stromberg, and served as "an antidote to anomie, which had resulted from the sweep of powerful forces of the recent past—urban, capitalistic, and technological forces tearing up primeval bonds and forcing people into a crisis of social relationships."[47] Two poems by Rupert Brooke (1887-1915) capture these naïve and high blown sentiments: "Peace" (1914) thanks God for giving Britain a war to cleanse "a world grown old and cold and weary"; and "The Soldier" (1915) declares that upon his death there shall be "some corner of a foreign field / That is forever England."[48] Fifty years later, Philip Larkin would describe the enthusiastic crowds that greeted Britain's declaration of war in his poem "MCMXIV": "as if it were all / An August Bank Holiday lark ... Never such innocence again."

The war proceeded as quickly as it had begun, with all the leading generals believing that swift, decisive battles would win the war by Christmas 1914. These same generals, however, never anticipated or seemed to learn that an infantry's size and fighting spirit (or *élan* as the French called it) were no match for the machine gun.[49] Each nation claimed to be "defending its existence," wrote English historian A. J. P. Taylor, "though the method of defense was to invade someone else's territory."[50] Attacking the German positions in Lorraine on August 14, 1914, barely two weeks into the war, the French suffered their highest casualties of the entire war and lost their best officers and soldiers.

The French then shifted to defense and, along with the British, halted the German sweep through Belgium at the Marne River on September 5, 1914, at the cost on each side of one-half million casualties.[51] "The Battle of the Marne was one of the decisive battles of the world," according to American historian Barbara Tuchman, "not because it determined that Germany would ultimately lose the war or the Allies ultimately win the war but because it determined that the war would go on." The combatant nations, Tuchman continues, "were caught in a trap, a trap made during the first 30 days out of battles that failed to be decisive, a trap from which there was, and has been, no exit."[52] The Germans dug in, the war of movement ended, and the trench warfare began along a front that eventually extended from the North Sea through Belgium and France all the way to Switzerland.[53] This frontline never varied more than a few miles over the next four years, despite the incredible slaughter, as armies on both sides attempted continually and futilely to break through.[54]

Between February and May 1915, the French launched further futile attacks in Champagne, San Mihiel, and Arras, as did the British at Festubert and Aubers Ridge—all with enormous casualties.[55] In March 1915, the Allied Powers (Anglo-French naval forces with Australia and New Zealand ground forces) landed on the Gallipoli Peninsula in a strategically brilliant plan along the Dardanelles to aid Russian and Serbian forces and to circumvent the impasse on the Western Front. But the Dardanelles campaign suffered from inadequate planning and inept execution, leaving Australian and New Zealand troops clinging to narrow beachheads overlooked by entrenched Turkish forces. After sustaining heavy losses and failing to move inland by October, the Allies recognized the Dardanelles campaign was a failure and successfully evacuated their troops from the Gallipoli Peninsula by the end of 1915.[56]

The Allied Powers concentrated once again on the Western Front and planned more frontal attacks at the Somme during 1916, while the Germans planned similar attacks at Verdun—all tactically and humanly disastrous. Proposing "to bleed the French white" at their weak Verdun salient, German General Erich von Falkenhayn attacked in February 1916. Equally determined to defend France's strategically unimportant salient, French General Philippe Pétain declared, "They shall not pass." Both armies paid a heavy price for the German offensive. The Germans suffered 281,000 casualties compared to the French 315,000 casualties. Armies fought "literally for the sake of fighting," wrote Taylor. "There was no prize to be gained or lost, only men to be killed and glory to be won"—all for no gain in what Taylor calls "the most senseless episode in the war."[57]

On July 1, 1916, the British launched their attack on the Somme—the worst location, circumstance, and timing for this offensive.[58] Fronted heavily with barbed wire, the Germans occupied the crested hills on the Somme, and sat securely in trenches 40 feet deep, with every modern convenience. The British needlessly alerted them to the coming attack by conducting various exploratory raids and five days of heavy bombardment along an 18 mile front. Then, the British attacked using inexperienced and inadequately trained soldiers and similarly inexperienced junior officers taught to expose themselves recklessly in battle, which resulted in their six-times-greater casualty rate. Captain W.P. Nevill literally kicked off the British attack with a football, followed by British soldiers, each weighed down by 66 pounds of equipment and all advancing slowly in uniform, solid lines toward the entrenched German positions. When the British artillery stopped firing, German soldiers emerged from their trenches, set up their machine guns, and began firing into the approaching British formations. Nevill died almost immediately, and by day's end the British had suffered the largest single-day losses by any army in the war—60,000 casualties, including 20,000 dead.[59]

Undeterred by the senseless carnage, British General Alexander Haig ordered the same uniform attacks all along the line every day thereafter with the same disastrous results on a diminishing scale. The subsequent attacks included a tragic British cavalry charge on July 14, 1916, replete with bugles and lances, all slaughtered by German machine guns. By its last attack on the Somme (November 13, 1916), the British had suffered 420,000 casualties, the French nearly 200,000, and the Germans about 450,000—simply because General Falkenhayn ordered German soldiers to retake every yard of lost ground by counterattack.[60]

After the Somme, the war dragged on for two more years, and the death toll mounted from incessant and futile frontal assaults. During its offensive at Aisne (April 1917), the French infantry was massacred for a mere 600 yards. French soldiers mutinied and 100,000 were court-martialed.[61] Undeterred by his disastrous Somme offensive, Haig devised a new offensive (July 31-November 7, 1917) at Ypres, called Passchendaele by the British, without ever inspecting the front line, anticipating the mud in rainy Flanders, or heeding the opposition of his Intelligence Staff or the warning of French General Foch about fighting both Germans and mud. The British suffered 300,000 casualties to gain a trivial amount of ground, and the Germans suffered 200,000 casualties, in what Taylor calls "the blindest slaughter of a blind war." After Passchendaele Haig's chief of staff visited the war zone for the first time and, finding his vehicle stuck in the mud, he literally wept: "Good God, did we really send men to fight in that?" His companion replied, "It's worse further up."[62]

On May 23, 1915, Italy had declared war on Austria-Hungary (and a year later on Germany) after entering a secret treaty with Britain and France which promised rich postwar rewards for Italy's alliance. On October 24, 1917, however, the Italian front finally collapsed at Caporetto before the advancing Austro-Hungarian Army supported by German reinforcements. Caporetto cost the Italian army 200,000 casualties in battle and 400,000 in desertions, and almost drove the Italians from the war. The Italian line finally held at the River Piave, where the Allies developed a unified southern strategy.[63] The Allied Powers fared even worse on the Eastern Front after Vladimir Lenin, with German assistance, arrived in Russia in April 1917 and took charge of fomenting discontent with the Russian Provisional Government. By November 1917, the Bolsheviks under Lenin had seized power, determined to end Russia's involvement in the war. In December 1917, the Bolsheviks signed an Armistice and, in March 1918, signed the Brest Litovsk Treaty with Germany. With Russia out of the war, the Germans moved their troops from the Eastern to the Western Front, which was now key to German victory. The Central Powers had succeeded on every other front: Russia had surrendered, Italy had retreated at Caporetto, and the Allies had evacuated Gallipoli.[64] What would turn the tide of battle from the Central Powers to the Allied Powers was the American entry into the war.

Throughout the first two years of World War I, President Woodrow Wilson assiduously maintained American neutrality, despite the British blockade and seizure of neutral shipping headed to the Central Powers and the German sinking of unarmed vessels, like the *Lusitania* on May 7, 1915, with the loss of 128 American lives. In January 1917, however, American commitment to neutrality began to weaken as Germany instituted unrestricted submarine warfare and began sinking American ships. The infamous Zimmermann telegram ultimately tipped the American scales from neutrality to belligerence. In April 1917, the British Secret Service intercepted, decoded, and transmitted to the United States a telegram from the German Minister of Foreign Affairs, Arthur Zimmermann, to the

German Minister to Mexico, proposing to ally Germany with Mexico in waging war against the United States and recovering Mexican territory in Texas, New Mexico, and Arizona.[65] Promptly, isolationist America entered the war to counter these provocative actions, to make the world "safe for democracy," and to protect its booming trade and its substantial loans with the Allies.[66]

On March 21, 1918, Germany launched its final offensive of the war at the Somme before American troops could make an important contribution to the Allied cause. The Germans advanced to within 71 miles of Paris, reaching the Marne on July 15. Following three days of intense fighting, the Allied Powers, with the aid of 85,000 American troops, once again held the Germans at the Marne and turned the tide of battle.[67] German Chancellor Hertling noted the dire implications for Germany of this second battle of the Marne: "On the 18th even the most optimistic among us knew that all was lost. The history of the world was played out in three days."[68] On August 8, 1918, the British and French, supported by hundreds of thousands of American troops, attacked across a wide front, and ultimately broke the Hindenburg line to end the war. By September 29, recognizing that his army had no chance for victory, German General Erich Ludendorff insisted that Germany seek an immediate armistice. To enhance Germany's negotiating position with the Allies, especially President Wilson, Ludendorff urged that Germany adopt, and turn over control of the war to, a democratic government.[69] This newly formed German government signed the Armistice, and at 11 AM on November 11, 1918 (the eleventh hour of the eleventh day of the eleventh month), the war was finally over. During the four years and three months leading up to the Armistice, the Great War had taken the grim toll among combatants of 9.45 million dead (averaging 6000 per day for 1500 days) and 15.4 million wounded, and with civilian casualties included, about 16 million dead and 20 million wounded.[70]

The Experience and Disillusionment of War

English Futurist and Marinetti disciple Christopher R.W. Nevinson (1889-1946) volunteered as an ambulance driver and observed firsthand war's dehumanizing brutality. In his early war-painting,

Figure 4. Christopher R. W. Nevinson, *Returning to the Trenches*, 1914-15,
Gift of the Massey Collection of English Painting, 1946.
National Gallery of Canada, Ottawa.
Photo Credit: © National Gallery of Canada.

Returning to the Trenches (1914-15), Nevinson portrays the grim
march of overburdened French soldiers returning to the front like
one huge war-machine (Figure 4). Despite its Futurist artistic techniques of angular shapes and "force-lines" of rifles, *Returning to the
Trenches* conveys no fighting élan or military optimism among this
mass of humanity. The Futurist bravado is missing because Nevinson has seen that "war is now dominated by machines, and that
men were mere cogs in the mechanism."[71] Reflecting this mechanized misery, Nevinson's soldiers, as English author and painter
Wyndham Lewis observed, "have a harried and harassed mel-
ancholy and chilliness."[72] *Returning to the Trenches* provided little
support for the dazzling recruitment propaganda that Nevinson
found at the time on the British Home Front.[73] As experienced in
the trenches on the Western Front, war was misery.

The 1916 Battle of the Somme was a turning point. According to

A. J. P. Taylor, "Idealism perished on the Somme." Volunteers had lost not only their enthusiasm for war but, more significantly, their faith "in their cause, in their leaders, in everything except loyalty to their fighting comrades. The war ceased to have a purpose. It went on for its own sake, as a contest in endurance."[74] Disillusionment with the war and its leaders and loyalty toward one's comrades permeate the later war literature, starting in 1917 with the British war poets who fought on the Somme, like Wilfred Owen (1893-1918) and Siegfried Sassoon (1886-1967). In "Dulce Et Decorum Est" (1918), Owen impugns the "old lie" that it is decorous and sweet to die for one's country.[75] He graphically depicts a soldier's agonizing death from gas poisoning, "guttering, choking, drowning," and bitterly admonishes a chauvinistic poet for urging young men to enlist in pursuit of "some desperate glory":

> If you could hear, at every jolt, the blood
> Come gargling from the froth-corrupted lungs,
> Obscene as cancer, bitter as the cud
> Of vile, incurable sores on innocent tongues, –
> My friend, you would not tell with such high zest
> To children ardent for some desperate glory,
> The old lie: Dulce et decorum est
> Pro patria mori.[76]

In "Futility" (1918), Owen laments the premature fate and unrealized potential of a soldier who froze to death overnight in the trenches: "Was it for this the clay grew tall?" The "fatuous sunbeams" cannot revive his frozen corpse as they had routinely awakened him at home, "whispering of fields unsown." Owen's sympathetic and ironic treatment of this half-lived life, in the words of one critic, "places the tragedy of an individual death on a plane of cosmic significance, or rather, this death, so futile in its finality, points to an ultimate futility in the whole order of things."[77] In "Strange Meeting" (1918), Owen explicitly criticizes the civilization responsible for the war through the device of a soldier's mythic descent into hell. There he confronts his alter ego, the very man he killed the prior day. Staring "with piteous recognition in fixed eyes," the stranger discloses: "I am the enemy you killed, my friend." Together these former enemies grieve about the "truth untold" of the "hopelessness" and "pity of war" and of the "the march of this retreating world" where "none will break ranks, though nations trek from progress."[78]

In May 1918, Owen wrote a preface for a book of poems he hoped to publish that carries both a warning and a lament:

> This book is not about heroes. English poetry is not yet fit to speak of them.
> Nor is it about deeds, or lands, nor anything about glory, honor, might, majesty, dominion, or
> power, except War.
> Above all I am not concerned with Poetry.
> *My subject is War, and the pity of War.*
> *The Poetry is the pity.*
> Yet these elegies are to this generation in no sense consolatory. They may be to the next. All a poet can do today is warn. That is why the true Poets must be truthful.[79]

(The italicized lines are quoted in Westminster Abbey's monument to First World War poets.) Owen dismissed words like glory and honor as belying the un-heroic character of trench warfare. He chided patriotic warmongering as an old lie, deemed enemy soldiers his brothers, and pictured modern civilization in full retreat.

Siegfried "Mad Jack" Sassoon served as a courageous second lieutenant in France, earned Britain's second-highest military honor, the Military Cross, but became disillusioned and embittered on the Somme. Sassoon wrote angry, sarcastic poetry directed at the war effort, at the government and generals who pursued it, and at the people on the home front who supported them.[80] Fully expecting to be court-martialed, Sassoon published a defiant letter to his commanding officer in July 1917, claiming "that the war is being deliberately prolonged by those who have the power to end it … . I believe that this war, upon which I entered as a war of defense and liberation, has now become a war of aggression and conquest."[81]

In his 1929 war memoir, *Good-Bye to All That*, Sassoon's friend and fellow officer Robert Graves (1895-1985) recounts his efforts to save Sassoon from court-martial by urging the Army to convene a

medical board instead. Graves knew that Sassoon was in no condition to endure a court-martial and imprisonment and "should not
be allowed to become a martyr to a hopeless cause in his present
physical condition." Accordingly, Graves undertook "to rig the
medical board" and to appear before it "in the role of the patriot
distressed by the mental collapse of a brother-in-arms–a collapse
directly due to his magnificent exploits in the trenches." Although
"conscious of a betrayal of truth," Graves observes the "irony of
having to argue to these mad old men that Siegfried was not sane!"
The board sent Sassoon to the Craiglockhart psychiatric hospital for
shellshocked soldiers, "Dottyville" as he called it, and dispatched
Graves as his escort.[82]

At Craiglockhart, Sassoon met and befriended Owen, also recovering from shellshock.[83] Both Sassoon and Owen left Craiglockhart and returned to France (Owen over the objection of his doctor),
not from any conviction about pursuing the war but, rather, to look
after their men.[84] In a letter to his mother shortly before his death,
Owen wrote: "I came out in order to help these boys—directly by
leading them as well as an officer can; indirectly, by watching their
suffering that I may speak of them as well as a pleader can."[85] After
convalescing in England, Graves and Sassoon voiced similar sentiments about their responsibilities as officers to return to the front
to support their troops.[86] Owen was awarded the Military Cross in
October and died on November 4, 1918, exactly one week before
the war's end.

Two important anti-war novels by French and German soldiers, respectively, Henri Barbusse (1873-1935)[87] and Erich Maria
Remarque (1898-1970),[88] echo these same themes of the brotherhood of the trenches, the futility of war, and the betrayal by society. In *Under Fire, The Story of a Squad* (*Le Feu* in French) (1916),
Barbusse describes the frontline experience of Corporal Bertrand's
infantry squad, mostly farmers and artisans of all ages—the *"poilu"*
or "shaggy beasts," as they were called. The squad has endured 15
months of incessant rifle, machine gun, and cannon fire in "a vast
and water-logged desert," and is "chained and riveted together in
fraternity."[89] The narrator from Bertrand's squad draws a distress-
ing picture of bodies mutilated by shellfire, hand-to-hand combat, executions for desertion, nighttime raids into No Man's Land,

drowned men unable to "extricate themselves from the mud," and increasing deaths among the squad, finally including the brave Corporal Bertrand.[90]

The squad constantly rails against the "truly unpardonable division" within France between "those who gain and those who grieve," and between the happy civilians and the unhappy *poilu*. In short, *Under Fire* is a *cri de coeur* against the "blasphemy" of war: "Shame on military glory, shame on armies, shame on the soldiers' calling, that changes men by turns into stupid victims or ignoble brutes."[91] Barbusse's novel opens surrealistically with men of culture and intelligence reading that "War is declared" and foreseeing thirty million soldiers of two slave armies "committing suicide." It closes with a socialist sermon against the "sword wavers, profiteers, and intriguers" who caused and benefited from the war on behalf of the victimized common soldiers, the universal brotherhood who must unite to ensure "no more war after this!"[92]

In *All Quiet on the Western Front* (1929), Remarque has 19-year-old Paul Bäumer narrate the experiences of his classmates and older German soldiers in his infantry squad during the last two years of the war on a vaguely specified portion of the Western Front.[93] In addition to his classmates, Bäumer's squad includes a locksmith, a peat-digger, a farmer, and a cobbler—Bäumer's 40-year-old mentor Kat Katczinsky. They experience artillery barrages, gas attacks, food shortages, military hospitals, patrols into a No Man's Land, guard-duty over Russian prisoners, and trench life, with its rats, latrines, boredom, and carnage. *All Quiet* portrays the alienation of these long-suffering young soldiers on the Western Front from the patriotic older generation on the Home Front. It also conveys their fierce loyalty to one another, their incomprehension of war's purpose, their loss of innocence, and their desperate determination to survive.[94]

On home leave Bäumer feels estranged from his family and familiar surroundings—from his mother dying of cancer, his father's colleagues still brimming with 1914 war spirit, and his glass case containing butterflies. Of his youthful passion for books, he says: "Words, Words, Words—they do not reach me." Bäumer inadvertently fails to salute an Army major who dresses him down, and deliberately lies to the mother of his dead squad member to spare her the awful knowledge of her son's agonizingly slow and painful death following amputation of his foot. "I ought never to have come on leave," he chides himself, longing to return to the front.[95] Back in the trenches, Bäumer hears the voices of his comrades:

> These voices, these quiet words, these footsteps in the trench behind me recall me at a bound from the terrible loneliness and fear of death by which I had been almost destroyed. They are more to me than life, these voices, they are more than motherliness and more than fear; they are the strongest, most comforting thing there is anywhere: they are the voices of my comrades.
>
> I am no longer a shuddering speck of existence, alone in the darkness;—I belong to them and they to me; we all share the same fear and the same life, and we are nearer than lovers, in a simpler, harder way; I could bury my face in them, in these voices, these words that have saved me and will stand by me."[96]

Bäumer verbalizes the same comradeship of the trenches that motivated soldiers Graves, Owen, and Sassoon.

In the Preface to the novel, Remarque sets forth his literary purpose:

> This book is to be neither an accusation nor a confession, and least of all an adventure, for death is not an adventure to those who stand face-to-face with it. It will try simply to tell of a generation of men who, even though they may have escaped shells, were destroyed by the war.

His Preface to the contrary notwithstanding, *All Quiet* is both an accusation that "the culture of a thousand years could not prevent the stream of blood being poured out," and a confession that Remarque himself is part of the "lost generation" of men "destroyed by the war." As Bäumer's classmate remarks, "The war has ruined us for everything."[97] Numerous scenes make the novel's pacifist leanings unmistakable: Bäumer thinks "a word of command might transform [the Russian prisoners] into our friends"; his squad questions the war's justification (both sides are simply protecting their fatherland, the Kaiser could have said No to the war, opposing leaders and generals have caused the war merely to "become famous" and, instead, should duke it out among themselves); and Bäumer promises the dead French soldier whom he has just killed and called "Comrade": "It shall never happen again."[98]

By the summer of 1918, Bäumer and his friends realize they are falling back, dying one by one, and losing the war: "We are not beaten, for as soldiers we are better and more experienced; we are simply crushed and driven back by overwhelming superior forces."[99] His generation "might have unleashed a storm," says Bäumer, had they returned home in 1916, but returning now we are "weary, broken, burnt out, rootless, and without hope. We will not be able to find our way anymore."[100] As Canadian historian Modris Eckstein's observes, *All Quiet* personalized the fate of the Unknown Warrior. War became a matter of individual experience rather than interpretive history; and Paul Bäumer was the Everyman who "sparked the intense reconsideration of the meaning of the war at the end of the twenties."[101]

As English historian Brian Bond reminds us, the real historical war ceased to exist after 1918, because it "was swallowed up by imagination in the guise of memory."[102] Yet memory of the First World War "changed reality" in postwar English culture, according to former Princeton Professor of Literature Samuel Hynes. The war caused a "sense of radical discontinuity of present from past" and created a new narrative, which Hynes calls the Myth of War:

[A] generation of innocent young men, with heads full of high abstractions like Honor, Glory, and England, went off to war to make the world safe for democracy. They were slaughtered in stupid battles planned by stupid generals. Those who survived were shocked, disillusioned and embittered by their war experiences, and saw that their real enemies were not the Germans, but the old men at home who had lied to them. They rejected the values of the society that had sent them to war, and in doing so separated their own generation from the past and from their cultural inheritance.[103]

Most of the war literature contributed to this postwar narrative—the Myth of War.[104]

The War Wounds of Western Civilization

The war gouged deep wounds in Western civilization that remained weeping over a long, turbulent twentieth century and are barely healed even today. Among the most severe of these wounds are the following: (1) the expendability of human life for political purpose, turning soldiers into cannon fodder and martyrs rather than heroes, (2) the mistrust and hostility within the postwar society toward its wartime leaders, (3) the war's continuation in the form of internal rioting and unrest, and (4) the latent hostility within existing and newly formed nations toward their multiracial citizenry. Each deserves special consideration because each contributed significantly to postwar cultural disintegration.

The Expendability of Life. World War I produced a shocking death toll because the Great Power leadership and its civilian population maintained their committed support for the bloodbath to the bitter end.[105] After the Battle of the Marne in 1914, the war became a vast industrialized siege that moved little over four years. Military leaders waged war along this virtually impregnable front essentially to destroy the other side's manpower in a strategy of mechanized human slaughter.[106] In pursuing their strategy, moreover, the leaders on both sides display their indifference to the lives even of their own soldiers. As American theologian Richard L. Rubenstein observed, "Both the British and the German generals made the same decision; their country's young men were expendable."[107] The imaginative violence of prewar Futurism had become war's reality; the nightmare *was* reality.

After the publication of Wilfred Owen's poems in 1920 with Sassoon's introduction, and in 1931 with Edmund Blunden's biography, Owen became recognized, not just as the greatest war poet, but as a "tragic, selfless, talented young man whose humanism in the face of wartime atrocities spoke out from every poem."[108] This assessment by English lecturer in literature George Walter is seconded by Samuel Hynes, who puts it even more bluntly: Owen was "neither hero nor coward, but a sacrifice."[109]

Once the soldier was seen as a victim, the idea of a hero became unimaginable: there would be no more heroic actions
in the art of this war. And if entire armies could be imagined composed of such victims—if indeed every army was
an army of martyrs—then Victory too must fade from the
story, and war become only a long catastrophe, with neither
significant action nor direction, a violence that was neither
fought nor won but only endured."[110]

In Ernest Hemingway's *A Farewell to Arms* (1929) about the
"white war" in Italy, the American ambulance driver Frederick
Henry echoes the same sentiment. Henry muses about war's unhe-
roic brutality in response to a compatriot's comment that the Italians could not have fought the Austrians in vain:

I was always embarrassed by the words sacred, glorious,
and sacrifice and the expression in vain. We had heard them
... and had read them, on proclamations that were slapped
up by billposters over other proclamations, now for a long
time, and I have seen nothing sacred, and the things that
were glorious had no glory and the sacrifices were like the
stockyards at Chicago if nothing was done with the meat
except to bury it. There were many words that you could
not stand to hear and finally only the names of places had
dignity. Certain numbers were the same way and certain
dates and these with the names of places were all you could
say and have them mean anything. Abstract words such as
glory, honor, courage, or hallow were obscene beside the
concrete names of villages, the numbers of roads, the names
of rivers, the numbers of regiments and the dates.[111]

Thus, soldiers sensed that they had become expendable victims
of disastrous political miscalculations and that memorials honoring
the war dead gravely misrepresented their sacrifice. In "On Passing the New Menin Gate" (1928), Sassoon mocks the sentimental
platitudes on a Brussels memorial to British war dead: "Their name
liveth for ever" carved on the "peace-complacent stone" bearing
"intolerably nameless names" cannot "absolve the foulness of their

fate.... Well might the Dead who struggled in the slime / Arise and deride this sepulchre of crime." Consequently, "to represent the war in traditional ways," explains Hynes, "was necessarily to *mis*-represent it, to give it meaning, dignity, order, greatness."[112]

Mistrust and Alienation. The returning soldiers felt estranged from civilian noncombatants, especially the political leadership—Old Men responsible for the war, like Lloyd George, who grandly described the British soldier as "a good sportsman" who "played the game" without quitting; and Kaiser Wilhelm who gloried in the war before fleeing to permanent exile in Holland.[113] In his 1920 poem, "Hugh Selwyn Mauberley," Ezra Pound describes soldiers who went to war "believing in old men's lies, then unbelieving / came home ... to old lies and new infamy"—or never came home:

> There died a myriad,
> And of the best, among them,
> For an old bitch gone in the teeth,
> For a botched civilization,
> ...
> For two gross of broken statues,
> For a few thousand battered books.[114]

The literature represented the war as relentless horror and the "botched civilization" as the culpable party. The soldier's estrangement, mistrust, and hostility reverberates throughout Sassoon's angry and sarcastic poetry about those supporting the aggressive war and Owen's ironic and sensitive poetry about the gruesome fate of those innocents fighting the meaningless war.

In *Goodbye to All That* Robert Graves wrote, "I couldn't stand England any longer," and thought "London seemed unreally itself. Despite the number of uniforms in the streets, the general indifference to, and ignorance about, the war surprised me."[115] Graves reported the same sentiments among soldiers returning from the Home Front; they "could not understand the war madness that ran about everywhere, looking for a pseudo-military outlet." Graves even found serious conversation with his parents "all but impossible."[116] Similarly, in *All Quiet on the Western Front*, Paul Bäumer finds himself a stranger during home leave; he cannot relate to his family or former neighbors and is eager to return to his comrades. "But a sense of strangeness will not leave me, I cannot feel at home amongst these things. There is my mother, there is my sister, there my case of butterflies, and there the mahogany piano—but I am not myself there. There is a distance, a veil between us."[117]

Robert Wohl describes the English myth of the "lost generation," referring "simultaneously to the severe losses suffered within a small and clearly defined ruling class and to the difficulties that survivors from this class (and others below it) had in adjusting to the political and social realities of postwar England."[118] The lost generation was England's "missing elite," the university and public school graduates brought up to rule, only to discover at the war's end that British power was declining and "that they were going to have to preside over the transformation of the country, the phasing out of their values, and the dissolution of the empire."[119] The English elite, moreover, were not unique in their disillusionment. Throughout Europe, Wohl found that "this feeling of betrayal and deceit was especially strong among returning veterans born in the 1890s." He describes the returning generation of First World War veterans throughout Europe as being caught between two worlds, "one dead, the other powerless to be born."[120]

Mistrust and resentment of the society responsible for the war is not limited to the writings of combatants but also is found in the literature of noncombatants like that of George Bernard Shaw (1856-1950) and D. H. Lawrence (1885-1930). Shaw wrote *Heartbreak House* (1919) during the war (1916-17) about the "cultured, leisured Europe before the war" that pursued the war. As the play's title implies, theirs was a "house without foundations."[121] *Heartbreak House* is set in a Sussex country cottage occupied by a weird assortment of representative upper-class English people who deconstruct and devalue every aspect of English society: industry, politics, marriage, and religion.[122] Rather than focus on the war raging across the English Channel, *Heartbreak House* exposes the decaying society, corrupted values, and human folly that led Edwardian England into war. "I tell you one of two things must happen," says Hector Hushabye near the play's end, "Either out of that darkness some new creation will come to supplant us as we have supplanted the animals, or the heavens will fall in thunder and destroy us."[123]

Lawrence wrote *Women in Love* (1920) at the same time that Shaw wrote *Heartbreak House,* during the costly British offensives at the Somme and Passchendaele in 1916-17.[124] But, like Shaw's *Heartbreak House,* Lawrence's novel ignores the war and focuses instead on the disintegration of a failed civilization.[125] Although *Women in Love* depicts societal struggles for women's and workers' rights and personal struggles for meaning by the sisters Ursula and Gudrun Brangwen and their lovers Rupert Birkin and Gerald Crich, the novel's central theme is a world in crisis: "The sisters found themselves confronted by a void, a terrifying chasm, as if they had looked over the edge."[126] For Lawrence, the nineteenth-century rise of industry, embodied in the ruthless coal-mining industrialist Gerald Crich, caused this humanitarian crisis. Crich turns men into machines and finally dies in the desolate, white, alpine winter. The graphic scene was Lawrence's metaphor for all that Crich represents—England's industrial power and wealth that caused the apocalyptic war. In Lawrence's fatally diseased world, humanity's salvation is love, marriage, and some new human race. Echoing Hector Hushabye's comment in Shaw's play about a possible new race, Rupert Birkin consoles himself at the end of Lawrence's novel: "If humanity ran into a cul-de-sac, and expended itself, the timeless creative mystery would bring forth some other being, finer, more wonderful, some new, more lovely race, to carry on the embodiment of creation."[127]

A paradigm shift occurred after 1918, when intellectuals and youths began questioning the purpose and necessity of the war. They had gladly welcomed the war, but subsequently, as Stromberg reports, they developed "a revulsion against war ... quite as powerful as the welcoming of it in 1914."[128] In his poem on the 1918 signing of the armistice, Thomas Hardy poses their unanswered and unanswerable question:

The Sinister Spirit sneered: "It had to be!"
And again the Spirit of Pity whispered, "Why?"[129]

Some individuals did offer answers. The Dadaist Tristan Tzara wanted to sweep away the prewar civilization into nihilism. The Fabian George Bernard Shaw and the novelist Henri Barbusse embraced the myths surrounding Stalin. And the militarist Ernst Junger, who wrote *Storm of Steel* (1920), laid the groundwork for Nazism and Fascism.[130] Disillusionment with war, according to Wohl, fostered "an openness to radical political ideologies and skepticism about all nineteenth-century political movements, including social democracy."[131] Stromberg emphasized that it also caused a passionate retreat into pacifism, which left the door open for Nazism to enter European society unchecked.[132] Little more than two decades after the First World War, the generation of 1914 found themselves in the Second World War. They had failed to preserve the hard-won peace following the First World War. "The French and British had lost it out of weakness," according to Wohl, "the Germans and Italians had lost it out of wounded pride and reckless national ambition."[133]

War's Continuation. While cultural critics lamented the unconscionable human sacrifice and lambasted the culpable civic leaders of the war just ended, other wars erupted across Europe in the form of internal violence. Strikes resumed in all of Britain's major trades (miners, railwaymen, munitions workers, cotton spinners, and even London police) and culminated in a general ten-day strike, May 3-13, 1926.[134] The IRA Volunteers and the Black and Tans both perpetrated terrorist acts, like Bloody Sunday (November 21, 1920), bringing about the Anglo-Irish treaty of 1921 and precipitating a gruesome civil war.[135] War-hardened veterans fought the labor wars and the Irish wars, which made these internal conflicts all the more violent. In January 1919, the communist Spartakus organization staged an uprising in Berlin and government troops murdered its leaders Rosa Luxemburg and Karl Liebknect. In May 1919, French workers staged a general strike, and in fall 1920, Northern Italian strikers seized factories.[136] At the war's end, Russia plunged into a barbaric civil war that cost 1.5 million deaths and 6 million total casualties. *In terrorem* Bolshevik rule resulted in killing of independent peasant farmers (*kulaks*), priests, and White Guards, in establishing concentration camps in 1920, and in reinstituting pogroms that cost 120,000 lives among Russian and Ukrainian Jews.[137] In effect, one authoritarian Russian Empire had replaced another, this time with Lenin as the Red Czar. The U.S.S.R. became the first country "to be based on terror itself since the short-lived tyranny of Jacobin Revolutionary France."[138]

Ethnic Hostilities. A pernicious impact and terrible irony of the war was the creation of vulnerable ethnic minorities in new nation-states throughout Central and Eastern Europe, which resulted from unprecedented use of Wilsonian "national self-determination" to establish a new European order. "The single most important reason for the fragility of peace in Europe," according to Ferguson, "was the fundamental contradiction between self-determination and the existence of these minorities."[139] Germans were an overwhelming majority in many areas (e.g., Sudetenland, South-Tyrol, and Alsace Lorraine), but they had no vote. Instead, they were forced into the nations of Czechoslovakia, Italy, and France, respectively.[140] Romania, Czechoslovakia, Yugoslavia, Bulgaria, and Hungary all had sizable at-risk minorities, especially Jews.[141] These newly created nations routinely denied political and legal rights to ethnic minorities, who effectively became stateless persons (*apatrides*) without judicial protection from police domination. Rubenstein writes that "none of the national minorities could either trust or be trusted by the states of which they were technically citizens."[142]

The war had already exposed the terrible vulnerability of these ethnic minorities: from 1915 to 1918, the Turks instituted an unprecedented genocidal campaign that killed 1 million Armenians in a population of about 1.8 million.[143] Two decades later, Germany was the epicenter of an even worse genocide. Many Germans believed that their cause had been just, that they had not lost the war, and that they had been "stabbed in the back" by their civilian politicians, socialists, and Jews who acquiesced to an oppressive Versailles Treaty in order to seize power.[144] Adolf Hitler and the Nazis exploited this libel by blaming the Jews for Germany's defeat. The Nazis also charged them with polluting German blood, disenfranchised and isolated them within Germany, and finally perpetrated on them and the rest of European Jewry an unprecedented genocide.[145] As William Butler Yeats foresaw within two months after the Armistice ending World War I, "The blood-dimmed tide is loosed…. The best lack all conviction, while the worst / Are full of passionate intensity." The war's indifference to life, destruction of empires, and disenfranchising of vulnerable ethnic minorities sowed the seeds of the Holocaust.

Postwar Disintegration of Western Culture

One iconic poem, by title and content, distilled these four war-wounds to Western civilization and became the mythic representation of war-ravaged Europe—*The Waste Land* (1922). His protests concerning his poetic intentions to the contrary notwithstanding, T.S. Eliot (1888-1965) spoke for the postwar generation about the cultural devastation wrought by a ruinous war.[146] The poem's collage of different languages, conversations, verse forms, literary allusions, and poetic excerpts reflects the resulting fragmentation of Western civilization and culture. In "The Burial of the Dead," displaced people vie for attention and significance: the Archduke's niece reminisces upon her barren postwar existence and her loss of childhood freedom; the speaker points to the "stony rubbish" and the "heap of broken images" remaining from the destroyed civilization and offers to show the reader "something different"; the celebrated mystic Mme. Sosostris seeks answers for the loss of life in tarot cards; and the war veteran imagines a spectral crowd flowing over London Bridge and remarks, "I had not thought death had undone so many."[147] The dead, including his friend Stetson, provide no answers for the war's carnage.

"April is the cruelest month" because it reminds the speaker of Easter and ancient fertility rites, yet it fails to assure resurrection and rebirth or even to inspire his poetic sensibility. *The Waste Land* transits from the corpse-filled trenches—"rats alley / Where the dead men lost their bones"—to a culturally dead landscape where the promise of genuine renewal and rebirth is barely visible.[148] Stark images of a desiccated, arid, and infertile ground, and disturbing scenes of impotent, loveless, and unproductive sexuality permeate the poem.[149] Eliot draws upon ancient myths and rituals to paint a bleak picture of the postwar urban wasteland, with its misused and meaningless sexuality, its loneliness and despair, its disorienting cacophony of competing voices, and its societal and cultural disintegration. The poetic tradition is in tatters and Western culture in crisis.

In his review of James Joyce's *Ulysses* Eliot predicted that subsequent writers would follow Joyce's new technique of "manipulating a continuous parallel between contemporaneity and antiquity."

Eliot considered the technique "a way of controlling, of ordering, of giving a shape and a significance to the immense panorama of futility and anarchy which is contemporary history" and also a way of "making the modern world possible in art."[150] In *The Waste Land* Eliot employs this same "mythical method" effectively to describe cultural fragmentation but less successfully to restore Western culture from its ruins.[151] Ultimately, the speaker looks East to give "a shape and a significance" to the West and adopts three instructions from the Hindu *Upanishads*—giving, compassion, and control—to provide "the Peace which surpasseth understanding."[152] Perhaps Eliot is suggesting that Europeans blend Eastern and Western religions to provide spiritual healing and transcendental perspective for postwar Europe.[153] In the poem's final outpouring of allusions, however, Eliot struggles to find coherence in the fragmentation of the old civilization and to create a new aesthetic order out of the "heap of broken images." Revealingly, Eliot's collage of allusions, quotations, history, and myths requires explanatory notes because the poet and his reader no longer share a common culture. The war has destroyed it.

In summary, the Great War had ended a century of sustained scientific and technological progress, accelerating economic growth, and unprecedented material prosperity and cultural vibrance in the West. Western civilization had dominated the globe politically and economically and bustled everywhere with cultural creativity.[154] The apparently stable and progressive prewar civilization, however, proved fragile and self-destructive. The growing European middle class conducted a devastating civil war; the prosperous European empires became debtor nations; and postwar Europe remained a battleground for internal ethnic and political strife.[155] The Myth of the war and the Myth of the Wasteland merged into a single narrative—a failed, war-torn civilization was groping to find meaning among the broken fragments of its past.

Eliot's wasteland imagery not only resonated with postwar Western civilization, but also provided a perfect narrative setting for the emergence of materialism. Could a providential God have permitted this unmitigated human catastrophe? Or was the idea of God now dead and the cosmos finally revealed as indifferent to human concerns? Was fundamental reality just mindless matter lacking meaning and purpose? Was humanity just the accidental byproduct of a blind evolutionary process, with survival belonging to the fittest? Materialism provided clear-cut answers to all these questions with the apparent backing of science. The critical remaining question was whether mainstream Western culture would resume its centuries-old engagement with materialism and its metaphysical search for cosmic meaning and purpose in the postwar wasteland. The following close look at postwar theology, philosophy, literature and art provides a surprising and disturbing answer—a deafening silence.

4

Postwar Christian Theology

The Bible has only *one* theological interest and that is not speculative: interest in God himself. It is this that I call the Bible's other-
worldliness, its unhistoricalness, its antipathy to the idea of sa-
credness. *God* is the new, incomparable, unattainable ... interest.
... He is not a thing among other things, but the *Wholly Other*. ...
He it is of whom the Bible speaks.
— Karl Barth, *The Word of God and the Word of Man* (1924)[1]

Personally, I am convinced that there is no more substantial nour-
ishment for the religious life than contact with scientific realities,
if they are properly understood. ... It is useless, in consequence,
and it is unfair, to oppose science and Christ, or to separate them
as two domains alien to one another. By itself, science cannot discover Christ—but Christ satisfies the yearnings that are born in
our hearts in the school of science.
— Teilhard de Chardin, *Science and Christ or Analysis and Synthesis* (1921)[2]

The First World War produced a revolution in European thought
more significant than the ancient Christian revolution or the Enlightenment scientific revolution, according to Baumer, because
in a short time it destroyed centuries-old "idols" and changed the
world outlook, "leaving men without landmarks, casting them
adrift on an endless sea of becoming."[3] The postwar revolution
was unique because it focused upon humanity itself as the basic
problem. Humankind faced an existential crisis, alienated from an
unfathomable universe, anxious about life's meaningfulness, and
fearful of life's potential absurdity.

Before the war, Young Hegelians had pointed to self-alienation
as the consequence of humanity's misguided projection upon an

undeserving God, but they considered such alienation remediable. By contrast to such self-alienation, much less the theological optimism and triumphalism of the prewar period, humanity's postwar cosmic alienation seemed an inescapable doom. The radically new state of mind, writes Baumer, rendered the old theological questions "not merely controversial, but meaningless, to a significant number of people, including theologians."[4] After the Somme, talking about God was difficult as well as contentious. "Nor can the antimetaphysical climate, exemplified by both existentialism and the positivistic explosion, make things easy for a certain kind of religious thinking. It made theological metaphysics suspect, thus driving religion into the realm of faith, which, for the foregoing, as well as other reasons, 'secularist man' could no longer accept."[5]

As belief in the transcendent receded, humanity turned inward, and postwar culture became increasingly secularized. Some accepted Nietzsche's death of God as a *fait accompli* and considered religious questions irrelevant, and others anguished over apparent cosmic indifference and sought meaningful new answers.[6] Baumer largely attributes this post-World War I surge of secularism, characterized by existential and psychic angst, to "the patent failure of religion to encompass, or even to fit satisfactorily into, the scientific worldview."[7] Five distinct theologies arose to address the postwar crisis of secularism: (1) Protestant neoorthodoxy, (2) Christian existentialism, (3) Catholic neo-Thomism, (4) evolutionary or process theology, and (5) American fundamentalism.[8]

Protestant neoorthodoxy, exemplified by Karl Barth, Emil Brunner, and Friedrich Gogarten, eschewed metaphysical statements and rejected nineteenth-century liberal theology's positions concerning God's immanence in human life and culture. Instead, neoorthodoxy presented God as *Wholly Other* (Barth's phrase quoted above), knowable only through biblical revelation and divine grace. Christian existentialism, exemplified by Rudolf Bultmann and Paul Tillich, was heavily influenced by Martin Heidegger. Bultmann tried to relate religion to postwar secularist culture by demythologizing Christianity from its prescientific cosmology and explaining Christ's message to those suffering from existential anxiety over death and impermanence. Bultmann, however, sought to preserve the essential gospel message (*kerygma*) by rejecting exis-

tentialism's view that autonomous man could achieve authenticity alone; only Christ's saving grace could deliver fallen humanity
from its abject state. Tillich rejected Barth's view of God as outside
the natural world. Instead, he spoke of God as both transcendent
and immanent—"the God above the God of theism" but also "the
ground of being and meaning."[9]

Roman Catholicism, even before the war, opposed secularist
modernism and upheld Thomistic rationalism, with Jacques Maritain (1882-1973) defending Thomism against its modernist critics,
like Henri Bergson. Maritain maintained that reason can grasp the
essence of a thing or the being of being, drawing the Thomistic distinction between form and matter and arguing that form constitutes
the essence and matter the individuality of a being. Thus, Maritain
rejected Kant's limitations on man's cognitive capacity to understand noumena and to prove God's existence.[10] He also challenged
Bergson's idea of duration, the continuous process of change, as
"the pure becoming of Heraclitus," and Bergson's emphasis of intuition as having "chosen to abandon being and the intellect." To
the contrary, argued Maritain, the consummate Thomist, "being is
the only thing that endures."[11]

The Jesuit scientist Pierre Teilhard de Chardin and philoso-
pher-scientist Alfred North Whitehead pioneered evolutionary or
process theology. Teilhard's evolutionary theology attempted to
explain God as inspiration for the ascent of consciousness from primordial matter toward a superconsciousness in man and ultimate
fulfillment in Christ. Similarly, Whitehead described the world as
becoming or in process, and God as its lure toward increasing novelty, creativity, and aesthetic perfection. He rejected the idea of a
static, detached, and authoritarian God presiding over an entirely
separate and distinct world. Thus, Teilhard's evolutionary theology and Whitehead's process philosophy were consistent with one
another and embraced much of modern science, not only evolution
but, in the case of Whitehead, mathematics and physics as well.
Furthermore, Whitehead chided traditional Christian theology for
absolutizing truth, denigrating novelty in the world, and disasso-
ciating God from the ongoing process of reality—God as an outside overseer rather than an inherent co-creator along with man.[12]
Predictably, Maritain dismissed Teilhard's evolutionary thought as

"theology-fiction" — "one more Christian gnosis" and "a sin against the intellect" — for forsaking the being of Christ and of the cosmos.[13]

In America, during and immediately after the war, a militant Christian fundamentalism exploded as the result of associating the war with Nietzschean thought, German militarism, and Darwinian evolution. For fundamentalists, this modern secularist culture constituted a serious threat to traditional Anglo-Saxon Protestantism and moral civilization. "Do you not know," asks George McCready Price, fundamentalism's purported scientific spokesman, "that the theory of evolution absolutely does away with God and with His Son Jesus Christ, and with His revealed Word, the Bible, and is largely responsible for the class struggle now endangering the world?"[14] Evolution posed a major exegetical problem for fundamentalists, who considered the Bible divinely inspired and inerrant even on matters of science. They opposed teaching of evolution in high schools. When that failed, they urged equal classroom time for teaching "creation science." And when that failed, they urged equal classroom time for teaching "intelligent design."

Only one of the foregoing five postwar theologies attempted to integrate Christianity with Darwinian evolution and the new scientific worldview, namely, evolutionary or process theology. The rest disengaged from modern science or, in the case of American fundamentalism, actively opposed it. Protestant neoorthodoxy considered human reason incapable of understanding God or his relationship to the world; Christian existentialism focused on humanity's psychic needs rather than its metaphysical concerns; Catholic neo-Thomism reverted to the medieval world of being and God as First Cause; and American fundamentalism opposed Darwinian evolution as inconsistent with Genesis. By contrast, Teilhard and White-head resisted the anti-metaphysical climate of postwar positivism, re-interpreted Christianity in light of modern scientific developments, and constructed a modern cosmology infused with mind, meaning, and purpose.

Barth's Neoorthodoxy

Barth (1886-1968) was born in Basel, grew up in Bern, and in 1904 began his university studies in Switzerland. In 1908, he transferred to the German universities of Berlin, Tübingen, and finally Marburg. Barth studied under the leading liberal Protestant theologians, including Harnack and Herrmann, and also served as an editorial assistant for the most influential liberal Protestant journal, *The Christian World*. Thereafter, Barth served as pastor in the village of Safenwil in Aargau, Switzerland (1911-1922), where he supported the trade union movement against the local industrialists, joined the Social Democratic Party in 1915 (becoming labeled "the red pastor of Safenwil"), and opposed state religion and Church endorsement of war. During his subsequent professorships in theology at Göttingen, Münster, and Bonn (1922-1935), Barth tried to free Protestant theology from what he considered its philosophical and anthropological influences.[15]

The 1914 Manifesto of Intellectuals in support of the war was a turning point for Barth because it bore the signatures not only of scholars and artists but also of Adolph von Harnack and six other liberal Protestant theologians, including Wilhelm Herrmann. Karl Barth had studied under Harnack and Herrmann at Marburg and Berlin, respectively, and was horrified to discover their signatures on the Manifesto. Barth concluded that the "old world of exegesis, ethics, dogmatics and preaching, which I had hitherto held to be essentially trustworthy, was shaken to the foundations, and with it, all the other writings of the German theologians."[16] Following his shocked response to the Manifesto supporting the Kaiser's war policy, Barth led a revolt against nineteenth-century liberal Protestant theology by a group of German theologians.[17] The group included Emil Brunner, Friedrich Gogarten, Eduard Thurneysen, and Rudolph Bultmann, who variously called their program "Theology of Crisis," "Dialectical Theology," and "Theology of the Word of God."

In his essay, "Between the Times" (1920), Gogarten explained that Crisis theologians saw disintegration everywhere and believed they stood between the death of the old world and the birth of the new world of theology.[18] Zahrnt explains their approach as follows:

Everything that had been regarded as good, true and beautiful, as reasonable, civilized and liberal, as noble and humane, and which for more than a century had composed the whole world, had been destroyed. In its destruction, this world was revealed for what it was, the very delicate and skillful artifact of man. It is true that it was not a world without God, but its God had been a "human God." ... All these theologians looked towards the crisis, the uttermost limits of human existential life, the judgment of God.[19]

In 1922, they began the journal *Between the Times* to express their revolutionary thoughts in the aftermath of the war. They forecasted the coming judgment of God against the all-too-human God created by nineteenth-century theology, and called for mankind to approach a "wholly other" God in total nakedness and abject surrender.[20] *Between the Times* continued until 1933 when the group disintegrated in disagreement, especially over Nazi policies.

Like other Crisis theologians, Barth confronted a huge problem of biblical interpretation (or hermeneutics), having rejected the liberal theological views of the Reformed Church as no longer adequate to the postwar world.[21] At university, theologians had taught "awe in the presence of history." This suggested the need for historical-critical research into the Bible and Christianity and implied the presence of a divine spirit in history, a historical pantheism, which led humanity toward higher levels of civilization.[22] Barth deemed such theology totally inadequate to a proper understanding and interpretation of the Bible. Instead of awe for history, Barth substituted awe for the Word of God. His new theology stressed divine revelation rather than human consciousness—how God speaks to man rather than how man thinks of God.[23] For Barth, God is not accessible from the study of history, from the psychology of the pious individual, or from the speculations of philosophy about the Absolute. Rather, God is accessible only from the Word of God.[24] Thus, Barth reinvented himself as a biblical theologian, preaching a new theology of revelation which focused on God, and rejecting the dominant liberal Protestant view, which focused on man's feelings, mind, culture, beliefs, and piety. In his famous *The Epistle to the Romans* (1918, 1921), Barth trumpeted his new theme of finding "the Word in the words."[25] Like Kierkegaard, he preached God's "infinite qualitative distinction" from man and God's Incarnation as a matter of faith and not of reason.[26]

The Bible created a human *crisis*, for Barth. The Bible drove humanity beyond its immediate world to the infinite; it awakened humanity to the limitations of human thought; and it inspired humanity to the ultimate truth beyond human reason.[27] Furthermore, since the Bible is the word of man as well as the Word of God, and since biblical witnesses make questionable judgments about history, science, religion, and theology, human reason alone is inadequate to understand the Bible; it requires the miracle of grace.[28] Consequently, *"faith* in Barth becomes almost entirely speechless," according to Zahrnt, "almost ceases to have any content, and invariably represents no kind of assertion on the part of man, but only his denial."[29] Barth's rejection of reason, specifically, hermeneutical inquiry into Jewish eschatology and Hellenistic philosophy, as the means of grasping the biblical subject matter ultimately caused his break from the other Crisis theologians. They thought some understanding of humanity's origin, nature, and destiny was prerequisite to understanding God.[30] By the time of this break in 1933, however, Barth already had overturned three centuries of Protestant theology, restored God as its central postwar theme, and emerged as a dominant force in twentieth-century Protestant theology.[31] When the Nazis came to power that year and attempted to control the Church, Barth led the opposition. He wrote the famous Barmen Declaration, which rejected Nazi superintendence of the Church, proclaimed Church allegiance to the Word of God, and challenged Nazi anti-Semitic policies. In addition, he refused to take the Nazi loyalty oath—the one German professor of theology refusing to do so.[32] Consequently, in 1935, the Nazis stripped him of his Bonn professorship and forced him out of Germany.[33]

In 1927, Barth had begun writing his *Church Dogmatics* with an emphasis on God's *Wholly Otherness*, but, in 1935, he changed his emphasis. Thereafter, he stressed God's Incarnation in Christ, Barth's "Christological concentration," which reversed the traditional view of redemption and grace as following the Creation and Fall. Instead, Barth declared that God contemplated human redemption through Christ from the very beginning of time, even before Creation.[34] For Barth, Christ comprehends all of history, brings God's grace to the world, and unites God and humankind. Consequently, all of creation, especially humanity, has a positive relationship with God, despite the sin and evil in the world. While evil seeks to evade God, it cannot escape God's grace.[35] Barth's faith in Christ's predetermined coming led him to reject the Calvinist doctrine of election—the conception of predestination whereby God chooses some for salvation and others for damnation. Rather, from the very outset, God elected Himself for earthly death and elected sinful humanity for eternal life, believers and nonbelievers alike.[36] While Barth does not declare universal salvation, he also does not reject it. But Barth charged believers with a special call to service in joyful thanksgiving for receiving the gift of grace and truth.[37] Because of his *Church Dogmatics,* Barth has been called the theologian of the Good News, far removed from the pessimistic orthodoxy and divine otherness of *The Epistle to the Romans.*[38] The Old Testament prophet of Crisis theology had become the New Testament evangelist of Christ's loving humanity.

In summary, Barth's neoorthodoxy rediscovered the deity of God, introduced a necessary corrective to liberal Protestant theology, and resonated in the disillusioned postwar world.[39] Barth's rejection of human reason in understanding God, however, also applied to God's Creation. Existence became comprehensible, for Barth, only Christologically, by analogy to man's understanding of Christ's humanity and divinity through Scripture.[40] Thus, human suffering is analogous to Christ's suffering, and marriage is analogous to Christ's relationship with the Church and the triune divinity. Understanding existence, for Barth, is a one-way street proceeding from God to humankind rather than the converse. Human reason, the individual's critical intelligence, plays no meaningful role in interpreting the universe, except by analogy to Scripture. Hence, Barth's epistemology marginalizes the human projects of scientific inquiry, of relating modern science to Christian teaching, and of participating meaningfully in God's creation. Furthermore, Barth's concept of universal redemption implies a lack of dignity, value, and spiritual significance to humanity's existential travails and efforts; it strips history of its ongoing drama and meaning; and it undermines humanity's quest to understand Creation and to promote progress. By diminishing the role of critical intelligence in humanity's quest to understand reality, Barth effectively ceded metaphysical inquiry to materialism.

Teilhard's Evolutionary Theology

Teilhard (1881-1955) was born in Clermont, France, the fourth of eleven children, in a religiously pious, well-to-do family. He developed an early interest in geology, boarded at the Jesuit school of Notre Dame Mongré from age twelve, took his initial vows as a Jesuit in 1901 at age twenty, and was ordained a priest in 1911 at age thirty. While pursuing his doctorate in paleontology, Teilhard read and quickly embraced Henri Bergson's *Creative Evolution*. Then the war broke out, and at age thirty-three, with a growing scientific reputation, Teilhard suddenly became an enlisted stretcher-bearer in the French auxiliary service attached to a colonial light infantry regiment of North African Zouaves. He tended to the wounded and dying at the Marne and Ypres in 1914, and to victims of German poison gas near the Belgian coast in 1915.[41] In 1916, he began a notebook, trying to make sense of the war's death toll and to find some overarching principle for the war's disintegration. In his first wartime essay "Cosmic Life," Teilhard explained how matter progresses into organisms of greater psychic tension and fragility before crossing the line into humanity itself.[42] In 1917, Teilhard was promoted to chaplain; in March 1918, he faced the last great German offensive of the war; and in May 1918, he took his final vows as a Jesuit. In July 1918, his regiment retreated and then counterattacked at Soissons, at which point Teilhard felt his number was finally up.[43] But he survived and was honored for his service; his Muslim soldiers praised his gallantry and the French Army awarded him the Médaille Militaire and Chevalier of the Legion of Honor.[44]

Despite his four-year experience of death at the front, including two brothers killed and two wounded, Teilhard developed a Hegelian perspective on wartime destruction as a phase of cosmic evolution toward God.[45] The chaotic war, for Teilhard, was one of the inevitable side effects of humanity's active participation in creative evolution, which he considered "an adventure, a groping, a risk."[46] Teilhard returned to his doctoral studies at the Museum, earned highest honors for his dissertation in 1920, and was elected president of the French Geological Society. His views on human evolution, however, soon collided with the Church's insistence on

God's "instantaneous creation."[47] Questioning the literalist interpretation of the Creation and Fall, Teilhard had proffered several
possible alternative explanations in an attempt to harmonize Genesis with evolution.[48] Neo-Thomist critics quickly charged Teilhard
with designing a contrary "biological philosophy," and Teilhard
started to worry whether he could satisfy his Jesuit superiors and
still remain true to his scientific beliefs.[49] His fears proved justified
as ecclesiastical opposition mounted in tandem with his writings,
which sought to bring Church doctrine in line with scientific discoveries.[50] After a year and a half of geological exploration in China, Teilhard returned home to find the Roman Curia outraged at
his earlier "irresponsible speculations" about the Fall and insistent
that he formally promise not to write or speak "anything contrary
to the Church's 'traditional' position on Original Sin."[51] Teilhard
capitulated as an act of fidelity rather than intellectual assent ("I
stand condemned by dolts and ignoramuses!"), but privately assured his friend and professional colleague Professor Édouard Le
Roy that he maintained his evolutionary views and "gospel of research."[52] In letters to close friends, Teilhard lamented the failure
of church officials to embrace scientific progress and thought "the
time has come for us to save Christ from the clerics, in order to save
the World."[53]

Teilhard wrote "Hominization" (1925), an essay arguing that
hominoids crossed the reflectivity threshold to become self-aware
and cooperative, and urging scientists to classify humans among
primates, given their small morphologic disparity. By then he
had already exceeded those "limited" evolutionists who accepted
evolution "only within established phyla" and excluded humankind because of an apparently "missing link."[54] In 1929, Teilhard
returned to China where he collaborated in work on a skull with
the morphology of the Neanderthal and the cranial capacity of
Pithecanthropus, which Teilhard considered a close link between
humans and apes.[55] His collaborative discovery of Sinanthropus
received widespread acclaim, and in 1937, he visited the United
States to discuss Sinanthropus at the Academy of Science in Philadelphia and to receive the Mendel Medal at Villanova. His Villanova remarks about humanity's evolutionary breakthrough were
published in the *New York Times* and other American and Canadian

newspapers under the banner "The Jesuit Who Believes Man Descended from the Apes." This produced the so-called "Villanova
Incident," which triggered a stiff rebuke from Rome.[56] Nevertheless, Teilhard continued to write private essays and completed the
third revision of *The Phenomenon of Man* (1928, 1930, 1939), which
he sent to Rome for approval. *The Phenomenon of Man* expanded
his wartime thoughts in "Cosmic Life" and constituted his "final
testament" about evolution's goal.[57] Trapped in China throughout
World War II, Teilhard participated in efforts to protect the Sinanthropus bones in Peking. With permission of the Jesuit Order,
he addressed scientists and diplomats at Shanghai University, but
again he upset some Jesuits by discussing evolution "as though it
were proven fact."[58]

Following World War II, Teilhard returned home to learn that
the Curia had rejected *The Phenomenon of Man* and required such
extensive revisions that he felt defeated.[59] In 1948, the Jesuit Father
General invited Teilhard to Rome to discuss his philosophical and
theological views, his several books, his invitation to apply for the
chair of prehistory at the College of France, and his invitation to lecture at Columbia University. The Father General refused Teilhard
everything—permission to accept the college chairmanship because
his evolutionist views would cause another "Villanova incident,"
permission to publish *The Phenomenon of Man* because it would im-
ply Jesuit endorsement, and permission to lecture at Columbia or
to discuss his philosophy in public. Leaving Rome empty-handed,
Teilhard complained to friends, "My general doesn't *want* to understand! ... Those people in Rome are living on another planet!"[60]
Recognizing that the Jesuits considered his writings misguided and
might expunge his entire life's work upon his death, Teilhard con-
sulted a canon lawyer about following his conscience to preserve
his writings, and then wrote a will leaving his papers to his friend
Mademoiselle Mortier.[61] "If I'd had it to do over," Teilhard mused,
"I wonder if I'd still have been a Jesuit!"[62] In 1951, Teilhard found a
scientific position at the Wenner-Gren Foundation in New York. On
Good Friday, 1955, he wrote, "evil is not 'catastrophic' (the fruit of
some cosmic accident), but the inevitable side effect of the process
of the cosmos unifying into God."[63] Two days later, on Easter Sunday, Teilhard died.

Teilhard's works appeared shortly after his death, fulfilling his lifelong mission to educate modern man, just as Thomas Aquinas had educated medieval man, by integrating science, religion, and philosophy in systematic thought.[64] In books like *The Phenomenon of Man*, Teilhard portrayed the universe as expanding in an energetic process of ever-greater complexity from elementary particles through increasingly higher organisms toward "hominization," the crucial evolutionary turning point at which humankind appears. Humanity constitutes a new stage of increasing complexity-consciousness that gives rise to planetary consciousness, which he called the "noosphere."[65] The evolutionary path, for Teilhard, inevitably moves humanity toward ever greater consciousness in a process called "noogenesis," which proceeds in three phases: First, centrifugal force promotes human freedom and individuality; second, centripetal force promotes human planetary socialization; and third, human "planetization" converges at the Omega point where the evolutionary process ends in self-transcending love and unity with God. While God does not preordain the cosmic evolutionary process, which remains subject to human direction, divine love draws evolution toward Christ at the Omega point.[66]

Thus, Teilhard considered divine love as both the inspiration and the endpoint for the cosmic evolutionary process, with Omega both "supremely present" and yet "independent of the collapse of the forces with which evolution is woven."[67] In addition, the mutual care and cooperation among humans with the active and necessary support of Christianity advances in cosmic evolutionary progress toward Omega.[68] Scientific study, moreover, contributes significantly to this progress, and "Christians have no need to be afraid of, or to be unreasonably shocked by, the results of scientific research, whether in physics, in biology, or in history."[69] Three days before his death, Teilhard reflected on the edict of Church officials that he perform scientific work "without getting involved in philosophy or theology," and considered it "psychologically unviable and, what is more, directly opposed to the greater glory of God."[70] Vigorous Church opposition to evolution lasted until 1950, when Pope Pius XII gave it conditional support; opposition finally folded in 1996, when Pope John Paul II declared evolution more than a hypothesis.[71]

Barth, Teilhard, and Modern Science

The war spurred Barth and Teilhard toward new theological positions, which caused major shifts in Christian theology. They shared some remarkable similarities along with some fundamental differences. Barth overturned three centuries of Protestant theology and restored God as its central theme, and Teilhard pioneered evolutionary theology within neo-Thomist Catholicism. Christ was central to their thinking: Christ united God and man in Barth's *Church Dogmatics,* and inspired evolutionary progress in Teilhard's *Phenomenon of Man.* For Barth, evil cannot escape God's loving kindness and divine election, and for Teilhard, evil is the "disunity" inherent in the evolutionary process toward Christ.[72] In ethics, Barth considered God's humanity "the source and norm of all human standards and human dignity," and Teilhard considered socialization, cooperation, and mutuality a necessary and inevitable result of increased human consciousness en route toward Omega.[73]

The two diverge, however, precisely on the point of present concern, namely, theology's engagement with the modern scientific worldview. Teilhard represented the kind of philosophic approach within Christianity that Barth rejected for failing to concentrate on Scripture and Catholic officials rejected for failing to adhere to Thomism and ecclesiastical dogma. Teilhard thought Christianity needed to embrace the modern spirit, which he considered "pantheist in tendency, immanent, organistic, evolutionary," and to revise traditional dogma, which was "expressed primarily in terms of personality, transcendence, juridical relationships, and immutability."[74] Teilhard considered a religion of progress and evolution "exactly in line with what the modern world is looking for as its God, ... a God who justifies, sets the crown upon, and receives as a supreme tribute, the incessant ... labour of the consummation, even on earth, of man."[75] Instead of becoming a brake to human endeavor, Teilhard urged the Church to become a stimulus, replacing the image of Christ as "hidden in the clouds" with an image of Christ "clothed in the energies of the world in which he is immersed."[76] He believed that "the incorporation and assimilation by Christian thought of modern evolutionary views is sufficient to break down the barrier that for four centuries has continually been arising between reason and faith." Furthermore, it allowed Catholics and non-Catholics to "meet as one through their basic faith in a progress of the earth," confident of "a divine guarantee that, in spite of all death, the fruit of our labour is *irreversible* and *cannot be lost.*"[77]

Teilhard's efforts to relate Christianity and science constituted a necessary corrective to *fin de siècle* Catholic rigidity, just as Barth's Crisis theology constituted a necessary corrective to nineteenth-century liberal Protestant theology. Barth's theology, however, became dogmatic and remote from modern secular life, and largely indifferent to scientific developments and metaphysical concerns. Teilhard's thought, by contrast, integrated Christianity and modern science, recognizing the shared role of God and humanity in cosmic evolution. Barth's rejection of any philosophy in theology and Catholicism's rejection of any non-Thomistic philosophy in theology led both Christian denominations away from reasoned engagement with modern science and metaphysical materialism after World War I.

Mainstream Theology's Disengagement from Science

Emil Brunner. Despite his dominance, Barth was not the only voice in Protestant theology. But those other voices—neoorthodoxy and biblical existentialism—also focused on humanity rather than cosmology. Following the demise of Crisis theology, Emil Brunner (1889-1966) wrote the first Christian anthropology since the First World War, *Man in Revolt* (1935), influenced by the I-Thou philosophy of Martin Buber. In Brunner's view, both Christian and secular thought basically concern what it means to be human. The individual seeks something higher, beyond what he or she is presently. The individual either discovers the origin of that "true" self in the Word of God, the divine Thou, or opposes his origins and becomes a "man in revolt."[78] For Brunner, "it is the understanding of man that divides faith from unbelief," and a "true" understanding depends on whether "God or man is the center."[79] Through the I-Thou relationship with God, the individual achieves self-understanding as a creature in God's image. Hence, faith is fundamentally relational (I-Thou), not rational-scientific (I-it). Indeed, the shift from a personal to an intellectual understanding of faith, for Brunner, was

"the most fatal occurrence within the entire history of the Church."
He attributed it to the Greek philosophical influence in the early
Church and the application of rationalist thinking to biblical Rev-
elation.[80]

Barth and Brunner parted ways over Brunner's natural theology, which was Brunner's way of reaching out to non-Christians.
Brunner considered God's revelation in Creation (nature) to be an
anthropological fact, an aspect of the divine-human encounter. By
contrast, Barth considered nature and grace, like faith and reason,
history and revelation, Germany and Christianity, and all the other
"jolly little hyphens," a constant source of error in Protestantism.[81]
Brunner's concern was preaching the Word of God to de-Chris-
tianized modern man; Barth's concern was correctness in theology,
not conversion of nonbelievers who in the end are saved anyway.
Brunner tried to steer his middle course between liberalism and
orthodoxy, between the subjectivism of reason and experience and
the objectivism of church dogma and biblical literalism. At bottom,
however, Brunner's theology remained anthropological, focused
upon man's inescapable need for a personal relationship with God,
who was revealed in Christ through the witness of scripture.[82] Thus,
Brunner's theology centered upon humanity and not the implications of modern science for Christian thought.

Friedrich Gogarten. Another leading Crisis and neoorthodox
theologian who fell out with Barth over the relationship between
theology and anthropology was Friedrich Gogarten (1887-1967).
Like Barth, Gogarten rejected the liberal Protestant interpretation
of history. But Gogarten still took human history into account as interpersonal encounters of the individual with God and with the individual's neighbors. In a refinement of Brunner's I-Thou relationship, Gogarten stressed the primary importance of the Other in the
relationship, whether the Thou be God or humanity. Consequently,
Gogarten became a lifelong critic of subjectivism and individualism, prompting his opposition to Weimar liberalism, his brief embrace of Nazi politics, and his attacks on Barth and the Confessing
Church.[83]

Because he wrote at length about the relationship of theology
and science, Gogarten's views deserve special attention. Pre-Christian humanity worshiped the cosmos as divine, which Gogarten

considered humanity's original sin. But post-Christian humanity worshiped God as God, *secularizing* and removing divinity from the world. While freeing humanity *from* the inappropriately divinized pre-Christian world, Christianity simultaneously entrusted humanity with responsibility *for* the divinely created and newly secularized world through the exercise of reason. Medieval Christianity, however, reunified God and the world, causing humanity to lose its freedom. Luther restored that freedom during the Reformation, when he *re-secularized* the Christian world. Luther distinguished between the kingdoms of God and the world, and thereby inaugurated the modern era of humanity's cultural autonomy.

As Zahrnt points out, Gogarten's secularized world has an ambivalent character: "While Christian faith cannot exist without secularisation, it is quite possible, once the process of secularisation was set in motion by faith, for it to continue without faith."[84] In other words, individuals may well forget their freedom and responsibility as "sons of God" to care for and rule the secularized world, and lose sight of their God-given inheritance and patrimony.[85] If individuals ignore their divine gift and presume to impart meaning to the world themselves, then secularization becomes *secularism*. In the condition of secularism, humanity's self-importance delivers the world of its status as God's gift and produces an alien system in which humanity serves itself and falls into meaningless chaos and despair.[86] Interestingly, Gogarten faults theology rather than science for modern secularism.

The Church has failed to understand and has corrupted secularization in two ways, according to Gogarten: first, by challenging humanity's freedom to use reason in stewardship of the earth, and second, by trying to reunite God with the world in a misguided "religious worship of the world and its laws."[87] Gogarten contends that faith and science must remain distinct and independent. Like politics, economics, and other human projects that require the use of reason, science must remain free to pursue knowledge, unfettered by any theological concerns about conflicting with faith.[88] For its part, science must remain "related only to individual data, never to the whole of existence."[89] Science ceases to be science; however, when it attempts to advance a metaphysical "world view." In that event, science loses its secularized character, encroaches upon the realm of divine mystery, and becomes idolatrous philosophy.[90] Conversely, faith should not attempt to supply a "Christian world view" to the open questions of science. In so doing, faith would desert secularization and degenerate into "Christian secularism."[91]

Zahrnt summarizes Gogarten's rather complex and artificial separation of scientific knowledge and Christian faith as follows:

> [S]cience is without faith, or else it ceases to be science; but only where faith exists can science be without faith. We cannot escape this dialectic relationship between faith and science. Since the process of secularisation has come into being, in essence since the coming of Christian faith into the world, the unity of knowledge and faith has been destroyed once for all, and cannot be restored by any device, however ingenious, on the part of faith or on the part of knowledge. Since that time, knowledge and faith have no longer been able to exist in a unity, but only in a duality, or more precisely in the juxtaposition which preserves the identity of both. Faith must not subject knowledge to itself, nor must knowledge attempt to eliminate faith.[92]

In short, science becomes idolatrous, encroaches upon divine mystery, and exceeds reason's capability and responsibility when it transcends data, undertakes metaphysics, and espouses a worldview.[93] Conversely, theology becomes secularism and loses secularization when it intrudes on scientific thinking and tries to reconnect God with such worldly concerns. Hence, Gogarten's theology distances itself from modern science and limits its engagement only to those circumstances, such as materialism presumably, when science engages in metaphysics. Despite his views on the importance of secularization and science, therefore, Gogarten strictly separated faith and reason, theology and science, and he discouraged any active engagement between these two realms.

Rudolf Bultmann and Paul Tillich. With Rudolf Bultmann and Paul Tillich, Protestant theology turns to issues of human finitude and self-transcendence.[94] Bultmann (1884-1976) demythologized the New Testament imagery, calling it a prescientific effort to express the transcendent. In Bultmann's view, the biblical mythology that describes God as intervening in the world lacks credibility and belies modern experience. Instead, this prescientific imagery in the Bible requires reinterpretation to capture its deeper meaning for human existence. Biblical truth lies in its existential message about self-understanding and its framework for human authenticity. In contrast with Barth's view of the Bible as God's self-revelation, Bultmann considered the Bible as God's interrelationship with humanity and guidance for authentic Christian existence.[95]

Tillich (1886-1965) identified the causes of postwar existential anxiety as the triple threat of non-being—ontic anxiety caused by fate and death, spiritual anxiety caused by fear of meaninglessness, and moral anxiety caused by non-achievement of possibilities. The authentic individual, for Tillich, affirms his or her being, despite the threat of non-being, by a courageous act of will. The courage to be, however, requires divine inspiration, which comes from a different God than the God of traditional theology. Tillich considers that God to be a pathologic transference to a parental figure. For Tillich, God is the depth dimension, the ground of being, the unconditional acceptance, and the God above God. In Tillich's view, classical theism is really idolatry, which reduces God to an idol of finite proportions. The individual becomes truly self-reliant only when drawing his or her source of being from something infinite, namely, the God above God.[96] In summary, existentialist theologians like Tillich and Bultmann undertook to relate the biblical message to the postwar human condition of depersonalization, anxiety, inauthenticity, and desire for self-transcendence. Like the neoorthodox theologians, however, the existential theologians did not consider it their mission to relate Christianity to the modern scientific worldview.

American Fundamentalism and the Crusade against Darwinism

Between 1917 and the early 1920s, Christian fundamentalism burst militantly onto the American scene over anxiety about the theological and cultural implications of Darwinian evolution. World War I had exposed humanity's darker side, and fundamentalists attributed this to modernist German "Kultur"—Nietzsche's "superman philosophy" that might makes right. For fundamentalists, Darwinian evolution symbolized modernism and militarism, which posed a threat to traditional Protestant society and American civilization.[97] In particular, fundamentalists feared that the teaching of evolution in public schools would cause American youth to lose their faith. William Jennings Bryan (1860-1925), who became a spokesman for the antievolution crusade, "became convinced that the teaching of Evolution as a fact instead of a theory caused the students to lose faith in the Bible, first, in the story of creation, and later in the other doctrines, which underlie the Christian religion."[98]

Fundamentalism derived its name from twelve booklets entitled *The Fundamentals*, published (1910-1915) to reform worldwide Christianity based upon a mixture of biblical literalism and inerrancy motivated largely by nineteenth-century millenarianism. Millenarianism was an apocalyptic movement that predicted Christ's imminent return in the seventh age of human history, the coming new millennium of tribulation. Importantly, the timing of the millennium depended upon the literal understanding of the Bible. Millennialists believed that any contextual error might invalidate the entire Bible, and they aimed to preserve the truth of Genesis, particularly God's special creation of humans, against the threat of evolutionary science. Although *The Fundamentals* identify evolution as a principal cause of disbelief, their tone was not militantly antievolution. Rather, their primary target was the proponents of higher criticism who considered the Bible a historical text rather than the divine word.[99] With World War I, however, the fundamentalist movement underwent a "dramatic transformation," according to Notre Dame Professor of History George M. Marsden. Fundamentalists thought the war presented a clear and present danger to the moral course of civilization, as exemplified by Darwinian evolution.[100]

The leaders of the antievolution movement, like Bryan and the Baptist minister William Bell Riley (1861-1947), claimed not to oppose science. Rather, they opposed evolution as an unscientific, unproven hypothesis because it failed the scientific test of factual demonstration in the tradition of Bacon and Newton.[101] "It is not 'science' that Orthodox Christians oppose," declared Riley. "They are opposed only to the theory of evolution, which has not been proved, and therefore is not to be called by the sacred name of *science*."[102] Bryan added that Darwinism is not only unscientific but un-Christian, and he aligned himself with Riley in an effort to prevent the teaching of evolution, which was appearing in the growing number of American public schools.[103] To this end, Bryan and the fundamentalists influenced the passage of a Tennessee law in 1925 (the Butler Act), which banned the teaching of evolution in public schools. Officials in Dayton, Tennessee, asked science teacher John T. Scopes to voluntarily serve as a defendant in a test case. This became the famous Scopes Monkey Trial. Bryan advised the prosecution, Clarence Darrow defended Scopes, and the courtroom became a legal circus played out in the national press.[104]

Bryan failed to recruit any scientists to defend the prosecutor's creationist position. Furthermore, he could identify only one supportive living scientist, George McCready Price (1870-1963), who declined to testify and warned Bryan against getting into the science. When Bryan identified Price as the one living scientist whom he respected on the subject of special creation versus evolution, Darrow sarcastically derided Price's scientific credentials: "Every scientist in this country knows [Price] is a mountebank and a pretender and not a geologist at all."[105] Called to the stand and cross-examined by Darrow, Bryan displayed embarrassing ignorance of biblical criticism and non-Christian religions. He also conceded that the world was more than 6000 years old, and that creation probably took more than just six twenty-four days.[106] As Wisconsin-Madison Professor of the History of Science and Medicine Ronald L. Numbers notes, "Bryan's admission at Dayton spotlighted a serious and long-standing problem among antievolutionists: their failure to agree on a theory of creation."[107] Without ever taking the stand, Scopes confessed to teaching evolution, and was convicted and fined $100 on a straightforward application of the Butler Act. Scopes appealed his conviction, which was reversed on a technicality. Although creationists lost their public sounding board and went underground after the Scopes trial, their pressure on local and state legislatures and school boards succeeded for decades in keeping Darwinism out of American high school texts. This changed after 1957, when the U.S.S.R. launched Sputnik. During the 1960s, the United States Government supported the rewriting and publication of the Biological Sciences Curriculum Studies in American public schools, which introduced new high school biology textbooks discussing evolution.[108]

In 1961, fundamentalists revived a claim in the book entitled *The New Geology* (1923) by George McCready Price that certain strata and fossils were relics of Noah's flood. The new interest in Genesis flood geology promoted "creation science" as an alternative to evolution and spurred establishment of the Creation Research Society in 1963. The Society espoused a worldwide flood, biblical inerrancy, and special creation of "all basic types of living things."[109] Creationist viewpoints, however, vary widely. For *general* creationists, God creates in nonspecific ways, and for *special* creationists, God creates in specific ways. God's specific ways differ, however, depending on whether the special creationists apply a *strict* (literal) or *progressive* (allegorical) interpretation of the Bible. Scientific creationists are usually special and strict creationists, who fall into one of two categories: Young-Earth Creationists (YEC) read the Bible literally to mean that God created the Earth in six days between 6000 and 10,000 years ago. Old-Earth Creationists (OEC) construe Genesis to mean six "God-sized" days and accept both the Big Bang theory and the 13.8 billion year age of the universe.[110] YEC and OEC alike reject Darwinian evolution outright under the biblical test of truth, but the OEC accept some evolution with strategic divine interventions.[111]

Fundamentalist opposition to the teaching of evolution in public schools began with a legislative prohibition against teaching evolution, changed to a legislative "balanced treatment" requirement for teaching creation science, and most recently turned into a school board requirement to teach "intelligent design." Various judicial setbacks spurred the evolution of fundamentalism's antievolution strategy. In *Epperson v. Arkansas*, 393 U.S. 97 (1968), the United States Supreme Court invalidated an Arkansas statute that prohibited the teaching of human evolution in the public schools. The Court held that the Establishment Clause of the First Amendment to the United States Constitution prohibits a state from requiring "that teaching and learning must be tailored to the principles or prohibitions of any religious sect or dogma." Following the *Epperson* Case, fundamentalists changed legislative tactics, urging schools to give scientific creationism equal time with Darwinian evolution. In *Edwards v. Aguillard*, 482 U.S. 578 (1987), the United States Supreme Court invalidated the Louisiana "balanced treatment" law, which prohibited the teaching of evolution in public schools without also teaching creation science, on grounds that the law violated the First Amendment. Following the *Edwards* decision, fundamentalists again changed tactics, this time claiming that Darwinian evolution cannot account for the "intelligent design" in nature. The Dover Area School District in Pennsylvania required the teaching of intelligent design (ID) in addition to evolution, which also prompted yet another court challenge. In *Kitzmiller v. Dover Area School District* (2005), a Federal District Court found that ID is theology, not science, and teaching ID in public schools violates the First Amendment.[112]

Postwar Christian Theology in Summary

Barth and Teilhard were pioneers in postwar theological thought, leading their respective Christian denominations toward antipodal positions with respect to modern science—Barth toward God as *wholly other* and away from metaphysics and science; Teilhard toward God as immersed in the world's ongoing evolution and away from God "hidden in the clouds." Barth succeeded throughout the twentieth century, whereas Teilhard failed during his lifetime until his ideas gradually emerged following posthumous publication of his writings. As a leader in Crisis theology and neoorthodoxy, Barth kept the realms of religion and science separate and succeeded in refocusing Protestant thought on the Bible as the Word of God and on God in his "infinite qualitative distinction" from humankind. Even the neoorthodox theologian Gogarten, who stressed the value of science in the secularized world, insisted that science and religion must remain walled off from one another. Existentialist theologians like Tillich and Bultmann interpreted the Bible for an alienated and anxious postwar humanity, focusing on the human condition rather than the metaphysical implications of modern science. Like Teilhard's evolutionary thought, Whitehead's process philosophy was an exception in postwar Christian theology, although Whitehead developed a following among some Protestant theologians in the United States later in the twentieth century.[113]

Catholicism remained staunchly dogmatic and resistant to any engagement with modern science, at least until the Second Vatican

Council (1962-65). Instead, Catholic apologists like Jacques Maritain used Thomism to challenge modern philosophic-scientific ideas. Invoking Thomist reasoning, Maritain contested Bergson's creative evolution and dynamic reality and Teilhard's evolutionary thought as presumptuous human speculation.[114] American fundamentalists were even more militant in their opposition to modern science, primarily Darwinian evolution. They launched an antievolution crusade during and immediately after World War I, and it continues unabated to the present. In short, throughout the postwar era, Protestantism and Catholicism failed to address the serious theological implications of modern science, especially evolutionary thought. Instead, they remained largely indifferent to modern scientific developments or, in the case of American fundamentalism, openly hostile to those developments. The failure of engagement cleared an unobstructed path for emergence of materialism. Furthermore, fundamentalist opposition to evolution provided a scientifically vulnerable target for the materialist challenge to the idea of a purposeful universe.

5

Postwar Western Philosophy

The [*Tractatus*] deals with the problems of philosophy, and shows,
I believe, that the reason why these problems are posed is that the
logic of our language is misunderstood. The whole sense of the
book might be summed up in the following words: what can be
said at all can be said clearly, and what we cannot talk about we
must pass over in silence.
  —Ludwig Wittgenstein, *Tractatus Logico-Philosophicus* (1921)[1]

Thinking only begins at the point where we have come to know
that Reason, glorified for centuries, is the most obstinate adversary of thinking.
  —Martin Heidegger commenting on Nietzsche (1936-40)[2]

Traditional rationalist philosophy was already under attack before
World War I, but now confronted its greatest challenge: finding
meaning in the fractured postwar reality. The three great European
philosophers of the postwar era were ideally positioned to confront
this challenge: Ludwig Wittgenstein with language analysis, Edmund Husserl with transcendental phenomenology, and Martin
Heidegger with phenomenological ontology. All three philosophers personally experienced World War I, which influenced their
philosophic views. Wittgenstein was a soldier on Austria's Eastern
and Southern Fronts and a war-prisoner of the Italians; Husserl
won the Iron Cross for his lectures in support of Germany's war
effort and was father of two soldiers, both wounded, one fatally,
at Verdun; and Heidegger was a German support soldier with a
medical deferment. They exerted a powerful influence on twentieth
century philosophy, they believed the quest to understand ultimate
reality was vitally important, and they considered scientific positiv-

ism inadequate, if not detrimental, to that goal. Furthermore, they began developing their philosophical views amid a paradigm shift in Western physics that radically altered the Newtonian conception of the universe and provided scientific grounds for challenging materialism, placing mind squarely in the center of reality, and supporting an idealistic metaphysics.

The scientific revolution began before World War I and continued through the 1920s. It included Max Planck's quantum theory, Albert Einstein's special and general theories of relativity, and Niels Bohr's and Werner Heisenberg's uncertainty principle in physics.[3] In classical Newtonian physics, the atomic components of matter were rigid, impenetrable, inert, and unchanging—constant in mass, volume, shape, and total quantity. Matter was susceptible to mathematical calculation but not susceptible to change, except in location; it remained motionless unless acted upon externally by forces like gravity.[4] Motion changed the distribution of matter within the universe over time but did not change its inherent nature. And time proceeded uniformly. Thus, matter moved in absolute space and time, which were independent and immutable. Matter and motion, space and time were absolutes. Quantum and relativity physics radically changed this predictable and deterministic Newtonian world order.

In 1902, Max Planck observed that subatomic matter released and absorbed measurable amounts of energy, which he called quanta. In 1905, Albert Einstein applied Planck's quantum theory to posit an interrelationship between matter and energy. In 1915, Einstein published his general theory of relativity that space and time are an interrelated continuum rather than absolutes and must be measured relative to the observer. This gave rise to Einstein's "four-dimensional space-time continuum."[5] Space was no longer absolute, static, or uniform; it had variable structures and its curvature affected gravity. Time was no longer absolute; a stationary clock ran faster than a clock moving with the observer. And matter was no longer indestructible, with a fixed size and shape; it was active and interchangeable with energy. Subatomic electrons remained in constant motion, and they behaved variously as either waves or particles. Furthermore, in 1927, Werner Heisenberg concluded that it was impossible to determine simultaneously both the position and velocity of electrons. In short, the four Newtonian absolutes of matter and motion, time and space collapsed before quantum and relativity physics and the indeterminacy principle.

Matter, that cornerstone of Newtonian physics, suddenly became fraught with uncertainty. Heisenberg thought that atomic particles lacked "even the quality of being" and possessed at most "a possibility for being or a tendency for being."[6] Reality, going back to Democritus, was thought to consist of indestructible atoms, but with the interchangeability of matter and energy and the duality of waves and particles, the classical conception of atomic matter as solid and unchanging had to give way. Furthermore, with measurements of space and time affected by the motion of the observer, the observer's mind had an effect on the characteristics of the outside world.[7] English astrophysicist and philosopher Sir Arthur Eddington (1882-1944) thought that Heisenberg's indeterminacy principle had undermined materialism and that mind had replaced matter at the center of reality.[8] Whitehead developed a philosophy of organism that described the world as organic and in flux, with time interrelated with space, transitoriness unified in percipient events.[9] Thus, the new physics seemed to make way for a new philosophic cosmology to replace matter with mind at the center.

Quite to the contrary, materialism persisted and prospered as a philosophic worldview, notwithstanding the profound challenge of the new physics to the Newtonian absoluteness of matter.[10] And materialism's postwar rise to dominance owes much to philosophy's disengagement from metaphysics. Although the scientific revolution posed new questions about the nature of the cosmos, philosophers generally sidestepped those questions. Instead, they began to question traditional philosophy itself—neo-Kantianism on the continent and Hegelianism in Britain—and to search for ways to place philosophy on a more solid scientific footing. The scientific spirit of the age demanded no less; it called for scientific proof of metaphysical claims for absolute knowledge.[11] The new physics had reinforced the long-standing positivist skepticism about metaphysics; Newton's static model no longer applied to the external world; and the theory of relativity and principle of indeterminacy showed the confounding effect of the observer's mind.[12] Although scientific recognition of the mind's effect on objective reality suggested new grounds for philosophic idealism like that of Hegel, for example, postwar philosophy rejected idealism in favor of empiricism (logical positivism) and existentialism (human authenticity). Logical positivism and existentialism arose immediately after World War I and remained influential well into the second half of the twentieth century

Wittgenstein, Husserl, and Heidegger stood at the forefront of these two philosophical movements and epitomized philosophy's post-World War I retreat from engagement in metaphysics. Wittgenstein emphasized the transcendent in existence and Heidegger the meaning of Being, so they seemed ideally positioned to confront the challenges of epistemological scientism and metaphysical materialism. Instead, they retreated from reasoned engagement and relegated metaphysics to the arts rather than philosophy. Given their concern for the meaning of reality, their philosophical retreat from metaphysical inquiry is stunning. Of these three philosophers, only Husserl rose to challenge scientism. He advocated a modified form of rationalism and promoted a metaphysics of consciousness, but the Nazis eventually thwarted his efforts. The logical positivists considered science the surest route to truth, subjecting factual propositions to empirical verification and dismissing metaphysics outright. Existentialists generally ignored metaphysical questions, focusing instead on how to live authentically in an indifferent universe. Thus, following the Great War, philosophy lost faith in traditional metaphysics and effectively abandoned cosmology, leaving materialism essentially unchallenged. Understanding how this happened requires a closer look at these philosophers and philosophical movements.

Ludwig Wittgenstein and Language Analysis

Wittgenstein (1889-1951) was born in Vienna, Austria, but his interest in the then-new field of aeronautical engineering took him to England in 1908 at age 19. There he eventually gravitated toward mathematics and its philosophical foundations.[13] This inspired him to read Bertrand Russell and Alfred North Whitehead's *Principia Mathematica* (1910) and to study logic at Cambridge University (1912-14), where he became Russell's protégé and friend.[14] Before

World War I, Wittgenstein had two dominant philosophic influences: Russell's logical atomism and Viennese culture. Both factored significantly in Wittgenstein's seminal work *Tractatus Logico-Philosophicus* (1921). At Cambridge, Wittgenstein found Russell endeavoring to reduce mathematics to logic and to invent a new language (logical atomism) for expressing facts with a mathematical rigor, which was applicable to all scientific disciplines.[15] In 1914, Russell declared that "logic is the essence of philosophy," and that discrete atoms of sense data form the elementary building blocks of all reality.[16] His new philosophical thinking led Russell to abandon his Hegelian roots. He challenged Britain's reigning post-Hegelian idealists, such as Francis Herbert Bradley, and developed the core principles of analytical philosophy at Cambridge and logical positivism in Austria.[17]

Those cultural concerns within *fin de siècle* Vienna of greatest influence on Wittgenstein were the critique of language, the separation of facts and values, and the meaning of life as a mystical rather than rational endeavor.[18] Fritz Mauthner (1849-1923), a Viennese journalist turned philosopher, contended that philosophical problems devolve to problems of language, which is primarily a social convention and incapable of grasping the real world.[19] The three most widely read authors in Viennese intellectual circles reinforced this view: Arthur Schopenhauer (1788-1860), Søren Kierkegaard (1813-1855), and Leo Tolstoy (1828-1910). These writers considered values, morality, and meaning in life to be beyond rational thought and essentially mystical in nature.[20] The neo-Kantian Schopenhauer had rejected Kant's rational morality and interpreted Kant's noumenal world as the blind, obstinate, and impetuous Will.[21] Kierkegaard had challenged the logic of Hegel's historical dialectic and transformed Hegel's Absolute Spirit into the Absolute Paradox of Christ's Incarnation, which required faith rather than reason.[22] Tolstoy had argued that morality rests upon feeling, that art rather than thought is the language of feeling, and that the meaning of life lies within life itself, and not in human reason.[23]

Back home in Vienna when war broke out in August 1914, Wittgenstein promptly enlisted in the Imperial Army and spent two years with an artillery unit on the Eastern Front. In 1916, he entered officer training and returned to his unit as a lieutenant. Later posted to the Italian Front, Wittgenstein fell prisoner to the Italians in October 1918, when the Austro-Hungarian Front collapsed, and was interned near Monte Cassino until August 1919. His war experience affected him profoundly. The war evoked his sense of service and self-sacrifice (volunteering for military duty and seeking posts ever closer to the fighting); it introduced him to ordinary soldiers and citizens (interacting regularly with common people he rarely met as a rich man's son); it prompted his reading of Tolstoy's *The Gospels in Brief* (carrying *The Gospels* everywhere, he became "the man of the book" to fellow soldiers and later told Russell it "saved my life"); and it led him to renounce his privileged life for one of austerity (relinquishing his 1912 inheritance to his siblings). After meeting with Wittgenstein in Holland in 1919, Russell reported that Wittgenstein was reading "people like Kierkegaard" and had become "a complete mystic."[24]

While home on leave in 1918, Wittgenstein had begun the manuscript for the *Tractatus,* which he completed during his captivity near Monte Cassino and published with Russell's help in 1921.[25] Before the war Wittgenstein had formed his principal thoughts, but he synthesized them while stationed on the Eastern Front. They included his ideas about language as a picture of reality and about ethics and the meaning of life as transcendental concerns beyond the reach of philosophy.[26] As indicated in his introduction to the *Tractatus,* Wittgenstein believed that understanding "the logic of our language" and limiting it "to the expression of thoughts" would solve all philosophical problems. By showing what can be *thought* is only what can be *said,* Wittgenstein believed he could prevent philosophy from improperly intruding into the "unsayable" realm of ethics, value, and the meaning of life—the realm he considered most important.[27]

Wittgenstein predicated the *Tractatus* on two major premises: First, language consists of propositions of thought made up of more elementary propositions; propositions are combinations of names; and names are the basic constituents of language.[28] Second, the structure of language corresponds to the structure of the world. The world is composed of facts existing as "states of affairs"; states of affairs consist of objects or things; and objects constitute the world's unalterable, simple, and ultimate constituents.[29] From these two major premises Wittgenstein concludes that language mirrors the world; that is, names correspond to objects, elementary propositions to states of affairs, and propositions to facts.[30] Thus, thought becomes a "logical picture of facts" perceived by the senses and expressed in propositions, which fall within the natural sciences and constitute "a picture of reality."[31] Thought and discourse extend to facts and not values, about which nothing can be said. Philosophy sets limits on what can be thought but has no propositions or doctrines of its own; instead it "aims at the logical clarification of thoughts."[32] With these sweeping statements in the *Tractatus*, Wittgenstein summarily collapsed philosophy into three limited activities: separating questions of fact from questions of logic, referring factual statements to the natural sciences, and analyzing the logical syntax of propositional statements.[33]

In Wittgenstein's scheme, metaphysical statements, which usually contain mixed questions of fact and logic, become subdivided into one or the other. Philosophy refers the factual content to the appropriate natural sciences, and analyzes any remaining logical content simply for coherence. This methodological bifurcation effectively forces philosophic speculations about the cosmos into Wittgenstein's category of "nonsense."[34] Such metaphysical statements are thereby rendered senseless and must be discarded, says Wittgenstein, so we can "see the world aright."[35] Seeing the world aright requires that we "throw away the [philosophical] ladder" because "what is higher" lies beyond the scope and capacity of philosophy—or the natural sciences, for that matter.[36] "God does not reveal himself in the world," because such higher matters concern only the world as a whole, namely, the fact that it exists at all.[37] Values, like religion and ethics, are "transcendental" and "mystical"; they lie beyond the limits of the factual world; they "cannot be put into words" but, instead, "make themselves manifest." They can be *shown* but cannot be *said*.[38] In other words, those matters that Wittgenstein considered most important in life fall within the province of the arts, not philosophy. Indeed, the greatest contribution of the *Tractatus*, for Wittgenstein, was its emphasis on transcendental and mystical matters that "we must pass over in silence."[39]

Wittgenstein's silence, of course, is thunderous; it abruptly ends the rationalist and idealist speculations of philosophy about reality.

Metaphysics is over. Although Wittgenstein maintained that philosophy has no doctrines, the Vienna Circle of logical positivists used the *Tractatus* as its blueprint for further philosophical development in the 1920s. The Vienna Circle took Wittgenstein's "atomic facts" to mean sense data, or empirical observations, as grounding all genuine knowledge. In addition, they denigrated transcendental and mystical matters as utterly meaningless, effectively dismissing what Wittgenstein deemed most important in life.[40] Whereas Wittgenstein thought philosophy must be silent about what really matters, namely, ethics, value, and the meaning of life, the logical positivists thought that philosophy itself elucidated all that really matters.[41]

Wittgenstein is partially at fault here for applying Russell's concept of "logical atomism" to his picture of the world as the totality of facts.[42] Wittgenstein thereby gave philosophic expression to the image of a fragmented world of disconnected facts—perhaps characteristic of postwar European culture but certainly not Wittgenstein's picture of the world as a whole.[43] Logical atomism emerges from two philosophical roots. The first is David Hume's analysis of causation, which holds that the most we can say about B consistently following A is that they are conjoined, not causally related, facts (the view prevalent among empiricists). The second is mathematical logic, which ignores causation altogether, abstracts from the nature of A and B, and considers these two unrelated facts—merely distributions in logical space having nothing to do with one another. By projecting such dictatorial logic onto a world of disconnected facts, Wittgenstein's *Tractatus* actually presents a metaphysic, the very undertaking he says philosophy must avoid. Furthermore, this metaphysic consists of the disconnected objects or things, in effect, the sort of meaningless matter characteristic of materialism. Paradoxically, the metaphysic of the *Tractatus* is also wholly at odds with Wittgenstein's own view of the world, which manifests transcendental and mystical meaning when seen "aright."

Believing that the *Tractatus* had solved all the problems of philosophy, Wittgenstein abandoned philosophy in 1920 to train as a teacher, and for six years thereafter he taught at a grammar school in a village south of Vienna.[44] In 1929, however, he returned to Cambridge University, submitted the *Tractatus* as his doctoral dissertation, and received his Ph. D. the next year (at age 40), with Bertrand Russell and G. E. Moore as his examiners. Following graduation, Wittgenstein received a five-year fellowship at Trinity College, Cambridge. In 1935-36, he lived in a Norwegian hut that he had built before World War I as his retreat, and there began to write his posthumously published *Philosophical Investigations* (1953). In 1937, Wittgenstein returned to Cambridge, and in 1939, succeeded G. E. Moore as Chairman of the Philosophy Department.[45] After the Anschluss, Wittgenstein had to choose between German and British citizenship and he relinquished his Austrian passport to become a British citizen. During World War II he served at Guy's Hospital in London and the Royal Victoria Infirmary in Newcastle. In 1947, Wittgenstein relinquished his Chairmanship and moved to Ireland where he finished *Philosophical Investigations*. He then returned to England where he lived with friends in Oxford and Cambridge until his death from cancer in 1951.

Wittgenstein ultimately abandoned the "picture theory" of language as a mirror of the factual world, which he set forth in the *Tractatus*. Instead, in *Philosophic Investigations* he adopted a new theory of language as the mastery of technique, namely, knowing how to use language and to participate in "language-games." Language games are the practices, customs, and assumptions from which linguistic expressions derive their meaning in a shared "form of life." Yet Wittgenstein still maintained, as he had in the *Tractatus*, that philosophic problems arise from misconceptions and misuse of language and that a proper grasp of the workings of language dissolve rather than resolve such philosophic problems. Thus, for the later Wittgenstein, philosophy continued to play only the limited role of clarifying language and correcting linguistic errors, like a physician treating an illness. "What is your aim in philosophy?" Wittgenstein asks, and replies: "To show the fly the way out of the fly-bottle."[46] For Wittgenstein, the relationship between language and the world as a whole still must be shown rather than stated. That relationship, like all transcendental and mystical matters, still remained unsayable.

Despite his spiritual epiphany during World War I and his subsequent mission to preserve the transcendent and mystical, Wittgenstein argued throughout his career that philosophical statements about reality constituted nonsense, that linguistic rules and behavior within the community provided the source of meaning, and that only art could *show* the transcendent mystery of reality. Ironically, his *Tractatus* pictured the materialist world of logical atomism, bereft of transcendent and mystical meaning—the very world of valueless matter that underlies materialism. Eventually, Wittgenstein must have recognized his unintended metaphysic, especially since the *Tractatus* purported to eliminate all metaphysics. Furthermore, Wittgenstein surely knew that the Vienna Circle was misusing his *Tractatus* for philosophical development and that his colleague Russell was embracing a philosophy of logical atomism. Though Wittgenstein abandoned the picture theory of meaning, he neither corrected his portrait of this bleak materialist reality, nor rebutted materialism itself.

Wittgenstein looked to poetry and art in order to "see the world aright" and to *show* its transcendental meaning, but he stripped philosophy of any role in *saying* anything about this metaphysical undertaking. Showing the world's transcendental meaning engages two important aspects of critical intelligence, being attentive and intelligent about experiencing the world as a whole. But Wittgenstein disengaged the other two aspects of critical intelligence from humanity's quest for meaning in its world, namely, being critical in examining and responsible in judging the aesthetic experience of existence. Indeed, for Wittgenstein, saying anything thoughtful and responsible about the world as a whole, the fact that the world exists at all, was essentially a source of philosophical nonsense. The relationship between language and the world can be shown by artists but cannot be stated by philosophers. Wittgenstein had eliminated philosophy's traditional practice of metaphysical inquiry.

Edmund Husserl and Transcendental Phenomenology

Husserl (1859-1938) was born to German-speaking liberal Jews in Prossnitz, Moravia, now part of the Czech Republic. He received his doctorate in mathematics from the University of Vienna in 1881, and later studied philosophical psychology there with Franz Brentano, who inspired his interest in philosophy and ultimately in phenomenology.[47] In 1886, Husserl converted to Christianity and transferred to the University of Halle to study psychology with a former Brentano student. In Halle he married Malvine Steinschneider, who also converted to Christianity, had three children, and published his first book, *Logical Investigations* (1900).[48] In 1900, he transferred to the University of Göttingen as an assistant professor and remained in Göttingen for the next 16 years, immersing himself in the new discipline of phenomenology, perched on the border of logic, ontology, and descriptive psychology. Husserl lectured and wrote on Kant, comparing his own transcendental phenomenology to Kant's transcendental logic, and published his second book, *Ideas: General Introduction to Pure Phenomenology* (1913).

As Husserl wrote in his 1931 preface to the English edition, *Ideas* is "exclusively directed to this one end: to discover a *radical beginning* to a philosophy" that "will be able to present itself as science."[49] Although his constant rallying cry "To the things!" sounds like a call to empiricism, Husserl focused upon knowledge as a mental activity, specifically the manner in which consciousness contemplates the phenomena of which it is conscious. While agreeing that phenomena are the only *given*, Husserl opposed three then-current philosophical positions on phenomena: Kant's division between phenomena and noumena, Hegel's historical dialectic within phenomena, and materialism's reduction of consciousness to physical matter.[50] Instead, Husserl claimed that *in* phenomena is given the very *essence* of reality and that phenomenology is "a theory of essence contained in pure intuition."[51] The essence of reality lies within consciousness as an absolute and necessary truth—a pure intelligibility that is separate and apart from phenomena. He attempts to get at this essential reality simply by investigating consciousness, an unprecedented epistemological methodology. Thus, his phenomenology is both a philosophy and a technique; it attempts to bridge the implicit Cartesian dualism between a presumably independent reality and a subjective consciousness of that reality by examining consciousness of phenomena within consciousness.[52]

The phenomenological technique employs four interdependent processes, collectively called "intentional constitution"; these processes purify and validate an intuitive grasp or knowledge of reality, the essence of being. First, the thinking self or ego "brackets" (*epoché* in Greek) or detaches itself from the external world outside of pure consciousness, avoiding any preconceptions and judgments about phenomena, in order to concentrate solely upon consciousness. Second, consciousness proceeds through six successive, reductive steps (the *eidetic reduction* from the Greek word *eidos* meaning structure) intended to reveal the structure or essence of consciousness itself and the intended object of consciousness. Third, *ideation*, which occurs during the last four reductive steps, reveals the essences of those structures within "the pure flow of consciousness." This is the very center of reality, which Husserl calls the *transcendental ego*. Fourth, *intentionality* is the final step during which the transcendental ego considers the intended object of consciousness from different aspects in order to intuit the essential aspects of its being, that is, essential reality as distinct from contingent existence.[53]

Whereas Descartes separated the subject (ego) and the object (phenomenon), thinking and extended substance, Husserl considered them intelligible only in combination, guaranteeing each other and thereby guaranteeing absolute knowledge of being-in-consciousness.[54] Kant thought that pure reason can attain absolute knowledge by limiting itself to phenomena and that practical reason can postulate the noumenal realm (God, freedom, immortality). But Husserl thought that pure reason can attain absolute knowledge of noumena as "intentionally constituted" within consciousness.[55] Thus, Husserl synthesized Descartes's ideal of an absolute foundation for knowledge with Kant's transcendental idealism. Yet he rejected Descartes's dualism by placing existence within consciousness, and he rejected Kant's limitation of pure reason to contingent existence (phenomena) by constituting essential reality (Kant's noumena) within the transcendental ego. For Husserl, knowledge of being-in-consciousness constitutes the only authentic access to the meaning of essential reality and, therefore, phenomenology is the only science of being: "Only a science transcendentally clarified and justified, in the phenomenological sense, can be the ultimate science. Only a world clarified by transcendental phenomenology can be a world definitively comprehended."[56]

In short, phenomenology clarifies and justifies the real world by constituting its essence in and for the consciousness. Phenomenology is the metaphysics of consciousness. Furthermore, the transcendental ego grows in intuitive capacity and in knowledge of essential reality with each phenomenological experience.[57] In the words of American Jesuit philosopher Quentin Lauer, Husserl's transcendental phenomenology constitutes "a heroic effort to re-establish metaphysics according to the canons set up by science."[58] While promoting phenomenology as the science of sciences, however, Husserl also emphasized the prescientific, primordial, and unsophisticated mode of ordinary experience in the life-world (*Lebenswelt*). By life-world, Husserl means everyday human perception and interpretation of the world from which science abstracts its objects. Husserl stressed the life-world in an effort to liberate philosophy and science from their narrow positivist outlooks and to refocus them on the world of human experience.[59]

When World War I broke out in August 1914, Husserl was at Göttingen and 55 years old. Despite the increasing horror of the war, Husserl was inspired by the spirit of the German people: "A magnificent stream of national will to win floods through every one of us and gives us an undreamt-of strength of will in this terrible national loneliness."[60] Husserl's daughter volunteered in a field hospital and his two sons were mobilized. His sons had "gone out to fight this war in the Fichtean spirit as a truly sacred war," remarked Husserl, believing that God supported Germany, even as the European nations aligned to destroy it.[61] In March 1916, however, his younger son, winner of the Iron Cross, was killed, and his older son was badly wounded, at Verdun. Husserl became depressed over the death of his son and numerous students.[62] In April 1916, Husserl assumed the Chair of Philosophy at Freiburg where he remained until his retirement in 1929. In his inaugural lecture, Husserl called for restructuring science and philosophy: "Most recently, the need for an utterly original philosophy has re-emerged, the need of a philosophy that ... seeks by radically clarifying the sense and the motifs of philosophical problems to penetrate to that primal ground on whose basis those problems must find whatever solution is genuinely scientific." Husserl added that philosophy's mission is to protect and promote the "spiritual life of mankind."[63]

In 1918, during the last months of the war, Husserl gave three lectures in Freiburg entitled *Fichte's Ideal of Humanity*, which earned him the Iron Cross for his assistance in the German war effort. Husserl's lectures invoked Fichte's ability to find spiritual resources in defeat and a moral dimension in idealism. Citing Fichte's desire for a moral world order and belief in God's revelation through self-understanding, Husserl exclaims: "How elevating is this philosophy for the noble self-consciousness of the human being and the dignity of his existence when it proves that the entire world-creation is achieved in the absolute intelligence for his sake."[64] Although predicting a German victory to his wife Malvine even in late 1918, Husserl soon recognized the ethical bankruptcy of his earlier position that Germany's war was just, a recognition that no doubt contributed to his emerging view of the crisis in Western civilization.[65] In 1921, as the leading philosopher in Germany, Husserl called for an overall phenomenological philosophy to address the intellectual and spiritual needs of postwar humanity. He tried to establish this philosophy as an international movement, advocating a human community and moral order of shared interests extending beyond national borders. This same call for a "higher humanism" is later echoed in his *The Crisis of European Sciences* (1937).[66] At Freiburg, Husserl met Martin Heidegger who helped Husserl to prepare his manuscripts for publication and joined Husserl in an article on phenomenology for the *Encyclopaedia Britannica* in 1929. That same year, Heidegger succeeded Husserl upon his retirement as Chairman of the Philosophy Department.

Husserl's postwar philosophy grew out of his grave concern that Western culture had lost direction because philosophy no longer provided answers to man's fundamental concerns. Husserl faulted the natural sciences for the "seeming collapse of rationalism," and he pursued phenomenology as the means of "saving human reason."[67] In *Crisis* Husserl describes "a change which set in at the turn of the past century in the general evaluation of the sciences" concerning "what they, or what science in general, had meant and could mean for human existence."[68] Husserl presented his grave concern as follows:

> The exclusiveness with which the total world-view of modern man, in the second half of the nineteenth century, let itself be determined by the positive sciences and be blinded by the "prosperity" they produce, meant an indifferent turning

away from the questions which are decisive for a genuine humanity. Merely fact-minded sciences make merely fact-minded people. The change in public evaluation was unavoidable, especially after the war, and we know that it has gradually become a feeling of hostility among the younger generation. In our vital need—so we are told—this science has nothing to say to us. It excludes in principle precisely the questions which man, given over in our unhappy times to the most portentous upheavals, finds the most burning: questions of the meaning or meaninglessness of the whole of this human existence. Do not these questions, universal and necessary for all men, demand universal reflections and answers based on rational insight?[69]

Husserl worried that the Western world had become drawn to science and blinded by the prosperity it produced, and had repudiated the Greek spirit of philosophic inquiry—inquiry that "bespeaks nothing but universal science, science of the world as a whole, of the universal unity of all being." Instead, humanity had adopted the mechanistic worldview of the natural sciences, which maintain that "there can be no pure self-contained search for an explanation of the spiritual, no purely inner-oriented psychology or theory of spirit beginning with the ego in psychical-self-experience and extending to the other psyche. The way that must be traveled is the external one, the path of physics and chemistry."[70] So long as the materialist focus of the natural sciences dominated the human spirit, Husserl thought Western man would never understand his true purpose. In *Crisis* Husserl situated phenomenology at the end of the long teleological process for safeguarding the primacy of reason as the means of understanding reality. He argued that the surrender of reason to the anti-rationalist forces of the natural sciences would constitute a betrayal of Western man. Scientific positivism, explained Husserl, "decapitates philosophy" by giving questions of fact a higher dignity than basic questions of meaning.[71] By the summer of 1935, Husserl finally despaired over the prevailing anti-rationalism, which he considered the root cause of the European crisis: "Philosophy of science, as serious, rigorous, indeed apodictically rigorous science—*the dream is over*."[72]

In April 1933, the National Socialist Party issued a decree prohibiting non-Aryans from holding positions in state service. Heidegger enforced that decree against his mentor, emeritus professor Husserl, who was devastated, given his own loyal support of Germany, his sons' military service in the war, and his daughter's service in a field hospital.[73] In September 1935, under a subsequent law against non-Aryans, Husserl lost his teaching license and German citizenship. Because of his resulting non-German status, Husserl also lost his place among the German delegation to the international philosophy congresses in 1936 and 1937. Freiburg dropped his name from the faculty list in 1936, and the National Socialists denounced his philosophy urging universal rationality because it included Jews and Negroes, represented "a barren spirit without blood lineage or race," and failed to understand "the attachment to the soil of genuine spirituality."[74] Despite his last years of decreasing friends and increasing isolation, Husserl remained remarkably productive.[75] He died in April 1938, shortly after his 79th birthday, with only one person from the Freiburg philosophical faculty attending his funeral (not Heidegger, who allegedly was sick). Father Van Breda, a Belgian Franciscan priest intending to research Husserl's unpublished manuscripts in Freiburg, met with Husserl's widow Malvine, and together they developed a plan to preserve Husserl's manuscripts from the Nazis. He used a Belgian diplomatic courier to send them to Leuven, where they are now part of the Husserl Archive. Father Van Breda also arranged for Husserl's widow to move to Belgium where she hid in a convent during the Nazi occupation. In 1946, Malvine traveled to the United States to join her two surviving children, who had emigrated there in 1933-34.[76]

Husserl's message was sound, but his methodology was inadequate. Husserl sought to liberate philosophy from the materialist influence of positive science by promoting transcendental phenomenology as the "science of sciences" and the life-world as the pre-scientific mode of experiencing essential reality. While emphasizing the subjectivity of consciousness, however, Husserl tried to objectify consciousness through phenomenology, assuming (erroneously) that scientific analysis alone can grasp essential reality. In so doing, he succumbed to scientism himself by reducing philosophy to a narrow scientific approach rather than broadly proceeding through reason's other fields of meaning in pursuing truth about reality. The search for meaning cannot limit our critical intelligence solely to the theoretical approach of science; it must take a wider view of existence than Husserl allowed in his phenomenological reduction within human consciousness. His narrow objectifying "science of sciences" omitted the subjective feelings, aesthetic insights, interpersonal involvements, and mythic and historical narratives about humanity's place in the world. By ignoring these other rich sources of access to nature, Husserl circumscribed and prejudiced his resultant analysis of essential reality, and undermined his mission to overcome scientism and materialism. It doomed his attempt to integrate mind into matter, to save human reason, and to overcome materialism.

In addition, Husserl never escaped the false dichotomy between consciousness and existence, subjectivity and the life-world, because he detached (bracketed) consciousness from the life-world even as he sought a philosophical goal within that very world.[77] Consciousness itself is already bracketed by the world in which it exists; and the intentionality of consciousness necessarily points to something in that world. Thus, Husserl's primacy of consciousness inevitably (and mistakenly) divides the individual between the two worlds—*ego* and experience. As Heidegger points out, however, the two are inseparable; the individual is being-in-the-world. Consequently, phenomenology cannot hope to explain Husserl's life-world by bracketing a small portion of it in consciousness. Furthermore, the life-world—man's common, pre-reflective mode of finding meaning in daily life– appears almost as an afterthought to Husserl. Moreover, his life-world, much like Wittgenstein's "form of life" and Heidegger's "world," is humanity's participation in, understanding of, and engagement with the world, which implies that the individual rather than the dedicated philosopher may be the true metaphysician.

Martin Heidegger and Phenomenological Ontology

Heidegger (1889-1976) was born into a poor Catholic family in Messkirch, Baden, located in southwest Germany. In 1913, he earned his doctorate at Freiburg University with a dissertation criticizing psychologism (the psychological approach to philosophy), and in 1915, he qualified as a lecturer with his thesis on Duns Scotus. Conscripted into the German army that same year, Heidegger avoided front-line duty through a "limited service" deferment because of his weak heart, and entered the postal and meteorological services. Otherwise, he seemed personally unaffected by the war, lecturing by night at University while still in uniform.[78] Upon discharge from the Army in 1918, Heidegger became an assistant to Husserl at Freiburg, achieved renown as a lecturer, and in 1923 became an associate professor at Marburg. In 1927, Heidegger published his most influential work, *Being and Time*, in order to meet a government requirement for full professorship, and then assumed the Philosophy Department chairmanship at Freiburg.

Husserl had led nineteenth-century philosophy out of the impasse between the idealists and the materialists, both speculative philosophies about the nature of reality, by pursuing phenomenology, Husserl's important new idea about accessing essential reality within transcendental consciousness. In *Being and Time* (1927), Heidegger stepped beyond Husserl's phenomenology in two important respects. First, he replaced Husserl's idea of the human being as consciousness-of-objects by substituting the human being as being-in-the-world. Heidegger's individual exists within the external world of his or her everyday cares.[79] He calls the human being *Dasein*, meaning in German "existence" or literally "being there." Second, he focused on the human being (Dasein) because Dasein is the one being "concerned *about* its very Being."[80] Thus, Heidegger concentrates on Dasein primarily to access the meaning of Being; he is using phenomenology for an ontological end. Being—in German, *Sein*, meaning literally "there is/it gives"—is not a thing, human being, or even existence as a whole. For Heidegger, Being is the "indefinable" *giveness* of existence in all its pervasive mystery.[81]

Dasein has three characteristics. The first is *existentiality*, meaning that it engages the world through its concerns and its understanding of how things are used and relate to one another (i.e., their possibilities). The second is *facticity*, meaning that it is thrown into and open to the world, which affects its mood, that is, Dasein's past experience affects its state of mind as it stands in the present and moves toward the future. And the third is *falling*, meaning that it identifies with the worldly desires and activities valued by others generally rather than by Dasein specifically. Consequently, the "fallen" or inauthentic Dasein (*das Man* or the One) accepts the choices of others, whereas the authentic Dasein (the Self) makes choices for its own reasons. Dasein cannot decide *whether* to be since it is a contingent being, "thrown" into the world. But Dasein can decide *how* to be since it has no fixed nature. Instead, Dasein exists or "stands out" as constituting possibilities limited only by its facticity—its inherent physical and mental limitations. Dasein experiences existential guilt about its basic inadequacies (what it is not, has not been, and can never be) and latent anxiety (*angst*) about its inherent finitude (its ever-present possibility of death, its being-toward-death). Dasein's underlying mood of anxiety about its contingency, guilt, and finitude contributes to its pre-conceptual understanding of Being, with its inexplicable giveness.

Dasein's engagement with the world contributes to its preconceptual understanding of Being.[82] Unlike Descartes's conception of humankind as mind and body, thinking and extended substance, Heidegger conceives of Dasein as a field of being, radiating into the surrounding world of beings, cares, and concerns. Dasein stands at the world's very center, interpreting, employing, and unifying those entities (beings) in the world, which are ready-at-hand, like tools and equipment, or present-at-hand, like rocks and trees. Its engagement with entities in the world is constant and practical, not disinterested and theoretical; Dasein and the world are complementary and interdependent. Dasein understands *a priori* its relationship with other people and its application of tools because existing with these other beings is a structural feature without which Dasein is incomplete. Conversely, without Dasein there would be neither Being nor "world" because Dasein is necessary to raise the question of Being and to give entities present or ready at hand their modes of being as such.[83]

Truth about Being emerges from Dasein's engagement in the world because Truth, for Heidegger, is the "unconcealment or uncovering" of things or beings, letting them be seen for what they are. Thus, Truth is not the correspondence of thought with outside existence, as it was for Aristotle and the Scholastics, or the coherence between thought and the perception of existence, as it was for

Descartes. Rather, Truth lies outside the mind; it is not a proposition but a disclosure. "If we go looking for truth inside the mind," writes Barrett, "we shall only find the mind already outside of itself in the world."[84] Because Dasein is necessary to illuminate beings, Dasein is the locus of Truth, which it uncovers through its moods and understandings. Dasein exists in Truth when it is fully aware of things in the world and in un-truth when it does not allow things to reveal themselves. Even when it is in the Truth, however, Dasein illuminates beings (itself as well as others) imperfectly or even misinterprets them because of Dasein's own finiteness. Hence, Truth and the Being are interrelated. Dasein's understanding of Truth emerges in language, which Heidegger considers the common understanding and attunement of one person to another. As such, language may occur in silence as well as sounds and printed words. "Men exist 'within language' prior to their uttering sounds," explains Barrett, "because they exist within a mutual context of understanding, which in the end is nothing but Being itself."[85]

Heidegger thought Western philosophy had gotten off on the wrong foot with Plato and Aristotle because it began to focus on beings and to forget Being itself. Plato had exalted human values over the rest of existence, had considered reality to exist in essences or ideal forms, and had deemed truth accessible through the mind rather than the senses. Once the truth of ultimate reality became a product of the mind, reality ceased to be the unhiddenness of Being, as it was for the pre-Socratic Greeks. This shift in Western philosophy formed the basis of humanism, according to Heidegger, which separated man from nature, concretized mental concepts as ultimate reality, and emphasized beings rather than Being. Descartes, for example, resolved doubt about his own being by concluding *Cogito ergo sum*, but then he proceeded to ignore "*the meaning of Being of the 'sum,'*" just as did Kant after Descartes.[86] In detaching beings or objects in the world from Being's encompassing presence, Greek philosophical thought had arrogated to man the intellectual capacity to understand and exerted power over beings. This led to the development of science.[87] For Heidegger, Nietzsche's Will to Power exercised through science fulfilled this Western philosophical undertaking by channeling humanity away from living harmoniously with nature and toward controlling and transforming nature. Furthermore, science and technology exert their Nietzschean Will to Power over Being itself, and not just beings.[88] Since the possibilities of technology are inexhaustible, the new technological era may continue indefinitely, but, for Heidegger, the philosophy that brought science and technology about was now exhausted.[89]

Science, which Heidegger views as the product of Western philosophy, has no capacity to elucidate the meaning of Being since it subdivides and projects a theoretical and reductionist view upon the world of beings. As English philosopher Michael Inwood explains Heidegger's view, the scientist "ignores the background against which his projection takes place ... Not to mention the nature of being as such or the informal overall understanding of being that enables him to highlight one area of being in particular."[90] What entities are in themselves (atoms and molecules) and what they are for Dasein (tools or trees) "is a distinction drawn from our own understanding of being, not from the Dasein-independent nature of things."[91] Without Dasein's preconceptual understanding of the world such distinctions would be impossible. Thus, science is "a secondary phenomenon, only one of Dasein's ways of being, derivative from and irretrievably dependent on other, more everyday ways of being."[92] Without Dasein, says Inwood, "every being would be on a par with every other being, with no foreground or background, no depth and no superficiality. We do not have the resources to describe such a condition: every description we propose is already encumbered with our own understanding of being, our own significant world."[93] Because science's theoretical constructs depend upon Dasein's prior, intuitive understanding of the world and Being, they have no claim to the priority which materialists have given them.

In his 1929 inaugural lecture to the Freiburg faculties, entitled and later published as *What Is Metaphysics?*, Heidegger explained that metaphysics historically had tried to grasp the whole of beings and had forgotten Being itself. Philosophy had ignored the utter contingency and inexplicable happening of Being, a contingency that Heidegger called, "the nothing." The nothing belongs to Dasein and Being, and "the question of the nothing proves to be such that it embraces the whole of metaphysics."[94] Dasein's latent mood of existential anxiety over its finitude and contingency reveals the

nothing, thereby rendering Dasein, and not the traditional philosopher, the real metaphysician:

> [M]etaphysics belongs to the "nature of man." It is neither
> a division of academic philosophy nor a field of arbitrary
> notions. Metaphysics is the basic occurrence of Dasein. It
> is Dasein itself. Because the truth of metaphysics dwells in
> this groundless ground it stands in closest proximity to the
> constantly lurking possibility of deepest error. For this rea-
> son no amount of scientific rigor attains to the seriousness
> of metaphysics. Philosophy can never be measured by the
> standard of the idea of science.[95]

With these remarks, Heidegger rejected Husserl's idea of philosophy as a science and questioned philosophy's capacity to grasp the
meaning of Being, even as Heidegger himself engaged in that exact
metaphysical undertaking. He famously ended his 1929 inaugural
lecture with the question: "Why are there beings at all, and why not
rather nothing?"—a question he never answered.[96]

At this point, shortly after *Being and Time*, Heidegger determined that his own focus on Dasein to access the meaning of Being
was the same humanistic, anthropocentric mistake characteristic of
all Western philosophy since Plato and Aristotle. With this revelation Heidegger made his famous "turn" away from the most existential aspect of his most influential work and toward an exclusive
focus on Being itself. Heidegger found the logical, propositional
language of traditional philosophy inadequate to his new purpose.
Consequently, he redirected his attention away from Dasein as the
"clearing" where Being reveals itself and toward Being itself for
disclosure of Truth. Since Truth is not an exercise of mind or will,
for Heidegger, but of freedom in the form of receptivity and acceptance, the individual needs to relax his or her will and let Being show itself.[97] Heidegger's approach, writes Barrett, is like being "drawn instead to the exalted rapture that may come to us in
a walk through the woods or over a country path, and which, if
we were poets, we could turn into a lyric poem."[98] Unsurprisingly,
Heidegger began looking to poets and artists since they let things
speak to and through them and let Being become present to them.

"Being is indeed just this presence," writes Barrett, "invisible and all-pervasive, which cannot be enclosed in any mental concept. To think it is to thank it, to remember it with gratitude, for our human existence is ultimately rooted in it."[99]

In his 1935 lectures on *The Origin of the Work of Art* published in 1950, Heidegger rejected the idea of art as the concern for beauty and pleasure and embraced art as the disclosure of Being. He focused on three forms of art: painting, architecture, and poetry, exemplified in Van Gogh's painting *A Pair of Shoes* (1887), the Greek temple, and the poetry of Hölderlin. Heidegger chose *Shoes* because this painting brings to light the character and function of these well-worn peasant shoes, ordinarily inconspicuous even to the farm laborer (Figure 5).

By depicting the leather, nails, and design of the shoes, the work shows, not just artistic form and qualities, but more importantly the truth of their being: how the shoes are manufactured and used, and what they mean to the peasant world. By contrast, the Greek temple shows the earthly setting and human striving for openness in the

Figure 5. Vincent Van Gogh, *A Pair of Shoes*, 1886, Van Gogh Private Collection.
Photo Credit: Bridgeman Art Library, New York, NY.

ancient Greek world. As a happening of truth or unconcealedness, the temple bridges the divide between the world's desire for clarity and the earth's tendency to hide things.[100] Poetry, Heidegger's third example, involves language, which Heidegger called "projective saying." Poetry is not just a means of communicating what we know but of naming something for the first time and stimulating conversation among readers, i.e., revealing its truth as relational meaning.[101]

In short, the essence of art is the founding of Truth about Being. Rather than rely upon Dasein alone, the later Heidegger turns to the artist, whose artistic work product has become the new clearing for Truth. Art resolves conflicts between concealment and unconcealment and provides the viewer or reader a conversion experience, a happening in a clearing of beings, an unconcealment of Being.[102] Furthermore, art causes a fundamental shift in perspective on Being, presenting the extraordinary and diminishing the ordinary, and disclosing Truth as a gift. Art constitutes a new historical beginning, for Heidegger, allowing Truth to leap forward.[103] In effect, the artist has displaced Dasein at center stage. Like some demigod open to the force of art, Truth, and Being, the artist creates and preserves a new world.

Heidegger remained at Freiburg from 1929 through the end of World War II, rejecting an offer in 1930 to assume the prestigious position of Philosophy Department Chairman in Berlin. During the Weimar Republic (1918-1933), he remained apolitical, but in May 1933, within ten days of being elected rector (president) of the University by the Freiburg's faculty, Heidegger joined the National Socialist Party. In that capacity Heidegger cooperated with the new Nazi regime, denying library privileges to Husserl because of his mentor's Jewish background, and advocating Germany's withdrawal from the League of Nations in the 1933 plebiscite. In April 1934, Heidegger resigned as rector over conflicts with faculty and party officials, and he played no significant role thereafter in Nazi affairs, although he never left the party. In 1944, the German government drafted a humiliated Heidegger into the home guard to dig anti-tank trenches along the Rhine. After Germany's surrender, Heidegger appeared before the "Denazification Commission," which forbade him to teach until 1949, a verdict supported by his erstwhile friend Karl Jaspers, the university authorities, and the French administration. In 1947, Heidegger published *On Humanism*, distancing himself from French existentialism, and in 1955, he lectured in France on "What Is Philosophy?" In 1966, Heidegger gave an interview to *Der Spiegel* (published after his death), seeking to justify his Nazi era conduct and despairing of Western civilization: "Only a god can save us." In 1976, Heidegger died and was buried next to his parents in the Messkirch churchyard, following a Catholic mass officiated by his nephew Heinrich Heidegger.[104]

In *Being and Time* Heidegger focused his phenomenological ontology on humanity's fundamental question, the meaning of Being. Yet he never wrote his intended sequel on Being itself, and ultimately declared that metaphysics and the rest of Western philosophy were at an end. He positioned Dasein as the sole legitimate metaphysician and urged an entirely new, non-philosophical kind of thinking about the meaning of Being. "Thinking," says Heidegger, "only begins at the point where we have come to know that Reason, glorified for centuries, is the most obstinate adversary of thinking."[105] By Reason, Heidegger no doubt means rationalism with its metaphysical claims, because his new "thinking" takes place outside philosophy and within poetry and art. In the end, therefore, Heidegger left the meaning of Being exactly where Wittgenstein left the mystery of the transcendent—in the hands of artists and poets.

Artists and poets exemplify the attentiveness and intelligence needed to allow Being to reveal itself. Consequently, they no doubt provide unique access to essential reality. But pursuing truth and meaning in existence requires our full critical intelligence, which includes criticizing and judging as well as being attentive and intelligent. Poets and artists come ill-equipped and ill-disposed to criticize and judge the merits of epistemological scientism and metaphysical materialism; that undertaking falls squarely within the traditional province of philosophy. Indeed, Heidegger's deemphasis of wise judging and responsible decision-making about the aesthetic experience may well have caused him to be led astray by the poetry and rhetoric of Nazism. Despite granting ontological status to art and poetry in uncovering the Truth of Being, Heidegger never criticized materialist metaphysics, even though it devalues Being as merely valueless matter. Furthermore, he never said whether the poet or artist is capable of answering his (and Dasein's) most fundamental question: why there are beings rather than nothing. Ultimately, he left metaphysics to the individual (Dasein), and left philosophy and human reason with nothing to say in response to his critical question. They have no role to play in critiquing and judging claims about the truth of Being, including those of materialist metaphysics.

Logical Positivism and Existentialism

These three philosophers, Wittgenstein, Husserl, and Heidegger, were innovators who inadvertently promoted two major postwar philosophical movements very much at odds with their philosophies, namely, logical positivism and existentialism. Wittgenstein had tried to avoid philosophical doctrines and to emphasize the transcendent, whereas his successors, the logical positivists, directed philosophy toward new doctrines that marginalized the transcendent. Husserl had developed transcendental phenomenology to investigate human consciousness as a means of accessing essential reality, and his protégé Heidegger had redirected phenomenology toward human existence to gain access to the meaning of Being. Yet Husserl's analysis of human subjectivity and Heidegger's analysis of human existence led to existentialism, which ignored Husserl's concern for essences and Heidegger's concern for Being. Instead, existentialism focused on human authenticity, an ontology of freedom in an essentially materialist world.

In the 1920s, the school around Moritz Schlick developed logical positivism in Vienna and quickly identified Wittgenstein's *Tractatus* as support for his philosophical endeavor.[106] The logical positivists held natural science, mathematics, and logic in high regard, and sought to advance philosophy by making it more scientific. They considered science to be capable of resolving issues objectively, by stripping them of subjective opinion and testing them against verifiable facts. "Science for the positivists," writes English philosopher Samir Okasha, "was thus a paradigmatically rational activity, the surest route to the truth that there is."[107] Their approach was rational in that every synthetic proposition was subjected to verification through empirical observation or was logically deduced from a verified proposition.[108] They placed their faith in science as the only road to ultimate truth. Most of the logical positivists came to the United States in the 1930s and exerted a powerful academic influence through the 1960s.[109]

While eminently rational, logical positivism was decidedly not rationalistic since it looked to experience rather than reason as the source of genuine knowledge. The logical positivists deemed metaphysical propositions to be meaningless since they were unverifiable by empirical science. In the words of Rudolf Carnap, a leading member of the Vienna Circle of logical positivists:

> Metaphysical propositions are neither true nor false, because they assert nothing, they contain neither knowledge nor error, they lie completely outside the field of knowledge, of theory, outside the discussion of truth or falsehood. But they are, like laughing, lyrics, and music, expressive. ... The danger lies in the deceptive character of metaphysics; it gives the illusion of knowledge without actually giving any knowledge. This is the reason why we reject it.[110]

Thus, the logical positivists rejected traditional philosophical questions of cosmic meaning and purpose, and focused instead on synthetic propositions to determine whether they were empirically verifiable or logically inferable.[111] Presumably the logical positivists would have recognized and rejected materialism as a metaphysic, despite materialism's purported basis in scientific fact. But their highly academic focus lay elsewhere, in the distinction between analytic and synthetic statements and the empirical verification of the synthetic statements.[112] In effect, they supported epistemological scientism and disregarded materialist metaphysics.

The existentialists, who emerged after World War I but gained their greatest prominence after World War II, adopted some aspects of Husserl's phenomenological method, especially his claim that all consciousness is consciousness *of* something other than mere consciousness itself. In other words, consciousness is intentional since the mind focuses beyond itself toward some *other*, signaling how we behave in the real world.[113] While adopting Husserl's view of intentionality, however, existentialists resisted his bracketing of existence to gain access to essence. Also, they embraced Husserl's life-world because of their interest in lived experience, but rejected Husserl's essences and theoretical concepts.[114]

Heidegger maintained that he was not an existentialist, which is apparent from his focus in *Being and Time* on the meaning of Being rather than on ethical issues.[115] Although he described the structures of human existence, Heidegger's approach was closer to Kant's than to either Kierkegaard's or Nietzsche's. Although Heidegger addressed the difference between authentic and inauthentic Dasein, he remained unconcerned about Dasein's specific behavior in the existential struggle for authenticity. Instead, Dasein was only a vehicle to further Heidegger's ontological inquiry.[116] In his *Letter on Humanism* (1947) responding to Sartre's *Existentialism Is a Humanism* (1945), Heidegger criticized Sartre's humanistic definition of man as a rational animal because reason produced the modern technological society, diminished man to an instrument of productivity, and distracted man from openness to Being. Openness to Being requires a poetic rather than a pragmatic individual, and true humanism is humanity's attention to Being, not its quest for personal authenticity.[117] Despite his use of many Kierkegaardean and Nietzschean ideas, therefore, Heidegger considered existentialism's focus on personal authenticity to be a distraction from his overarching concern for Being.

Existentialists ignored rather than rejected metaphysical questions, even though their view of the natural world inevitably affected their approach to the human condition. Baumer remarks on this curious and counterintuitive disregard of nature among existentialists:

Conceivably, the existentialists might have found in the new physics support for their philosophy of freedom. But they do not seem to have looked at it that way. They were in revolt against positivistic science, as well as against idealism. True philosophy, seeking man's authentic "existence," had more to do with the objective and impersonal, the deterministic and materialistic, than with "nature" studied by scientists, than with the Hegelian Absolute. ... In Karl Jaspers' words, "the abstract sciences lacked the sentiment of a humanistic culture."[118]

Existentialists remained primarily interested in humanity and not nature, in ethics and not cosmology. Indeed, they focused on the human quest for authenticity as if inquiry into the natural order were largely irrelevant.

The existentialists' worldviews certainly influenced their approach to human authenticity, but they generally refrained from metaphysics in favor of an ontology of freedom formulated against a meaningless, materialist backdrop. Atheistic existentialists, like Nietzsche and Sartre, urged man to a heroic stance before an indifferent universe, whereas theistic existentialists, like Kierkegaard and Gabriel Marcel, urged man to respond authentically to a caring Deity.[119] Thus, for Sartre, "Existentialism is nothing else but an attempt to draw the full conclusions from a consistently atheistic position."[120] For Kierkegaard, by contrast, it is the task of becoming a true Christian by holding fast to an "objective uncertainty" with "the most passionate inwardness."[121]

Sartre spent more time than most existentialists in developing his ontology, which is similar to Cartesian dualism of mind and matter. Sartre distinguished consciousness (being-for-itself) from substance (being-in-itself), with consciousness experiencing universal contingency and absurdity of being. For Sartre, however, interpretation of existence was not a rational inquiry into the essence of reality, but a creative act of individual expression. Sartre says that "man is nothing else but that which he makes of himself."[122] As Barrett explains, "For Sartre, Doing takes precedence over Being, and the will to action becomes the central feature of man."[123] Sartre's ontological interest is illustrative of existentialism in general: existentialism addresses human authenticity primarily on the basis of a preconceived and generally un-rationalized cosmology. Therefore, existentialism never constituted a significant foil to materialist metaphysics. Although the materialist world is deterministic and leaves little room for human freedom, existentialists evolved a heroic philosophical stance against this materialist backdrop, but without seriously confronting its underlying metaphysics.

Postwar Philosophy and Materialism

In summary, World War I sounded the death knell for metaphysics and ended philosophy's historical engagement with scientism and materialism. As Whitehead admonished, philosophy must serve as the "constant critic of partial formulations" and "harmonize the ultimate concepts of science with the ideas drawn from a more concrete survey of the whole of reality."[124] After World War I, however, Western philosophy abandoned its role of criticizing epistemological claims like scientism and harmonizing such partial metaphysical formulations as materialism within a broader survey of reality. Consequently, the proponents of materialism, in Whitehead's words, "pushed philosophy out of the effective currents of modern life."[125]

With traditional philosophy sidelined, logical positivism and existentialism presented no genuine foil to materialism. Logical positivism embraced scientism and ignored metaphysics, and existentialism sought personal freedom within an indifferent cosmos. Europe's leading philosophers of the post-World War I era, Wittgenstein, Heidegger, and eventually Husserl, lost faith in human reason to seek the truth about the world as a whole and the meaning of Being. Consequently, Western philosophy effectively consigned itself to scientism, with its singular trust in the scientific method as the only avenue to genuine truth, and to materialism, with its assured claims of a meaningless and purposeless world. Following philosophy's default, materialism vaulted to virtually unchallenged status as the sole arbiter of reality. As a result, Western humanity confronted materialism's colorless, odorless, tasteless, and indifferent reality within which to search for some existential meaning. As Husserl and Whitehead warned, the positive sciences had supplanted philosophy in modern life, and this loss of metaphysical interest within philosophy constitutes one of the great tragedies of the Great War.

6

Postwar Western Literature

If people bring so much courage to this world the world has to kill them to break them, so of course it kills them. The world would break everyone and afterward many are strong at the broken places. But those that will not break it kills. It kills the very good and very gentle and very brave impartially. If you are none of these you can be sure it will kill you too but there will be no special hurry.
— Ernest Hemingway, *A Farewell to Arms* (1929)[1]

Here was a new generation, ... grown up to find all Gods dead, all wars fought, all faiths in man shaken.
— F. Scott Fitzgerald, *This Side of Paradise* (1920)[2]

A sense of loss, betrayal, and estrangement reverberates throughout the important literature of all the major combatant nations during and after World War I. In *Under Fire* (1916) Henri Barbusse's narrator rails at the "truly unpardonable division" in France between the victimized common soldiers and those back home who caused and profited from the senseless war.[3] In Erich Maria Remarque's *All Quiet on the Western Front* (1929) Paul Bäumer feels emotionally detached from everyone and everything in Germany during home leave and longs to rejoin his comrades at the Front, who are "weary, broken, burnt out, rootless, and without hope."[4] Robert Graves characterizes his war memoir *Good-Bye to All That* (1929) as his "bitter leave-taking of England"; it "looked strange to us returned soldiers" and Graves found that "civilians talked a foreign language" and serious conversation even with his parents was "all but impossible."[5] In Ernest Hemingway's short story "Soldiers Home" (1925), Harold Krebs returns to Oklahoma after serving in all the major American campaigns of World War I to find his family and community acting as if the war had never happened. Krebs becomes disillusioned, withdrawn, and resentful of society's lack of support, sympathy, and respect for his wartime service.[6]

In his poem *Hugh Selwyn Mauberley* (1920) Ezra Pound typifies the sentiments conveyed in much of the war literature considered in Chapter 3 on the war's cultural impact. Young men went off to the war "believing in old men's lies": they "walked eye-deep in hell," left behind "the best, among them," and returned "home to old lies and new infamy" — all for "a botched civilization."[7] According to Wisconsin-Madison Professor of English Frederick J. Hoffman, the returning American soldier "was forced into himself, was shocked into a painful suspicion of the words and acts of others; he retreated into embarrassed silence and suspicious disapproval when he encountered any public display of formal emotion or belief." Consequently, "what was left was the isolated person, who had in almost every case to start anew."[8] Samuel Hynes painted a similar portrait of the disaffected British veteran. After World War I, twentieth-century literature turned inward, describing the individual's psychological retreat within and away from anxiety over societal and cosmic alienation.[9]

Franklin Baumer labeled this postwar phenomenon "subjectivism" and identified its three distinct characteristics as (1) epistemological despair, (2) relativism or behaviorism, and (3) self-deprecation.[10] *Epistemological despair* means "despair of ever finding out who 'man' is," of ever unraveling his genuine self, his true underlying identity.[11] Whereas the hero of the nineteenth-century novel stood out as an unforgettable character, the converse is true after the First World War, as French novelist Nathalie Sarraute points out in her essay "The Age of Suspicion" (1950). The principal character of the modern novel seems "to vacillate and fall apart," and to lose "that most precious of all possessions, his personality — which belonged to him alone — and frequently, even his name."[12] Twentieth-century authors and readers alike no longer believed in these characters, who "now become the converging point of their mutual distrust." Sarraute attributed this state of modern literature to "the infinitely profuse growth of the psychological world and the vast, as yet almost unexplored regions of the unconscious."[13]

In his *Introductory Lectures on Psychoanalysis* (1916), Sigmund Freud (1856-1939) had questioned man's rational autonomy, declaring "that mental processes are in themselves unconscious and that of all mental life it is only certain individual acts and portions that are conscious."[14] Following World War I, Freud gained popularity as people sought out his writings to understand how the world's most advanced civilization could have perpetrated such a barbaric war. In *Civilization and Its Discontents* (1929) Freud explained that civilization provided humanity with security and order by repressing humanity's aggressive instincts. As civilization became more advanced, however, it became more repressive of these aggressive instincts, and human frustration and tension correspondingly increased. For Freud, the war was perfectly understandable because "civilized society is perpetually threatened with disintegration. The interest of working in common would not hold it together; instinctual passions are stronger than reasonable interests."[15] Freudian psychology struck the latest blow to humanity's classical image. After Copernicus, humanity was no longer the center of the universe, and after Darwin, it was no longer different from the ape, but after Freud, it was no longer master even of its own mind. Following the war an avalanche of literature confirmed Freud's disturbing revelation about the human psyche.

The second characteristic, distinct from but related to epistemological despair, is *relativism* or *behaviorism*—the complete lack of any fixed human nature, the individual's "infinite plasticity." Outside influences—time, place, culture, society, education, and environment—completely shape the individual's entire personality.[16] Who can forget Aldous Huxley's *Brave New World* (1932), with its chilling description of the Central London Hatchery and Conditioning Center? The Center breeds people like robots for particular roles and societal castes. The Center's Director proudly describes this shocking process for conditioning human behavior as "one of the major instruments of social stability!"[17]

The third characteristic, *self-deprecation*, is the individual's thinking ill of him or herself from a feeling of insignificance, powerlessness, and inherent evil. Baumer illustrated this wholesale unraveling of humanity's classical image of itself by contrasting two works by the English philosopher and broadcast personality

C. E. M. Joad: his autobiography *Under the Fifth Rib* (1933) and his *Guide to Modern Wickedness* (1939). Joad's autobiography describes the transition from his prewar confidence in human rationality and perfectibility while studying at Oxford to his subsequent postwar disillusionment described in the latter work. In that second work Joad declares that "man's true enemy is within himself; it lies in the strength of his own uncontrolled passions and appetites."[18] In short, literature after World War I entered the mysterious and troubling world of the human psyche, leaving behind cosmic questions about the death of God and turning instead to existential questions about "the death of Man."[19]

This subjectivist strain dominates writing and accompanies the loss of belief in the transcendent after the war, described in Chapter 4 on theology. By focusing inward upon the individual, postwar literature, including expository as well as fictional writing, largely disengaged from questions about cosmic meaning and purpose.[20] Instead, as illustrated below in the exemplary literary genre of British, American, and European novels, this postwar literature essentially accepted the condition of cosmic alienation. Consequently, Western literature after World War I interposed little opposition to the materialist portrait of a meaningless universe. Furthermore, in the decade after the war hundreds of new books appeared that extolled the gifts of science, which only reinforced the growing postwar commitment to scientism.

One of these books was Harold Stearns' *Civilization in the United States* (1922), which Hoffman called "a historical landmark in the post-World War I years."[21] Stearns' book is a compilation of articles by various contributors such as the American journalist and critic H. L. Mencken and American literary critic, biographer, and historian Van Wyck Brooks. Hoffman describes *Civilization in the United States* as "a curious document of disaffection, pointing to and reiterating the failure of culture, entertainment, family life, religion—of everything but science, and even it scored only partial success in the survey of American life and institutions."[22] In short, only science emerged from the war's cultural devastation relatively unscathed, due primarily to its continuing gifts to human knowledge, technology, and power. Science received a huge boost in popularity as Einstein's general theory of relativity was hailed worldwide as "epochmaking" and a "new theory of the universe." Happening within a year after the end of World War I, the announcement was universally welcomed, in the words of Einstein biographer Walter Isaacson, by a world that was "weary of war and yearning for a triumph of human transcendence."[23] With science's position reasonably secure after the war, expository writing about science often took aim at the rest of Western culture, including the role and value of literature. The primary target of this critical writing was literature expounding belief in the transcendent or in a meaningful and purposeful reality. Therefore, our analysis begins with critical writing about the implications of modern science for literature before venturing into fictional writing after the war.

Modern Science and the Role of Postwar Literature

Two works in particular stand out, for Hoffman, as reflecting the attitude toward science in the era following World War I: "A Free Man's Worship" (1903, 1917) by the British philosopher Bertrand Russell, and *The Modern Temper* (1929) by the American critic and journalist Joseph Wood Krutch. Russell espoused a scientific perspective on the modern world, and Krutch lamented the injury to traditional belief and aesthetics as the result of that science. In the following passage from his essay "A Free Man's Worship," Russell eloquently described his view of the purposeless universe, devoid of meaning, which modern science had given to humanity:

> That man is the product of causes which had no prevision of the end they were achieving; that his origin, his growth, his hopes and fears, his loves and his beliefs, are but the outcome of accidental collocations of atoms; that no fire, no heroism, no intensity of thoughts and feelings, can preserve an individual life beyond the grave; that all the labors of the ages, all the devotion, all the inspiration, all the noonday brightness of human genius, are destined to extinction in the vast death of the solar system, and that the whole temple of man's achievement must inevitably be buried beneath the debris of a universe in ruins—all these things, if not quite beyond dispute, are yet so nearly certain, that no philoso-

phy which rejects them can hope to stand. Only within the scaffolding of these truths, only on the firm foundation of unyielding despair, can the soul's habitation henceforth be safely built.[24]

To maintain human dignity within the indifferent cosmos bequeathed by science, Russell advocated the following naturalist philosophy:

disdaining the coward terrors of the slave of Fate, to worship at the shrine that his own hands have built; undismayed by the empire of chance, to preserve a mind free from the wanton tyranny that rules his outward fate; proudly defiant of the irresistible forces that tolerate, for a moment, his knowledge and his condemnation, to sustain alone, a weary but unyielding Atlas, the world that his own ideals have fashioned despite the trampling march of unconscious power.[25]

In short, humankind must rationally endeavor to improve its lot in life, while simultaneously accepting its dismal fate in a meaningless world. In Russell's naturalist philosophy, constructive use of science and human intelligence can better the human condition: "It is science, ultimately, that makes our age different, for good or evil, from the ages that have gone before. And science, whatever harm it may cause by the way, is capable of bringing mankind ultimately to a far happier condition than any that has been known in the past."[26] In *What I Believe* (1925), Russell rejected religious notions of good and evil as unscientific and also rejected cosmic philosophies, whether optimistic or pessimistic, because they arise from "the same naïve humanism: the great world, so far as we know it from the philosophy of nature, is neither good nor bad, and is not concerned to make us either happy or unhappy. All such philosophies spring from self-importance, and are best corrected by a little astronomy."[27]

While Russell confronted the indifferent universe with a confident faith in the promise of science, Krutch mourned the loss of traditional faith, which science had taken from humanity. In *The Modern Temper* (1929), Krutch reflected on the dire implications of science for the world of poetry, mythology, and religion that had reigned in the West before the war:

> Formerly he had believed in even his darkest moments that the universe was rational if he could only grasp its rationality, but gradually he comes to suspect that rationality is an attribute of himself alone and that there is no reason to suppose that his own life has any more meaning than the life of the humblest insect that crawls from one annihilation to another.[28]

Gradually over the prior centuries, science had eroded God's control of the universe and humanity's convictions about cosmic meaning and purpose, leaving people bereft of their stabilizing beliefs and cast into an alien environment:

> His teleological concepts molded [his world] into a form which you could appreciate and he gave to it moral laws which would make it meaningful, but step-by-step the outlines of nature have thrust themselves upon him, and for the dream which he made is substituted a reality devoid of any pattern which you can understand.[29]

Among the several kinds of prewar stabilizing beliefs that science has destroyed, Krutch identified the following four: First, science has disproved or at least seriously questioned the value of *humanism* in resolving the conflict between thought and feeling, leaving science alone as a potential source of human happiness ("Science has always promised two things not necessarily related — an increase first in our powers, second in our happiness or wisdom, and we have come to realize that it is the first and less important of the two promises which it has kept most abundantly").[30] Second, *love* has lost the promise of happiness as science has removed the mystery of sex ("if love is coming to be less often a sin, it has come also to be less often the supreme privilege," and, instead, has become "gradually so accessible, so unmysterious, and so free that its value is trivial").[31] Third, *literature* no longer can achieve real tragedy because tragedy requires a genuine belief in humankind's nobility and potential heroism ("We can no longer tell tales of the fall of noble men because we do not believe that noble man exists." "Our cosmos may be farcical or it may be prophetic, but it has not the dignity of tragedy and we cannot accept it as such").[32] And fourth, *aesthetic principles* provide no relief—"though the human mind may be made to work in accordance with them, external nature will not, and the ultimate dilemma may be stated thus: the proposition that life is a science is intellectually indefensible; the proposition that life is an art is pragmatically impossible."[33]

Krutch concluded his long lamentation by observing that materialism has taken "possession of each field of human speculation as soon as a connection had been established" and, further, that materialism and science have converged to expose metaphysical certitudes as mere phantoms.[34] Science has unmasked metaphysics as an art pretending to be a science, and "metaphysics, which promised so much, thus ends by confirming the very despair which it set out to combat."[35] Despite his dejection concerning "the tyranny which scientific thought has come to exercise over the human spirit," Krutch finds a limited consolation from knowing "at least that we have discovered the trick which has been played on us and that whatever else may be we are no longer dupes."[36] Thus, Krutch finds this one purportedly positive outcome of science's systematic destruction of the prewar belief systems—now humanity can correctly understand and consciously accept its dismal fate.

With science offering the one clear road to truth, however terrible that truth may be, the very role of literature was called into question, and Krutch was only one among these questioners. In *The Literary Mind: Its Place in an Age of Science* (1931), Max Eastman, an American journalist and critic, suggested that science is the inevitable successor to literature in interpreting experience:

> Literature, then as a thing distinct from science, may be a pure communication of experience; it may interpret experience in spheres as yet untouched by science; it may offer interpretations as intellectual things to be enjoyed without a tense regard to their validity. ... To which we must add that in these spirited activities, serious and yet set free from the tether of verification, new ideas and suggestions of infinite value to science may be born.[37]

Literature may open up avenues for scientific exploration but, for Eastman, literature must give way once science has given answer: "Poetry is compelled by its very nature to yield up to science the task of interpreting experience, of finding out what we call truth, of giving men reliable guidance in the conduct of their lives."[38]

British psychologist and critic I. A. Richards taught poetry at Cambridge University and wrote *Principles of Literary Criticism* (1924), which profoundly influenced the modern poetic. Richards maintained that science appeals to the intellect, and poetry appeals to emotional interests and attitudes:

> In its use of words poetry is just the reverse of science. Very definite thoughts do occur, but not because the words are chosen as logically to bar out all possibilities but one. No. But because the manner, the tone of voice, the cadence and the rhythm play upon our interests and make *them* pick out from among the indefinite number of possibilities the precise particular thought which they need.[39]

Although poetry and belief had been historically linked, modern science now challenged those traditional beliefs as unverifiable pseudo-statements, which left poetry with a purely human focus:

> Countless pseudo-statements—about God, about the universe, about human nature, the relations of mind to mind, about the soul, its rank and destiny—pseudo-statements which are pivotal points in the organization of the mind, vital to its well-being, have suddenly become, for sincere, honest, and informed minds, impossible to believe. For centuries they have been believed; now they are gone, irrevocably; and the knowledge which has killed them is not a kind upon which an equally firm organization of the mind can be based.[40]

Modern science had separated nature from the transcendent and rendered spiritual notions of the universe, in Richards' view, "probably nonsense."[41] This conclusion led Richards to value the poetry of Thomas Hardy for its honest confrontation of an indifferent, materialist universe. Richards thought that science had exposed as pseudo-statements those belief systems to which poetry previously was linked. Hereafter, poetry must serve a different role. Poetry can enrich life, enhance the human personality, and ultimately save us from despair: "it is a perfectly possible means of overcoming chaos."[42]

While some writers bemoaned science's diminution of literature, other writers considered science even more comforting than literature. In an article in the *New Republic* (January 26, 1927), the American novelist, poet, and critic Edmund Wilson found science "not abject, but, just at present, particularly heroic. ... In the last century it was often literature which magnified humanity and almost invariably science which made us feel insignificant. Today, the situation seems reversed: it is science which restores us to importance and fiction and poetry which often make us feel like worms."[43] Even this brief sampling shows that many respected essayists considered science to support a meaningless cosmos and to pose a serious challenge to the traditional role and continuing value of fictional literature because of its historical alignment with a meaningful cosmos. Could fiction create genuine tragedy in a world lacking human dignity and ultimate meaning? Was fiction only a temporary reprieve from existential despair, and could it provide any genuine comfort from cosmic indifference?

Not everyone, of course, accepted science as the sole road to truth, as Hoffman pointed out:

> Other critics refused to believe that science had so fully usurped all significant fields of knowledge, or had reduced the problem of truth to such an unbending criterion as "verifiability." They also suggested that scientists were not nearly so convinced of their reading of the universe as they were alleged to be. ... The arts are not philosophy or sociology, and they should not pretend to be; *as* arts they may (and should) in their special ways communicate significant truths either ignored or disparaged by science.[44]

The response to science from a religious perspective ran the full gamut—from return to religious fundamentalism, to religion based on science, to provisional religious beliefs pending new scientific discoveries, to complete separation of religious and scientific thought. In *God without Thunder* (1930), John Crowe Ransom, the American poet and critic, aligned himself with the religious fundamentalists against the modernists. Ransom argued that science's refusal to accept myth improperly discards much of human thought and experience.[45] The Harvard geologist Kirtley F. Mather argued on behalf of non-traditional religion "based on facts and experiences, a religion developed by rigidly scientific methods of thought."[46] Columbia Professor of Philosophy William Pepperell Montague proposed a new religion without sacrosanct authority: "Such dogmas as remain, and there would be many, would be transformed into hypotheses. The most fantastic theory of the supernatural, if held as a hypothesis, is honorable, and belief in it is honest and to be expected."[47]

At the other end of the spectrum, Herbert Croly, the American journalist and founder of the *New Republic,* claimed that science's "achievements have only intensified that moral chaos, of which the war with its barren victory, its peace without appeasement, and the ominous Bolshevist menace, are different but closely connected expressions." For Croly, science's imperative must include reconciliation with religion: "Scientific inquiry must posit the existence of the world which the human mind is capable, after a fashion, of understanding. The religious life must posit the existence of a world in which human purposes can, after a fashion, get themselves realized."[48]

In summary, a large body of critical literature of the post-World War I era sought various ways of coping with the dominant influence of modern science, ranging from Russell's courageous acceptance of the godless universe that science had revealed, at one extreme, to Ransom's bold reaffirmation of fundamentalist religion, at the other, and much in between. The great difficulty for many writers, as Hoffman explained, was finding meaning in a universe defined by science and devoid of the transcendent:

> The tragedy for many of these men and women was that there could scarcely be a tragic or heroic act without a structure of myth and an acceptable mode of belief within it. This

was a genuine dilemma; symbolically it might be considered the condition of the spiritual wasteland. The agony of the spiritual quest in a world that regarded spiritual matters with indifference was one of the most profound emotional experiences of the 1920s.[49]

Modern science engendered defensiveness among essayists about the continuing role and value not only of religious beliefs but also of literature itself because of its historical link to such beliefs. With that perspective, our analysis turns to some of the important British, American, and European novels of the era immediately following the war.

Modernism and the British War Novel

The term "modernism" generally refers to an international aesthetic movement toward distinctively new forms and concepts of literature and the other arts, which began in the 1890s and reached its high watermark during the post-World War I decade.[50] According to Florida Professor of English R. B. Kershner, modernism began in the decades just before the war "as a series of ceaseless avant-garde experiments that constituted an attack on tradition and in some ways on art itself." Modernism advocated both new subjects and new artistic forms in general adherence to Ezra Pound's dictum: "Make it new."[51] New novelistic forms included unusual, sometimes unreliable, and even multiple narrators, including the stream of consciousness narration. Among the modernists were novelists D. H. Lawrence, Virginia Woolf, James Joyce, Ernest Hemingway, and F. Scott Fitzgerald.[52]

The nineteenth-century novel that preceded the modernist movement is generally associated with the rise of realism and described as "representing complex characters with mixed motives who are rooted in a social class, operate in a developed social structure, interact with many other characters, and undergo plausible, everyday modes of experience."[53] Realism depicted a relatively stable, if often troubled, world. Jane Austen (1775-1817) revealed characters primarily through their own words; she used marriage as a metaphor for social and political revitalization; and she emphasized a traditional value system with her typical comedic endings in a happy marriage, as in *Emma* (1816). Charles Dickens (1812-1870) addressed social issues, as in *Hard Times* (1854), which depicted the harsh working conditions in England's industrial communities and the moral hypocrisy among wealthy factory managers like those in Dickens's fictional Coketown. In France, Gustave Flaubert (1821-1880) emphasized art over morality in *Madam Bovary* (1857), while searching for the right word, style, and structure in the story of an otherwise intellectually undistinguished bourgeois adulteress. Emile Zola (1845-1902) applied his journalistic technique in novels like *Germinal* (1885), written expressly to show the French miner as "crushed, starving, a victim of ignorance, suffering with his children in a hell on earth … a victim of the facts of existence—capital, competition, industrial crises."[54] In the same genre, but representing a multinational critique, Joseph Conrad (1857-1924) in *Heart of Darkness* (1902) exposed the hypocrisy of the civilizing ideals underlying European imperialism.

Virginia Woolf claimed that "on or about December, 1910, human character changed," referring to the exhibition of postimpressionist paintings presented in London by her friend Roger Fry. Woolf's larger point was that artistic distortions and exaggerations, like those in the exhibition paintings by Cézanne, Van Gogh, Gauguin, and Duchamp, present a greater and more compelling truth than the exact representation of external reality in traditional art.[55] The modernist novel represents this change, exemplified in the transition from the confident, omniscient narrator of nineteenth-century works by Austen, Dickens, Flaubert, and Zola to the ironic, vague, impressionistic narration by Charlie Marlow in Conrad's *Heart of Darkness*.[56] In "Modern Fiction" (1925), Virginia Woolf argued that "life or spirit, truth or reality" no longer lie in the nineteenth-century novelistic conventions because ideally "there would be no plot, no comedy, no tragedy, no love interest or catastrophe in the accepted style." Instead, the modernist novel would *look within* to "examine for a moment an ordinary mind on an ordinary day" during which it "receives a myriad of impressions—trivial, fantastic, evanescent, or engraved with the sharpness of steel."[57] "Life," Woolf asserted, "is not a series of gig-lamps symmetrically arranged; life is a luminous halo, a semi-transparent envelope surrounding us from the beginning of consciousness to the end." For Woolf, therefore, life involves "atoms as they fall upon the mind in the order in which they fall ... however disconnected and incoherent in appearance" because, for the modern novelist, the point of interest "lies very likely in the dark places of psychology."[58]

While novelists like Conrad were already doing substantially modernist work before the war, and while Woolf considers 1910 a turning point for modernism, many others see the war as "the decisive break," according to Kershner:

> [T]he massive disenchantment with sentimental patriotism generalized itself in a feeling of rejection of the older generation's entire set of values. It seemed to many that an art expressing a new sensibility and new values would have to reject conventional forms. Certainly there was a strong linkage between rejection of the war and aesthetic experimentation. James Joyce both by personal conviction and as an Irishman was a noncombatant. Many artists and intellectuals among Virginia Woolf's Bloomsbury group were pacifists, as was D. H. Lawrence."[59]

Whether World War I was its initiator or merely its accelerator, modernism (or high modernism, as it was called after the war) flourished in the decade of the 1920s, hastening its freighted postwar journey into "the dark places of psychology."[60]

Among the important British postwar novels inspired by the war and not already considered in Chapter 3 are Virginia Woolf's *Mrs. Dalloway* (1925) and Ford Madox Ford's *Parade's End* (1924-28). Virginia Woolf and Ford Madox Ford had entirely different experiences of the war. Woolf was a leading member of the Bloomsbury, an informal group of the English literary and aesthetic avant-garde, which stood at the forefront of principled opposition to the war. Ford served as an infantry officer during the war, was gassed, and suffered from shell shock.

Woolf sets *Mrs. Dalloway* in London's governing district of Westminster on a single day in the middle of June 1923, when Mrs. Clarissa Dalloway, "the perfect hostess," plans a party for England's ruling elite.[61] *Mrs. Dalloway* concerns the continuing psychological damage caused by a society that ignores its war victims in attempting to return to normalcy. Although almost four years have passed since the Treaty of Versailles (June 28, 1919), war and death haunt this novel and lurk behind the glitter and flutter of London society.[62] From the center of consciousness of each character, Woolf explores postwar reality by juxtaposing a politician's wife with a survivor's guilt. [63] Returning veteran Septimus Smith, his Italian wife Rezia, and German immigrant Doris Kilman live daily with the war's consequences, whereas Peter Walsh, Clarissa Dalloway, and the prominent politicians at Clarissa's party, including the Prime Minister, ignore society's ongoing responsibility for the postwar condition.[64] It is not the deferred effects of shell shock, as Dr. Bradshaw opines, but society's indifference that is the proximate cause of Septimus's suicide. In a terrible irony, Peter Walsh hears the ambulance that removes Septimus's mangled body and thinks only of the ambulance: "one of the triumphs of civilization."[65] In her June 29, 1920, diary entry Virginia Woolf wrote: "Our generation is daily scourged by the bloody war."[66]

Woolf biographer Roger Poole considers *Mrs. Dalloway* one of the finest war novels because of its uniquely "empathetic reconstitution of a mind thrown off balance by the experiences of sheer horror" — Septimus Smith's "internalized, inexpressible, incommunicable" fate.[67] Wilfred Owen memorialized the shell-shocked condition of veterans like Septimus in his poem "Mental Cases" (1918):

These are the men whose minds the Dead have ravished.
Memory fingers in their hair of murders,
Multitudinous murders they once witnessed.[68]

In the voice of Septimus, Woolf emphasized that society had no sympathy for madness after the war: "Once you stumble, Septimus wrote on the back of a postcard, human nature is on you. ... So he was deserted."[69] In a sense, Septimus Smith is Everyman, suffering from what Poole calls "the burden of the incommunicable" — a random shell missed him and killed his friend and lover Evans just before the Armistice; so, "if Evans can die like that, then we all can die like that."[70] As Septimus remarks, "it might be possible that the world itself is without meaning."[71]

Ford's tetralogy *Parade's End* (1924-28) is a World War I novel without battle scenes, a tragedy without resolution, and a love story without lovemaking. Instead, *Parade's End* focuses on the historical change during the World War I era viewed through the eyes of the anachronistic Christopher Tietjens, the last English Tory.[72] Tietjens is a large, untidy, 26-year-old Yorkshire gentleman, "an eighteenth-century figure of the Dr. Johnson type," a throwback to the Jane Austen era that D. H. Lawrence admired and to the English gentry before the middle-class built the British Empire. Staunchly noble, morally correct, socially humane, and classically educated, Tietjens resides in, but is not of, the greedy, venal, and unprincipled Edwardian society, which is disintegrating and unwittingly teetering on the brink of ruin.[73] Despite, indeed because of, his inherent goodness, Tietjens is endlessly persecuted, betrayed, and disparaged by everyone closest to him, including his wife Sylvia and his close friend Macmaster.[74]

Some Do Not ..., the first novel in the tetralogy, opens prewar in the oft-cited scene of Tietjens and Macmaster traveling in a well appointed railway car, part of the English official class that "administered the world."[75] After predicting the 1914 European conflagration "with financial statistics as to the approaching bankruptcy of various European powers and the growing acquisitive skill and rapacity of the inhabitants of Great Britain," Tietjens goes to war, gets injured, and returns home to recuperate. An exploding bomb dropped by a German airplane has caused Tietjens's amnesia and speech loss, and he is rebuilding his mind by reading the *Encyclopaedia Britannica*.[76]

The middle two novels, *No More Parades* and *A Man Could Stand Up*, show Tietjens's continuing psychological stress, while performing admirably as an Army captain in charge of replacements and, subsequently, as a front-line commander.[77] He copes with dire and tragic personnel issues: Lieutenant McKechnie, a classical scholar and brave officer who has gone mad; O Nine Morgan, a Welsh private who dies in his arms, killed by the shrapnel from a German "candlestick" bomb; a self-interested quartermaster who denies Tietjens needed supplies, jeopardizing Tietjens's troops simply to look good for promotion. Despite his competence and compassion as an officer, however, Tietjens is unappreciated and mistreated by his superiors and wrongly disparaged as a socialist and French spy. *The Last Post* ends the tetralogy with Tietjens living in a country cottage, surviving as an antiques dealer, and selling English antiquities to wealthy Americans.

Samuel Hynes applauds *Parade's End* as a masterly presentation of "the whole historical myth—the war-before-the-war, the gap of the war itself, and the war-after-the-war—in one intelligible story, and in a form that is appropriate to the Myths: a fragmented, elliptical, difficult form."[78] *Parade's End* exposes the unreliable values and unstable world of Edwardian England that led to war and left Britain after the war with an uncertain and unpromising future. Recalling the band's playing *Land of Hope and Glory* and the adjutant's saying *There will be no more parades* upon disbanding a Kitchener Battalion in 1914, Tietjens sees the whole march of Western civilization coming to a halt: "No more Hope, no more Glory, no more parades for you and me anymore. Nor for the country... Nor for the world, I daresay."[79] In the final book of the tetralogy, *The Last Post*, Tietjens and his dying brother Mark reconcile themselves to the coming end of the Tietjens dynasty. Referring to their reconciliation, American editor and writer Robie Macauley states:

> Both their strength and their failure lie in the fact that they have been true to something in the world where no one is truly anything. They are an anachronism and, as an anachronism, must disappear. It is inevitable that one theory of Truth, one systematic idea of how man may lead a 'good' life, will be swallowed up in a world of Untruth, but that is according to history's law—not its equity.[80]

Warwick Professor of English Bernard Bergonzi calls Tietjens "an Anglican saint" because Tietjens consistently forgives his tormentors throughout his long martyrdom at the hands of his wife, his friends, his military superiors, and his civilian leadership.[81] Bergonzi salutes *Parade's End* for its profound treatment of key themes in British literature of the Great War: "the suppression of the Hero as a tangible ideal; a nostalgic love of rural England, combined with an anguished sense that centuries of English tradition were being overthrown; the alienation of the soldier from the civilians."[82]

Woolf and Ford convey a profound sense of a lost civilization—the eighteenth-century Tory world of Jane Austen where the
British Empire assured universal stability, moral balance, and civic
propriety. World War I radically upset such stability, balance, and
propriety: for Woolf, by fostering a moral indifference to the consequences of that horrific catastrophe and by leaving its victims like
Septimus Smith to struggle alone with the terrible burden of personal loss; and, for Ford, by fostering the venal culture of Edwardian England that persecutes, betrays, and marginalizes people of
integrity like Tietjens. Hoffman writes that "no American literature
of the 1920s came quite so close to the heart of the cultural issue
that Ford's tetralogy so brilliantly documents."[83] This sense of lost
civilization left individuals like Clarissa Dalloway and Christopher
Tietjens isolated in the postwar world, even in the midst of civic
bustle. Talk of death intrudes into Clarissa's party, and the Tietjens
dynasty is dying out. Both Woolf and Ford portray British cultural
devolution and, along with Septimus Smith, raise the new possibility "that the world itself is without meaning."

American Novels of the Great War

America had not wanted to enter World War I and only launched
its first all-American offensive in September 1917, more than three
years after the war began.[84] This delay led many young American
writers to volunteer for the American Ambulance Service: E.E.
Cummings and John Dos Passos with the Norton-Harjes in France,
and Ernest Hemingway with the Red Cross ambulance section in
Italy. They volunteered for personal reasons to experience and test
themselves in a world crisis rather than for patriotic reasons, like
their European counterparts, to defend country and tradition.[85] In
A Farewell to Arms, for example, when the English nurse Catherine
Barkley questions the American Frederick Henry about why he
volunteered for the Italian ambulance corps, Frederick answers, "I
don't know. There isn't always an explanation for everything."[86]
These American quests for dangerous adventure, however, often
ended in real personal trauma: E.E. Cummings endured false imprisonment in a ghastly French prison from August 1917 to January
11, 1918, for fraternizing with the French *poilu* over the objections

of his superiors and for sharing his cynicism about the French war administration in intercepted letters home. Hemingway suffered a near-death experience in Italy on July 8, 1918, from 238 fragments of a mortar shell that exploded while he was carrying a more severely wounded comrade to safety.[87]

For participating Americans, World War I was strange, writes Hoffman, because it was "an affair they were not quite genuinely committed to sharing." Consequently, their wounds were "personally suffered and not in any way to be interpreted as a contribution to the cause." Rather, they provoked a sense of personal violation:

> The shock was immediate and for a long time irremediable. Danger, violence, battle chaos, death, were in every case dissociated from both geography and culture. The postwar American was almost abnormally sensitive to a form of experience that may best be described by the term "violation," a term that indicates what happened to their sense of dignity and security as a result of the events that had little or nothing to do with them.[88]

Hoffman found few English writers who "had a comparable feeling of outrage" as do their American counterparts.[89]

Four important American novelists wrestled with the effect of the war: E.E. Cummings, John Dos Passos, Ernest Hemingway, and F. Scott Fitzgerald. In the autobiographical novel, *The Enormous Room* (1922), E. E. Cummings (1894-1962) described his arrest and four-month imprisonment along with his friend and coworker William Slater Brown on trumped-up charges of "treasonable correspondence" growing out of their fraternizing with the *poilu*.[90] The novel re-creates their Dante-esque descent into the hell of La Ferté Macé prison in Orne, 100 miles west of Paris. The prison is a bedlam of "weird cries, oaths, laughter ... by at least 30 voices in 11 languages," which left Cummings "trembling with this chaos" and feeling he had "gone completely crazy."[91] La Ferté Macé is a triage camp housing men of various nationalities suspected of espionage, women prostitutes found in the restricted Army Zone, and wives of prisoners incarcerated voluntarily to be with their husbands—all awaiting a Commission's quarterly determination of their guilt or innocence. With remarkable grace these endearingly portrayed inmates endure questionable arrests on mostly spurious and often nonexistent charges, indefinite incarceration in grossly squalid conditions, and brutal mistreatment under the cruel administration of Prison Director Apollyon. *The Enormous Room* celebrates these abused prisoners as "the finest people," chronicles Cummings's own spiritual growth under hellacious conditions, and excoriates the prison bureaucracy and French civilization responsible for such depravity.[92]

John Dos Passos (1896-1970) considered military life "slavery" and "an enormous, tragic digression in people's lives which brought death to the intellect, to art, to everything that mattered."[93] His novel *Three Soldiers* (1921) dramatizes his viewpoint by showing the damaging effect of the military machine on three young enlisted men from different geographic, ethnic, socioeconomic, and educational backgrounds.[94] The central figure among the three is John Andrews, a 22-year-old Harvard-educated musician and composer. While washing windows stateside, Andrews mentally orchestrates the monotonous rhythms of the Army training routine and viscerally recoils at the "blind hatred stirring" among men after attending an anti-German indoctrination film.[95] While still on active duty in France after the Armistice, Andrews is apprehended, handcuffed, and beaten by MPs for lacking his required military pass and failing to salute a superior officer. *Three Soldiers* ends with Andrews being placed under arrest as a deserter facing 20 years to life imprisonment, while sheet music from his uncompleted musical composition about John Brown, "a madman who wanted to free people," blows page by page over his apartment floor.[96] Of John Andrews, Indiana Professor of Humanities Claudia Matherly Stoltz writes: "No glory, no heroism of the type one associates with war novels, but a man presented as a hero nonetheless because he is courageous enough to make a stand for and to pay the consequences of his individual beliefs."[97]

Ernest Hemingway (1899-1961) wrote three books about the Great War: a collection of short stories, *In Our Time* (1925), and two novels, *The Sun Also Rises* (1926) and *A Farewell to Arms* (1929). As revised for republication in 1930, *In Our Time* is organized like an autobiographical novel and contains sixteen epiphanic short stories and sixteen italicized prose poems (chapters) depicting scenes from World War I, the subsequent Greco-Turkish War, bullfighting, and violence and death in America.[98] It opens with the short story "On the Quai at Smyrna" about traumatized Greek refugees escaping the brutal Greco-Turkish War, and closes with the italicized prose poem "L'Envoi" about the deposed Greek king responsible for his nation's postwar chaos.[99] The centerpiece of the book is the prose poem about Nick Adams and his friend Rinaldi, both seriously wounded in the Italian campaign. Nick "sat against the wall of the church where they had dragged him to be clear of the machine-gun fire in the street"; he has been hit in the spine and "both legs stuck out awkwardly." Rinaldi "lay still in the sun breathing with difficulty" with his "face downward against the wall"; the street is littered with the dead, including two Austrian soldiers. Waiting for the stretcher bearers, Nick tells Rinaldi, "You and me we've made a separate peace." In a single paragraph Hemingway captures the loathsomeness of war, the destruction of private lives, and the impotence and stoicism of Nick and Rinaldi. The surrounding eight short stories about Nick Adams describe his personal maturation as a young man growing up in America, a soldier in the crucible of war, a spouse in a failing marriage, and a traumatized veteran in search of a new existential code.[100] Although the Nick Adams stories anchor *In Our Time*, Hemingway adds characters and scenes to develop his major themes: the brutality of war, the hypocrisy of the era, and the need for stoic personalized values.

A Farewell to Arms portrays two characters disillusioned by the capricious chaos of the Great War, Frederick Henry and Catherine Barkley. They discover love as a religious experience that gives meaning to their lives. After her fiancé is killed on the Somme ("They blew him all to bits"), Catherine teaches Frederick the world's absurdity and says, "You're my religion. You're all I've got."[101] Frederick reciprocates her love after his two near-death experiences from an exploding shell on the Alpine Front and from a murderous Italian Peace Brigade, which is arbitrarily shooting suspected deserters during the Caporetto retreat.[102] Thereafter, the two lovers briefly enjoy the feeling of being "the same one."[103] Escaping to Edenic Switzerland, they live on borrowed time because they know the absurd world "kills the very good and very gentle

and very brave impartially."[104] Reflecting on the meaningless carnage during Italy's "white war," Frederick concludes that "abstract
words such as glory, honor, courage, or hallow are obscene," and
Catherine despairs that "they just keep it up until they break you,"
before dying shortly after the birth of a stillborn child.[105]

Though written before *A Farewell to Arms*, Hemingway's *The
Sun Also Rises* is its logical sequel, focusing on the "lost generation"
of American expatriates in post-World War I Paris. Primary among
them is Jake Barnes, the quintessential Hemingway hero: knowledgeable, wounded, vulnerable, and brave. In love with Brett Ash-
ley but unable to consummate their relationship because of his war
injury, Jake is "hard-boiled about everything in the daytime, but at
night it is another thing."[106] He tries to live by his code of conduct to
give meaning to his life, stoically enduring the trauma of his war injury with dignity and courage: "All I wanted to know is how to live
in it. Maybe if you found out how to live in it you learned from that
what it was all about."[107] By contrast, Jake's antagonist Robert Cohn
is not "one of us," but instead is an outsider who behaves badly:
sleeping with Brett, intruding on Jake's fishing trip, and picking
fights with Jake and the bullfighter Pedro Romero. Whereas Jake
embodies the Hemingway code of stoic endurance, Cohn repeatedly violates it. Jake's fishing trip in Burguete, Spain, celebrates not
just the camaraderie with friends Bill Gorton and Bill Harris, but
also the ritualistic, spiritually healing rite of fishing. Like Nick Adams in "Big Two-Hearted River" from *In Our Time*, Jake also recu-
perates from loss, suffering, and death in the Great War. By contrast
with hedonistic France, Spain represents community and values:
Jake visits the monastery of Roncesvalles (made famous in the *Song
of Roland*) and shares bread and wine with the Basques en route to
Pamplona, giving the trip a sacramental quality. In addition, Jake is
the lone bullfighting "aficionado" on the Spanish trip, sharing with
the hotel owner Montoya a spiritual passion for bullfighting, that
ritualistic confrontation with death.[108] Like the bullfighter Villalta
in *In Our Time*, the extraordinary Romero in *The Sun Also Rises* embodies the characteristic Hemingway values of courage and style in
the face of death. As Jake says, "Nobody ever lives their life all the
way up except bullfighters."[109]

F. Scott Fitzgerald (1896-1940) wrote his autobiographical

novel, *This Side of Paradise* (1920), about the quest of young Amory Blaine for self-discovery.[110] Blaine gradually transitions from a morally weak, aristocratic egoist in boarding school, through Princeton, World War I service, and postwar employment, to emerge as a more courageously self-aware individual.[111] After the war Blaine exclaims that "my whole generation is restless" because of its loss of ideals (Woodrow Wilson "had to compromise over and over again"), its loss of faith ("I think four men have discovered Paris to one that discovered God"), and its loss of leadership ("There were no more wise men; there were no more heroes"). Blaine "had grown up to a thousand books, a thousand lies; he had listened eagerly to people who pretended to know, but knew nothing." This realization leaves him "brood[ing] over a new generation, the chosen youths from the muddled, unchastened world, still fed romantically on the mistakes and half-forgotten dreams of dead statesmen and poets."[112] *This Side of Paradise* captures the disillusionment of the younger generation in postwar America, striving for meaning in a discredited civilization.[113]

With its undercurrent of crass materialism, self-love, and foreboding, *This Side of Paradise* prefigures Fitzgerald's *The Great Gatsby* (1925), about the futile romantic quest of the fabulously wealthy Jay Gatsby for the beautiful, married, and equally wealthy Daisy Buchanan. *Gatsby* is the tragic story of one veteran of the Great War, Jay Gatsby, told by another veteran, Daisy's younger second-cousin Nick Carraway. In October 1917, a month before embarking for France, Jay Gatsby, the penniless young Army officer "without a past," had an affair and fell obsessively in love with Daisy, a rich Louisville socialite. Then, in June 1919, while delaying his postwar return to Daisy for lack of financial means to support her extravagant lifestyle, Gatsby lost Daisy in marriage to the wealthy Chicagoan Tom Buchanan. For three years thereafter Gatsby aggressively acquired largely tainted money to finance his illusory dream of winning Daisy back.[114] Nick and Gatsby bond over reminiscences of their common war experience in "some wet, grey little village in France." Gatsby purportedly did "extraordinarily well in the war," advanced from lieutenant to major, commanded divisional machine guns in the Argonne Forest, and received various awards for bravery, including a declaration from Montenegro.

After the war he joined the American Legion to pursue his questionable business dealings with Meyer Wolfsheim.[115] The war also provides much of Gatsby's mystique ("they say he's a nephew or cousin of Kaiser Wilhelm's. That's where his money comes from"; "he was a German spy during the war"; "he was a nephew to von Hindenburg and a second cousin to the devil"). Hearing Gatsby's fantastic and contradictory stories, Nick "had reached the point of believing everything and nothing about him." Ultimately, however, Nick comes to judge Gatsby the best of that "rotten crowd" of New Yorker socialites, and tells Gatsby, "You're worth the whole damn bunch put together."[116]

Gatsby depicts the postwar hedonism, venality, and moral indifference that corrupted the American dream of success, and left a "valley of ashes" — materialism's wasteland of disillusionment, sterility, and despair. Daisy negligently kills Myrtle Wilson and also indirectly causes Gatsby's death: "They were careless people, Tom and Daisy — they smashed up things and creatures," says Nick, "and then retreated back into their money or their vast carelessness, or whatever it was that kept them together, and let other people clean up the mess that they made."[117] Embodying the American dream of success, Gatsby rose from humble origins to extraordinary, albeit tainted, wealth, but he also possessed "some heightened sensitivity to the promises of life" and "an extraordinary gift for hope, a romantic readiness" that was incorruptible.[118] As Brown Professor of English Arnold Weinstein observes, "the achievements furthered by the dream may be tawdry and corrupt, although the dream never can be."[119] While describing the loss of values and the social dissolution of the post-World War I era, *Gatsby* also celebrates the enduring American belief that individuals can create themselves and their reality.

In comparison to a sophisticated British soldier like Christopher Tietjens, American war heroes seem naïve and stunned by the horror of war, although they share the same revulsion for patriotic abstractions used to inspire fighting spirit, alienation from the society they left, and withdrawal into themselves. Nick Adams, Frederick Henry, and Jake Barnes discover through the war's wanton brutality that the world lacks meaning; it injures and kills the weak and the strong with capricious indifference. Consequently, they retreat from society for spiritual healing and renewal, Nick to the Northern Michigan woods, Frederick to the Swiss mountains, and Jake to Basque country. For Hemingway, existence amid meaninglessness requires strict adherence to the stoic virtues of discipline and courage, exemplified for him by bullfighting with the consummate skill of Villalta and Romero. Instead of reacting like Hemingway to an indifferent universe, Cummings and Dos Passos reacted to demeaning institutions: for Cummings, the brutal French penal system that ignores human rights and abuses human dignity; and for Dos Passos, the military bureaucracy that enslaves men, molds them into brutes, stifles their intellect, and saps their basic humanity. Cummings and John Andrews suffer for their self-expression: Cummings for fraternizing with the *poilu*, and Andrews for deserting to compose music. Fitzgerald broadened his focus to cover postwar society in general, with Amory Blaine and his generation disaffected by society's lack of any wise men or heroes, and with Nick Carraway repelled by its corruption and greed. For all these American writers, World War I was the cause of personal disaffection, isolation, and alienation.

The Postwar Continental Novel

The novels of Franz Kafka and Jean-Paul Sartre resonate with intense introspection and anxiety over existence in a universe lacking any transcendent meaning. Franz Kafka (1883-1924) brought clarity, rigor, and rationality to his writing about personal revulsion lying *within* (man's psychic makeup) and about nightmarish dread lying *without* (man's immediate bureaucratic society and wider environment). Kafka wrote *The Metamorphosis* (1915) in 1912, before the war, about his sense of shame and unworthiness, his struggle to recover his humanity, and his place within the family. Beginning with the famous line, "As Gregor Samsa awoke one morning from uneasy dreams he found himself transformed in his bed into a gigantic insect," the book develops from this nightmarish, surreal, and implausible premise into a realistic dramatization of Gregor's futile attempt to cope with paternal hostility and deceit and to recover from revulsion at his personal condition.[120]

When Austria declared war on Serbia on July 28, 1914, Kafka attempted unsuccessfully to enlist in the Austro-Hungarian army as a Czech citizen. Princeton Professor of German and Contemporary Literature Stanley Corngold explains that Kafka wrote *The Trial* (1925) during the last five months of 1914 to alleviate a profound sense of personal failure from escaping the draft and from dodging his engagement to Felice Bauer.[121] In *The Trial* Joseph K. is awakened and arrested one morning on undefined charges. Thus begins his long, desperate, and futile effort against insuperable obstacles to find a court in which to prove his innocence, only to become resigned to his brutal execution for unknown crimes. Joseph K. finds no legal recourse, no ascertainable answers, and no ultimate redemption because, for Kafka, grace and truth are personally unattainable and corruption lies within his very being.

The *Castle* (1926), written in 1922 and, like *The Trial*, published posthumously, is the story of a land surveyor by the name of K. (again without a surname) who is summoned by the Castle authorities only to learn that his job offer as a surveyor was a miscommunication. Although the authorities accommodate him with a demeaning alternate position as school janitor, K. doggedly seeks redress by attempting to contact the inaccessible Lord of the Castle and to petition the inscrutable Castle bureaucracy, but different obstacles repeatedly thwart his efforts. Of course, K. is Kafka himself, feeling summoned by some higher authority for some higher purpose but unable to access or understand it and ultimately left estranged and homeless. Franklin Baumer writes that Kafka "finds God alternatively remote, cruel by human standards, incommensurable with the human mind, and probably nonexistent."[122]

Jean-Paul Sartre (1905-1980) achieved maturity during the 1930s while launching his critique of the ineffectual and self-righteously smug postwar French bourgeoisie, whom he called "*Les salauds*" or "the stinkers."[123] Sartre established the relationship between existentialism and literature and made his early reputation with the novel *Nausea* (1938), permeated with the decadent *salauds*.[124] In *Nausea*, Antoine Roquentin, a writer doing historical research for a biography of the Marquis de Rollebon, experiences the contingency of his own existence, triggered by viewing the roots of the chestnut tree while sitting on a park bench. "Existence had suddenly unveiled itself," says Roquentin, "we hadn't the slightest reason to be there, none of us," and that was "the key to my Nauseas, to my own life ... to this fundamental absurdity."[125] Existence was not necessary but contingent, and he was superfluous (*de trop*): "Everything existing is born without reason, prolongs itself out of weakness and dies by chance."[126]

William Barrett considered *Nausea* probably Sartre's best book by effectively conjoining the intellectual and creative artist. American poet Hayden Carruth considered Roquentin's confrontation with the chestnut tree "one of the sharpest pictures ever drawn of self-doubt and metaphysical anguish."[127] Roquentin's mood of disgust plunges him into an authentic experience of his own existence, a recognition that he, like the chestnut tree, has no ultimate reason for existing. Roquentin has encountered the void, the Nothingness, his own contingency and finitude, and he finds it disgusting, fearsome, and nauseating. The Nothingness, by definition, is unknowable, non-rational, and absurd. When the search for rational answers confronts the radical meaninglessness of existence, the result is nausea. Roquentin had tried unsuccessfully to escape from his predicament through traditional avenues. He considers the rational humanism of the Self-Taught Man who rejected belief in God while a POW ("I do not believe in God; His existence is belied by science. But, in the internment camp, I learned to believe in men"). But Roquentin dismisses such humanism following his final and grossly ludicrous encounter with the Self-Taught Man in the town library.[128] He also considers his life in town with its activity and commerce, his desire for travel, and his final pursuit of his former mistress Anny all to no avail. Roquentin remains nauseated by his consciousness of being *de trop*. His only way out, much debated by critics, is through his own writing, though not biography but fiction, and through self-acceptance.[129] Typical of existentialist writers, Sartre finds it difficult to give *Nausea* any finality because of his open-ended view of life as a state of constant becoming.[130]

Kafka and Sartre represent the two faces of secularism in the aftermath of World War I. Kafka is anguished over his feeling of cosmic homelessness, poignantly dramatized in K.'s desperate and futile pursuit of access to the Lord of the Castle and in Joseph K.'s relentless and unavailing effort to defend his innocence before some judicial tribunal. Kafka finds no relief, no remedy, no understanding in his inscrutable universe, and remains tormented by his inability to find answers and by his abject sense of personal inadequacy. By contrast, Sartre accepts cosmic meaninglessness, rejects religious belief, and tries to create meaning in a world without meaning. Antoine Roquentin's existential drama is about discovering the cause of his metaphysical anguish—the utter contingency of his existence—accepting his condition, and giving meaning to his life by personal endeavor.

Literature and Materialism

Despite the industrialized slaughter during World War I wrought by modern technology, science emerged relatively uninjured in postwar public opinion and popular literature. Bertrand Russell trumpeted the promise of modern science, while Joseph Wood Krutch mourned the loss of metaphysical truths that science had unmasked as falsehoods. Creative literature offered no assurance of a meaningful reality; moreover, prominent postwar critics claimed that science had marginalized the value of literature in this regard. Max Eastman thought poetry must yield to science the role of interpreting experience, and I. A. Richards relegated poetry to assuaging human anxiety over the loss of cosmic meaning and purpose. In short, modern literary criticism directed literature away from metaphysical concerns and toward human suffering resulting from loss of a meaningful universe, doubts about personal identity, and feelings of insignificance, powerlessness, and depravity.

The leading novelists of the post-World War I era consistently obliged these critics. British literature powerfully evokes the sense of a lost civilization shattered by the war and of damaged individuals alienated not only from their indifferent and corrupt society but also from a seemingly meaningless and purposeless reality. American literature turned wartime injury into personal violation and postwar existence into cosmic alienation, a quest, not to answer big philosophical questions about the world, but simply to learn "how to live in it." Continental literature portrayed a similarly meaningless world, with characters variously tormented by a feeling of unworthiness, self-doubt, and metaphysical anguish; by an inability to justify themselves either to society or to a higher power; and by a struggle to find meaning within cosmic indifference. Thus, the central characters in the leading British, American, and Continental novels are injured, tormented, and alienated. They confront cultural disintegration and cosmic indifference, wracked by doubt yet striving to endure.

In summary, the First World War engendered a metaphysically dark literature that abandoned any quest for cosmic meaning and purpose—science had rendered that quest a fool's errand. Literature did not show the world's transcendent and mystical meaning, as Wittgenstein expected, or disclose the truth about Being, as Heidegger promised. Rather, literature turned away from metaphysical engagement and toward psychic unrest. It turned inward to explore the human struggle to cope within a materialist universe— mindless, meaningless, and indifferent. It observed human beings adrift in society and in the universe, strangers to themselves and to their war-shattered civilization. Consequently, literature provided no effective counterweight to scientism or materialism. Postwar literature accepted their premises, reinforced their epistemological and metaphysical claims, and explored ways of finding meaning within meaninglessness.

7

Postwar Western Art

How are we to bring order to the chaos of this infinite, formless variation: man? The principle of "love thy neighbor" is hypocritical. "Know thyself" is a Utopian idea, but a more acceptable one, which also contains spite. No pity. What remains to us after the carnage is a putrefied humanity. ... Thus DADA was born of the need for independence, of mistrust of the community. Those who belong to us keep their freedom. ... Does anyone think that, by a minute refinement of logic, he had demonstrated the truth and established the correctness of these opinions? Logic imprisoned by the senses is an organic disease. To this element philosophers always like to add: the power of observation. But actually this magnificent quality of the mind is the proof of its impotence.
 — Tristan Tzara, *1918 Dada Manifesto*[1]

World War I broke out almost exactly in the middle of a half-century of change in artistic theory and practice that Yale Professor of Art George Heard Hamilton considered "as radical and momentous as any that had occurred in human history."[2] This period of change occurred between the last Impressionist exhibition in 1886 and the start of World War II in 1939, and involved the dramatic emergence of abstract (or non-objective) art. Abstract art rejected the traditional aesthetic, dominant since the Renaissance, that art should represent objects and events as they appear in the natural world, and that artists should use form, light, and color as observed in three-dimensional visual space. By contrast, post-impressionists like Paul Cézanne (1839-1906) and Paul Gauguin (1848-1903) began to flatten space, distort color, depart from Renaissance perspective, and record experience originating in their minds rather than in the objective world. By the start of the twentieth century, therefore, avant-garde artists already were investigating new techniques to manifest their interior, personal experience of reality.[3]

With the advent of Cubism just before the Great War, the work of art ceased being a description or illusion of the natural world. Instead, writes Hamilton, the work of art became "its own reality, a real thing, subject to the laws of art rather than of nature, imposing its own system of relations upon nature."[4] Traditional criteria of shape, color, and dimension appropriate for representational art were no longer adequate to interpret such non-objective art, with its new, quintessentially modern aesthetic values.[5] In his innovative *Les Demoiselles d'Avignon* (1907) discussed in Chapter 3 (Figure 2), Pablo Picasso (1881-1973) pioneered new ways of treating the traditional elements of mass, line, and color without regard to the representation of external reality, and presaged the advent of abstraction and Cubism.[6] Significantly, *Les Demoiselles* included primitive, bestial, and non-human heads, which implicitly cast doubt on human reason. In Picasso's hands the human head, from which the individual derives intelligence and communicates understanding, was becoming mere illusion.[7] With the advent of Cubism just before the First World War, the artist began to picture reality as fractured, blurred, and in flux, and even to question the capacity of human reason to understand that reality.[8] World War I had a profound effect upon that prewar artistic trend.

Cubism, Futurism, and Expressionism were the three prewar movements in art that had the greatest effect on Dadaism and Surrealism, which arose in direct response to World War I. In 1916, Dadaism erupted as outspokenly anti-art, challenging outright the prevalent prewar aesthetics and the decadent bourgeois society responsible for the catastrophic and insane war. In 1924, Surrealism emerged from Dadaism in Paris and continued Dada's confrontational, anti-bourgeois, and anti-rationalist attitude by delving into the dream world of the human unconscious. Appreciation of Dada and Surrealism, however, requires some consideration of the theory and practice within their predecessor movements: Cubism, Futurism, and Expressionism. These three movements are represented here by the following artist-soldiers: French Cubist Fernand Léger, English Futurist Christopher Nevinson, and German Expressionists Ernst Ludwig Kirchner and Otto Dix. The selected Dadaists represent the five important Dada centers: Hans (Jean) Arp in Zürich, Marcel Duchamp in New York, Kurt Schwitters in Hanover, George Grosz in Berlin, and Max Ernst in Cologne and Paris. Since Max Ernst straddled both Dadaism and Surrealism, his work provides an appropriate transition to Surrealism before considering the significance of Dadaism and Surrealism to materialism. Did these war-inspired movements make room for human reason and metaphysical inquiry in the post-World War I era? Did they live up to the Wittgenstein's expectations that art show the world aright, with transcendent meaning and purpose? Or, like postwar writers, did Dadaism and Surrealism turn postwar art inward upon the unconscious and away from external reality, leaving metaphysical concerns in the hands solely of materialists?

Cubism, Futurism, and Expressionism in Peace and War

Cubism. In 1907, Picasso met and became friends with Georges Braque (1882-1963), who was already experimenting with Cubism. Before long, the two artists were collaborating in the development of Cubism—one of the great aesthetic transformations, a watershed in modern art.[9] In their initial "analytic" phase (1909-12), they examined real objects from different perspectives, lighting them from different directions, exploring their mass from inside and out, and depicting interpenetrating and shifting planes of color. While always referring to the natural object and never constituting pure abstraction, their analytical styles nevertheless became increasingly abstract and converged in two climactic and remarkably similar masterpieces, Braque's *The Portuguese* (1911) and Picasso's *Ma Jolie (Woman with Guitar)* (1911-12). Both paintings depict figures playing a stringed instrument rendered in typically Cubist language of opposing and interpenetrating curves, rectilinear shapes, lines, and planes.

In their subsequent "synthetic" phase (1912-14), they used fragments of real, unrelated, and recognizable objects to construct works, using a bright and expressive palette rather than the monochromatic and restrained palette of their analytical phase. Picasso created the first Cubist collage, *Still Life with Chair Caning* (1912), in which he pasted an oilcloth having a chair-cane pattern onto the canvas and also painted fragments of objects (a pipe, glass, knife, and scallop shell) and of words ("JOU" for "Journal"). He then framed the work unconventionally with actual rope.[10] *Still Life with Chair Caning* explores the ambiguity between reality and art: the oilcloth is real but its caning is illusion, the *trompe l'oeil* pipe appears real but is an illusion, the rope is real but it serves as the frame for a pictorial illusion.[11] Picasso's use of everyday objects for artistic effect in his synthetic phase of Cubism contributed significantly to the development of both Dada and Surrealism.[12] Picasso's collaboration with Braque ended in 1914, when Braque went off to war.

Futurism. In 1909, on the front page of the Paris newspaper *Le Figaro,* the Italian poet Filippo Tommaso Marinetti published his Futurist manifesto advocating a dynamic new society, poetics, and art, and rejecting Italy's reactionary reliance on its classical and Renaissance past. He celebrated "love of danger, the habit of energy and fearlessness," and he glorified "war—the world's only hygiene—militarism, patriotism, the destructive gesture of freedom-bringers, beautiful ideas worth dying for, and scorn for women."[13] One year later a group of Italian artists published their "Manifesto of the Futurist Painters," exalting originality and a new artistic sensibility that used "dynamic sensation" to achieve Marinetti's principles of energy and velocity.[14] In late 1911, four Italian Futurists visited Paris, saw Cubist paintings for the first time, and immediately recognized Cubism's value as an expressive technique for capturing continuous movement. To this Cubist vocabulary of dynamic sensation, they added their characteristic "lines of force" technique since "objects reveal in their lines calm or frenzy, sadness or gaiety."[15]

In his representative Futurist painting *Elasticity* (1912), Umberto Boccioni combined lines of force with Cubist fragmentation to convey in vivid color the sequential movement of a machine-like horse and its black-booted rider racing across a mechanized landscape of high tension poles and factories (Figure 6). In works like *Elasticity,* Futurism left the conceptual studio of analytic Cubism for the outside world of dynamic sensation. Boccioni joined the Italian artillery and executed a number of war paintings. But by 1916, Boccioni was dead, along with the architect Antonio Sant' Elia, another important leader of the Futurist movement.[16] World War I not only

Figure 6. Umberto Boccioni, Elasticity, 1912, Private Collection, Milan, Italy
Photo Credit: Scholar/Art Resource, NY

decimated Futurism's leadership, it also sapped the movement's moral standing and intrinsic vitality. Consequently, by the end of the war, Futurism was a spent aesthetic force.

Expressionism. During 1905, Expressionism arose in several different countries as a movement aimed at recording the artist's personal response to the surrounding world by emphasizing or distorting every aspect of the artist's technique. French *Fauves* (Wild Beasts), for example, employed color and form symbolically to evoke mood.[17] But Expressionism is most associated with German art, especially two movements, *Die Brücke* (The Bridge) (1905-14) and *Der Blaue Reiter* (The Blue Rider) (1910-16). Prewar Expressionism often addressed the spiritual emptiness and psychological effects of the modern industrialized world, as seen in Ludwig Kirchner's *The Street* (1913), discussed in Chapter 3 (Figure 3). In two remarkably prescient paintings, both entitled *Apocalyptic Landscape* (1913), the Berlin Expressionist Ludwig Meidner pictured visions of Armageddon a year before World War I. The first painting portrays a naked man asleep in the foreground by a fire, dreaming about the violent lightning storm that rages in the background, splinters the buildings, and threatens the survival of those few figures located in the valley below the dark whirlwind. The second painting (Figure 7) portrays a large city with fires spreading and buildings crumbling from the violent force of bombs exploding throughout the sky and city below. "I feared such visions," Meidner said, "yet the final results gave me an especially warm feeling of satisfaction, a slightly Satanic joy."[18].

Of these three movements, Cubism seems least suited to address the effects of World War I, given its analytical rather than expressive content and its focus on still life and human forms, at least as Cubism was practiced by Braque and Picasso. But French Cubist Fernand Léger used his particular Cubist style effectively to portray fellow soldiers mechanized for combat. Futurism seems most

Figure 7. Ludwig Meidner, *Apocalyptic Landscape*, 1913, Jüdisches Museum der Stadt Frankfurt am Main, Germany.
© Ludwig Meidner-Archiv, Jüdisches Museum der Stadt Frankfurt am Main.
Photo Credit: Bridgeman Art Library, New York, NY.

suited, with its militaristic credo and "lines of force" technique. But English Futurist Christopher R. W. Nevinson eventually turned away from Futurism to a more representational style for recording war's dehumanizing brutality. Expressionism seems particularly well suited to record the artist's experience of war, focused as it is on the artist's personal feelings. And indeed it was. But the war so tormented Ernst Ludwig Kirchner and transformed Otto Dix that, ironically, both German artists ultimately abandoned Expressionism in search of different expressive styles.

Fernand Léger—Cubism at War. In 1910, after viewing the works of Braque and Picasso at Kahnweiler's Paris gallery, Fernand Léger (1881-1955) apparently destroyed all his prior works of art and developed his own Cubist style.[19] Unlike Braque and Picasso, Léger's Cubism rejected fragmentation even as he accepted fracture of objects; he embraced physical activity and industrialization rather than intellectual conceptions and still life; and he found aesthetic appeal in equating men-as-machines. In his prewar work, best expressed in *Nudes in the Forest* (1910), Léger was already painting inhuman, robotic, sexless figures consisting of rounded or flattened mechanized parts that blend confusingly with the surrounding natural environment. In 1915, the war took Léger out of his Paris studio and "thoroughly abstract" style and into frontline service among the *poilu* and a "period of a pictorial liberation."[20] Léger endured some of the heaviest fighting on the Western Front while assigned to dangerous service in the Argonne Forest as a sapper (a fortifications and demolitions expert). As the result of a gas attack in the spring of 1917, he was invalided out of his regiment and into a hospital near Paris.[21] During his war service, Léger "discovered the French people," came to admire "the exuberance, the variety, the humor, the perfection of certain types of men," and "found them poets, inventors of everyday poetic images." Léger also was "dazzled by the breech of a 75-millimeter gun which was standing uncovered in the sunlight: the magic of light on white metal." At war, Léger discovered men and machines: "once I had got my teeth into that sort of reality I never let go of objects again."[22]

The war's effect on Léger's Cubist style is evident in *Soldier Smoking* (1916), which he painted in a subdued, austere palette

Figure 8. Fernand Léger, *Soldier Smoking*, 1916,
© Artists Rights Society (ARS), New York/ADAGP, Paris.
Photo Credit: Bridgeman Art Library, New York, NY.

while on leave in Paris that summer. *Soldier Smoking* (Figure 8) portrays a wounded soldier smoking his pipe while recovering from
battle injuries evident from the head bandage and the red patch on
the man's left cheek, right hand, and right forearm. The soldier's
cylindrical arms, armored jacket, and metallic inner structure convey the effect of "light on white metal." The soldier's rigid posture suggests a continued commitment to duty and fighting spirit,
wounds notwithstanding. Unlike Léger's prewar painting *Nudes in
the Forest*, which conflates and abstracts human and environmental
forms, *Soldier Smoking* presents a very recognizable and formidable
figure, who occupies the entire canvas. The wounded soldier suggests that very "perfection of certain types of men" whom Léger
came to admire at the front. *Soldier Smoking* displays the quiet confidence and imposing force of the *poilu*, symbolized in the puffs of
his pipe smoke, which look like cannonballs.

 While convalescing in 1917, Léger painted a mechanized and
gravely serious game of cards entitled *The Card Game* (1917). In this

Figure 9. Fernand Léger, *The Card Game,* 1917, Collection Kröller-Müller Museum, Otterlo, The Netherlands.
© Artists Rights Society (ARS), New York/ADAGP, Paris.
Photo Credit: Kröller-Müller Museum, Otterlo, The Netherlands.

work Léger draws upon a traditional eighteenth-century artistic theme, which Cézanne subsequently employed in a series of five oil paintings during the early 1890s, entitled *The Card Players.* But Léger's work lacks Cézanne's quiet mood and peasant setting.[23] In Léger's *The Card Game* (Figure 9) the three card players are awesome machines, pausing from the industrialized game of war, for which they appear ideally suited. Cramped within the walls of their narrow trench, the robotic players confront each other on three sides of a large, rigid, mustard-colored table, a color probably inspired by Léger's recent gas attack.[24] Instead of the subdued sepia color of *Soldier Smoking,* Léger painted his card players in gunmetal gray, wearing their chevrons and medals.[25] The subject of Léger's *Card Game* is the unsentimental but dignified uniting of man and machine for industrial warfare, consistent with Léger's optimistic view of the modern world even in the midst of war.

Léger's depiction of the human as machine has none of the

pejorative, dehumanizing connotations of Christopher Nevinson's mechanized soldiers in *Returning to the Trenches* (1914-15), discussed in Chapter 3 (Figure 4). Nor does it impart the fanatical belligerence of the Futurist Boccioni, the debilitating psychosis of the Expressionist Kirschner, or the satirical bitterness of Dadaists. Indeed, Léger's positive portrait of man as machine is anomalous within World War I art, as amply demonstrated by even a cursory glance at Richard Cork's magnificent and seminal book *A Bitter Truth: Avant-Garde Art and the Great War*. How strange to see Léger's robotic soldiers presented in a positive light, while stripped of their most human qualities. Long after the war, Léger retained this positive view of modern technology and urban humanity, exemplified in his Cubist paintings like *The City* (1919).[26] He found sculptural beauty in the machine culture and integrated recognizable human figures into the industrialized urban kaleidoscope simply as mechanical objects. Despite his benign intentions, however, humankind has lost much of its traditional value and intrinsic significance in Léger's artistic celebration of modernity.

Christopher R. W. Nevinson—From Futurism to Realism. Soon after leaving the Slade School of Art in 1912, Christopher R. W. Nevinson (1989-1946) became a devoted follower of Marinetti's Futurist movement.[27] Like a true Futurist, when the war broke out, Nevinson volunteered for Red Cross service as an ambulance driver in France since a limp prevented him from enlisting. As he told the *Daily Express* in February 1915, "This war will be a violent incentive to Futurism for we believe that there is no beauty except in strife, and no masterpiece without aggressiveness."[28] Although better known in England than internationally, Nevinson serves as a useful exemplar of Futurism and its fate. Not only did Nevinson go to war and survive it, but the war experience led him to abandon philosophic and artistic Futurism.

His Futurist technique is on display in his early war paintings like *Returning to the Trenches* (1914-1915) and *A Bursting Shell* (1915). *Returning to the Trenches* (1914-15) uses angular shapes and "forcelines" of rifles reminiscent of Boccioni's *Elasticity* (1912), but this work noticeably lacks Boccioni's Futurist bravado. Instead, *Returning to the Trenches* suggests the war's dehumanizing brutality, and for this reason drew a hostile reaction from a chauvinistic British press and citizenry during its March 1915 exhibition.[29] In *Bursting Shell* (see book cover), one of his last Futurist works. Nevinson depicts an aerial view of a bomb explosion with its brilliant spiraling light in five triangular shards radiating from the center of the picture. A contemporary art critic labeled *A Bursting Shell*: "Futurism pure and simple, without hidden remnant of realistic tendencies."[30] The graphic, swirling, rainbow colors and dark, radiating shards dramatize the shell's destructive power and create the type of dynamic sensation glorified by the 1910 Manifesto of the Futurist Painters.

By 1915, however, the war had eroded Nevinson's Futurist convictions, which he formally repudiated in a letter to Marinetti.[31] As an ambulance driver in France, Nevinson had encountered too much human tragedy to sustain his early Futurist militancy. His philosophic about-face is reflected in his subsequent art, like *La Mitrailleuse* (1915), a darkly realistic portrait of French soldiers manning a machine-gun post. In his weekly column for *L'Europe Nouvelle* French poet and art critic Guillaume Apollinaire (1880-1918) complimented Nevinson for *La Mitrailleuse*. He admired Nevinson's "way of rendering and making palpable the soldiers' suffering, and of communicating to others the feeling of pity and horror that have driven him to paint," and "the way in which man and machine are fused in a single force of nature."[32]

Nevinson's doubts about Futurism had begun shortly after his initial crossing from Dover while he attended countless wounded and dying soldiers at a makeshift Red Cross shelter in Dunkirk.[33] Nevinson returned to the subject of the Dunkirk shelter, nicknamed the "Shambles," in his compassionate and moving painting with the bitterly ironic title *La Patrie* (1916). By then, having abandoned his Futurist style, Nevinson painted *La Patrie* (Figure 10) in a representational idiom that conveys the stricken faces and unrelieved agony of the gravely injured and dying soldiers in the Dunkirk shed. Nevinson himself best describes the scene that he portrays so sensitively:

They lay on dirty straw, foul with old bandages and filth, those gaunt, bearded men, some white and still with only

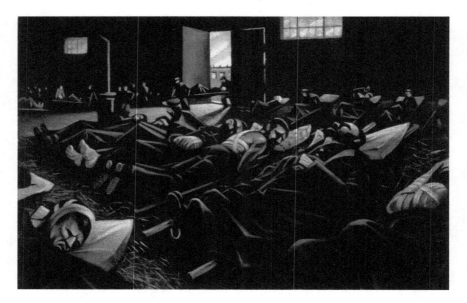

Figure 10. Christopher R. W. Nevinson, *La Patrie*, 1916, Birmingham Museums and Art Gallery, UK.
Photo Credit: Bridgeman Art Library, New York, NY.

a faint movement of their chests to distinguish them from the dead by their side. Those who had the strength to moan wailed incessantly. ... The sound of those broken men crying for their mothers is something I shall always have in my ears.[34]

Futurism's innovations of force-lines technique and dynamic sensations ultimately had proven inadequate for Nevinson to convey the personal misery and degradation of service on the Western Front.

In April 1917, the British Department of Information appointed Nevinson an official artist, which caused him to depart from the moral outrage of his earlier war canvases and to venture into depictions of the heroic exploits of aircraft. Nevertheless, he created one further controversial antiwar painting entitled *Paths of Glory* (1917), which depicts two dead British soldiers. He exhibited the painting over the objection of the War Office, pasted a brown paper on it bearing the word "censored," and incurred an official reprimand under the Defense of the Realm Act.[35] Thereafter, Nevinson's work never returned to Futurism or achieved the effectiveness of his representational art set on the Western Front.

Ernst Ludwig Kirchner — Expressionism at War. In 1905, after finishing architectural school in Dresden, Ernst Ludwig Kirchner (1880-1938) inaugurated Germany's first modern art movement, *Die Brucke* (The Bridge), an artists' association with four fellow architectural students seeking freedom from the constraints of Wilhelminian society.[36] The most gifted and best trained of the *Die Brucke* artists, Kirchner initially painted in a *Fauve* style heavily influenced by Matisse.[37] In 1911, following *Die Brucke's* split over stylistic differences, Kirchner moved to Berlin and developed his own expressive style, combining harsh, non-naturalistic color, angular hatchings, geometric shapes, and elongated human figures.[38] He created eleven paintings as well as numerous pastels, drawings, and prints of Berlin street scenes exemplified by *The Street* (1913), discussed in Chapter 3 (Figure 3). *The Street* depicts the moral hypocrisy of pre-war Berlin with its fashionable yet predatory prostitutes (cocottes) and their prospective bourgeois johns.[39]

After war broke out, Kirchner volunteered for military service on July 1, 1915, was assigned to the field artillery, but failed to cope with the military's physical regimen. He was discharged in September on grounds of mental illness and on condition that he enter a sanatorium. Thereafter, Kirchner deteriorated mentally and physically in various sanatoria, while remaining mortally fearful until the war's very end of being recalled to frontline duty.[40] During the same period, however, Kirchner created some of his most powerful paintings, like *Artillerymen in the Shower* (1915) and *Self-Portrait as a Soldier* (1915). As one observer wrote in a letter dated November 25, 1916, "His art grows the more his body fails."[41]

Artillerymen (Figure 11) portrays naked soldiers shorn of their uniforms and dignity and crammed together in a small, low-ceilinged shower room. They look jaundiced and emaciated, with elongated thin legs and orange hash marks emphasizing their exposed rib cages. They seem anonymous and fungible, with their dark eyes and stylized faces. Except for the two figures on the far left, they all stand largely isolated and alone despite their physical proximity.

Figure 11. Ernst Ludwig Kirchner, *Artillerymen in the Shower*, 1915, The Solomon R Guggenheim Museum, New York, NY.
Photo Credit: The Solomon R Guggenheim Foundation/Art Resource, NY.

Dodging the shooting streams of shower water as if they were enemy gunfire, the soldiers appear completely vulnerable.[42] The blue floor and green walls and ceiling give the shower room a cool, oppressive atmosphere, evocative today of photographs of World War II concentration camps. The presence of an overseeing officer wearing a uniform with cap and boots and apparently barking orders intensifies the scene, as does the sinister, devilish-looking soldier in the foreground, crouching to stoke the flaming boiler. Kirchner depicted the Kaiser's formidable military as frail, gawkish, anonymous youths, vulnerable to both their autocratic military superiors and their mechanized foreign adversaries.

While the *Artillerymen* implies Kirchner's own personal isolation, physical deterioration, and mental depression, *Self-Portrait as a Soldier* (1915) expresses it unmistakably. *Self-Portrait as a Soldier* (Figure 12) places Kirchner in the foreground, looking gaunt, sickly, depressed, and blank-eyed. He wears his old blue uniform with its 75th Artillery Regiment designation and his military cap with its

Figure 12. Ernst Ludwig Kirchner, *Self-Portrait as a Soldier* (1915), Allen Memorial Art Museum, Oberlin College, Ohio.
Photo Credit: Bridgeman Art Library, New York, NY.

target-like insignia. He stretches toward the viewer his gangrenous right arm severed at the wrist, while in the background stands an unfinished canvas and a nude model (probably his lifelong companion from the Berlin years, Erna Schilling). Kirchner's grisly fantasy of permanent maiming and artistic impotency from military service accurately captured his desperate mental state.[43] His steep emotional decline and lost artistic optimism from the *Die Brücke* period is palpable.

Kirchner never truly recovered from his brief war experience. His mental instability led him away from Berlin to pastoral Davos, Switzerland, and also away from his prior artistic self-confidence to a postwar state of "self-dissolution." [44] In Davos, Kirchner developed a "new style" that departed from his expressive, figurative idiom toward a more abstract and pastoral subject matter, a largely unsuccessful phase of his art.[45] In 1933, the Nazis began interfering with his artistic opportunities, and in 1937, they declared his art degenerate. The Nazis removed more than 600 of his works from

German museums, and then ridiculed, sold, or destroyed them.[46] In March 1938, when the German Army marched into Austria to effect the Anschluss and bivouacked barely twenty kilometers from Davos, Kirchner destroyed his art to avoid its falling into Nazi hands and killed himself.[47]

Otto Dix—From Expressionism to Postwar Dadaism. Otto Dix (1891-1969) provides a fitting conclusion to this discussion of Expressionist soldier-artists. His war art displays a dramatic transition from Nietzschean bravado to moral disgust about the war, and his brief postwar flirtation with Dada provides a useful transition to that war-inspired artistic movement.[48] Trained initially as a decorative painter, Dix entered Dresden's School of Applied Arts in 1910 to study ornamental design. He became a fervent devotee of Friedrich Nietzsche and even produced a life-size bust of Nietzsche, his only known sculpture. In 1914, Dix enthusiastically volunteered for military service, believing that war would revitalize staid Wilhelminian Germany.[49] Dix's *Self-Portrait as a Soldier* (1914), painted soon

Figure 13. Otto Dix, *Self-Portrait as a Soldier*, 1914, Municipal Gallery, Stuttgart. © 2013 Artist Rights Society (ARS), New York / VG Bild-Kunst, Bonn. Photo Credit: Kunstmuseum Stuttgart.

after his assignment to the Dresden artillery regiment, pictures a fierce, pugnacious, bull-necked, baldheaded brute, itching for a fight (Figure 13).[50] His head turns to stare menacingly at the viewer, with the white of his eyes magnified against the dark shading and pronounced sculpting of his head. The blood-red cloak wrapped about his shoulders and his name and year scratched like graffiti on the wall behind him accentuate this frightening self-portrait of the blood-thirsty German warrior.

Dix's several subsequent self-portraits painted during the war suggest increasing doubt about his outspoken Nietzschean convictions. *Self-Portrait with Artillery Helmet* (1914) shows a more restrained and cautious soldier, defensively hiding in the shadow of his elaborate artillery helmet; his narrowed, barely visible eyes look defensive and uncertain. *Self-Portrait as Mars* (1915) is a Futurist painting of the square- and clenched-jawed god of war. He seems composed under his star-studded helmet, but is dissected from every angle by the chaotic scenes of death and destruction reeling about him. Dix's *Self-Portrait as Shooting Target* (1915) dis-

Figure 14. Otto Dix, Self-Portrait as Shooting Target, 1915, Otto Dix Foundation, Vienna
© 2013 Artist Rights Society (ARS), New York / VG Bild-Kunst, Bonn
Photo Credit: Kunstsammlungen, Gera.

plays a significant attitudinal change (Figure 14) and deserves comparison with Kirchner's *Self-Portrait as a Soldier* (Figure 12). In each self-portrait the artist appears in the same artillery uniform and soft visor-less military hat with their two central, round insignia one above the other. Kirchner appears sickly, emaciated, maimed, and traumatized, already a casualty of war by 1915. Dix no longer poses as the warrior god Mars but as more like a war victim, wide-eyed and stoically awaiting execution by enemy fire. Cork considers Dix "torn between seeing himself as aggressor and victim" who presents "a nihilistic image, where despair is countered by an obstinate ability to mock the mortal danger he confronts."[51] Dix's experience on the Western Front has visibly transformed his combative Nietzschean spirit into a sober awareness of war's absurd self-destructiveness.

Trained as a heavy machine gunner, Dix fought in the 1915 autumn campaign in Champagne, in several 1916 battles on the Somme, and in the March 1918 final German offensive on the Western Front, with intermittent duty during 1917 on the Eastern Front. He incurred multiple wounds, one almost fatal, and eventually rose to the rank of vice-sergeant-major, earning the Iron Cross (second class), the Friedrich-August Medal, and the Saxon Service Medal with Swords.[52] Throughout the war, Dix retained his conviction about the restorative effect of Nietzsche's life-and-death cycle. But amid pauses in hostilities, Dix made hasty gouache paintings on paper, like *Signal Flare* (1917) and *Setting Sun (Ypres)* (1918), which portrayed the ferocity and bestiality of battle like no other artist.[53] His growing sense of war's horrible futility finally became a primal scream in graphic drawings and paintings after the war.

In Dada-inspired works Dix targeted the callous military elites and civilian population indifferent to the presence of horribly maimed soldiers. In one such macabre painting, *Skat Players* (1920), Dix depicts three grotesquely deformed war veterans playing cards indoors (Figure 15). The veteran on the left is hideously scarred by a burn that cost him his right ear, most of his hair, and probably his right eye. He holds his cards between the toes of his one uninjured right leg, hears through a long snaking listening device resting on the card table, wears a permanent grimace exposing teeth on the right side of his mouth, and crosses the wooden stump serving as

Figure 15. Otto Dix, *Skat Players*, 1920, Nationalgallerie, Staatliche Museen, Berlin, Germany.
© 2013 Artist Rights Society (ARS), New York / VG Bild-Kunst, Bonn.
Photo Credit:bpk, Berlin/ Nationalgallerie/ Joerg P. Anders/ Art Resource, NY.

his left leg with the two wooden stumps of the card player to his left. The center player has neither arms nor legs and holds a card between his teeth. He has an artificial left eye that stares rivetingly at the viewer, and bears a scar circling half his head and down his brow, which knits in place a large plaster covering. The legless player on the right proudly wears his Iron Cross, together with an artificial jaw and a patch over his missing nose. He deftly plays a card with an artificial right limb craned over his bald head, while holding his remaining cards in his intact left hand. The contrast between Dix's and Léger's card players could not be more striking. Dix's hideously maimed soldiers with their artificial limbs have lost their former military swagger, since technology could not restore their war-ravaged bodies. Their very presence in society serves as an indictment of the war and those responsible for it. By contrast, Léger's machinomorphic card players (Figure 9) are products of the modern technological age, physically capable of enduring the brutality of industrialized warfare.

Dix's intense moral revulsion at war and its consequences attracted the interest of Berlin Dada. But Dix soon gravitated toward a more realistic artistic idiom, the *Neue Sachlichkeit* (New Objectivity), in antiwar drawings and paintings of immense power. Hamilton calls Dix's painting *The Trench* (1920-23), which the Nazis destroyed after making it the centerpiece of their 1938 exhibition of Degenerate Art, and his great *War Triptych* (1932) "perhaps the most powerful as well as the most unpleasant anti-war statements in modern art."[54] Dix's *War Triptych* cost him his professorship at the Dresden Art Academy in 1933, after which he retreated to his German country estate near Lake Constance where he pursued his antiwar art, including the mesmerizing *Flanders (After Henri Barbusse "Le Feu")* (1934-36).[55]

In summary, all four artist-soldiers recorded war's terrible reality in their art, but none more graphically than Expressionists Kirchner and Dix. Both Léger and Nevinson recognized that war turns men into machines. But Léger interpreted this dehumanization as a helpful adaptation to industrialized war and modern society, whereas Nevinson thought that it stripped man of his dignity. In *Soldier Smoking* and *The Card Game* Léger used his Cubist style to convey his respect and admiration for the strength and determination of the French *poilu*. Nevinson, by contrast, used Futurist lines of force in *Returning to the Trenches* to portray the same *poilu* as dynamic cogs in the dehumanizing war machine. By late 1915, Nevinson was in full retreat from Futurism in works like *La Mitrailleuse* and *La Patrie* since the aesthetics of velocity and dynamic sensation proved inadequate to convey war's awful human toll. Nevinson's full moral outrage at British war policy surfaced in *Paths of Glory*, a disturbing portrait of dead soldiers, which he exhibited courageously despite war censorship.

Kirchner portrays the abject vulnerability of the ordinary soldiers in *Artillerymen in the Shower*, and his own physical and psychological trauma in *Self-Portrait as a Soldier*. Similarly, Dix's war-time self-portraits convey his psychic transition from brutish warrior to stoic target, and *Signal Flare* and *Setting Sun (Ypres)* convey frontline brutality and carnage like the work of no other artist. War changed Kirchner from a confident artistic innovator to a terrified artistic émigré, and Dix from a swaggering militarist to an outraged pacifist. Kirchner symbolized war's toll on his mental stability and artistic talent in his haunting *Self-Portrait as a Soldier*, with his blank stare and severed hand. Dix displayed his moral disgust at war's gruesome human injuries in the Dadaist *Skat Players*, and his moral revulsion over war itself in the *War Triptych* and *Flanders*. Léger's anomalous embrace of mechanized man notwithstanding, the dominant effect of works by these other three, more representative soldier-artists conveys war's destructive and dehumanizing effect on body and soul. The indictment by these soldier-artists of the apocalyptic war and the civilization responsible for it is unequivocal, graphic, and compelling.

Dadaism: Zürich, New York, Hanover, Berlin, Cologne, and Paris

Dada arose primarily from outrage over the unprecedented and senseless slaughter of the Great War and the civilization that initiated and could not stop it.[56] Dada arrived independently in Zürich in February 1916, and in New York about the same time, following Marcel Duchamp's and Francis Picabia's arrival there from France in October 1915.[57] The Zürich Dadaist Richard Huelsenbeck claimed that he and Hugo Ball discovered the word Dada in a dictionary and deemed it appropriate: "the child's first sound expresses the primitiveness, the beginning at zero, the new in our art." Ball added the following: "Dada is 'yes yes' in Romanian, 'rocking horse' and 'hobbyhorse' in French. For Germans it is a sign of foolish naïveté, joy in procreation, and preoccupation with the baby carriage."[58] Dada "paradoxically stood for everything and nothing," according to Glasgow Professor of Art History David Hopkins: "It amounted to a kind of absurd admixture of affirmation and negation, a kind of pseudo-mysticism. Art was a dead religion. Dada was born."[59]

Dada had no specific creed. Its intent was to attack the cultural, political, and social forces responsible for the crisis and to provide a kind of shock therapy to redeem humanity through moral revolution. "Dadaists assailed the Western humanist belief in the supremacy of reason, the efficacy of the rational ego, and the essential goodness of human nature," according to Oxford Professor of German and cultural critic Richard Sheppard.[60] They especially targeted Western aesthetic values, which they regarded as decadent, bourgeois, and egotistical. "We were seeking an art based on fundamentals, to cure the madness of the age," wrote Zürich Dadaist Hans (Jean) Arp, "and the new order of things that would restore the balance between heaven and hell."[61] While owing much to Cubism, Expressionism, and Futurism, Dadaism focused on lived experience rather than avant-garde aesthetics. Dadaists ignored concerns about art's relationship with reality, innovations in autonomous art, investigation of nonobjective art, or art about art.[62] They rejected art's autonomy and refused to separate art from modern human experience and the "praxis of life."[63] According to Hopkins, Dada and its successor movement Surrealism "shared the defining avant-garde conviction that social and political radicalism should be bound up with artistic innovation. The artist's task was to move beyond aesthetic pleasure and to affect people's lives; to make them see and experience things differently."[64]

While ranging from Romania to Japan, Dada's most important centers were Zürich, New York, Hanover, Berlin, Cologne, and Paris. The Dada artists in Zürich focused on cabaret performances by dislocated expatriates; New York on modern machinery, commercialism, and the human psyche; Hanover on recreating a new postwar culture; Berlin on radically critiquing postwar politics and society; Cologne on the psychic underpinnings of modern culture; and Paris on disrupting the postwar return to normalcy.[65] Using circulated texts and personal contacts, Dada artists spread their works and messages widely through group dynamics that fostered radical innovation. For American Curator of Art Leah Dickerman, this helped to explain "why so many of those artists who have had the greatest impact on twentieth-century art founded their careers, and defined the terms of their mature practice, within the crucible of Dada."[66]

Hans (Jean) Arp—Zürich Dada and the Unconscious. Hans (Jean) Arp (1886-1966) was born in the Alsacean city of Strasbourg to a German father and French mother, hence his German and French given names. He studied art in Strasburg, Weimar, and Paris and made wide connections in French and German art circles. When war broke out, Arp dodged the German draft by moving to Paris, only to have the French suspect him as a German spy and force him to move to neutral Zürich.[67] There, in 1915, he met and later married Sophie Taeuber, a professor of textile design at the Zürich School of Applied Arts, who collaborated with Arp and influenced his significant innovations in abstract art. A central figure in Zürich Dada, Arp created what he and Taeuber called "applied" rather than fine art in an effort to "approach the pure radiance of reality" by avoiding traditional artistic constraints and personal subjectivity.[68]

In a series of collages, including *Untitled (Collage with Squares Arranged According to the Laws of Chance)* (1916-1917), Arp tried to eliminate rational control and to engage unconscious forces by dropping torn pieces of paper on a grid and pasting them where they fell (Figure 16). Holding human reason and egoism responsi-

Figure 16. Hans (Jean) Arp, *Untitled* (Collage with Squares Arranged According to the Laws of Chance), 1916-1917, The Museum of Modern Art, New York, NY.
© 2013 Artist Rights Society (ARS), New York / VG Bild-Kunst, Bonn. Digital Image © The Museum of Modern Art/Licensed by SCALA/Art Resource, NY.

ble for the war, Arp sought new meaning through art that involved his own unconscious and nature's unpredictability. "The 'law of chance,'" Arp later wrote, "which comprises all other laws and surpasses our understanding ... can be experienced only in a total surrender to the unconscious."[69] Chance, however, was not mere randomness because Arp assumed some world-ordering power lay behind the inscrutable flux of nature, some "unfathomable raison d'être ... an order inaccessible in its totality."[70]

Arp's metaphysical conviction about nature's underlying order arose out of his early attraction to the pre-Socratic philosophers like Heraclitus, who viewed reality as a paradoxical mixture of form and flux, and to Eastern mysticism, which considered reality a balance of the warring factions of creation and destruction.[71] Arp tried to achieve this balance of conflicting natural energies in his art. In late 1917, he began experimenting with freeform or "automatic" processes, which reflected his increasing faith in nature's formative powers.[72] Seeking to avoid conscious control, he moved his hand quickly across a paper and then had a carpenter cut the spontaneously drawn shapes with a handsaw. The resultant organic forms in his reliefs reflect his faith in natural chance over human logic.[73]

In summary, Arp engaged the unconscious and mistrusted reason; he encountered reality mystically rather than rationally; and he created applied art intended to reflect the inaccessible order underlying the flux of reality. Consistent with his artistic approach, Arp explained Dada's mission as follows:

> Dada is aimed to destroy the reasonable deceptions of man and recover the natural and unreasonable order. Dada wanted to replace the logical nonsense of the men of today by the illogically senseless. ... Dada is for the senseless, which does not mean nonsense. Dada is senseless like nature. Dada is for nature and against art.[74]

Arp's mystical theories and artistic approach contributed to Zürich Dada's relatively more constructive Dada image.[75] Ultimately, Arp came to see God's influence as the ordering principle in the material world and converted to Roman Catholicism.

Marcel Duchamp—New York Dada and the Ready-Made. Marcel Duchamp (1887-1968) was born into a French family of artists. He worked as an illustrator after graduating from the Julian Academy in Paris, began exhibiting in 1909, and embraced Cubism as a member of the Puteaux group. The doctrinaire leaders of the group embarrassed Duchamp, however, by asking him to remove his *Nude Descending a Staircase No. 2* (1912) from the Independents Salon because of its title. Exempt from military service because of a minor heart defect, Duchamp abandoned chauvinistic Paris and warring Europe in 1915. He headed for neutral New York where his *Nude* already had created a sensation at the Armory Show exhibition in 1913.[76] In New York, Duchamp invented Dada and shook up the conservative American art scene until his return to Paris in mid-1921. By the time of his New York arrival, Duchamp had abandoned Cubism and other painting innovations of color and form. He considered such "retinal" art to constitute self-deluding humanism, inconsistent with the impersonal culture of modern industrialized society.[77] Instead, Duchamp determined to create art that employed the following three elements: (1) radical Cartesian doubt ("doubt in myself, doubt in everything. In the first place never believing in truth"); (2) science against science ("the precise and exact aspects of science ... in order to discredit it, mildly, lightly, unimportantly. But irony was present"); and (3) intellectual rather than physical dexterity ("painting once again at the service of the mind").[78]

Duchamp's most curious application of the intellectual versus the physical in art was his so-called "ready-made," a bold challenge to the reigning aesthetics, in which he substituted an ordinary, mass-produced article for a hand-made work of art. Starting with his *Bicycle Wheel* (1913) and then his famous *Fountain* (1917), Duchamp's ready-mades usurped the place of sculpture. *Bicycle Wheel*, a so-called "assisted ready-made," consists of a bicycle wheel placed atop a stool. Simultaneously, *Bicycle Wheel* impugns the hierarchical convention of a sculpted object resting upon a base and aestheticizes two ordinary objects from the world of mass production. Duchamp's ready-mades posed a basic question about the nature of art itself. Etymologically, as Hopkins noted, art means "to make," but Duchamp had done little of that with his "conceptual provocations" like *Bicycle Wheel* and *Fountain* (Figure 17).[79]

Figure 17. Marcel Duchamp, *Fountain*, 1917, Philadelphia Museum of Art, Philadelphia, Pennsylvania, U.S.A.
© Succession Marcel Duchamp /ADAGP, Paris /Artists Rights Society (ARS), New York 2013.
Photo Credit: The Philadelphia Museum of Art/Art Resource, NY.

In April 1917, as an elaborate joke undertaken for its shock value, Duchamp submitted his now iconic *Fountain* (signed "R. Mutt") to the New York Society of Independent Artists exhibition, which supposedly was available to any artist willing to pay the exhibition fee. Duchamp had dual goals: first, to discredit the organizers' claims for aesthetic democracy, and second, to offend the current standards of propriety.[80] With his thought-objects, like *Fountain*, Duchamp intended not only to attack artistic and social norms but also to preserve individuality in a mass society indifferent to the ongoing human slaughter taking place in a brutal world war—a war that, in April 1917, the United States was just entering.[81]

Both Duchamp and his friend Francis Picabia equated human sexuality with mechanism. Duchamp illustrates this equation in *The Bride Stripped Bare by her Bachelors, Even* (or *Large Glass*) (1915-23), a composition of oil, water, and lead foil on two glass panels

Figure 18. Marcel Duchamp, *The Bride Stripped Bare by her Bachelors, Even* (or *Large Glass*), 1915-23, Philadelphia Museum Of Art, Philadelphia, Pennsylvania, U.S.A.
© Succession Marcel Duchamp /ADAGP, Paris /Artists Rights Society (ARS), New York 2013.
Photo Credit: The Philadelphia Museum of Art/Art Resource, NY.

(Figure 18). And Picabia does the same in *Portrait of a Young American Girl in a State of Nudity* (1915), a line drawing of a spark plug equating it with female sexuality. Duchamp's *Bride* (and her suitors) and Picabia's *Young American Girl* are depicted as mechanisms. In *Bride* (Figure 18) Duchamp uses mucus-colored mechanomorphs to deconstruct human sexuality, especially in the nine male bachelors. He described the bachelors as "malik molds" who are trapped and "will never be able to pass beyond the mask."[82] Duchamp's and Picabia's artistic characterization of human sexuality as mechanical (humans-as-machines) is a shockingly anti-humanist position, characteristic of New York and also Berlin Dada.[83]

Kurt Schwitters—Hanover Dada and Merz. Kurt Schwitters (1887-1948) was born into a family of well-to-do shopkeepers, and attended the Hanover School of Applied Arts and the Dresden Art Academy. When war broke out, Schwitters avoided the draft by bribing a doctor and feigning insanity. He spent the war years in the auxiliary military service and used his free time to paint and write poetry, both influenced by Cubism and Expressionism.[84] At the end of the war, Schwitters developed a different form of abstract collage (or assemblage) made from urban detritus, such as discarded bus tickets, wrappers, newspapers, string, and other refuse. He labeled his collages and other art, "Merz" (after the word "*Commerzbank*" used in one of his collages).[85] In addition, he composed and widely publicized an expressionistic parody of a sentimental love poem, "An Anna Blume" (To Eve Blossom), and a long, wordless sound poem, "Ursonate" (The Primal Sonata). He also built an enormous, organic "Merzbau" (Cathedral of Erotic Misery) throughout his house, which he described as an "abstract (cubist) sculpture in which people can go."[86] Schwitters' ultimate aesthetic goal was to develop a total artwork (*gesamtkunstwerk*) that encompassed all of the arts.

"Art is a primordial concept," declared Schwitters, "exalted as the godhead, inexplicable as life, indefinable and without purpose." Believing that art served an important spiritual function, he called his art "a prayer about the victorious end of the war, victorious as once again peace has won in the end; everything had broken down in any case and new things had to be made out of the fragments: and this is Merz."[87] Schwitters' *Revolving* (1919) exemplifies both his artistic viewpoint and his technique (Figure 19). In the tradition of Synthetic Cubist collage, *Revolving* employs oil painting on canvas and construction with discarded material—wood, metal, cord, cardboard, wool, wire, leather. The circles and rods in *Revolving* constitute the artist's effort to make a new conceptual mechanism out of the fragmented parts of a broken machine, as if to create a new culture from the shattered remains of postwar German culture.[88] The reconstructed mechanism in *Revolving* evokes the indomitable human spirit to pick up the pieces of the old world broken by the war and to use them to rebuild a newer world.

Although Schwitters came late to Dada, he persisted the longest.[89] In 1923, he launched his *Merz Magazine*, which characterized his Merz artwork as anti-Dada: "We are Kurt Schwitters, not

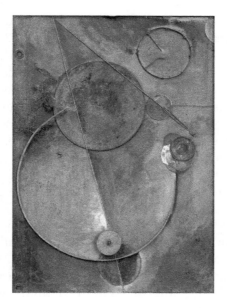

Figure 19. Kurt Schwitters, *Revolving*, 1919, The Museum of Modern Art, New York, NY, U.S.A.
© 2013 Artists Rights Society (ARS), New York / VG Bild-Kunst, Bonn.
Digital Image © The Museum of Modern Art/Licensed by SCALAR/Art Resource, NY.

dada, but MERZ." Drawing an implicit contrast with the political negativity of Berlin Dada, Schwitters emphasized the redemptive purpose of his art: "Merz, and only Merz is able to transform ... the entire world into a work of art."[90] In 1937, however, the Nazis interrupted his restorative mission by confiscating his art works in German museums and exhibiting them as Degenerate Art. Nazi opposition prompted Schwitters to emigrate from Germany to Norway where he began a new Merzbau, and then to Britain where he remained for the rest of his life.

George Grosz—Berlin Dada and Mechanistic Humanity. George Grosz (1893-1959) was born Georg Gross, but in 1916, he anglicized his given name and slavicized his family name, as an anti-German protest. When he was nine years old, his widowed mother became manager of an officers' casino where Grosz had an early association with German officers. After the war broke out, Grosz enlisted but was soon released for medical reasons. In 1917, he was drafted, then transferred to a mental hospital, and finally discharged as unfit for service. He studied at the Dresden Art Academy and the Berlin Museum of Applied Arts, among other art schools. During the war, Grosz painted and produced photomontages that were antimilitary, resulting in his being charged several times with insulting the German Army and committing public offense. Grosz's Dadaist painting *The Funeral (Dedicated to Oskar Panizza)* (1917-18), for example, depicts a hellish carnival of grotesques in a riotous funeral procession hurtling down a major thoroughfare amid bars, strip joints, and skyscrapers toward fiery damnation. *The Funeral* is typical of Grosz's highly critical images of Berlin as the depraved locus of brutish militarists, despicable profiteers, pitiful war wounded, and myriad destructive forces. "No one since Daumier," asserts Hamilton, "has left such a complete record of a particular historical situation, a horrifying, intensely circumstantial German report on Berlin between 1914 and 1924."[91] Following the war, Grosz joined the German Communist Party and Club Dada. In June 1920, Club Dada produced its notorious "Dada Fair," which lampooned the German military and its war policy, and also brought Club Dada to an end. When the Nazis came to power, Grosz left Germany for the United States where he taught at the Colombia University School of Fine Art.[92]

Dada reached Berlin in 1918, following Richard Huelsenbeck's arrival from Zürich. Unsurprisingly, Berlin Dada became politically radical, given the societal turmoil from losing the war, the economic crisis from war reparations, and the brutal suppression of communist sympathizers, including the murders of Rosa Luxembourg and Karl Liebknecht. Berlin's Club Dada consisted of two highly political types: communist sympathizers, like George Grosz, Wieland Herzfelde, and John Heartfield; and anarchist sympathizers, like Raoul Hausmann and Johannes Baader.[93] Consistent with New York Dadaists, Berlin Dadaists openly opposed Expressionism and prewar avant-garde art as humanistic, spiritual, and "retinal art." Huelsenbeck lambasted it in his *1920 Berlin Dada Manifesto*: "On the pretext of carrying out propaganda for the soul, they have, in their struggle with naturalism, found their way back to

Figure 20. George Grosz, *Daum marries her pedantic automaton "George" in May 1920. John Heartfield is very glad of it*, 1920, Galerie Nierendorf, Berlin, Germany.
Art © The Estate of Georgia Grosz /Licenced by VAGA, New York, NY.
Photo Credit: Erich Lessing / Art Resource, NY.

the abstract, pathetic gestures which presuppose a comfortable life free from content or strife."[94] Berlin Dadaists rejected traditional painting in favor of sonic poetry and photomontage, new art forms which they pioneered. They often depicted humans as machinery in the manner of their New York counterparts.

In his self-critical watercolor/photomontage, *Daum marries her pedantic automaton "George" in May 1920. John Heartfield is very glad of it* (1920), Grosz displayed his strong anti-humanist view of modern man as a hybrid machine. *Daum* (Figure 20) refers in part to Grosz's own recent marriage to Maud (*Daum* plays on her name), and in part to Berlin's decadence as the city of prostitutes and automatons.[95] Daum (on the left) looks like a barroom floozy, and George (on the right) looks like a ridiculous machine. Grosz's Club Dada colleague Wieland Herzfelde (John Heartfield's brother) considered *Daum* to be an attack on the bourgeois institution of marriage, which "unfailingly transforms the man into a constituent part of itself, into a small cog within a larger system of wheels and gears"; marriage partially frees the woman, while the man "addresses other sober, pedantic and calculating tasks."[96] Unlike Duchamp's *Bride*, however, Grosz's *Daum* still shows woman as human and at least semi-autonomous, whereas Duchamp's bachelors and Grosz's husband remain inhuman mechanisms.

Berlin Marxists, like George Grosz, embraced a kind of Sartrean existentialism and rejected the idea of Geist or spirit guiding the world. By contrast, the non-Marxist, anarchistic Berlin Dadaists, like Raoul Hausmann and Johannes Baader, found an elusive and fluid pattern within nature's chaos.[97] Synthesizing Christianity, Buddhism, and Taoism, as Arp had done in Zürich, Hausmann believed that pattern underlies matter and leads to spirit. Similarly, Johannes Baader held a monistic pantheism, curiously based on the monist materialism of the German Darwinian biologist Ernst Haeckel.[98] In the first issue of *The Dada* (June 1919), Hausmann made his famous statement:

> Dada is the only savings bank that pays interest in eternity. The Chinaman has his tao and the Indian his brama. Dada is more than tao and brama. … Gotama thought of entering Nirvana and after he was dead, he stood not in Nirvana but in dada. … The dada hovered above the waters before God created the world and when he spake: let there be light! lo there was not light, but dada. And when the Twilight of the Gods broke in upon us, the only survivor was the dada.[99]

The secular mysticism espoused by the anarchist side of Berlin Dada (as well as Arp and Schwitters) never touched New York, Cologne, or most of Paris Dada.[100]

Max Ernst—From Cologne Dada to Paris Surrealism. Surrealism evolved from Dada in Paris and was largely a French movement, although Max Ernst gave it a German footprint when he moved there from Cologne in 1922. Max Ernst (1891-1976) was born into a well-to-do Catholic family with a father who was an amateur painter. Ernst enrolled in Bonn University in 1910, became influenced by Cubism, Futurism, and Expressionism, and joined a group of painters in 1912. When the war broke out, Ernst enlisted in the field artillery, and rendered meritorious service on both the Western and Eastern Fronts, which earned him the Iron Cross, first and second class. After the war he pursued art rather than university studies and joined Cologne Dada along with Hans Arp, who had moved to Cologne from Zürich. In 1922, Ernst moved to Paris where he became a major force in the Surrealist movement.[101]

In Cologne, Dada jelled around the "Cologne Dada Fair" of April 1920. There Ernst exhibited startling collages and photomontages of colliding images that bitterly attacked traditional art and religious iconography. Unlike Berlin Dada, Cologne Dada was essentially apolitical.[102] Hopkins explains that "employed by Ernst in Cologne, collage had summoned up a world that was profoundly inimical to human control; whole systems of ideas and regimes of representation appeared to be in conflict."[103] For example, in a slightly later work, *Santa Conversazione* (Sacred Conversation) (1921), Ernst used anatomical diagrams, photographs, and bird illustrations in a sacrilegious collage of the Virgin's Immaculate Conception, placing a dove as the Holy Spirit over the principal woman's exposed womb (Figure 21).

Ernst focused specifically on the civilization rather than the politics responsible for the current turmoil:

> Contrary to general belief, Dada did not want to shock the bourgeoisie. The bourgeoisie were already shocked. No, Dada was a rebellious upsurge of vital energy and rage; it resulted from the absurdity, the whole immense stupidity of that imbecilic war. We young people came back from the war in a state of stupefaction, and our rage had to find expression somehow or another. This it did quite naturally through attacks on the civilization responsible for the war. Attacks on speech, syntax, logic, literature, painting and so on.[104]

Consistent with his apolitical agenda, Ernst downplayed the physicality of the disparate materials in his ideational photomontages. Instead, he painted over and re-photographed them to give his

Figure 21. Max Ernst, *Santa Conversazione* (*Sacred Conversation*), 1921, Private Collection.
© Artists Rights Society (ARS), New York/ADAGP, Paris.
Photo Credit: Courtesy of Fondation Beyeler, Basel.

works a seamlessness. The photomontages of Berlin Dadaists, by contrast, display the cutting and reassembling of newspaper and magazine imagery, thereby emphasizing their rending of the depraved social fabric.

Ernst's artwork bridged Dada and Surrealism in three respects: First, his collages, like *Santa Conversazione,* created disturbing new worlds, or counter-realities, using fragments of materials from daily life. As a Dadaist, he rejected the old world, but as a Surrealist, he created a new world. Whereas Braque and Picasso introduced fragments of newspaper clippings and sheet music into their collages as witty allusions, Ernst used such familiar materials to evoke a strange new reality with troubling psychological implications. Indeed, with his painterly technique, Ernst created collages that effectively became "dream painting," Surrealism's very keystone.[105] Second, Ernst made what he called "frottages," using surface rubbings over wood-graining to conjure images of flora and fauna.

Ernst discovered this rubbing technique on a rainy evening in August 1925, after being struck by the symbolism in the floorboards of his seaside room.[106] Deriving them in this way, Ernst considered his frottages just like the "automatic writing" being developed in Surrealist prose and poetry.[107] Thus, the frottages bridge the two movements by implicating Surrealist psychic as well as Dadaist chance operations. Third, Ernst's Dadaist collages involved overpainting to produce a seamless, dreamlike space and an imaginative illusionism. Dada manifestoes generally proscribed painting in artworks because of its elitist implications, but Ernst used painting to suggest the "individual reverie" of Surrealism rather than the "political edge" of Dada.[108]

Ernst completed his transition from Dada to Surrealism by the time of his move to Paris. In his Surrealist oil painting, *Pietà or Revolution by Night* (1923), for example, Ernst introduced Freudian dream psychology (Figure 22). Using the Christian iconography of

Figure 22. Max Ernst, *Pietà or Revolution by Night*, 1923, Tate Gallery, London, Great Britain.
© Artists Rights Society (ARS), New York/ADAGP, Paris.
Photo Credit: Tate, London / Art Resource, NY.

the *Pieta*, presumably inspired by Michelangelo's famous sculpture, Ernst portrays a father holding his son—an undoubted reference to Ernst's own father Philippe, a pious Catholic, who had painted his young son Max as the infant Jesus. Ernst's *Pieta* suggests a dream state in which subconscious fears and desires become manifest; it also conflates Christian iconography with personal biography. Like *Santa Conversazione, Pieta* is a sacrilegious work in which Ernst evokes Philippe as God the Father holding his Son, but, by implication from the son's gray coloration, the father has turned his son into stone.[109] As typified by Ernst's *Pieta*, Surrealists focused on the unconscious in order to emphasize human irrationality rather than to redress human psychoses. Indeed, Surrealists accepted man's riven subconscious. Instead, they used art to increase public awareness of the unconscious and to dissect bourgeois morality, especially as regards sexuality.[110]

Dada Transitions to Surrealism

In 1919, Dada reached Paris when Francis Picabia arrived there from New York; Duchamp followed in 1921, and Ernst in 1922. Parisian Dada, however, galvanized around the French poet Andre Breton (1896-1966), who gradually assumed Guillaume Apollinaire's role as catalyst for the avant-garde after the latter's death in 1918. Breton admired the *1918 Dada Manifesto* (quoted above), which the Zürich group published in its magazine *Dada*, because of its highly critical yet potentially redemptive posture: "After the carnage we are left with the hope of a purified humanity."[111] In 1920, Tristan Tzara, author of the *Dada Manifesto*, left Zürich and reached Paris. Zürich Dada had ended the prior year, and thereafter Paris became the principal Dada center.

Although they opposed France's conservative government, Paris Dadaists were less overtly political than Berlin Dadaists. But Paris Dadaists were outspokenly negative about traditional art. Duchamp brought to Paris his *L.H.O.O.Q.* (1919), a reproduction of the *Mona Lisa* with a penciled-in mustache and goatee. Spoken in French the letters LHOOQ become "*Elle a chaud au cul,*" roughly "She has a hot ass." Thus, the work mocked reproductions and questioned the concept of a masterpiece. Breton publicized Duchamp's assisted ready-made *L.H.O.O.Q.* with the rhetorical question: "Could it be that Marcel Duchamp reaches the *critical point* of ideas faster than anyone else?" Breton thereby firmly established Duchamp's reputation as a cerebral artist.[112] In a similar vein, Picabia published a 1920 journal containing his illustration *Tableau Dada*, which consists of a stuffed monkey surrounded by the words "Portrait of Cézanne, Portrait of Rembrandt, Portrait of Renoir."[113]

In its second season Dada experienced a rift over the 1921 mock trial of Maurice Barres, a radical libertarian turned ultra-nationalist during the war. The trial drove a wedge between Tzara and Breton, which foretold Dada's demise. Tzara protested any claim of moral authority over another, and Breton rejected Dada's "acknowledged commitment to indifference."[114] Tzara's (and also Picabia's) objection to a collective moral code constituted a critical fault line between Dadaism and Surrealism.[115] In May 1922, Breton organized a Congress of Paris to respond to Dada's pursuit of "insolent negation" and "scandal for its own sake," and to set the future direction of avant-garde activity.[116] During a two-year hiatus (1922-24), called *"movement flou"* (or hazy/indistinct movement), Dada artists explored the irrational through self-induced trances, assimilated Freudian theories of the unconscious, and developed techniques of automatic writing (rapid flurries of drafting without preconceived ideas). Then, in 1924, Breton issued a manifesto that gave birth to Surrealism "based on the belief in the superior reality of certain previously neglected associations, and the omnipotence of dreams, and the disinterested play of thought."[117] Breton's Surrealist manifesto rejected self-referential and autonomous art, embraced the irrational, exempted itself from aesthetic concerns, and erased any distinction between "art" and "life" —all clearly legacies of Dada.[118]

Although initially focused on poetics rather than visual arts, Surrealism increasingly embraced the visual arts, especially Ernst's kind of "dream painting." Surrealist painting took one of two directions: either realistic "dream painting" that creates alternative realities with academic exactitude, like the work of Ernst, Salvador Dali (1904-1989), and Yves Tanguy (1900-1955), or spontaneous blotches of forms, or "automatic drawings," like the work of Joan Miro (1893-1983).[119] Breton defended Surrealist painting, despite its strong appeal to bourgeois taste, which stood at odds with his

Marxist leanings, and despite its obvious need for aesthetic technique, which occurs in dream painting and automatism.[120] Because of Breton's inability to provide an adequate theoretical justification, Hopkins thinks that painting "ends up as Surrealism's Achilles heel."[121]

In his pioneering work, *The History of Surrealism*, Maurice Nadeau described Surrealism as "the heir and extender" of Cubism, Futurism, and Dada, convinced that man had produced the "terrible civilization" responsible for the Great War by becoming "a cerebral monster with hypertrophied rational faculties."[122] For the Surrealists, the human being was more than reason and logic, reality was more than what the senses could reveal, and the "unknown realm" of man's dreams was "the true source of his acts, his thoughts, his life."[123] Surrealism asserted that humankind was a dreamer as well as a "reasoner" and "was not the creature molded by a century of positivism, of associationism, of 'scientism,' but a being of desires, instincts and dreams as psychoanalysis revealed him."[124] In short, for Nadeau, Surrealism tried to restore the whole individual by placing emphasis "on the night side of being, on the imagination, on instinct, desire, and the dream, on the irrational or merely ludic forms of behavior."[125]

Dada, Surrealism, and Materialism

The crisis of World War I had triggered a radically energized, iconoclastic, but short-lived movement, Dadaism, which led to a similarly iconoclastic but longer-term, successor movement, Surrealism. Dadaists declared themselves anti-art, challenging the prewar avant-garde aesthetics as decadent, bourgeois, egotistical, and divorced from the lived experience of ordinary people. Consequently, Dada challenged the very movements that influenced it, like Cubism, Expressionism, and Futurism, as self-indulgent efforts serving only the artists and their discredited capitalist society, which caused the catastrophic war. Dada "became an instrument of ballistics" and "hit the spectator like a bullet," observed German literary and art critic Walter Benjamin, and, therefore, was useless for "contemplative immersion."[126] Dadaists produced spectacles that engaged the audience, forced a reaction, and reenacted the wartime chaos. They were cultural saboteurs, who militarized art to combat the smug and destructive reasoning that spawned "a botched civilization." Dadaists were utterly dismissive of philosophic reason in human affairs. In his *1918 Dada Manifesto* Tristan Tzara castigated logic as a disease, and in his *1920 Berlin Dada Manifesto* Richard Huelsenbeck savaged Kantian noumena: "The urinal, too, is a thing in itself"—no doubt a reference to Duchamp's *Fountain*.[127] Having assimilated Bergson's views on intuition, Dadaists aimed at liberating intuition and unconscious as more dynamic and fundamental human faculties for coping with a mysterious universe.[128] They emphasized the human body over the Cartesian ego, the unconscious over the conscious, and the irrational over the rational side of human nature—all ostensibly to bring human nature into balance and to cope with the chaotic flux of reality.[129]

Following World War I, humanity certainly needed to acquire new psychic balance, but Dada's shock therapy was incapable of providing the stable setting needed for a reasoned inquiry into humanity's ultimate concerns. Moreover, German and French Dadaists differed over Freudian psychology. The Berlin Dadaists suspected Freudianism as an attempt to adjust man to a defective society and to suppress man's Dionysian impulses needed to reform society; and the Parisian Dadaists, including Max Ernst, accepted Freud's diagnosis of an unconsciously directed and conflicted humanity and favored social adaptation to an essentially Marxist model.[130] Neither view of Freud, however, emphasized reason or focused upon metaphysical concerns. Furthermore, Berlin and New York Dadaists characterized humans as machines committed to a mechanized world. This human-machine or mechanomorphic iconography appears in George Grosz's *Daum marries*, Marcel Duchamp's *The Bride Stripped Bare*, and Picabia's *Portrait of a Young American Girl*. Their anti-humanist rendition of the body as a machine not only separated mind from matter but portrayed mind as mechanical and untrustworthy, and discredited individualism in favor of Marxian collectivity. Although some Berlin and Zürich Dadaists mystically aligned body and soul in a curious metaphysical monism, Berlin Dadaists, according to Hopkins, "sought a robust materialism and shunned humanist platitudes."[131]

Dada's riotous exposé of man's innate irrationality responsible for the war evolved into Surrealism's more constructive effort to put humanity in touch with those same irrational forces, and Surrealism survived well into the 1940s. While placing humanity in touch with its unconscious, however, Surrealism continued Dada's denigration of human reason as a useful source for finding meaning in the postwar world. Moreover, by challenging reliance upon reason and emphasizing the subconscious, both Dadaism and Surrealism turned inward toward the human psyche and away from metaphysical concerns. They portrayed humanity either as a troubled psyche focused upon its own unconscious forces or a mindless mechanism moving robotically in a materialist universe. Those few non-materialists, like Arp and the Berlin anarchists, who imagined a vague mystical force beneath the inscrutable world of chance and flux, provided no credible counterpoint to materialism. By diminishing the role of reason and discounting the value of metaphysical inquiry, they did little to restore purpose and meaning to the universe. In short, Dadaism and Surrealism either embraced a materialist worldview or failed to show a world of transcendent value or intrinsic meaning, which left materialism effectively unchallenged.

8

Materialism from World War I to the Present

> With me the horrid doubt always arises whether the convictions of man's mind, which has been developed from the mind of the lower animals, are of any value or at all trustworthy. Would anyone trust in the convictions of a monkey's mind, if there are any convictions in such a mind?
> — Charles Darwin, Letter to W. Graham (1881)[1]

World War I radically changed Western theology, philosophy, literature, and art, causing them to lose faith in human reason and its ability to find cosmic meaning for a civilization devastated by the war. Western culture disengaged from metaphysical concerns and, instead, focused upon the postwar condition of human anxiety and alienation from an apparently absurd world. Relieved of serious challenge from Western culture, the materialist neo-Darwinian conception of nature gradually strengthened its hold on the Western mind and ultimately succeeded in reframing the intellectual discourse about ultimate reality as devoid of meaning. Then, starting in the last quarter of the twentieth century and continuing through the present, an avalanche of popular books aggressively promoting the atheistic implications of materialism descended upon the general public. The books include *Chance and Necessity* (1972) by Jacques Monod, *The Blind Watchmaker* (1986) and *The God Delusion* (2006) by Richard Dawkins, *Darwin's Dangerous Idea, Evolution and the Meaning of Life* (1995) by Daniel Dennett, and *The Grand Design* (2012) by Stephen Hawking. These authors have assured a wide general audience that science represents the only certain road to truth, that science demonstrates a materialist reality, indifferent to humankind, and that the idea of God or a transcendent power is no longer intellectually defensible.

Materialism's escalated onslaught against cosmic meaning and purpose finally revived Western culture from its metaphysical slumber. Prominent modern spokespersons like Georgetown theologian John F. Haught and British philosopher and theologian Keith Ward, among others, have risen in defense of a world with transcendent meaning and spiritual value—a world with God. This chapter takes the measure of materialism and its critique of theism after bringing Western culture and materialism forward to the point of their present engagement.

Western Culture and Cosmology Through the Late Twentieth Century

Theology. Karl Barth died in 1968, *the* dominant influence on Protestant neoorthodoxy throughout the twentieth century. Barth emphasized God as *Wholly Other* and deemphasized the human projects of scientific and metaphysical inquiry as theologically insignificant. His fellow Crisis theologians developed their own variations on this same theological theme and remained influential leaders in Protestantism throughout their lives: Emil Brunner died in 1966, Friedrich Gogarten in 1967, and Rudolf Bultmann in 1976. Paul Tillich stood at the forefront of Protestant existentialism and remains influential to this day, long after his death in 1965. The evolutionary thought of Pierre Teilhard de Chardin was exceptional among postwar Christian clerics for its constructive engagement with modern science, but Teilhard's posthumously published writings did not reach the general public until after his death in 1955. Indeed, the Catholic Church did not formally accept Darwinian evolution as more than a hypothesis until 1996. Significantly, *Modern Christian Thought, the Twentieth Century* (2006), a major treatise on Christian theology in the last century, makes no mention of evolutionary theology and only two brief references to Charles Darwin and Darwinism, the very backbone of materialism.[2]

This leaves American fundamentalism as the one Christian voice since World War I consistently outspoken on Darwinism. Fundamentalists adopted a religious mission to oppose evolution or at least to limit its influence in society based upon their literalist reading of the Bible and their conviction of biblical inerrancy even as to science. As Whitehead warned, however, "religion will not regain its old power until it can face change in the same spirit as does science." Instead, religion must disengage its essential message "from the bonds of imperfect science" and from "the imaginative picture of the world entertained in previous ages."[3] American fundamentalists did not heed Whitehead's advice and, instead, have waged a war against materialists over evolution's supposed threat to religious belief. Unfortunately, mainstream religious thought remained a bystander in this controversy by not effectively coming to grips with the religious implications of modern scientific developments until late in the twentieth century. By then materialism's godless cosmology had attained the status of scientific dogma and become firmly entrenched in Western secular culture.

Philosophy. Existentialism and logical positivism were the polar opposite philosophical offspring of World War I, and both fled metaphysics, but in opposite directions. Existentialism turned toward humanity's psychic distress from two successive world wars, and logical positivism toward science's position "as the ultimate ruler of human life," to quote William Barrett.[4] Existentialism emerged in the aftermath of World War I, but reached its high point only after World War II. Jean-Paul Sartre, its most visible proponent, died in 1980. Existentialism remained influential until "flaming out" after the French student riots of May 1968, the so-called "Sartrean revolution."[5] The logical positivists exited Vienna during the Nazi era and emigrated from Europe mostly to the United States, where they remained influential throughout the 1960s.[6]

Existentialism's successor movements—structuralism in the 1960s and post-structuralism in the 1970s and 1980s—took a linguistic turn, which continued to avoid metaphysics. Structuralism analyzed the basic structure of language, considered as sets of linguistic signs, rather than language's content or relationship to the world.[7] Post-structuralists reacted against the rigidity of structuralism's assumed unifying linguistic systems and grand narratives, embracing instead what Emory Professor of Philosophy Thomas R. Flynn calls "an ethical practice without metaphysical commitment or inviolable laws and principles."[8] In short, existentialism and its successor movements of structuralism and post-structuralism remained disengaged from metaphysical inquiry, just as the logical positivists had.

Literature. Much of high modernist literature following World War I situated humanity in an existential struggle for meaning in an alien universe—a worldview fully consistent with materialism—and this literary theme persisted well into the postmodernist era following World War II. Ernest Hemingway, arguably the most influential writer of the twentieth century, had a prominent career spanning four decades, from *In Our Time* (1925) until his death in 1961.[9] He won the Pulitzer Prize for his last major work published in his lifetime, *The Old Man and the Sea* (1952), received the Nobel Prize in 1954, and became the literary voice for an age of skepticism.[10] From Nick Adams and Jack Barnes recovering from the trauma of war, to the old fisherman struggling alone at sea with a huge marlin ("I do not care who kills who," he tells the fish), Hemingway portrays stoic courage and unflinching resolve in the face of mortal danger and cosmic indifference.[11] Postmodernist writers like Samuel Beckett (1906-1989) pursued Hemingway's absurdist theme by attempting "to reveal the meaninglessness of existence and the underlying 'abyss,' or 'void,' or 'nothingness' on which any supposed security is conceived to be precariously suspended."[12]

Postmodernism in literature, like post-structuralism in linguistics, questioned the meaningfulness of language, perceived as the mere manifestation of power and ideology in contemporary society.[13] In his influential work *The Postmodern Condition: A Report on Knowledge* (1979), Jean-François Lyotard characterized modernism as "making an explicit appeal to some grand narrative, such as the dialectics of Spirit, the hermeneutics of meaning, the emancipation of the rational or working subject, or the creation of wealth." By contrast, postmodernism expressed "incredulity toward metanarratives" and supported performance and efficiency in search of utility rather than truth.[14] Thus, the postmodern mind rejected totalizing theories, whether philosophical, literary, or artistic, which purported to explain all of existence, and, instead, promoted skepticism rather than any particular theory.[15]

Art. Postmodern art is a legacy of Dada and Surrealism, which continued into the latter half of the twentieth century.[16] *Bed* (1955) by Robert Rauschenberg (b. 1925), for example, is a neo-Dada work that consists of painting on a quilt and combines everyday detritus like nail polish and striped toothpaste, reminiscent of collages by

Kurt Schwitters. Abstract expressionist works, like *Blue Poles* (1952) by Jackson Pollock (1912-1956), suggest the "psychic automatism" of surrealism as a means of accessing the unconscious.[17] *Tilted Arc* (1981) by Richard Serra (b. 1939) was a quintessential postmodern work that consisted of a massive steel blade erected in Foley Square, New York. *Tilted Arc* measured twelve feet high and 120 feet long and weighed seventy-two tons. It signified simultaneously the urban role of industrial steel, the seemingly weightless balance between sculpture, space, and viewer, and the human obstructions posed by modernity, in this case an "Iron Curtain" that impeded people wanting to cross Foley Plaza.[18] By its brute form, *Tilted Arc* resisted the idea of decorative public art and urban assimilation, for one critic, "by registering the inescapable strangeness of urban space" and by returning "to one of the central themes of literary and philosophical modernity: that consciousness is marked by its sense of transcendental homelessness."[19] In short, Western culture continued to emphasize existential angst, to turn away from metaphysics, and to offer materialism a relatively uncontested platform until late in the twentieth century.

Materialism through the Late Twentieth Century

In the absence of cultural concern for metaphysics, "scientific materialism" had taken hold of academe within the first decade following World War I and gradually thereafter became entrenched in the Western mind.[20] In his 1925 Lowell Lectures at Harvard, Whitehead coined this term for his Harvard audience, noting with alarm that materialism's abstract system of concepts which had successfully guided science since the Enlightenment had become "the fixed scientific cosmology" in every university in the world. "We have mistaken our abstraction for concrete realities," Whitehead warned, and "it is quite unbelievable."[21] Some men of letters, like Aldous Huxley, did criticize materialism, and some scientists thought quantum and relativity physics supported non-materialistic interpretations of nature. Einstein was not a materialist, and while not believing in organized religion or a personal God, he held a "religious" feeling of wonder about the "subtle, intangible and inexplicable" harmonizing force behind nature.[22] Baumer cites efforts by several European scientist-philosophers to bridge the mind-matter dualism and oppose materialism.[23] But he also reported that materialism "persisted as a philosophy of nature, among Marxists, and, no doubt, also among many men of science."[24] By mid-twentieth century, most scientists had adopted materialism as their working hypothesis, and ever since, the secular intellectual community has accepted and promoted materialism within Western culture.[25]

In his 1948 article for *The Atlantic Monthly*, Princeton Professor of Philosophy W. T. Stace asserted that science had given modern man the materialist picture of the world: "Nature is nothing but matter in motion. The motions of matter are governed, not by any purpose, but by blind forces and laws." Stace credited Whitehead for identifying this materialist worldview and observed that "belief in the ultimate irrationality of everything is the quintessence of what is called the modern mind."[26] Science had undermined "the religious basis of our ideals," and "we must now boldly and honestly face the truth that the universe is non-spiritual and indifferent to goodness, beauty, happiness, or truth."[27] Thus, in 1948, Stace confirmed that the materialist worldview, with its "immense spiritual emptiness," had become "the quintessence" of the modern mind. In 1972, Monod reaffirmed Stace's position: modern science "wrote an end to the ancient animist covenants between man and nature, leaving nothing in place of that precious bond but an anxious quest in a frozen universe of solitude."[28] Thus, materialism had become the modern metaphysical paradigm, as exemplified in the positions of the following four outspoken materialists: Hawking, Monod, Dawkins, and Dennett.

Hawking's Grand Design — the Gravity Explanation

Traveling back almost 14 billion years in *The Grand Design* (2010), co-authored with Leonard Mlodinow, renowned British physicist Stephen Hawking opens the materialist story with the Big Bang. Based upon the recent discoveries of physics, Hawking argues that gravity alone caused the Big Bang and spontaneously created the universe out of nothing. The "most general supersymmetric theory of gravity," which he calls M-theory, involves highly sophisticated concepts such as eleven space-time dimensions able to contain both vibrating strings and point particles, among other dimensions.[29] M-theory is "the unified theory Einstein was hoping to find" and "the *only* candidate for a complete theory of the universe."[30] M-theory "predicts that a great many universes were created out of nothing," and obviates need for "the intervention of some supernatural being or God."[31] "Because there is a law like gravity," Hawking continues, "the universe can and will create itself from nothing. ... Spontaneous creation is the reason there is something rather than nothing, why the universe exists, why we exist. It is not necessary to invoke God to light the blue torch paper and set the universe going."[32] Gravity provides the entire explanation; God is superfluous.

In addition to the Big Bang, M-theory also explains the laws of nature that govern every aspect of the universe, with no exceptions, including humanity.[33] Thus, "scientific determinism must hold for people as well," leaving the (presumably predetermined) idea of free will completely untenable:

> Though we feel that we can choose what we do, our understanding of the molecular basis of biology shows that biological processes are governed by the laws of physics and chemistry and therefore are as determined as the orbits of the planets. Recent experiments in neuroscience support the view that it is our own physical brain, following the known laws of science, that determines our actions, and not some agency that exists outside those laws. ... It is hard to imagine how free will can operate if our behavior is determined by physical law, so it seems that we are no more than biological machines and that free will is just an illusion.[34]

Only because we find it "impractical" to apply physical laws to predict human behavior, says Hawking, do "we use the effective theory that people have free will."[35] Consequently, "scientists have become the bearers of the torch of discovery in our quest for knowledge," and "philosophy is dead" since it has failed to keep up with scientific developments.[36]

Hawking's contention that science has outstripped philosophy as the primary means of discovering truth is unabashed scientism. In *The Grand Design*, he begins by posing and ends by answering fundamental questions about reality—questions that mimic the most profound concerns of traditional Western philosophy:

> How can we understand the world in which we find ourselves?
> How does the universe behave?
> What is the nature of reality?
> Where did all this come from?
> Did the universe need a Creator?
> Why is there something rather than nothing?
> Why do we exist?
> Why this particular set of laws and not some other?[37]

Only the second of his foregoing eight questions is a "how" question, which characteristically falls within the domain of science. The rest are "why" questions, which occupy the long history of Western philosophy.

Ironically, despite his dismissive elegy over philosophy, Hawking is unwittingly dabbling in philosophy himself—but not very successfully. He claims that the universe spontaneously created itself from nothing, which is logically impossible. He claims that gravity preexisted creation, but gravity certainly is not nothing. And he claims that a natural law (gravity) actually caused nature, when a law like gravity depends entirely on nature's preexistence in order to function. How can a law of nature exist before and apart from the very bodies or objects to which it applies? Gravity predicts the Earth's rotation around the sun, but it did not create these celestial bodies, and it most certainly cannot explain itself. Hawking has effectively empowered a natural law with the creative powers of God without ever answering the obvious question of who created gravity. Thus, Hawking's three contradictory assertions do not offer a promising start to his explanation of everything.[38] Could Hawking's philosophical reach possibly exceed his scientific grasp?

Hawking has attributed creative powers to a natural law (gravity) as if it were a causative agent, when the two ideas (law and agency) are wholly distinct. In effect, Hawking has conflated Aristotle's four types of causes, illustrated by the following example of a house: (1) the *material cause* is the raw material such as bricks and boards of which the house is made; (2) the *formal cause* is the

architect's blueprint for the house; (3) the *efficient cause* is the con-
tractor's construction to the architect's blueprint; and (4) the *final
cause* is the purpose for building the house, for example, the prospective owner's desire for a roof over his head. Science tradition-
ally asks the "how" questions, focusing on the material cause, and
only those "why" questions that are limited to the functions of raw
materials, for example, the reason for using bricks. But science does
not ask, and it cannot hope to answer, the "why" questions about
purpose, in this case, why the prospective owner wanted a house.
Scientific reasoning is simply not equipped to answer such questions of purpose. Those questions are philosophical. Hawking has
reduced gravity or M-theory to a final cause or purpose, as if a law
of nature were a causative agent. But natural laws do not cause or
create anything.[39]

Like many materialists, Hawking writes admiringly about the
exquisite design of the universe:

> The laws of nature form a system that is extremely fine-
> tuned, and very little in physical law can be altered without
> destroying the possibility of the development of life as we
> know it. Were it not for a series of startling coincidences
> in the precise details of physical law it seems, humans and
> similar life-forms would never have come into being.[40]

But, also like many materialists, Hawking attributes this extraordinary design, including human life and mind, solely to matter and
energy rather than to God or any ultimate mind or agency. Such
extreme reductionism, however, inevitably undermines human rationality; mind becomes no more than the firing of neural synapses.
Hawking does not trouble himself with Darwin's question (quoted above) about why the convictions and values of such a mind
would be trustworthy. Former Cambridge Professor of Mathematical Physics John Polkinghorne explains the logical implications of
such reductionism:

> For, not only does it relegate our experiences of beauty, mor-
> al obligation, and religious encounter to the epiphenomenal
> scrapheap, it also destroys rationality. Thought is replaced

by electro-chemical neural events. Two such events cannot confront each other in rational discourse. They are neither right nor wrong. They simply happen. ... The very assertions of the reductionist himself are nothing but blips in the neural network of his brain. The world of rational discourse dissolves into the absurd chatter of firing synapses. Quite frankly, that cannot be right and none of us believes it to be so.[41]

Hawking's contention that the rational arises from the irrational—that our minds are entirely reducible to meaningless matter—gives us no reason to trust our minds, including Hawking's reductionist contention.

Monod's Chance and Necessity—The DNA explanation

In *Chance and Necessity*, French biochemist and Nobel laureate Jacques Monod takes up the materialist story ten billion years after the Big Bang. Then, about four billion years ago, macromolecules emerged by chance alone from the earth's prebiotic soup and eventually formed the biosphere. Based upon his inspection of "the more general properties that characterize living beings," Monod contends that chance alone guides the universe and is responsible for all living things, including man: "from the bacterium to man the chemical machinery is essentially the same, in both its structure and its functioning."[42] DNA is the "fundamental biological invariant," the genetic code that faithfully replicates itself from within each living organism and thereby "guarantees the invariance of the species." This reproductive invariance enables living beings to fulfill their purpose, which Monod calls teleonomy.[43] The teleonomic character of living things, however, implies no purpose in nature because it "owes almost nothing to the action of outside forces" and, instead, is "a secondary property deriving from invariance."[44] Thus, for Monod, DNA is at once the product of a unique chance event and also the means "of preserving the effects of chance and thereby submitting them to the play of natural selection."[45] Once incorporated in the DNA, the chance mutation is faithfully replicated; hence, "the accident enters into that of necessity, of the most implacable certainties."[46] For Monod then, DNA is not only the "secret of life," but the key to "the origin and descent of the whole biosphere."[47]

This explanation of the universe, for Monod, "is today the *sole* conceivable hypothesis, the only one that squares with observed and tested fact."[48] Thus, he concludes that "objective knowledge" disproves the idea that nature has purpose. This idea is just an "animist projection" of the teleonomic character of living organisms—an intellectually indefensible effort "to render nature decipherable and morally meaningful."[49] Objective knowledge, which Monod considers "the *only* authentic source of truth," demonstrates humankind's "total solitude, his fundamental isolation."[50] This observation prompts Monod to espouse the "ethic of knowledge," the "transcendent kingdom of ideas," as a means of personal fulfillment amidst humanity's existential struggle—"alone in the universe's unfeeling immensity, out of which he emerged only by chance."[51]

Monod's materialist thesis is disarming and initially confusing because it employs the language and to some extent the approach of a rationalist thinker. He begins with a general observation of the nature of things, namely, that living organisms are teleonomic and "in their structure and performance they act projectively—realize and pursue a purpose."[52] As Stace observed, the medieval rationalists assumed that "everything must have a purpose," but the scientific movement since Galileo has "consciously and deliberately expel[led] the idea of purpose as controlling nature." Instead, science is "exclusively an inquiry into causes," not purpose.[53] For all his rationalist trappings, however, Monod is a thoroughgoing materialist. "Living beings are chemical machines," and their teleonomic functioning "in the final analysis" depends upon the ability of proteins "to 'recognize' other molecules (including other proteins) by their *shape*, this shape being determined by their molecular structure."[54] Therefore, living matter at all levels (*a fortiori*, nonliving matter as well) consists essentially of atoms and molecules operating according to certain natural laws.[55]

Like Descartes, Monod initially divides reality into mind and matter, but Monod's initial dualism quickly collapses into the monism of matter. As a typical materialist, Monod ultimately reduces mind to matter, although the specific operation of the brain still lies at the frontiers of science:

There lies the frontier, still almost as impassable for us as it was for Descartes. Not until that barrier has been passed will dualism cease to be a force, and to that extent a truth, in the lives of all of us. We today are no less in the habit of differentiating between brain and mind than they were in the eighteenth century. Objective analysis obliges us to see that this seeming duality within us is an illusion.[56]

In other words, Monod contends that science eventually will prove that the human mind, with its desire for truth and capacity to understand, is basically just brain matter and its physical processes. It is the outcome of evolution and learned experience, and, as such, fully reducible and explainable in terms of physics and chemistry. Thus, Monod falls squarely within Whitehead's definition of the materialist since he "presupposes the ultimate fact of an irreducible brute matter, or material, spread throughout space in a flux of configurations."[57]

Monod's materialism is vulnerable to Whitehead's critique of its inherent illogic. Monod's basic and admitted postulate is that nature is "objective" and interpretable only through use of the scientific method: "The cornerstone of the scientific method is the postulate that nature is objective."[58] This postulate from which materialists like Monod propound their cosmology is a metaphysical statement based upon "a simple faith in the order of nature."[59] In other words, when Monod presumes to be "abolishing Aristotelian physics and cosmology" by applying the inductive reasoning of modern science to nature, he in fact is relying upon an antecedent rationalism, namely, a metaphysical conviction that nature is rationally ordered.[60] "There can be no living science," says Whitehead, "unless there is a wide-spread instinctive conviction in the existence of an *Order of Things*, and, in particular, of an *Order of Nature*."[61]

Monod also fails to recognize that inductive reasoning is incapable of proving that nature is uniform because it assumes this very premise and would be begging the question. This is Hume's point: inductive reasoning is not rationally provable and relies on a fundamental faith in the uniformity of nature.[62] Hence, Monod's exclusive reliance upon the scientific method as the means of interpreting nature predetermines the result; the method cannot demonstrate purpose and inevitably leads to the conclusion that nature lacks purpose. As Whitehead explained, nature's teleology "cannot be justified by any inductive generalization"; a broader use of reason than induction is necessary.[63] Indeed, Monod admits that his postulate about nature's objectivity is "forever undemonstrable." Yet he fails to recognize either the implicit rationalist underpinnings for his postulate of objectivity or the implicit admission of his methodological limitations for ascertaining whether nature has purpose.[64]

Monod's "thoroughly Cartesian" view that the cell and all living beings are "chemical machines" suffers an additional logical failure, which Whitehead calls the "fallacy of misplaced concreteness."[65] Monod has abstracted the physical and chemical constituents of a living organism, and assumed that they define the essence of the whole organism. Monod has mistaken his scientific abstractions for concrete realities. He has accepted the quantifiable aspects of matter, Locke's primary qualities, "as the most concrete rendering of fact."[66] For example, Monod has assumed that once having identified all the physicochemical constituents and neurochemical processes of the brain, science can fully explain human consciousness and thought. These subjective qualities of mind, however, are intrinsically and undeniably as real as the underlying brain matter itself. They are inextricably interwoven with, but different from, the brain, but Monod has denied their essential reality. Science's reductive analysis of the brain is immensely valuable to our understanding, but the scientist-philosopher commits a metaphysical fallacy by assuming that this scientific reduction can or will fully explain the human mind. Monod has unjustifiably conflated scientific reduction with metaphysical reductionism and proffered it as scientific truth. He has taken a metaphysical leap and called it empirical science when reductionism is just "an unproved and unprovable belief."[67]

Monod's reductionism of all living creatures to their constituent elements also must confront the logical critique of Hungarian physical chemist and philosopher Michael Polanyi (1891-1976), who contends that life and mind are "emergent" phenomena which cannot be fully explained in terms of lower or chronologically precedent phenomena.[68] Polanyi analogizes nature to a hierarchy, each successive layer of which relies upon, but is not reducible to, the lower. Rather, each higher level is composed of higher organizational principles, which harness the lower processes, just as living organisms harness physical and chemical processes, but are not fully explainable in terms of these lower levels. Polanyi would contend that Monod's reductionist thesis—that biology is merely physics and chemistry—is an illogical statement for the same reason that it is illogical to attempt to reduce a town to bricks and mortar, a painting to brush strokes and pigments, or a book to words, phrases, and grammatical rules. Something more is at work in the higher life forms than can be fully explained simply by identifying their constituent elements—a higher organizational principle (the architect, artist, or writer) has imposed an order upon the lower processes. The physical and chemical processes are necessary but not sufficient conditions for life.

Monod addresses Polanyi's argument that physical forces and chemical interactions "do not fully account for" living systems by contending that he is merely hiding in "our present day ignorance alone."[69] Similarly, Monod charges religions—"a disgusting farrago of Judeo-Christian religiosity"—with hiding in those areas not yet fully explained by the scientific method and relying upon the so-called "God of the gaps."[70] Monod's defense of metaphysical reductionism, his belief that science will eventually "reduce the properties of a very complex organization to the 'sum' of the properties of its parts," reveals both a naïve faith in the scientific method, and an implicit admission that he lacks an adequate answer for Polanyi's emergence thesis. Indeed, Monod admits that in a "very real sense the organism does effectively transcend physical laws—even while obeying them—thus achieving at once the pursuit and fulfillment of its own purpose."[71] Although letters, words, and sentences following grammatical rules are necessary to write this book, it is not simply reducible to them because the book also has meaning and purpose. Apprehending the latter requires the reader's critical analysis and judgment to take account of, without being limited to, the letters, words, and grammatical rules.

Similarly, metaphysical inquiry—the search for meaning and purpose in nature—requires more than reductionist analysis. The individual must apply his or her critical intelligence to a wider view of reality than reductionist analysis, a broader empiricism, so to speak, that also takes account of human consciousness and thought. By applying critical intelligence to an enlarged field of vision beyond reductionist empiricism, the individual can logically and credibly find a larger meaning in evolutionary biology. For example, Polanyi explains that the ontological discontinuity of emergence is fully consistent with evolution and temporal continuity. Haught capsulizes his argument as follows:

> [T]here is no logical incoherence in thinking of nature as a hierarchy of distinct dimensions integrating a continuous, unbroken chain of physico-chemical occurrences, (just as the architect's designs do not interrupt the continuity of the bricklaying process, but simply impose a determinate structure onto it.) In fact, allowances can also thus be made for the role of chance in the emergence of life and in the mutations that are required for the evolution of new species.[72]

In other words, it is logically possible to accept science's methodological reduction of life and mind to physics and chemistry without necessarily concluding that such reduction is their entire explanation.

While Polanyi challenges the logic of reductionist materialism with arguments about ordering principles and emergence, organismic thinkers like Teilhard and Whitehead challenge its analytic illusion, namely, the materialist thesis that you can fully understand and explain the whole simply by breaking it down. In their view, any whole organism necessarily transcends the sum of its parts. Consequently, the process thinkers depart from the materialists by integrating mind and matter at every level and by eschewing the scientific abstraction "foisted onto philosophy" by materialism that matter with simple location in space and time is "the most concrete rendering of fact."[73] Whereas materialists consider consciousness as an epiphenomenon explainable by and reducible to matter, organismic philosophers permeate matter at every level with consciousness (Teilhard) or mentality (Whitehead).

The point here is not to make the case for the emergent or organismic viewpoints per se, but to show that such non-materialist views of nature are consistent with scientific analysis and evolutionary theory when viewed through a non-reductionist lens. Consequently, Monod cannot justifiably dismiss such philosophers as hiding in "our present day ignorance" because Monod's contention rests precariously on his own logical fallacy of misplaced concreteness—his erroneous belief that reductionist scientific abstractions constitute essential reality. He also overlooks the intrinsic reality of his own inquiring mind, a major materialist shortcoming, even as he confidently relies on it in advocating his materialist metaphysics.

Monod's determination that reality is basically mindless matter inexorably leads him to find a meaningless and purposeless universe. Thus, like most materialists, he adopts a tragic vision of the universe as remorselessly indifferent. Chance and necessity have become the decrees of fate, and science and objective knowledge his ultimate concern. Scientific objectivity wards off chaos and provides meaning, certainty, and security amid life's "enormous lottery presided over by natural selection" and man's "total solitude, his fundamental isolation." Yet, for all his railing against "the invention of myths and religions," and against animist ideologies vying with science's quest for objectivity, Monod seems naïvely unaware of the myths to which he has submitted.[74]

There is a cognitive dissonance, moreover, between his materialist thesis and his repeated wonder at "the stunning richness of the biosphere and the amazing variety of forms and behavior it displays," and at "the unfathomable profundity of the genetic and cultural heritage and of the personal experience, conscious or otherwise, which together constitute this being of ours."[75] While rhapsodizing about the beauty of the biosphere, Monod denies any intrinsic metaphysical value or validity to his aesthetic experience. Such qualitative values do not factor in his quantitative world of science and objective truth, so Monod considers them epiphenomenal and lacking intrinsic reality. Whitehead, by contrast, accords fundamental value and importance to this aesthetic quality, which discloses a deeper reality than does "clear" or "objective" reductive science. Monod's own crabbed view of reality, limited as it is to scientific reasoning, causes him to deny the metaphysical significance of his own perceptions of the universe.

In summary, Monod's thesis suffers fundamentally from an absence of perspective. Like Hawking, he gives science alone the role of "clarify[ing] man's relationship to the universe," and he accords to biology "a central position" in this effort.[76] But science, including biology, provides only a partial view of reality, abstracted from the whole. Rather, it is for philosophy "to harmonize the ultimate concepts of science with the ideas drawn from a more concrete survey of the whole of reality."[77] Indeed, philosophy is "the critic of abstractions" like reductionist materialism; it is not merely one among sciences; it is "the survey of sciences, with the special object of their harmony, and of their completion."[78] Science in general and biology in particular are incapable alone of fully clarifying man's relationship to the universe. Thus, Monod has not proven and cannot prove the truth claims for his materialist metaphysics. Epistemological scientism and metaphysical reductionism produce only a limited understanding of reality and deliberately omit the fact of human consciousness and mind. Monod has turned the scientific method into a metaphysical truth, but his metaphysical reach extends well beyond the grasp of his scientific discipline.

Dawkins's Blind Watchmaker — the Neo-Darwinian Explanation

Richard Dawkins, formerly Professor of the Public Understanding of Science at Oxford University, asserts in his 1996 Introduction to *The Blind Watchmaker* (1986) that Darwinism "provides the only satisfying explanation for why we all exist, why we are the way we are. It is the bedrock on which rest all the disciplines known as the humanities." Consequently, he adds, "all human works are the products of brains, brains are evolved data processing devices, and we shall misunderstand their works if we forget this fundamental fact."[79] Thus, Dawkins sets out to explain "not just that the Darwinian world-view *happens* to be true, but that it is the only known theory that *could*, in principle, solve the mystery of our existence ... [n]ot just on this planet but all over the universe wherever life may be found."[80]

By Darwinism, of course, Dawkins does not mean simply the random variation and natural selection described by Darwin, because they cannot alone account for evolution. In addition, Darwinian evolution requires isolation to prevent interbreeding and, most importantly, genetic heredity.[81] During his life Darwin was unaware of Gregor Mendel's 1865 work showing that heredity factors, namely genes, passed intact from one generation to another.[82] Thus, heritable genes provided the mechanism for transferring to successive generations those preferential traits produced by random variations.[83] The application of genetic inheritance completed Darwin's theory of species evolution in what is now called "neo-Darwinism" but is referred to herein simply as "Darwinism." Today most scientists and knowledgeable people accept Darwinism, although it is not clear to what, if any, extent Darwinism has led them to atheism or agnosticism.[84]

Dawkins explains that the apparently premeditated design of complex living organisms resulted from a slow cumulative process over immense time, obviating the need for a supernatural deity. Challenging the argument from design advanced by the eighteenth-century theologian William Paley, Dawkins asserts that "the only watchmaker in nature is the blind forces of physics, albeit deployed in a very special way." Whereas the watchmaker has foresight, Dawkins asserts:

> Natural selection, the blind, unconscious, automatic process which Darwin discovered, and which we now know is the explanation for the existence and apparently purposeful form of all life, has no purpose in mind. It has no mind and no mind's eye. It does not plan for the future. It has no vision, no foresight, no sight at all. If it can be said to play the role of watchmaker in nature, it is the *blind* watchmaker.[85]

Dawkins considers that David Hume's rebuttal to the argument from design was persuasive but not fully satisfying to atheists because Hume offered no alternative explanation for nature's apparent design. For Dawkins, Darwin provided the full explanation, and "made it possible to be an intellectually fulfilled atheist."[86]

Although he attributes all living matter to the laws of physics, Dawkins resists being labeled a reductionist since he does not try "to explain complicated things *directly* in terms of the *smallest* parts," or "as the *sum* of the parts." Rather, he considers himself a "hierarchical reductionist," who "explains a complex entity at any particular level in the hierarchy of organization, in terms of entities only one level down the hierarchy; entities which, themselves, are likely to be complex enough to need further reducing to their own component parts; and so on."[87] Thus, the hierarchical reductionist explains things in terms of their successively smaller units, "which are ultimately explained in terms of the smallest fundamental particles. Reductionism, in this sense, is just another name for an honest desire to understand how things work."[88]

Recognizing the improbability of any single act of chance producing nature's enormous complexity, Dawkins undertakes to "explain its coming into existence as a consequence of gradual, cumulative, step-by-step transformations from simplest things, from primordial objects sufficiently simple to have come into being by chance."[89] Genetic mutations at each evolutionary stage are random, but their natural selection is a nonrandom survival process: "Each successive change in the evolutionary process was simple enough, *relative to its predecessor*, to have arisen by chance. But the whole sequence of cumulative steps constitutes anything but a chance process, when you consider the complexity of the final end-product relative to the original starting point."[90] Thus, the physical process of *cumulative selection*, for Dawkins, "is the blind watchmaker, blind because it does not see ahead, does not plan consequences, has no purpose in view. Yet the living results of natural selection overwhelmingly impress us with the appearance of design as if by a master watchmaker, impress us with the illusion of design and planning."[91]

Having dealt with the "philosophical aspects" of Darwinism, Dawkins turns to the details: DNA patterns, or genes, arranged along chromosomes accurately transmit genetic information in a process aimed "selfishly" at their own survival and the propagation in their gene pool. Genes also program individual organisms to be selfish.[92] Cumulative selection following random genetic mutations over immense time explains all of life, for Dawkins, and seems "powerful enough to make the evolution of intelligence probable, if not inevitable."[93] Furthermore, Dawkins adds that "to explain the origin of the DNA/protein machine by invoking a supernatural Designer is to explain precisely nothing, for it leaves unexplained the origin of the Designer. You have to say something like 'God was always there', and if you allow yourself that kind of lazy way out, you might as well say 'DNA was always there', or 'Life was always there', and be done with it."[94]

So, Dawkins undertakes to prove that either of two theories potentially explains the emergence of life itself: (1) the inorganic mineral theory, which suggests that the DNA/protein machinery may have come into existence as recently as three billion years ago based upon self-replicating inorganic crystals such as silicates; and (2) the organic primeval soup theory, which suggests that carbon chemistry suitable for life produced large molecules that became self-replicating.[95] Given that the universe consists of 100 billion billion planets, Dawkins reasons that the calculated chance of spontaneous self-replication once in about one billion years seems "if anything in danger of erring on the side of being too plausible!" Consequently, for Dawkins, "the present lack of a definitively accepted account of the origin of life should certainly not be taken as a stumbling block for the whole Darwinian worldview."[96]

In his Preface to *The God Delusion* (2006), Dawkins ramps up his attack on the idea of God —a "scientific hypothesis about the universe" that is "spectacularly weak"—by laying into the pseudo-scientific fundamentalist Christian challenges to Darwinian evolution based upon special creation, intelligent design, and irreducible complexity in nature.[97] Citing his book *Climbing Mount Improbable* (1996), Dawkins describes his rebuttal to this argument as follows:

> One side of the mountain is a sheer cliff, impossible to climb, but on the other side is a gentle slope to the summit. On the summit sits a complex device such as an eye or a bacterial flagellar motor. The absurd notion that such complexity could spontaneously self-assemble is symbolized by leaping from the foot of the cliff to the top in one bound. Evolution, by contrast, goes about the back of the mountain and creeps up the gentle slope to the summit: easy! The principle of climbing the gentle slope as opposed to leaping up this precipice is so simple, one is tempted to marvel that it took so long for a Darwin to arrive on the scene and discover it.[98]

Given the implausibility of "the God hypothesis," Dawkins searches out the natural selection pressures that favored such misguided religious behavior and concludes that it is possibly a "misfiring" of several brain modules, an aberrant byproduct of a once-useful childhood propensity to believe what one's parents or tribal elders believed because it favored the child's survival.[99] How neat to charge your opponent's argument, and not your own, with brain misfirings. These misfirings, Dawkins claims, have promoted the "natural tendency towards a *dualistic* theory of mind," which "acknowledges a fundamental distinction between matter and mind" and "believes that mind is some kind of disembodied spirit that *inhabits* the body and therefore conceivably could leave the body and exist somewhere else."[100] By contrast, Dawkins identifies himself as an "intellectual monist" who "believes that mind is a manifestation of matter — material in a brain or perhaps a computer — and cannot exist apart from matter."[101] He then offers a four-fold Darwinian explanation of altruism: man's genetic kinship, generosity motivated by the expectation of returned favors, benefits derived from a reputation for kindness, and personal stature from such reputation.[102] In short, for Dawkins, Darwinism fully explains life, humanity, mind, religion, and morality.

Dennett's Dangerous Idea — Darwin's Algorithmic Design

In *Darwin's Dangerous Idea* (1995), Tufts Professor of Arts and Sciences Daniel C. Dennett reinforces Dawkins's position on Darwinism and its metaphysical implications. "In a single stroke," Dennett asserts, "the idea of evolution by natural selection unifies the realm of life, meaning, and purpose with the realm of space and time, cause and effect, mechanism and physical law."[103] To a skeptical world, Dennett had shown "a scheme for creating Design of Chaos without the aid of Mind."[104] Since neo-Darwinian evolution is now accepted among scientists, Dennett declares we must reject a providential God — "*that* God is, like Santa Claus, a myth of childhood, not anything a sane, undeluded adult could literally believe in. *That* God must either be turned into a symbol for something less concrete or abandoned altogether."[105]

For Dennett, as for Dawkins, Darwinism answers not only the

"how" questions about the development of life but also the "why" questions about teleology and final cause, providing "for the first time, a stable system of explanation" — "the Principle of Accumulation of Design."[106] Dennett regards Darwin's "dangerous idea" as a simple reductionism, namely, an algorithmic process that demystifies existence and dispatches the need for a "skyhook" — the idea of God.[107] "Darwin's dangerous idea is that Design can emerge from mere Order via an algorithmic process that makes no use of pre-existing Mind."[108] Citing Dawkins's "selfish gene," which uses an organism as a survival machine to enhance its continued replication, Dennett identifies the ruthless process of random variation coupled with natural selection as the machinery of nature that "unifies all of biology and the history of our planet into a single grand story."[109] Since Darwin's "universal acid" shows "how even the laws of physics might emerge from chaos or nothingness without resort to a Special Creator, or even a Lawgiver," Dennett sees a fundamental conflict between science and religion, and religion is the loser.[110]

Although they focus and elaborate on Darwinism rather than DNA, the biologist Dawkins and philosopher Dennett add little to the materialist argument of the biochemist Monod in *Chance and Necessity* and, therefore, are susceptible to the same critique. They have erroneously assumed that inductive reasoning can answer metaphysical questions about meaning and purpose; they have mistaken their reductionist abstractions for concrete reality; they have discounted human consciousness and intelligence as if they were not intrinsic to "objective" reality; they have assumed that their minds are trustworthy while simultaneously attributing them entirely to a mindless evolutionary process; they have failed to recognize that their inductive reasoning alone necessarily leads to a meaningless and mindless cosmos; and they have failed to apply their critical intelligence to the broad empiricism required for any comprehensive metaphysics.

Darwin, Design, and the Dover Decision

Dawkins and Dennett have obviously undertaken more than a scientific defense of Darwinian evolution. They have zeroed in on what they consider to be Darwinism's religious implications, namely, the death of the "God hypothesis." As apologists for reductive and evolutionary materialism, Dawkins and Dennett have issued a pointed challenge to theism. They assert that a providential God is illusory since random genetic mutation, blind natural selection, and immense cosmic time fully account for all of life. In addition, they have effectively rebutted the intelligent design (ID) theorists who claim that Darwinism cannot account for the "irreducible complexity" in aspects of nature. While Dawkins's rebuttal has dignified ID as conventional theism, in fact ID does not represent theology's best effort to maintain intellectual space for belief in God after Darwin.

As discussed in Chapter 4, special creationists of the young earth and old earth persuasions believe that the Bible is divinely inspired, inerrant even on matters of science, and reliable evidence that God created nature and life in specific ways. As the United States Supreme Court has held, however, creation science or creationism is not science but religion.[111] It fails to consider the wide array of information from multiple scientific disciplines supporting Darwinian evolution and, instead, considers the Bible to be a scientifically accurate and superior account of life, irrespective of modern scientific discoveries. In comparing the Bible to the *Origin of Species*, explains Haught, creationism "trivializes religion by artificially imposing scientific expectations upon the sacred text whose objective is in no sense one of satisfying scientific curiosity." Instead, creationists overlook the real biblical message about trust and gratitude for the gift of life and about openness "to the ultimate mystery of the universe."[112]

In contrast to scientific creationists, ID theorists eschew biblical authority and advance a purportedly scientific argument that the irreducible complexity of many biochemical systems belie "Darwin's gradualist process of natural selection sifting random mutations."[113] In this new twist to William Paley's old argument from design, Lehigh Professor of Biochemistry Michael Behe asserts that gradual evolution by natural selection cannot alone account for the irreducible complexity discovered in biology.[114] Baylor mathematician William A. Dembski adds a mathematical argument to Behe's biochemical argument by asserting that as a matter of statistical probability "biological complexity is not exclusively the result of material mechanisms but also requires intelligence."[115] Additionally, American philosopher of science Stephen C. Meyer asserts that intelligent design provides a better explanation than Darwinism for the specific and complex information needed to account for the sudden appearance of new animal body parts and organizations during the Cambrian explosion 350 million years ago.[116]

Like creation science, however, ID theory is religion masquerading as science. The ID theorists' claim—that some master intelligence rather than blind natural selection is necessary to account for the otherwise improbable and irreducible complexity of genes, proteins, and body organization—offers no explanation of evolution's obvious imperfections. Furthermore, it insulates itself from empirical testing and, consequently, is not proper science.[117] The former Harvard Professor of Entomology E.O. Wilson also observes that ID rests entirely upon a default argument with no positive supporting evidence, and it offers no mechanism "to explain the transcription from supernatural force to organic reality."[118] Although ID theorists like Behe and Dembski assert that intelligent design rests on empirical evidence and deductive logic presupposing no Creator or theology, the *Dover Area School District* case laid bare both the religious motives and the scientific flaws of ID theory.

In 2004, the Board of Education in Dover, Pennsylvania directed high school biology teachers to mention ID as an alternative to Darwinian evolution and invited students to read *Of Pandas and People* to learn about ID and problems and gaps in evolutionary theory. A group of parents challenged the directive in federal court on grounds that teaching ID in public schools violates the First Amendment prohibition against establishment of religion. Behe testified as the school board's principal scientist in the case. Brown Professor of Biology Kenneth R. Miller, author of the standard biology textbook found wanting by the Dover school board for failing to mention ID, testified as the principal scientist for the parents challenging the school board directive.

First, the court traced the well-documented history of the ID Movement (IDM). It began with the fundamentalist fervor against Darwinism beginning in the 1920s, continued as an anti-evolution movement through the 1960s, emerged as scientific creationism enacted into Louisiana's "balanced treatment" law that the United States Supreme Court struck down in the 1987 *Edwards* case, and culminated in ID theory. The court found that the IDM was a religious response to the *Edwards* decision intended "to change the ground rules of science to make room for religion, specifically, beliefs consonant with a particular version of Christianity."[119] ID is a form of creationism based upon the old religious argument for the existence of God and "anyone familiar with Western religious thought would immediately make the association that the tactically unnamed designer is God."[120] Furthermore, *Of Pandas and People* was sponsored by a Christian organization and written by creationists who "deliberately and systematically" replaced its prior references to creation, God, creationism, and Genesis with the phrase ID after the *Edwards* decision.[121] Finally the court found that "the Goal of the IDM is not to encourage critical thought, but to foment a revolution which would supplant evolutionary theory with ID."[122]

Second, the court concluded that ID is not science because it invokes supernatural causation, "the same flawed and illogical contrived dualism that doomed creation science in the 1980s," and has been "refuted by the scientific community," including the National Academy of Sciences and the American Association for the Advancement of Science.[123] Whereas science is "limited to the search for natural causes to explain natural phenomena," ID "is predicated on supernatural causation."[124] Furthermore, irreducible complexity, the centerpiece of ID theory, "is a negative argument against evolution, not proof of design," and scientific evidence fails to support Behe's three selected examples of irreducible complexity. Scientific studies have shown possible precursors to the purportedly irreducible complex bacterial flagellum; several peer-reviewed studies have disproven the alleged irreducible complexity of the blood-clotting cascade; and innumerable peer-reviewed publications, books, and immunology textbooks have "confirmed each element of the evolutionary hypothesis explaining the origin of the immune system."[125] Consequently, the court concluded that ID "cannot be judged a valid, accepted scientific theory as it has failed to publish in peer-reviewed journals, engage in research and testing, and gain acceptance in the scientific community."[126]

The *Dover* case was a scientific debacle for ID and irreducible complexity, but in no sense did the case pit science against God, as Dawkins and Dennett do regularly. This supposed conflict is false and unwarranted, but creationists and ID theorists have mistakenly accepted it as real. The contention of Dawkins and Dennett that evolution fully accounts for nature's design and totally discredits theism assumes erroneously that Darwinism and God occupy the same explanatory slot. Creationists and ID theorists bit on this sophistic bait, conflating science and religion themselves, and responding as if their only choice were between God and Darwinism. Moreover, by arguing that divine intervention is necessary to bring about life on earth, they have sold God short. As Miller noted in an article on the *Dover* case, they implicitly assume "that the universe is *not* so intelligently designed as to make the evolution of life even possible or inevitable."[127] Despite its elements of chance and waste, however, Darwinian evolution is not inconsistent with a perception of order, meaning, and purpose in the universe. As the Catholic Church has concluded, "even the outcome of a truly contingent natural process can nonetheless fall within God's providential plan for creation."[128]

Both sides of this misbegotten debate have fixated on nature's design rather than its drama and meaning, and have missed the essential point that a perfect world would be finished, static, dead, and futureless. "If life were perfectly designed right now, as Dawkins's implicit theology demands," writes Haught, "there could be no drama at all. Perfect design would mean that the work of life has been finalized. There would be no story but only stiff and static structures to talk about."[129] He warns the debaters that "the flawlessly engineered world they prefer would be dead on delivery. Since it would already be perfect, it would also be finished; and if finished, it would have no future."[130] Therefore, by associating teleology or purpose with design or order in the universe the debaters have overlooked the potential existential significance and value of evolution itself.

Teilhard and Whitehead, for example, describe the universe as self-actuating, with humanity emerging over time to play a creative role in the divinely inspired adventure of the universe toward aesthetic harmony, beauty, and perfection. As discussed in Chapter 5, Teilhard considers that underlying evolution is a movement in the direction of complexity and consciousness, the product of non-coercive divine inspiration operating invisibly beneath the seeming randomness of evolutionary change. Whitehead considers that "the teleology of the universe is directed to the production of Beauty," and that "God's purpose in the creative advance is the evocation of intensities."[131] In this quest for greater beauty and intensity lies the risk of disorder and suffering, acknowledges Whitehead, but "the immanence of God gives reason for the belief that pure chaos is intrinsically impossible."[132] In a word, the debate over design has trivialized the idea of God and is woefully out of step with mainstream theology, which fully accepts Darwinian evolution.[133]

The Pretensions of Materialism

For Hawking, Monod, Dawkins, and Dennett, the combination of complex gravity, DNA, and evolution fully explain the universe and earthly life, rendering theism an irrational self-delusion. In advancing their position, however, these materialists have segued from science into philosophy. They have found personally satisfying scientific answers to their "how" questions about the cause of the cosmos, life, and mind, and have used them to answer the most vexing "why" questions of traditional Western philosophy: Why is there something rather than nothing? Why do we exist? Why do we possess a mind? Why do we question the meaning of existence? Darwinian evolution may explain *how* nature produced the human mind, but it cannot explain *why* we have a mind, *why* our minds seek understanding, *why* we trust our minds to interpret reality, or *why* we think reality is worth investigating. These "why" questions lie beyond the intellectual bounds of empirical science. Science can provide answers about the causes of events in the world but it cannot provide answers about the meaning, value, and purpose of the world. In searching for the latter answers, humanity must look to philosophy and theology, as it has always done.

These four materialists ignore such concerns about the epistemological limitations of the scientific method when concluding that the universe at bottom is mindless matter. What materialists mean by matter, of course, is fraught with uncertainty. The ancient Greek Democritus thought material reality consisted of indestructible atoms, but today's conception of atomic matter is problematic, with the interchangeability of matter and energy, the duality of waves and particles, and the contribution of mass to subatomic particles and perhaps the whole universe via the Higgs boson, the so-called "God particle." However materialists choose to define it, matter is the sole source of mind for them. By contrast, the theistic arguments for God "show that mind is the ultimate reality, and that materialism is a delusion caused by misuse of modern science," explains Keith Ward; and "once you are a committed materialist, God has to be a delusion."[134] The fundamental dispute between theism and materialism, therefore, boils down to whether ultimate reality is mind or matter.

In presenting their case for matter, materialists largely ignore the great Western philosophers —Plato and Aristotle, Descartes and Locke, Kant and Hegel—who argued that mind or spirit lies hidden outside the material world of appearances. Indeed, as Ward points out, even the dissenters from theism like David Hume and A.J. Ayre were not materialists and considered the world to be constructed from "impressions and ideas" or "sense-data."[135] Instead of systematically addressing these opposing philosophical views, materialists uncritically adopt the scientific method as their source of ultimate truth without any discussion of the method's provenance, assumptions, or limitations. As discussed in Chapter 1, however, the scientific method was built upon Enlightenment faith in nature's inherent order and rationality, and inductive reasoning implicitly rests upon this antecedent metaphysical conviction, drawn from medieval theology and rationalism. Ignoring this history, materialists have turned the scientific method itself into a metaphysic. But reductionism is a metaphysical leap, not a scientific proof; questionable philosophy, not verifiable science. Inductive reasoning, scientific concepts, and methodological reductions are indispensable for discovering and explaining *how* things happen, but they cannot explain *why* things happen.

Dawkins denigrates the "God of the gaps" as a scientific hypothesis, which it most certainly is not. The idea of God is a metaphysical statement about the ultimate source of contingent reality, existing outside of time and space and beyond the realm of science. God has a personal answer to questions about why things are as they are. Dawkins also blames the idea of God for impeding scientific understanding: "if you don't understand how something works, never mind: just give up and say God did it."[136] Ward rightly characterizes this as "one of the most obviously false statements in the history of human thought" since Christianity's conviction about nature's intelligibility actually inspired the Enlightenment leaders of science:

> Scientific explanation should be pushed as far as it can go. Belief in God supports this push, because it guarantees that the universe is ultimately intelligible. But it adds that scientific explanation is not the only form of explanation. Scientific explanation drives you back in the end, to eternity and necessity—to the realm of timeless and necessary mathematical truths, to ultimately intelligible laws and fundamental forces. But what is also needed for a final explanation is appeal to consciousness, value, creativity and purpose. Personal explanation complements, but does not replace, scientific explanation. Both are necessary to a truly final explanation of the universe.[137]

The idea of God is not, as Dawkins and Dennett assert, a "lazy way out" of scientific questions or a "sky-hook" solution; rather, as Teilhard urges, it "satisfies the yearnings that are born in our hearts in the school of science."

The scientific method and "objective" knowledge cannot usefully serve as the exclusive source of truth about reality, as materialists claim, because they contain an inherent bias toward a mindless, purposeless, and meaningless universe. Science alone cannot find otherwise. Consequently, scientism is an epistemological and metaphysical dead end. The investigation of meaning and purpose requires broader modes of inquiry and different ways of seeing into the mystery of existence than simply science. It requires critical thinking and responsible judgment following careful attention to ideas drawn from a broad survey of experience, including science. Most importantly, it requires attention to attentiveness itself, as Canadian Jesuit philosopher and theologian Bernard Lonergan (1904-1984) has urged.[138] The investigation must take cognizance of humanity's conscious striving for understanding and truth, which materialism overlooks.

In practice, everyone accepts the irreducible and immaterial reality of the human mind. Even the materialists trust their minds, their desire for truth, and their implicit conviction about the value of truth. They do not dismiss these qualities of mind as merely the arbitrary firings of brain synapses signifying nothing valuable. Their commitment to science and correct thinking, exemplified in Monod's "ethic of knowledge" and "postulate of objectivity," transcends mere adaptive brain processes. The human mind with its striving for meaning and truth is unquestionably real, and no conception of reality is credible or complete that ignores its essential reality. Science alone, however, cannot explain why the cosmos produced the human mind because it cannot answer these "why" questions. Yet the emergence of the human mind during the cosmic evolutionary drama begs for a more comprehensive and convincing explanation than materialism provides. It calls for an explanation commensurate with this profoundly important occurrence.

The attribution of the human mind solely to a blind evolutionary accident occurring within senseless matter suggests a magical happenstance inconsistent with the empirical explanatory basis upon which materialism purportedly rests. The materialists' conclusion that some 150,000 years ago unintelligent matter alone produced human intelligence seems like miraculous alchemy, turning material dross into intellectual gold. Rather, the emergence of mind invites a teleological explanation of existence, a cosmic predisposition toward the development of human consciousness and mind. Theism proffers one such explanation, namely, that a permanent cosmic intelligence pre-existed the Big Bang and that mind (God) rather than matter is fundamental reality. Furthermore, the idea of God complements and does not compete with scientific discoveries, like the Big Bang theory and Darwinian evolution; it invests them with cosmic meaning, value, and purpose. It imbues the universe and human life with inherent beauty, goodness, and futurity—an alternative conception of reality entirely lost to materialism's pretentious claims to scientific truth.

What engenders unwarranted confidence in the materialist conception of reality is scientific hubris, a willful disdain and disregard for other, more comprehensive ways of seeing and interpreting human experience of the world than science alone can provide. In *Mind and Cosmos* (2012), the prominent New York University Professor of Philosophy Thomas Nagel concludes that materialism is inherently incapable of adequately accounting for human consciousness and mind because it rests upon "conceptual and probabilistic contortions" and constitutes "a heroic triumph of ideological theory over common sense."[139] Although an atheist himself, Nagel perceives a "natural teleology" in the universe, "a cosmic predisposition to the formation of life, consciousness, and the value that is inseparable from them."[140] Consequently Nagel urges contemporary enlightened culture to "wean itself of the materialism and Darwinism of the gaps," which he considers "antecedently unbelievable," and "almost certainly false."[141] In short, reductive materialism does not deserve its current prominence, and most certainly does not deserve its claims to scientific truth. The secular intellectual community must broaden its perspective and recognize science's epistemological and metaphysical limitations along with its wondrous achievements and enormous capabilities.

9

Conclusion

The aim of science is to seek the simplest explanations of complex facts. We are apt to fall into the error of thinking that the facts are simple because simplicity is the goal of our quest. The guiding motto in the life of every natural philosopher should be, Seek simplicity and distrust it.
— Alfred North Whitehead, *The Concept of Nature*[1]

I want to urge you as much as I can, dear friend, to be patient toward all that is unsolved in your heart and to try to love the questions themselves like locked rooms and like books that are written in a very foreign tongue. Do not seek to have answers, which cannot be given to you because you would not be able to live them. And the point is to live everything. Live the questions now. Perhaps you will then gradually, without noticing it, live along some distant day to answer.
—Rainer Maria Rilke, *Letters to a Young Poet*[2]

World War I precipitated a revolution in Western thought unprecedented for its speed and radicalism. The Christian revolution had transformed the ancient world gradually over centuries, and the scientific revolution had introduced modernity without destabilizing the divinely ordered universe. The nineteenth century was an age of revolutions—an age of anarchy, writes Matthew Arnold—with the Romantic Movement, the Young Hegelians, and Darwinian Evolution, among others, and with Nietzsche calling for a transvaluation of values. But these nineteenth-century revolutions, like those preceding them, came with new icons to replace the fallen ones. The Romantics saw God in nature, the Young Hegelians saw humanity as god, and the Bergsonians saw evolution's *élan vital* as of God, if not God himself. With World War I, however, the nineteenth century perturbations became a giant tsunami, opening an unbridgeable gap between the civilizations before and after. The dangerous new era in Western culture that Nietzsche anticipated had finally arrived; the world had become "unchained" and had left humanity "straying as through an infinite nothing."[3] This was no "normal" revolution; the war radically altered the Western worldview. People were adrift in a seemingly indifferent universe, permanent strangers in an alien cosmos devoid of recognizable guideposts or standards. This was not the self-alienation of the Young Hegelians; this was *cosmic alienation*. For Franklin Baumer, "These words signified not merely the toppling, but the abandonment, of absolutes. *This* was what was new, above everything else: not iconoclasm *per se*, which is characteristic of every revolution of the mind, but the realization, widespread in the twentieth century as never before, that icons were always changing and would continue to change."[4]

Suddenly, the world had become untrustworthy, the transcendent in doubt, and the old theological questions meaningless. The war had shattered long-standing beliefs, removed traditional absolutes, and compelled entirely new answers. The following century did little to restore cosmic meaning for Western civilization because World War I, sadly, was not "the war to end all wars." War continued in the violent labor and political wars, the Russian civil war, the Second World War, the Korean War, and so on. The twentieth century, writes Niall Ferguson, was "without question the bloodiest century in modern history, far more violent in relative as well as absolute terms than any previous era."[5] Faced with unsettling and unrelieved turmoil in the extended wake of World War I, Western culture sought answers amid surrounding uncertainty, but its answers did not redress the bleak picture of the universe that appeared in 1918. Instead, with three prominent exceptions, Western culture largely ignored metaphysical concerns, especially the implications of modern science for cosmic meaning and purpose. The most prominent exceptions were materialism, fundamentalism, and evolutionary or process thought. Materialism found metaphysical certainty in science, fundamentalism in the Bible, and process thought in change itself. This chapter offers a perspective on the opposing metaphysical paradigms of materialism and fundamentalism, proposes a basis for dialogue between them, and urges process thought as an alternative paradigm for the changing world that followed the Great War.

Comparing Two Incommensurable Worldviews

The opposing protagonists in the debate over the metaphysical implications of Darwinian evolution represent two fundamentally different worldviews. The creationists and ID theorists inhabit a world believed to be created and overseen by a personal God thoroughly involved with humankind. The materialists inhabit a world believed to be the product of an impersonal necessity ruled by indifferent physical laws. These are the disparate worlds of faith and reason, moral man and intellectual man, Jerusalem and Athens, Hebraism and Hellenism. William Barrett describes Hebraic man as "passionately committed to his own mortal being," and Hellenic man as the "the philosopher or pure scientist, [who] looks upon existence with detachment."[6] These two protagonists approach the Darwinian debate from the vantage point of their different worldviews—two worldviews that are *incommensurable* and have remained so ever since the breakdown of the medieval synthesis of faith and reason. They are incommensurable, by definition, because they lack any common measure or standard of comparison. There is no neutral third paradigm that can embrace them both and adjudicate or resolve their fundamental differences over whether or not the universe is ultimately the product of transcendent design. But, as Haverford Professor of Philosophy Richard J. Bernstein has shown, they can participate in a dialogue and achieve an understanding of their differences and agreements.[7]

Materialism and Scientism. Materialism has deep roots in Western philosophy, beginning with the atomistic philosophy of Democritus in the fourth century B.C.E., with its uncanny resemblance to modern science. For Democritus, nature consisted of an infinite number of indestructible atoms existing in space or the void, colliding without purpose or design by a creator or designer, and forming various atomic clusters that comprise everything in nature. Atomistic materialism accounted for humankind and human thought, the latter resulting entirely from physical processes.[8] Epicurus (341-270

B.C.E.) elaborated Democritus's physics, claiming that the eternal atoms would "swerve" as they fell in space, forming the clusters that constituted all beings, including divine beings. Epicurus enhanced Democritus's physics with an ethics, and Lucretius (98-55 B.C.E.) memorialized both the physics and the ethics in poetry, *On the Nature of Things (De Rerum Natura)*, celebrated by Stephen Greenblatt in *The Swerve* (2011).[9] For Epicurus and Lucretius, humanity need not fear God or death; God does not reward, punish, or interfere with humanity, and death simply returns atomic matter to nature. Instead, humanity should pursue the good life, which, for Epicurus and Lucretius, meant maximizing pleasure and minimizing pain by controlling desires, overcoming fears, and exalting pleasures of the mind.[10]

"The problem with Epicurus and Lucretius," wrote Greenblatt, "was not their paganism—after all, Aristotle too was a pagan—but rather their physics. Atomism absolutely denied the key distinction between substance and accidents, and therefore threatened the whole magnificent intellectual edifice resting on Aristotelian foundations."[11] According to Greenblatt, the Catholic Church suppressed Lucretius's poem after its rediscovery in 1417 for over two centuries until the Enlightenment, not because of atomism *per se*, since the world obviously was made of something, but because atomism denied the Eucharistic dogma of transubstantiation, the bread and wine (accidents of nature) becoming the actual body and blood of Christ (substance of God) upon consecration.[12] Today, the point of disagreement between materialism and fundamentalism still remains the physics, not its Eucharistic implications, but its denial of the spiritual realm and claim that matter rather than mind is ultimate reality.

Modern science has elaborated upon the ancient physics about matter and space. Today we understand that atoms have subatomic particles, appear as waves as well as particles, change their mass via the Higgs boson, and are interchangeable with energy. We also understand that space is interrelated with time and, to quote Hawking, "is curved and distorted by the mass and energy in it."[13] While modern science has refined our understanding of matter and space, it has not changed the essential and ancient materialist claim that at bottom reality is just mindless matter. What has changed between

the ancient and the modern materialists is scientism, the epistemological claim that "objective" science is the only reliable source
of truth and that everything else, as Bernstein explains this viewpoint, is "pseudo-knowledge"—merely "noncognitive emotional
responses or private subjective preferences."[14] Bernstein attributes
this objectivist state of mind to "Cartesian Anxiety," referring to
Descartes's effort to find a "fixed foundation" for knowledge and
thereby to "escape the forces of darkness that envelop us with madness, with intellectual and moral chaos."[15] Cartesian Anxiety has a
seductive appeal, and leads to a desire for certainty and objectivism, an "Archimedean point" on which to ground all knowledge.
Furthering this quest for certainty is a fear that without objectivism we inevitably face the quagmire of relativism. Calling this a
false dichotomy, Bernstein urges proponents of scientism to look
beyond the objectivist "belief that there are or must be some fixed,
permanent constraints to which we can appeal and which are secure and stable," and to recognize instead that epistemological scientism "is deficient; it leaves out something vitally important, or
fails to recognize that there are other legitimate forms of experience
and knowledge."[16]

Whitehead reminds us that science is reductionist, its aim "is to
seek the simplest explanations of complex facts," but that philosophy must not "fall into the error of thinking that the facts are simple because simplicity is the goal of our quest. The guiding motto
in the life of every natural philosopher should be, Seek simplicity
and distrust it."[17] Materialists have fallen into the error of believing
that science's reductionist abstractions about complex facts provide
the full explanation of ultimate reality. Philosophy should serve as
the critic of such abstractions and endeavor to harmonize scientific
concepts with the ideas drawn from a broader perception of reality.[18] Materialists, however, have forsaken the responsibility they
undertook as philosophers by assuming that science in general and
biology in particular can fully clarify humanity's relationship to the
universe. To the contrary, this important metaphysical endeavor
requires a broader empiricism than science allows and a broader
application of critical intelligence than inductive reasoning.

Materialists must recognize that science abstracts from reality
as a whole and limits the field of knowledge, and that they can

open themselves to other forms of knowledge and experience when addressing questions of meaning and purpose in existence without sacrificing objectivity. This broad concept of reason involves what Bernstein describes as "a continuous dialectical tacking" between the details of inductive discovery and the global mystery of reality.[19] While advances in evolutionary biology can explain the causal mechanism for the organization of living beings, evolution itself does not necessarily constitute an ultimate explanation for our existence. It does not predetermine the kinds of organisms, or address the origin of life or the universe, or explain nature's constant, creative striving for newer and higher forms of order. Science looks only for cause and not for purpose in nature; it can explain *how* Darwinian evolution constitutes the mechanism but cannot explain *why* it happens to be nature's mechanism. If nature and the cosmos harbor any ultimate purpose, science alone cannot uncover it. In approaching the question of whether reality has any ultimate meaning, therefore, materialists must learn to ask different questions beyond the bounds of science.

Dennett asserts that Darwin's idea is a "universal acid" that "eats through just about every traditional concept, and leaves in its wake a revolutionized worldview, with most of the old landmarks still recognizable, but transformed in fundamental ways."[20] But, this same universal acid apparently does not cut through Dennett's unquestioned assumption that his sweeping statement deserves our serious attention, even though it flows from a mind that he claims is solely the product of a mindless evolutionary process. As Dennett's statement implies but his philosophy denies, our minds are inherently real and considered trustworthy. They are not just epiphenomena of evolutionary brain matter, but also essential reality. Dennett has not heeded Heidegger's teaching; we are fundamentally beings who seek to understand and interpret reality, who question the very meaning of being: "Why are there beings at all, and why not rather nothing?"[21] Our questioning minds are the very essence of our being, yet science alone is incapable of answering our most fundamental concerns. Science cannot investigate or explain the idea of nothingness or its relation to being. Evolution may explain how nature produced the human mind, but it does not explain why we have a mind, why our minds seek understanding, why we trust our minds to interpret reality, or why we think reality is worth investigating.

The human mind with its insatiable thirst for understanding is an inseparable and intrinsic part of nature, and its quest for meaning does not simply stand "out there" to be discovered scientifically. Meaning is realized through a "happening" of understanding, as philosophers like Whitehead and Bernstein remind us.[22] To ascertain whether there is meaning and purpose in nature, we must become open to, and have an encounter with, reality—letting reality "speak to us" in a continuous process that never achieves finality. Bernstein explains that meaning "is always *coming into being* through the 'happening' of understanding," and Haught explains that such understanding requires "other ways of seeing, understanding and knowing than those available to scientific inquiry."[23] Furthermore, "because science deliberately leaves out any concern with value, meaning, importance, subjectivity, intentionality or purpose," Haught adds, "it cannot even in principle tell us whether or not these are features of the real world."[24] The quest for meaning requires other methods of seeing the world, which involve our intuition, subjectivity, aesthetics, and historical sense.[25] Reductionism is a demonstrably effective approach to scientific inquiry and to technical development, but is wholly inadequate to find purpose in nature. Furthermore, scientism and "objective" knowledge inevitably bias the results toward finding a universe without purpose. Scientism is methodologically incapable of finding otherwise; it is a philosophical dead end.

Fundamentalism. With the widespread acceptance of Darwinian evolution, fundamentalists inevitably encountered the materialist views that divine providence does not guide nature and that reality is mindless and godless. Instead of recognizing and addressing materialism as a philosophic point of view rather than a scientific truth, fundamentalists ill-advisedly chose to do battle on the underlying science. They challenged Darwinian science with creationism and ID, both forms of "natural theology," which seeks evidence of God in nature. Fundamentalists looked for the divine hand in the remarkable scientific complexity of certain organisms, assuming that the cause must be either an intelligent designer or a mindless process.[26] Such mono-causal, either/or thinking prejudges the ongoing scientific investigation of life-forms and oversimplifies nature; it seeks to objectify and demystify existence with a single explanation. Introducing a master intelligence into the interstices of evolutionary biology is a scientific nonstarter and an unconvincing counterargument to materialism. In addition, as Haught explains, "it is theologically misguided in assuming that a 'master intelligence' would influence and interact with the created world in a way that could be scientifically detectable."[27] ID reduces divine mystery to an explanatory pigeonhole.

Darwinian evolution constitutes the current scientific paradigm, which neither ID nor creationism will ever likely supplant. In order to remain relevant, therefore, fundamentalists need to accept rather than challenge Darwinian evolution, recognizing that no single discipline (science or theology) can provide an exhaustive explanation of existence and that evolution can have profound spiritual implications.[28] Their search for ultimate meaning requires the use of a far wider lens that takes into account modern science as well as biblical scholarship.[29] For example, what if fundamentalists were to reinterpret the bronze-age cosmology of Genesis in light of Darwinian (and cosmic) evolution in order to help explain and give meaning to an evolving universe? What if God made humankind through gradual evolution from cosmic dust rather than special creation from Edenic soil? What if Original Sin is not Adam and Eve's disobedience in a lost earthly paradise but humanity's pervasive neglect of its creative responsibilities to an unfinished cosmic future? What if cosmic perfection lies not behind us in a mythical Edenic past but before us in an idyllic absolute future?[30]

The perfect, instantly created world of Genesis, which fundamentalists take so literally, would have no vitality, no promise, no future.[31] By contrast, evolutionary thought, like that of Whitehead and Teilhard, offers a theologically compatible view of nature and nature's God. Whitehead sees evolution as a cosmic and human adventure toward aesthetic value, integrating intensity with harmony, novelty with stability, and complexity with order. He thinks of God as a persuasive rather than controlling love, luring the universe toward perfection, and as the source of order and novelty in increasing levels of complexity.[32]

Haught describes evolutionary theology as engaging both neo-

Darwinian and cosmic evolution in thinking about God and God's involvement with humanity and the world:

> Evolutionary theology claims that the story of life, even in its neo-Darwinian presentation, provides essential concepts for thinking about God and God's relation to nature and humanity. However, it also agrees with Polkinghorne and others that all serious theological reflection on biological evolution today must be situated in the more expansive context of "cosmic evolution." It would be artificial in the extreme to relate theology to neo-Darwinian evolution without taking into account the entire physical universe that has sponsored the emergence of life.
>
> Evolutionary theology, unlike natural theology, does not search for definitive footprints of the divine in nature. It is not terribly concerned about "intelligent design," since such a notion seems entirely too lifeless to capture the dynamic and even disturbing way in which the God of biblical religion interacts with the world. Instead of trying to prove God's existence from nature, evolutionary theology seeks to show how our new awareness of cosmic and biological evolution can enhance and enrich traditional teachings about God and God's ways of acting in the world. In other words, rather than viewing evolution simply as a dangerous challenge that deserves an apologetic response, evolutionary theology discerns in evolution a most illuminating context for our thinking about God today.[33]

Whatever the content of its particular evolutionary theology, however, fundamentalists must conceive of divine providence as something other than special design within nature in order to be credible and relevant today.

Toward a Dialogue between Materialism and Fundamentalism

As incommensurable worldviews, materialism and fundamentalism are susceptible to comparison but not resolution, to dialogue but not agreement, because there is no neutral algorithm to resolve this dispute between their competing paradigms of an indifferent versus a purposeful reality. Materialism is deeply rooted in the Greek tragic world of necessity—impersonal, remorseless, and in-different—and fundamentalism in the ancient Abrahamic world-view—personal, relational, and governed by an actively involved God. Nevertheless, as Bernstein urges, through mutual respect, openness, and genuine willingness to listen and understand, these two paradigms can enlarge and enrich themselves by a "fusion of horizons" through a dialogical encounter that seeks validation through argument.[34] Materialism and fundamentalism must rec-ognize that their war of words over Darwinian evolution is fun-damentally a metaphysical and not a scientific dispute. They both consider Darwinian evolution to be incompatible with divine prov-idence—materialism because it involves blind chance and mindless natural selection, and fundamentalism because it removes the de-signing hand of God. Neither position, however, is entirely defen-sible. Materialism argues from a narrow, abstract, and reductionist view of reality using a methodology incapable of finding purpose in nature, while ID theory argues from a theological view of real-ity incapable of empirical testing. Thus, each debating position is overly simplistic and has something to learn from the other.[35]

Dialogue might begin with both sides acknowledging the lim-its of their methodology: the scientific method cannot investigate questions of ultimate meaning and purpose in the universe, and ID and creationism are not testable scientific propositions. The dia-logical goal, according to German sociologist and philosopher Jur-gen Habermas, "is to bring about an agreement that terminates in the intersubjective mutuality of reciprocal understanding, shared knowledge, mutual trust, and accord with one another." Commu-nicative action "has nothing to do with propositional truth, but has everything to do with the truthfulness of intentional expres-sions and with the rightness of norms."[36] To Habermas's assertion, American philosopher Richard Rorty adds that dialogue, such as here proposed between proponents of fundamentalism and ma-terialism, will not provide metaphysical comfort but can help in "coping with the contingencies of human life" and in developing "a renewed sense of community." Rorty adds that "what matters is our loyalty to other human beings clinging together against the dark, not our hope of getting things right."[37]

The Unholy Grail of Certitude

In their different ways the proponents of materialism and fundamentalism both are looking for the psychological comfort of certitude before the immense mystery of existence. In an effort to objectify and demystify existence with a single explanation, they have simplistically determined that nature allows only one of two possible choices, a mindless process or an intelligent designer. In *Consilience* (1998), Edward O. Wilson epitomizes this narrow quest for metaphysical certainty when reporting his personal encounter with the powerfully competing lures of creationism and materialism.[38] Growing up a fundamentalist Baptist, Wilson apparently interpreted biblical cosmology literally as scientific truth. Then, upon discovering evolution in college, he turned to scientism as his belief system and adopted the materialist worldview. The certitude provided by either position has an undeniably powerful, if ultimately misguided, psychic appeal. As Bernstein urges, we must confront Cartesian Anxiety, liberate ourselves from the false fixation of certainty, and confront the mystery of existence with an open mind that draws upon all aspects of our experience, including science. In practice, we routinely place our trust not just in empirical evidence, but also in our intuition, feelings, and aesthetic sense when making our most important life choices, such as whom we love. Scientific analysis cannot explain or account for the beauty, inspiration, and wonder of human love, yet we trust our primal, non-theoretic modes of cognitive experience in responding to this interpersonal mystery. Fundamentally, the approach of neo-Darwinian materialism, like that of creationism and ID theory, is narrow-minded and represents a lack of courage to face honestly the ineluctable mystery of reality.

Understanding engages our subjective as well as theoretic modes of contact with the world—our desire to know, our feelings for the subjectivity of other people, our historical sense about the long cosmic process, and our aesthetic sense of surrounding beauty, which we have historically aligned with truth. This personal search for truth is elusive and unending. As the Austrian poet Rainer Maria Rilke stressed about humanity's quest for truth (quoted above), we must "try to love the questions themselves," indeed, "to live them." Materialism short-circuits that inquiry about potential cosmic purpose by denying any validity to nonscientific modes of thought. But scientism is a myopic approach to reality that leads inexorably toward materialism's bleak metaphysics, a world devoid of dramatic coherence, aesthetic aim, and inherent goodness. Materialism prejudges the inquiry and imprisons humans in a colorless, odorless, senseless, and valueless reality—a godless universe—because scientism can provide no other. Fundamentalism short-circuits that inquiry by focusing on the literal words rather than the spiritual message of the Bible about our world. As Teilhard recognized upon emerging from the trenches of the Great War, "We are moving! We are going forward!" Experience leads us to recognize, says Teilhard, that nature is "becoming" and in "self-creation," that humanity too is in "the full flood" of change, and that "our nobility consists in serving, like intelligent atoms, the work proceeding in the Universe."[39]

Materialism's dominance over modern consciousness almost to the exclusion of a purposeful worldview remains the unfortunate legacy of the Great War. At primary fault in enabling this unchallenged rise of ideological materialism to its undeserved intellectual reign is postwar Western culture. From World War I until very recently, theology, philosophy, literature, and art have remained largely disengaged from materialism's unwarranted epistemological and metaphysical truth-claims and thereby have carelessly ceded unjustified preeminence to the neo-Darwinian materialist worldview and its increasingly strident New Atheism.

Notes

Chapter 1. Introduction

1. William Shakespeare, *Julius Caesar,* ed. Lewis B. Wright (New York: Washington Square Press, 1964), 3.2, 56-57.

2. "August 1914 is the axial date in modern Western history, and once past it we are directly confronted with the present-day world," William Barrett, *Irrational Man* (Garden City: Doubleday Anchor Books, 1958), 28; "The Great War was to be the axis on which the modern world would turn," Modris Eksteins, *Rites of Spring: The Great War and the Birth of the Modern Age* (Boston: Houghton Mifflin Company, 1989), 237; the Great War "was a hideous embarrassment to the prevailing Meliorist myth which had dominated the public consciousness for a century. It reversed the Idea of Progress," Paul Fussell, *The Great War and Modern Memory* (Oxford: Oxford University Press, 1975), 8; "The first half of the twentieth century, especially after 1914, marked a revolution in European thinking almost beyond compare," Franklin L. Baumer, *Modern European Thought: Continuity and Change in Ideas, 1600-1950* (New York: McMillan Publishing Co., 1977), 402; "The First World War ... altered the ways in which men and women thought not only about war but about the world, about the culture and its expressions ... it changed reality," Hynes, Samuel, *A War Imagined: The First World War and English Culture* (New York: Atheneum, 1991), xi.

3. George Macaulay Trevelyan, *Grey of Falloddon* (Boston: 1937), 302, in Hynes, *A War Imagined, 3.*

4. H.G. Wells, *The Outline of History,* Vol. II (London: 1920), 748, in Hynes, Samuel. *A War Imagined,* 323.

5. Charles F. G. Masterman, *England after War* (London: 1922), ix, in Samuel Hynes, *A War Imagined,* 313-15.

6. Roland N. Stromberg, *Redemption by War: The Intellectuals and 1914* (Lawrence: Regents Press of Kansas, 1982), 193-94.

7. Alfred North Whitehead, *Science and the Modern World* (New York: The Free Press, 1967), 17.

8. Ibid., 17, 54-55; Thomas Nagel, *Mind and Cosmos, Why the Materialist Neo-Darwinian Conception of Nature Is Almost Certainly False,* Oxford: Oxford University Press, 2012), 127; John F. Haught, *Is Nature Enough? Meaning and Truth in the Age of Science* (Cambridge University Press, 2007), 25; William Barrett, *Death of the Soul: From Descartes to the Computer* (New York: Anchor Books, 1986), 7, 57; W.T. Stace, "Man against the Darkness," *The Atlantic Monthly* (Sept. 1948): 55; John Wellmuth, *The Nature and Ori-*

gins of Scientism (Milwaukee: Marquette University Press, 1944), 14; and John Russell, *Science and Metaphysics* (New York, Sheed and Ward, 1958), 10.

9. Stephen Hawking and Leonard Mlodinow, *The Grand Design* (New York: Bantam Books, 2012), 5, 180.

10. Jacques Monod, *Chance and Necessity*, trans. Austryn Wainhouse (New York: Vantage Books, 1972), 13.

11. Richard Dawkins, *The Blind Watchmaker: Why the Evidence of Evolution Reveals a Universe without Design* (New York: W. W. Norton, 1986), 7-10.

12. Daniel C. Dennett, *Darwin's Dangerous Idea: Evolution and the Meaning of Life* (New York: Simon & Schuster, 1995), 18 (emphasis in original).

13. Friedrich Nietzsche, *The Gay Science* (1882) in *The Portable Nietzsche*, trans. Walter Kaufmann (New York: Vintage Books, 1967), 95. Nietzsche tells of the madman who entered the marketplace in daylight carrying a lantern and crying, "God is dead... And we have killed him." Recognizing from everyone's silence that he had "come too early," the madman asks, "are we not straying as through an infinite nothing?"

14. Nietzsche, *The Twilight of the Idols* (1889) in L. Nathan Oaklander, *Existentialist Philosophy, an Introduction*, 2d ed. (Prentice Hall, 1996), 122. Nietzsche considers Christianity inherently unworthy of belief because divinely inspired altruistic love is irrational. Nietzsche, *Human, All Too Human* in Oaklander, *Existentialist Philosophy*, 130. Personally lacking altruistic love, humanity feels sinful and guilty and searches for the external rather than the internal causes for bad feelings, which Nietzsche calls a *"psychology of error."* Nietzsche, *Human, All Too Human* (Part Two, Volume 2, *The Wanderer and His Shadow*), in Oaklander, *Existentialist Philosophy*, 139. Similarly, Nietzsche considers the Christian distinction between man's soul and his actions irrational; "there is no 'being' behind the doing, effecting, becoming: 'the doer' is merely a fiction added to the deed—the deed is everything." Nietzsche, *On the Genealogy of Morals* in Oaklander, *Existentialist Philosophy*, 118. The soul is essentially man's free will because otherwise man's action would be unintentional or irrational and, consequently, not punishable. The freedom to act is inherent and man is the sum total of his actions. In short, Nietzsche considers the Christian notion of the soul as the creation of the weak, who refuse to accept existential reality and need another world to reward their suffering of life's tribulations.

15. Steven E. Aschheim, *The Nietzsche Legacy in Germany, 1890-1990* (Berkeley: University of California Press, 1992), 86, 203-05, 213. German Protestants construed Nietzsche's critique of decadence as an impetus for regeneration and a call for church reform; and some Catholics invoked Nietzsche's revaluation of values as a call for a "Dionysian Catholicism."

According to Aschheim, "in Nietzsche's system of thought, the Catholic, Protestant and mystic streams of Christian experience all found their place." Ibid., 206. "All these religions had to channel Nietzsche's potentially anarchic notions of will, vitalism, immoralism, and individualism into manageable sociopolitical and intellectual frameworks." Ibid., 210.

16. Nietzsche, *The Will to Power* (1895) in Oaklander, *Existentialist Philosophy*, 106; Nietzsche, *Beyond Good and Evil* (1886) in Oaklander, *Existentialist Philosophy*, 108, 115.

17. John F. Haught, *What Is Religion? An Introduction* (New York and New Jersey: Paulist Press, 1990), 145-57.

18. Ibid., 153.

19. W.T. Stace, "Man against the Darkness," *The Atlantic Monthly* (Sept. 1948): 54.

20. Whitehead, *Science and the Modern World*, 17.

21. John F. Haught, *Is Nature Enough? Meaning and Truth in the Age of Science* (Cambridge: Cambridge University Press, 2007), 8.

22. Ibid., 14.

23. "Their vision of fate, remorseless and indifferent, urging a tragic incident to its inevitable issue, is the vision possessed by science. Fate in Greek Tragedy becomes the order of nature and modern thought." Whitehead, *Science and the Modern World*, 10.

24. Kitto, *The Greeks* (London: Penguin Books, 1991), 60-61, 176-77, 196-97, 199-200; Francis J. Ambrosio, *Philosophy, Religion, and the Meaning of Life* (Chantilly, Virginia: The Teaching Company, 2009), Course Guidebook, 12.

25. Baumer, *Modern European Thought*, 312 (John Dalton's atomic theory, Antoine Lavoisier's persistence of matter through chemical change, and Helmholtz's view of the constancy of energy).

26. Ibid., 342.

27. Ibid.

28. Ibid., 313.

29. Whitehead, *Science and the Modern World*, 17, 54-55; Haught, *Is Nature Enough?*, 25; William Barrett, *Death of the Soul: From Descartes to the Computer* (New York: Anchor Books, 1986), 7, 57; Stace, "Man against the Darkness," 55; John Wellmuth, *The Nature and Origins of Scientism* (Milwaukee: Marquette University Press, 1944), 14; and John Russell, *Science and Metaphysics* (New York: Sheed and Ward, 1958), 10.

30. Wellmuth, *The Nature and Origins of Scientism*, 1-2.

31. Bertrand Russell, *Religion and Science* (New York: Oxford University Press, 1961), 189, 243.

32. Wellmuth, *The Nature and Origins of Scientism*, 12-14; Tom Sorell, *SCIENTISM: Philosophy and the Infatuation with Science* (London: Routledge, 1991), 24-40, 176. Although Sorell disputes that scientism began

with empiricism, he recognizes that the views of Bacon, Descartes, and other seventeenth-century scientists and philosophers genuinely anticipated the twentieth-century rise of scientism and its confidence in scientific reasoning.

33. Whitehead, *Science and the Modern World*, 6-8.

34. Barrett, *Death of the Soul*, 36.

35. Ibid., 42.

36. Samuel Enoch Stumpf, *PHILOSOPHY: History & Problems*, 2nd ed. (New York: McGraw-Hill, 1983), Glossary, G-2, G-3.

37. Ibid., 160-61, 174-77. Anselm argued from the premise that everyone believes God is "that than which nothing greater can be thought." This idea must have actual existence because it would be a contradiction to deny the existence of an idea of God that the mind is already posited. By contrast, Aquinas bases his proof of a First Cause by pointing out that there must be a first mover in a series of causes, rather than an infinite series of regressions, and this actuality is God.

38. Whitehead, *Science and the Modern World*, 12-13.

39. David Hume, *An Inquiry concerning Human Understanding*, Section IV, Part I, in *The Philosophy of David Hume*, ed. V. C. Chappell (New York: Modern Library, 1963), 325-30.

40. Whitehead, *Science and the Modern World*, 44.

41. Ibid., 16.

42. Ian Babour, *Issues in Science and Religion* (Englewood Cliffs, New Jersey: Prentice-Hall, 1966), 36.

43. Whitehead, *Science and the Modern World*, 51.

44. Ibid., 55, 59.

45. John F. Haught, *Science and Religion, from Conflict to Conversation* (New York: Paulist Press, 1995), 72-99 (emphasis in original).

46. Whitehead, *Science and the Modern World*, 66-67.

47. Ibid., 18.

48. Haught, *Is Nature Enough?*, 43-50.

Chapter 2. God, Science, and Reason in Enlightenment Culture

1. Robert Browning, *Pippa's Song*, in *The Oxford Book of English Verse (1250-1900)*, ed. Arthur Quiller-Couch (New York: Blue Ribbon Books, 1900), 701.

2. William Wordsworth, "The Tables Turned, An Evening Scene on the Same Subject" (1798), lines 29, 20, 25-28, in *The Norton Anthology of English Literature*, ed, M. H. Abrams and Stephen Greenblatt, 7th ed., vol. 2 (New York: W. W. Norton, 2000), 228.

3. Stumpf, *PHILOSOPHY: History & Problems*, 213, 215.

4. Ibid., 215-16.

5. Baumer, *Modern European Thought*, 52.

6. Stumpf, *PHILOSOPHY: History & Problems*, 234-37.

7. René Descartes, *Meditations on the First Philosophy in Which the Existence of God and the Distinction between Mind and Body Are Demonstrated*, Meditation V, *Of the essence of material things, and, again, of God, that He exists*, in Vol. 28 of *Great Books of the Western World: Bacon, Descartes, Spinoza*. ed. Ralph M. Eaton (New York: Charles Scribner's Sons, 1955), 139.

8. Baumer, *Modern European Thought*, 51-52.

9. John Locke, *An Essay Concerning Human Understanding*, Chap. XIX, Sec. 14 (1690) in *Great Books of the Western World: Locke Berkeley Hume*. Vol. 33, ed. Mortimer J. Adler (Chicago: Encyclopaedia Britannica, 2007), 387-88 (emphasis in original).

10. Baumer, *Modern European Thought*, 73-75.

11. Ibid., 78.

12. Ibid., 62.

13. Mortimer Chambers, Barbara Hanawalt, Theodore K. Rabb, Isser Woloch, and Lisa Tiersten, *The Western Experience*, 10th ed. (New York: McGraw-Hill, 2010), 455-56. The English title of Newton's Latin masterpiece is *The Mathematical Principles of Natural Philosophy*.

14. Edwin Arthur Burtt, *The Metaphysical Foundations of Modern Physical Science: A Historical and Critical Essay*, rev. ed. (London: Routledge & Kegan Paul, 1950), 281, 288, 294.

15. Theodore M. Greene, Introduction to *Kant Selections*, ed. Theodore M. Greene (New York: Charles Scribner's Sons, 1957), xxxi.

16. Ibid., xxxii.

17. Stumpf, *PHILOSOPHY: History & Problems*, 270-77; Theodore M. Greene, Introduction to *Kant Selections*, xxxii-iv.

18. Whitehead, *Science and the Modern World*, 4 (emphasis in original).

19. Barrett, *Death of the Soul*, 45.

20. Stumpf, *PHILOSOPHY: History & Problems*, 270-79.

21. Ibid., 46.

22. David Hume, *An Inquiry concerning Human Understanding*, ed. Charles W. Hendel, Jr. (New York: Liberal Arts Press, 1955), 142-43.

23. Ibid., 143.

24. Ibid., 146.

25. Ibid., 146-47.

26. David Hume, *An Inquiry Concerning Human Understanding* in *Hume Selections*, ed. Charles W. Hendel, Jr. (New York: Charles Scribner's Sons, 1955), 193.

27. Whitehead, *Science and the Modern World*, 4, 51.

28. Greene, Introduction to *Kant Selections*, xxxiv-xxxv.

29. Livingston, James C. *Modern Christian Thought: The Enlightenment and the Nineteenth Century,* 2nd ed. (Minneapolis: Fortress Press, 2006), 59-60; Greene, Introduction to *Kant Selections,* xxxvii-xli.

30. Livingston, *Modern Christian Thought: The Enlightenment and the Nineteenth Century,* 59-60.

31. Immanuel Kant, *Critique of Pure Reason* in *Kant Selections,* 22.

32. Kant, *Theory of Ethics* in *Kant Selections,* 279-81, 336-38; Livingston, *Modern Christian Thought: The Enlightenment and the Nineteenth Century,* 62-63.

33. Livingston, *Modern Christian Thought: The Enlightenment and the Nineteenth Century,* 63. Kant, *Theory of Ethics* in *Kant Selections,* 360-68. Because perfect concordance of virtue and happiness (the *supremum bonum*) is not achievable in a single lifetime, Kant postulates that the soul is immortal; and because moral duty requires pursuit of moral perfection, Kant postulates that "it is morally necessary to assume the existence of God" to mete out the level of happiness in the hereafter appropriate to the individual's dutiful performance in the here and now. Livingston, *Modern Christian Thought: The Enlightenment and the Nineteenth Century,* 64.

34. Kant, "Preface to the Second Edition" of *Critique of Pure Reason* in Greene, *Kant Selections,* 12.

35. Barrett, *Death of the Soul,* 75.

36. Livingston, *Modern Christian Thought: The Enlightenment and the Nineteenth Century,* 63; Greene, Introduction to *Kant Selections,* liv.

37. Greene, Introduction to *Kant Selections,* li, liv.

38. "Our beliefs about the universe do enter into our views of morality. Our ethical being is projected against some imagination of the cosmos as a whole. This is true for the atheist as for the theist, for a Nietzsche as well as a Kant." Barrett, *Death of the Soul,* 111.

39. Quoted in Barrett, *Death of the Soul,* 90.

40. Livingston, *Modern Christian Thought: The Enlightenment and the Nineteenth Century,* 121.

41. Stephen D. Crites, "The Gospel According to Hegel," *The Journal of Religion* 46 (1966): 246-63, 247.

42. Stumpf, *PHILOSOPHY: History & Problems,* 314-15.

43. Ibid., 316.

44. Ibid., 324-25; Crites, "The Gospel According to Hegel," 261.

45. Whitehead, *Science and the Modern World,* 63-64.

46. Livingston, *Modern Christian Thought: The Enlightenment and the Nineteenth Century,* 116.

47. Arnold, Matthew. *Culture and Anarchy and Other Writings,* ed. Stefan Collini (Cambridge: Cambridge University Press, 1993), 22, 83, 85, 100; Baumer, *Modern European Thought,* 260.

48. Arnold, *Literature and Science* (1885) in *The Norton Anthology of English Literature*, 1555.

49. Ibid., 161-62.

50. Baumer, *Modern European Thought*, 260.

51. Ibid., 162-63, 302-14.

52. Ibid., 263.

53. Ibid., 264.

54. Crites, "The Gospel According to Hegel," 258.

55. Søren Kierkegaard, *Philosophical Fragments Johannes Climacus*, ed. and trans. with introduction and notes by Howard V. Hong and Edna H. Hong (Princeton: Princeton University Press, 1987), 9, 11, 13, 19. Unlike the Socratic teacher, who is merely a midwife for man's discovery of an immanently residing truth, Kierkegaard's teacher is Christ the Redeemer, and mankind "owes that divine teacher everything."

56. Ibid., 78.

57. Livingston, *Modern Christian Thought: The Enlightenment and the Nineteenth Century*, 388.

58. Kierkegaard, *FEAR AND TREMBLING* and *THE SICKNESS UNTO DEATH*, trans. Walter Lowrie (New York: Doubleday Anchor Books, 1954), 70, 72, 77; Kierkegaard, *Concluding Unscientific Postscript* in Walter Kaufmann, *Existentialism from Dostoyevsky to Sartre* (New York: New American Library, 1975), 118.

59. Baumer, *Modern European Thought*, 444-45, 445n10. Since his complete works were not translated into German until 1909-1911, Kierkegaard had his greatest influence in postwar Germany, with theologians like Karl Barth.

60. Livingston, *Modern Christian Thought: The Enlightenment and the Nineteenth Century*, 222.

61. Ibid.

62. Ibid., 223-24.

63. Ibid., 127-38.

64. Arnold, "Dover Beach" (1851), lines 26-28, in *The Norton Anthology of English Literature*, 1492.

65. Ibid., lines 29-37, in *The Norton Anthology of English Literature*, 1492-93.

66. Arnold, Stanzas from the Grande Chartreuse" (1852), lines 85-6, in *The Norton Anthology of English Literature*, 1493-98.

67. Alfred, Lord Tennyson, *In Memoriam A. H. H.* (1950), lines 1-4, in *The Norton Anthology of English Literature*, 1231.

68. Ibid., section 55, lines 17-20 in *The Norton Anthology of English Literature*, 1251.

69. Ibid., section 54, line 18; section 56, line 15 in *The Norton Anthology of English Literature*, 1250-51.

70. Ibid., stanza 96, lines 11-12, in *The Norton Anthology of English Literature*, 1266.

71. James C. Livingston, *Modern Christian Thought: The Enlightenment and the Nineteenth Century*, 200; *The Norton Anthology of English Literature*, 1448-51.

72. *The Norton Anthology of English Literature*, 1657.

73. *The Norton Anthology of English Literature, The Twentieth Century and After*, 8th ed., Vol. F (New York: W. W. Norton, 2006), 1851-52; Baumer, *Modern European Thought*, 377-78. Until the age of twenty-five, Hardy considered becoming an Anglican priest, but based upon Darwinian evolution, he lost his belief in divine governance and stoically accepted a mechanistic worldview.

74. In "The Darkling Thrush" (1900). Hardy finds little cause for the thrush "to fling his soul/ Upon the growing gloom" of the "Century's Corpse." Ibid., 1871.

75. Ibid., 1877-78.

76. Baumer, *Modern European Thought*, 305-06.

77. Stumpf, *PHILOSOPHY: History & Problems*, 326-34; Frank Thilly, *A History of Philosophy* 3rd ed., rev. Ledger Wood (New York: Holt, Rinehart and Winston, 1957), 520-24.

78. Thilly, *A History of Philosophy*, 522.

79. Ibid.

80. Ibid., 525; Baumer, *Modern European Thought,* 315-16.

81. Ibid., 75-94; Baumer, *Modern European Thought*, 260; Jacques Barzun, *Classic, Romantic and Modern* (Chicago: University Of Chicago Press, 1961), 98-99.

82. Whitehead, *Science and the Modern World*, 75, 146.

83. Friedrich Schleiermacher, *Second Speech, The Nature of Religion* in *Friedrich Schleiermacher on Religion: Speeches to Its Cultured Despisers* (New York: Harper & Row, 1958), 36-37.

84. Ibid., 37-39.

85. Ibid., 41.

86. Ibid., 45.

87. Ibid., 45-46.

88. Ibid., 72-73.

89. Ibid., 78-79.

90. William Blake, "Auguries of Innocence," lines 1-4, in *The Complete Poems*, ed. Alicia Ostriker (London: Penguin Books, 1977), 506.

91. Schleiermacher, *Second Speech, The Nature of Religion*, 45, 48.

92. Livingston, *Modern Christian Thought: The Enlightenment and the Nineteenth Century*, 93.

93. Blake, *Jerusalem* , verse 15, lines 14-20, in *The Complete Poems*, 662.

94. Baumer, *Modern European Thought*, 274.

95. Whitehead, *Science and the Modern World*, 81-86.

96. William Wordsworth, "The Tables Turned, An Evening Scene on the Same Subject" (1798), lines 29, 20, 25-28, in *The Norton Anthology of English Literature*, 228.

97. Wordsworth, Preface to *Lyrical Ballads, with Pastoral and Other Poems* (1802) in *The Norton Anthology of English Literature*, 250; and *Lines Composed a Few Miles above Tintern Abbey, on Revisiting the Banks of the Wye during a Tour, July 13, 1798* , lines 93-102, in *The Norton Anthology of English Literature*, 237.

98. Wordsworth, *Tintern Abbey*, lines 75, 152, 122-23, in *The Norton Anthology of English Literature*, 236-38.

99. Whitehead, *Science and the Modern World*, 83-84.

100. *The Norton Anthology of English Literature*, 699-700; Whitehead, *Science and the Modern World*, 85.

101. Percy Bysshe Shelley, *Mont Blanc, Lines Written in the Veil of Chamouni* (1817), lines 1-11, in *The Norton Anthology of English Literature*, 720.

102. Ibid., lines 40, 97, in *The Norton Anthology of English Literature*, 721, 722.

103. Shelley, "Ode to the West Wind," lines 1, 3, 7, 69-70, in *The Norton Anthology of English Literature*, 730-32.

104. Whitehead, *Science and the Modern World*, 87.

105. Ibid., 94.

106. Barrett, *Death of the Soul*, 46, 112-113.

107. Darwin, *Descent of Man* in James C. Livingston, *Modern Christian Thought: The Enlightenment and the Nineteenth Century*, 254. Darwin's full title is *On the Origin of Species by Means of Natural Selection, or the Preservation of Favored Races in the Struggle for Life.*

108. Irwin W. Sherman & Vilia G. Sherman, *Biology, A Human Approach* (Second Edition) (New York: Oxford University Press, 1979), 508 (In 1650, the Irish Archbishop James Usher calculated the date of creation as 4004 B.C.); Livingston, *Modern Christian Thought*, 251-53.

109. Sherman, *Biology*, 508-12.

110. Darwin, *Origin of Species* in Francisco J. Ayala, "Design without Designer, Darwin's Greatest Discovery" in William A. Dembski and Michael Ruse, eds., *Debating Design: From Darwin to DNA* (New York: Cambridge University Press, 2004), 59, 59n7.

111. Darwin, *Descent of Man* in Livingston, *Modern Christian Thought: The Enlightenment and the Nineteenth Century*, 254.

112. Livingston, *Modern Christian Thought: The Enlightenment and the Nineteenth Century*, 250, 253.

113. Ibid. 253; Sherman, *Biology*, 500-01.

114. John F. Haught, *Making Sense of Evolution: Darwin, God, and the Drama of Life* (Louisville: Westminster John Knox Press, 2010), 14-17; Adrian Desmond and James Moore, *Darwin* (New York: Warner Books, 1991), 636.

115. Livingston, *Modern Christian Thought: The Enlightenment and the Nineteenth Century*, 255-56.

116. Ibid., 259-62.

117. Ibid., 257-58.

118. Ibid., 265.

119. Stumpf, *PHILOSOPHY: History & Problems*, 367-75; Thilly, *A History of Philosophy*, 579-82; and Hakim, Albert B. *Historical Introduction To Philosophy*, 2nd ed. (New York: Macmillan, 1992), 688-92.

120. Henri Bergson, *Creative Evolution* (1907) in Hakim, *Historical Introduction To Philosophy*, 694 (emphasis in original).

121. Henri Bergson, *The Two Sources of Morality and Religion* (New York: Henry Holt, 1935), 209.

122. Bergson, *Creative Evolution* (1907) in Hakim, *Historical Introduction To Philosophy*, 698.

123. Heinz Zahrnt, *The Question of God: Protestant Theology in the Twentieth Century*, trans. R. A. Wilson (New York: Harvest Book, 1966), 15; Schleiermacher, Friedrich. *Second Speech, The Nature Of Religion*, 45.

124. Schleiermacher, *Second Speech, The Nature Of Religion*, 80, 90.

125. Zahrnt, *The Question of God*, 15.

126. Adolph von Harnack, *What Is Christianity?* trans. Thomas Bailey Saunders (New York: Harper & Row, 1957), 11, 14.

127. Ibid., 17; Livingston, *Modern Christian Thought: The Enlightenment and the Nineteenth Century*, 289-90; Harnack, *What Is Christianity?*, 31.

128. Livingston, *Modern Christian Thought: The Enlightenment and the Nineteenth Century*, 289.

129. Zahrnt, *The Question of God*, 15.

130. Livingston, *Modern Christian Thought: The Enlightenment and the Nineteenth Century*, 359-64.

131. Le Roy (1870-1954), a mathematician turned philosopher and Teilhard's scientific colleague and friend, tried to align Catholicism with Darwinian evolution and Bergsonian philosophy. Ibid., 376-77.

132. Alfred Loisy, *The Gospel and the Church*, trans. Christopher Home, 2nd English ed. (London, 1908) in Livingston, *Modern Christian Thought: The Enlightenment and the Nineteenth Century*, 365.

133. Loisy, *The Gospel and the Church*, 210-11 in Livingston, *Modern Christian Thought: The Enlightenment and the Nineteenth Century*, 369.

134. Livingston, *Modern Christian Thought: The Enlightenment and the Nineteenth Century*, 379. In 1910, the Church required all priests and

priesthood candidates to sign an anti-Modernist statement and instituted a campaign called "Integralism" that caused the end of both Modernism and biblical study within Catholicism until after World War II.

135. Baumer, *Modern European Thought*, 377.

Chapter 3. The Great War and Cultural Breakdown

1. William Butler Yeats, "The Second Coming" (1920), lines 3-8, in *The Norton Anthology of English Literature: The Twentieth Century and After*, 2036.

2. The dictionary definition of *civilization* is "a relatively high level of cultural and technological development," and *culture* is "enlightenment and excellence of taste acquired by intellectual and aesthetic training ... in the arts, humanities, and broad aspects of science" (as distinguished from vocational and technical skills). *Merriam-Webster's Collegiate Dictionary*, 10th ed. (Springfield, Massachusetts: Merriam-Webster, 1998), 210, 282.

3. Kenneth Clark, *Civilisation: A Personal View* (New York: Harper & Row, 1969), 4.

4. Ibid., 4, 14, 347.

5. Fussell, *The Great War and Modern Memory*, 7-8.

6. William Barrett, *Irrational Man* (Garden City: Doubleday Anchor Books, 1958), 28, 31.

7. Matthew Arnold, *Culture and Anarchy And Other Writings*, ed. Stefan Collini (Cambridge: Cambridge University Press, 1993), 79; Clark, *Civilisation*, 1, 24.

8. John Maynard Keynes, *Economic Consequences of the Peace* (London, 1940), chapter 1, in Niall Ferguson, *The War of the World: Twentieth-Century Conflict and the Descent of the West* (New York: Penguin Books, 2006), 4.

9. Niall Ferguson, *The War of the World*, lx-xi, 16, lx.

10. Ibid., 16. The Austro-Hungarian Empire, for example, included eighteen nationalities dispersed across five distinct kingdoms in a remarkable assimilation of diverse ethnicities. According to Ferguson, the Empire's Jewish minority succeeded largely because of "the *fin-de-siècle* combination of global integration and the dissolution of traditional professional barriers." Ibid., 41-42.

11. Ibid., 91. All but one of Victoria and Albert's nine children married royally, and when Victoria died in 1901 "members of the extended kinship group to which she belonged thus sat on the thrones not only of Great Britain and Ireland, but also of Austria-Hungary, Russia, Denmark, Spain, Portugal, Germany, Belgium, Greece, Romania, Bulgaria, Sweden and Norway." Ibid., 96.

12. Barbara W. Tuchman, *The Proud Tower: A Portrait of the World Before the War 1890-1914* (New York: Ballantine Books, 1962), 241.

13. Ferguson, *The War of the World,* 92. In 1914, the Great Powers were hardly an armed camp, moreover, since they spent barely three percent of GNP on defense and employed only about one and one half percent of their population in the Armed Forces. Ibid., 92-93.

14. Ibid., 81.

15. Samuel Hynes, *A War Imagined: The First World War and English Culture* (New York: Atheneum, 1991), 5-6; Barbara W. Tuchman, *The Proud Tower,* 431. "Between 1900 and 1913 no fewer than 40 heads of state, politicians and diplomats were murdered, including four Kings, six prime ministers and presidents," and including President McKinley (1901) as well as an almost successful attempt on President Roosevelt. Ferguson, *The War of the World,* 73.

16. Roland N. Stromberg, *Redemption by War: The Intellectuals and 1914* (Lawrence: The Regents Press of Kansas, 1982), 90-91.

17. Ibid., 98-100, 106; Lloyd Kramer, *European Thought and Culture in the 20th Century* (Chantilly, Virginia: The Teaching Company, 2002), Course Guidebook, 49-50, 55-57.

18. Ferguson, *The War of the World,* 21-26.

19. Ibid., 33.

20. Tuchman, *The Proud Tower,* 182.

21. Robert Rosenblum, *Cubism and Twentieth-Century Art* (New York: Abrams, 1968), 14-16, 25.

22.Tuchman, *The Proud Tower,* 337-39.

23. Ibid., 343.

24. Stromberg, *Redemption by War,* 190, 20.

25. Hamilton, *Painting and Sculpture in Europe 1880-1940* (Baltimore: Penguin Books, 1972), 280. One year after Marinetti's Manifesto a group of Italian artists published their "Manifesto of the Futurist Painters," exalting originality and introducing a new style that used "dynamic sensation" and "lines of force" to achieve Marinetti's principles of energy and velocity.

26. Filippo Tomasso Marinetti, "Manifesto of Futurism," *Le Figaro,* February 20, 1909, in Amy Dempsey, *Styles, Schools and Movements* (London: Thames & Hudson, 2002), 88; Hamilton, *Painting and Sculpture in Europe 1880-1940,* 279.

27. Stromberg, *Redemption by War,* 27, 7.

28. Joseph Conrad, *Heart of Darkness* Norton Critical Edition, 4th ed. (New York: W. W. Norton, 2006), 30, 7.

29. Joseph Conrad, *Lord Jim* (New York: Signet Classic, 1961), 119, 22.

30. T.S. Eliot, *The Love Song of J. Alfred Prufrock* in *The Norton Anthology of English Literature: The Twentieth Century and After,* 2290, lines 4-7, 27, 51. *Prufrock* was written in 1910-11 but published in 1915, 1917. Except for the

war poetry, I have generally used publication dates rather than composition dates.

31. Nicole Brandmueller, "The Expressionist in Berlin," in *Ernst Ludwig Kirchner: Retrospective*, ed. Felix Kramer (Frankfurt: Stadel Museum, 2010), 102-03.

32. Robert Greenberg, *Great Masters: Mahler—His Life & Music* (Chantilly: The Teaching Company, 2001), Course Guidebook, 2, 21

33. Ferguson, *The War of the World*, 80-86; Stromberg, *Redemption by War*, 179. While many historians think that World War I was the anticipated and inevitable consequence of militarism, imperialism, or Darwinian struggle among nations, Ferguson and Stromberg argue convincingly that war came as a complete shock to virtually all Europeans.

34. George Bernard Shaw, Introduction to *Heartbreak House* (New York: Classic Books International, 2009), 1.

35. A.J.P. Taylor, *The First World War: An Illustrated History* (New York: Perigee Books, 1980), 13-25.

36. Ibid.

37. Christopher Clark, *The Sleepwalkers: How Europe Went to War in 1914* (New York: HarperCollins, 2012), 561-62.

38. Vejas Gabriel Liulevicius, *World War I: The "Great War,"* (Chantilly, Virginia: The Teaching Company, 2006), Course Guidebook (Part 1), 26; Modris Eksteins, *Rites of Spring*, 57-62.

39. Taylor, *The First World War*, 53, 114. In Britain, with a small standing army and no compulsory military service, 500,000 men volunteered in the first month, and volunteers ran over 100,000 per month for the next year and a half, raising more than 3 million volunteers. Stromberg, *Redemption by War*, 3; Taylor, *The First World War*, 146.

40. Romain Rolland, *Au-dessus de la melée*, in Stromberg, *Redemption by War*, 1.

41. Stromberg, *Redemption by War*, 178-85, 188.

42. Ibid., 2.

43. Ibid., 2, 37-38; George Walter, Introduction to *The Penguin Book of First World War Poetry*, ed. George Walter (London: Penguin Books, 2006), viii.

44. Stromberg, *Redemption by War*, 157-62.

45. Ibid., 177.

46. Ibid., 187.

47. Ibid., 191, 198.

48. Rupert Brooke, "Peace," line 5 in Walter, *The Penguin Book of First World War Poetry*, 11; Brooke, "The Soldier," in Ibid., 108. During his sermon on Easter Sunday 1915, Dean Ing of St. Paul's Cathedral read Rupert Brooke's poem "The Soldier," making him famous. After Brooke died in

April 1915, on the Greek island of Skyros (unheroically or at least ingloriously) of septicemia from a mosquito bite while en route to Gallipoli, Winston Churchill wrote his obituary. Ibid., xv, xxii.

49. Taylor, *The First World War*, 22-24. In January 1915, Field Marshal Earl Kitchener, British Secretary of State for War, recognized that the German lines "cannot be carried by assault, and also cannot be completely invested." Nevertheless, British General Sir John French and his successor in command General Sir Douglas Haig ignored Kitchener's advice and remained committed to the offensive. Haig famously remarked: "The machine gun is a much overrated weapon and two per battalion were more than sufficient" (by the war's end every British battalion had 43 machine guns "and cried out for more"). Ibid., 67, 86.

50. Ibid., 22.

51. Fussell, *The Great War and Modern Memory*, 9.

52. Barbara W. Tuchman, *The Guns of August* (New York: Ballantine Books, 1962), 440.

53. Taylor, *The First World War*, 34. After the Battle of the Marne, German and British forces undertook flanking maneuvers toward the English Channel in a "race to the sea" but only succeeded in extending the front from the English Channel to Switzerland.

54. Ferguson, *The War of the World*, 117-18.

55. Taylor, *The First World War*, 83.

56. Michael Howard, *The First World War: A Very Short Introduction* (Oxford: Oxford University Press, 2007), 46; Taylor, *The First World War*, 84, 104.

57. Taylor, *The First World War*, 121, 126, 123.

58. Ibid., 132-33.

59. Ibid., 136, 140; Paul Fussell, *The Great War and Modern Memory*, 27; Niall Ferguson, *The Pity of War* (Great Britain: Penguin Press, 1998), 293. By contrast, the Germans suffered 6000 casualties that day. John Keegan, *The First World War* (New York: Vintage Books, 1999), 295-96. On D-Day in World War II, the Allies sustained 10,000 casualties, including 2500 dead, during the largest amphibious landing in history. D-Day Museum, Portsmouth, "D-Day and the Battle of Normandy: Your Questions Answered, "http://www.ddaymuseum.co.uk/d-day/d-day-and-the-battle-of-normandy-your-questions-answered#casualities (accessed Sept. 13, 2012).

60. Taylor, *The First World War*, 140.

61. Ibid., 177. One French Regiment went to the front bleating like sheep being led to the slaughter.

62. Ibid., 191-94. Ludendorff added a final footnote that the British soldiers were "lions led by donkeys." Ibid., 287. English historian Brian Bond, however, provides a different and more positive perspective from

Taylor's on British military leadership. Bond, Brian. *The Unquiet Western Front: Britain's Role in Literature and History* (Cambridge: Cambridge University Press, 2002), 20-22. 63. Taylor, A.J.P. *The First World War*, 89, 196-98.

64. Ferguson, *The War of the World*, 117.

65. William E. Leuchtenburg, *The Perils of Prosperity, 1914-32* (Chicago: University Of Chicago Press, 1958), 12-28.

66. Ferguson, *The War of the World*, 171.

67. Taylor, *The First World War*, 230-31.

68. Leuchtenburg, *The Perils of Prosperity*, 36.

69. Ibid., 233-37.

70. Ferguson, *The Pity of War*, 295; Richard L. Rubenstein, *The Cunning of History, The Holocaust and the American Future* (New York: Harper Colophon Books, 1978), 7. France suffered 1.4 million dead and 2 million wounded; Britain 723,000 dead and almost 1.66 million wounded; Germany 2 million dead and 4.2 million wounded; and America 114,000 dead and almost 206,000 wounded. The casualty rate among major combatants ran about fifty percent, except for France which ran higher. Indeed, the French war toll was catastrophic, considering its relatively low birth rate and older population: ten percent of the adult population and half of the French male population ages 20-32 died, leaving millions maimed for life. Mortimer Chambers, et al. *The Western Experience*, 10th ed. (New York: McGraw-Hill, 2010), 800.

71. Nevinson in Hynes, Samuel. *A War Imagined*, 162.

72. Wyndham Lewis, "The London Group. 1915 (March)," *Blast No. 2* (London, 1915), 77, in Richard Cork, *A Bitter Truth: Avant-garde Art and the Great War* (New Haven : Yale University Press in association with Barbican Art Gallery, 1994), 72, 317n18.

73. Christopher R. W. Nevinson, *Paint and Prejudice* (London, 1937), 104, in Cork, *A Bitter Truth*, 72, 317n19.

74. Taylor, *The First World War*, 140.

75. Wilfred Owen, "Dulce et Decorum *Est*" (1917-18), in *The Norton Anthology of English Literature, The Twentieth Century and After*, 1974.

76. Ibid., lines 16, 21-28. The poet was Jessie Pope. Ibid., 1974n4.

77. Owen, "Futility," Ibid., 1976, lines 13, 3, 12; Bernard Bergonzi, *Heroes' Twilight* (Manchester: Carcanet Press, 1996), 123.

78. Owen, "Strange Meeting" (1918) in *The Norton Anthology of English Literature, The Twentieth Century and After*, 1975-76, lines 6-7, 40, 24, 16, 25, 32, 29.

79. *The Norton Anthology of English Literature, The Twentieth Century and After*, 1980 (emphasis added); Walter, introduction to *The Penguin Book of First World War Poetry*, xxx-xi.

80. *The Norton Anthology of English Literature, The Twentieth Century and*

After, 1960-63. Sassoon variously satirizes the noncombatant headquarters officers who cavalierly kibitz about the frontline death of some "Poor young chap," in "Base Details"; the "cheery old card" of a general and the "incompetent swine" on his staff who planned the disastrous attack at Arras, in "The General" (1918); the gleeful British audiences who cackle at anti-German musicals and disregard war's brutal reality ("I'd like to see a Tank come down the stalls"), in "Blighters" (1917); the jingoistic Bishop who pontificates about "a just cause" and "the last attack / On Anti-Christ" but omits any mention of the war's disastrous human toll, in "They" (1917); and the naïvely romantic women who "believe / That chivalry redeems the war's disgrace," in "Glory of Women" (1918).

81. Ibid., 1960.

82. Robert Graves, *Good-Bye to All That* (New York: Anchor Books, 1998), 261-63.

83. Hynes, *A War Imagined,* 174-75.

84. Ibid., 186; Walter, introduction to *The Penguin Book of First World War Poetry,* xxx-xi.

85. Harold Owen and John Bell, eds. *Wilfred Owen: Collected Letters* (London: 1967), 580, in Hynes, *A War Imagined,* 186.

86. Graves, *Good-Bye to All That,* 233.

87. Born in 1873, Barbusse enlisted in the French army in 1914 at age 41 and served for 17 months on the front until invalided out at the end of 1915. *Le Feu,* dedicated "to the memory of the comrades who fell by my side at Crouÿ and on Hill 119 January, May, and September 1915," was the most widely read war novel in England during 1917-18. Hynes, *A War Imagined,* 203, 205.

88. Remarque was born in Osnabrück on June 22, 1898, and christened Erich Paul Remark. He saw frontline experience in Flanders where he was wounded in the left knee and under one arm on July 31, 1917, and hospitalized for 15 months (August 1917-October 1918). Modris Eksteins, "Memory" in *Bloom's Modern Critical Interpretations, Erich Maria Remarque's All Quiet on the Western Front* (new edition) (New York: Bloom's Literary Criticism, 2009), 59-60. In May 1933, the Nazis symbolically burned *All Quiet* as "politically and morally un-German." Ibid., 77.

89. Henri Barbusse, *Under Fire, The Story of a Squad,* trans. Fitzwater Wray (n.p.: Digireads.com Book, 2010), 7-29, 124.

90. Ibid., 173.

91. Ibid., 138.

92. Ibid., 5-6, 183, 177.

93. Erich Maria Remarque, *All Quiet on the Western Front* (New York: Ballantine Books, 1982) (*Im Westen Nichts Neues,* literally *Nothing New in the West*).

94. Ibid., 170-73.

95. Ibid., 185.

96. Ibid., 212.

97. Ibid., 263, 87.

98. Ibid., 192-94, 205-06, 226.

99. Ibid., 286.

100. Ibid., 294.

101. Modris Eksteins, "Memory" in *Bloom's Modern Critical Interpretations, Erich Maria Remarque's All Quiet on the Western Front*, 70-71.

102. Bond, 26. Bond maintains that World War I was "for Britain, a necessary and successful war," but acknowledges that Britain's optimistic views about the front produced a "backlash against the concealment of painful truths and, worse, outright deception," which gave critics, like Paul Fussell, a legitimate target over the shocking gulf between the real and the sanitized war. Ibid., 11.

103. Hynes, *A War Imagined*, xii.

104. Not all the important war literature shares his narrative about the Myth of War. May Wedderburn Cannan (1893-1973) continued to support the British cause long after the war and rejected the sentiment that soldiers "went to the war with Rupert Brooke and came home with Siegfried Sassoon." *The Norton Anthology of English Literature, The Twentieth Century and After*, 1981. Similarly, in *In Parentheses* (1937), David Jones (1895-1974) gives a heroic character to death in the trenches, but ends his epic in July 1916, after which he acknowledges that "things hardened into a more relentless, mechanical affair, took on a more sinister aspect." Ibid., 1990.

105. Rubenstein, *The Cunning of History*, 7; Stromberg, *Redemption by War*, 183-84. According to Bond, the "idea of sacrifice in a just cause did not collapse into cynicism for the war generation," but, instead, for the generation which followed. Bond *The Unquiet Western Front*, 14, 24, 106.

107. Rubenstein, *The Cunning of History*, 9.

108. Walter, Introduction to *The Penguin Book of First World War Poetry*, xxv; Hynes, *A War Imagined*, 437.

109. Hynes, *A War Imagined*, 437.

110. Ibid., 215.

111. Ernest Hemingway, *A Farewell To Arms* (New York: Charles Scribner's Sons, 1957), 177-78.

112. Hynes, *A War Imagined*, 108, 274. Honoring the sacrifice of these war dead while simultaneously believing their sacrifice pointless ultimately produced a schism within the postwar body politic, as Britain and Germany both created chivalric war memorials that reaffirmed their respective nation's continuity with its past. Stefan Goebel, *The Great War and Medieval Memory: War, Remembrance and Medievalism in Britain and Ger-*

many, 1914-1940 (Cambridge: Cambridge University Press, 2007), 287. By contrast, the emerging postwar sensibility described by Hynes rejected such historical continuity with a false, dead, and gone past.

113. Hynes, *A War Imagined,* 117; Howard, *The First World War,* 111.

114. Ezra Pound, "Hugh Selwyn Mauberley (Life and Contacts)," section V, lines 88-91, 94-95, in Walter, *The Penguin Book of First World War Poetry,* 248.

115. Graves, *Good-Bye to All That,* 238, 142.

116. Ibid., 228.

117. Remarque, *All Quiet on the Western Front,* 160.

118. Robert Wohl, *The Generation of 1914* (Cambridge: Harvard University Press, 1979), 120. Bond gives a contrary view in *The Unquiet Western Front,* 24-25.

119. Wohl, *The Generation of 1914,* 121.

120. Ibid., 225, 228.

121. Shaw, *Heartbreak House,* 133.

122. Ibid., 43, 77, 126, 139. Boss Mangan, "a Napoleon of industry and disgustingly rich," robs Mazzini Dunn and destroys companies "as a matter of business"; Hesione Hushabye and Ellie Dunn expose modern marriage as a business proposition rather than a love match; Mangan's business syndicate cynically promotes him "as the director of the great public department" for its own commercial purposes; and Captain Shotover declares, "The Church is on the rocks, breaking up." Hector Hushabye concludes, "We are useless, dangerous, and ought to be abolished." Ibid., 123.

123. Ibid., 122.

124. D. H. Lawrence, Foreword to *Women in Love* (New York: Viking Press, 1950), vii-x.

125. In a November 1915 letter Lawrence wrote, "I think there is no future for England, only a decline and fall. That is the dreadful and unbearable part of it: to have been born into a decadent era, a decline of life, a collapsing civilization." George J. Zytaruk and James T Bolton, eds. *The Letters of D. H. Lawrence,* vol. II (Cambridge: 1981), 441, in Hynes, Samuel. *A War Imagined,* 136, 482n26.

126. Lawrence, *Women in Love,* 4.

127. Ibid., 460.

128. Stromberg, *Redemption by War,* 178.

129. Thomas Hardy, "'And there was a great calm' (On the Signing of the Armistice, Nov. 11, 1918)," *Late Lyrics and Earlier* (London: 1922), 55-58 in Hynes, *A War Imagined,* 256.

130. Stromberg, *Redemption by War,* 195-97.

131. Wohl, *The Generation of 1914,* 230.

132. Stromberg, *Redemption by War,* 195-97.

133. Wohl, *The Generation of 1914,* 234.

134. Hynes, *A War Imagined,* 355-56.

135. Ibid., 355.

136. Liulevicius, *World War I: The "Great War,"* Course Guidebook (Part 3), 46.

137. Ferguson, *The War of the World,* 152, 156-59.

138. Ibid., 159.

139. Ibid., 160, 168.

140. Ibid., 161.

141. Ibid., 159-74.

142. Rubenstein, *The Cunning of History,* 13, citing Hannah Arendt, *The Origins of Totalitarianism* (New York: Harcourt Brace, 1951), 275.

143. Ibid., 176-79.

144. Howard, *The First World War,* 116. By urging the formation of a new republic to sue for peace, General Ludendorff saved the Army from responsibility for Germany's surrender and created grounds for the "stab in the back" myth. Leuchtenburg, *The Perils of Prosperity,* 48-49.

145. Ferguson, *The War of the World,* 245-69.

146. Pericles Lewis, "The Waste Land," The Modernism Lab at Yale University, http://modernism. research. yale. edu/wiki/index.php/The_Waste_Land (accessed October 26, 2010). Eliot denied, as "nonsense," any intention to express "the disillusionment of the generation."

147. T. S. Eliot, *The Waste Land,* lines 20, 22, 27, 63, in *The Norton Anthology of English Literature: The Twentieth Century and After,* 2296-97.

148. Ibid., lines 115-16, in *The Norton Anthology of English Literature: The Twentieth Century and After,* 2299.

149. Ibid., 2298-2305. These include an unhappy tryst between an neurotic woman and a laconic man in an upper-class boudoir, and a barroom report of the conversation between two women concerning the bodily deterioration of the lower-class wife of a returning soldier caused by her medication for an abortion, in "A Game of Chess"; and the unromantic sex between the typist and the carbuncular clerk, a proposed homosexual encounter with Mr. Eugenides, the unfulfilled relationship between the "virgin" Queen Elizabeth and Robert Dudley, and the mechanical copulation in a canoe, in "The Fire Sermon."

150. T. S. Eliot, "*Ulysses,* Order, and Myth" (1923) in *The Norton Anthology of English Literature: The Twentieth Century and After,* 2294.

151. Ibid., 2305, line 314. In "Death by Water" Phlebas the Phoenician forgot "profit and loss" and drowned just as Mme. Sosostris prophesied, but his death may only signify every man's fate rather than constitute a sacrifice presaging rebirth. In "What the Thunder Said" Christ's two disciples en route to Emmaus show no recognition of "the third who walks

always beside you"; the chaste knight finds nothing but decay and illusion in his unavailing quest to the Chapel Perilous; and the speaker sees an endless historical cycle of birth and destruction of fallen cities from Jerusalem, Athens, Alexandria to Vienna and London. Ancient myths and history seem to offer little consolation, only "the arid plain." Ibid., 2305n1.

152. Ibid., 2307n3, 2308n6. *Datta, dayadhvam, damyata* mean "give, sympathize, and control"; and *Shantih* means "the Peace which surpasseth understanding."

153. Ibid. 2300-05, lines 310, 308. "The Fire Sermon" concludes with a reference to St. Augustine's coming to Carthage after a lustful youth ("O Lord Thou pluckest me out") and to Buddha's sermon about lust ("burning"), thereby blending Eastern and Western religions. Eliot says, "The collation of these two representatives of eastern and western asceticism, as the culmination of this part of the poem, is not an accident." Ibid., 2305n9.

154. "In 1900 the West really did rule the world," according to Ferguson, because it "produced more than half the world's output" and controlled most of the world's land surface and population. Ferguson, *The War of the World,* lxvii-lxviii, 16.

155. Ibid., 189-90; Modris Eksteins, *Rites of Spring,* 256-57.

Chapter 4. Postwar Christian Theology

1. Karl Barth, *The Word of God and the Word of Man* (1924) in *Great Books of the Western World, Philosophy and Religion: Selections from the Twentieth Century,* ed. Mortimer J. Adler (Chicago: Encyclopaedia Britannica, 2007), 471 (emphasis in original).

2. Pierre Teilhard de Chardin, *Science and Christ* (New York: Harper & Row, 1965), 36.

3. Baumer, *Modern European Thought,* 402.

4. Ibid., 410-11, 418-24.

5. Baumer, *Modern European Thought,* 442.

6. Ibid., 441.

7. Ibid., 425, 442.

8. Ibid., 443. Because of existentialism's emphasis on human authenticity as distinct from neoorthodoxy's emphasis upon God's *wholly otherness,* I have separated it from neoorthodoxy, thereby adding a fourth theology to Baumer's three. In addition, I have included American fundamentalism, which Baumer did not address because of his European focus.

9. Paul Tillich, *The Courage to Be* (New Haven: Yale University Press, 1979), 186.

10. Baumer, *Modern European Thought,* 428, 450-51; *Stanford Encyclopedia of Philosophy,* "Jacques Maritain," http://plato.stanford.edu/entries/maritain/(accessed May 17, 2012).

11. Jacques Maritain, *Bergsonian Philosophy and Thomism*, trans. Mabel L Andison and J. Gordon Andison (New York: Philosophical Library, 1955), 278, 280.

12. Whitehead, *Science and the Modern World*, 185-92.

13. Jacques Maritain, *The Peasant of the Garonne: An Old Layman Questions Himself about the Present Time*, trans. Michael Cuddihy and Elizabeth Hughes (New York: Holt, Rinehart and Winston, 1968), 119, 122, 264-65 (emphasis in original).

14. Ronald L. Numbers, *"Aggressors, Victims, and Peacemakers*, Historical Actors in the Drama of Science and Religion" in *The Religion and Science Debate: Why Does It Continue?*, ed. Harold W. Attridge (New Haven: Yale University Press, 2009), 37.

15. Livingston and Fiorenza, *Modern Christian Thought: The Twentieth Century*, 63, 97.

16. Ibid., 62.

17. "One day in August 1914 stands out in my personal memory as a black day," Barth later recalled. "Ninety-three German intellectuals impressed public opinion by their proclamation in support of the war policy of Wilhelm II and his counselors. Among these intellectuals I discovered to my horror almost all of my theological teachers whom I had greatly venerated. In despair over what this indicated about the signs of the time, I suddenly realized that I could not any longer follow either their ethics and dogmatics or their understanding of the Bible and of history. For me at least nineteenth-century theology no longer held any future." Barth, "Evangelical Theology in the Nineteenth Century," *The Humanity of God* (Richmond: John Knox Press, 1963), 14, in Zahrnt, *The Question of God*, 16.

18. Livingston and Fiorenza, *Modern Christian Thought: The Twentieth Century*, 66.

19. Zahrnt, *The Question of God*, 45.

20. Ibid.

21. Ibid., 18.

22. Ibid., 19.

23. "It is not the right human thoughts about God which form the content of the Bible, but the right divine thoughts about men. The Bible tells us not how we should talk with God but what he says to us." Hans Urs von Balthazar, *Darstellung und Deutung seiner Theologie* (Cologne, 1961), 182, in Heinz, *The Question of God*, 19.

24. Livingston and Fiorenza, *Modern Christian Thought: The Twentieth Century*, 66. Zahrnt writes that "in opposition to every merely historical, psychological and speculative view of Christianity, Barth rediscovered the revelation of God as the decisive category of theological thought, and thereby restored to theology its own proper theme, which it had lost." Zahrnt, *The Question of God*, 20.

25. Karl Barth, *Epistle to the Romans* (London: Oxford University Press, 1933), 1, in Zahrnt, *The Question of God,* 22.

26. "If I have a system, it is limited to a recognition of what Kierkegaard calls the 'infinite qualitative distinction' between time and eternity, and to my regarding this as possessing negative as well as positive significance: 'God is in heaven, and thou art on earth.' The relation between such a God and such a man, and the relation between such a man and such a God, is for me the theme of the Bible and the essence of philosophy. Philosophers named this KRISIS of human perception—the Prime Cause: the Bible beholds at the same cross-roads—the figure of Jesus Christ." Barth, *Epistle to the Romans,* 10, in Zahrnt, *The Question of God,* 24.

27. "Behold, I make all things new! The affirmation of God, man, and the world given in the New Testament based exclusively on the possibility of a new order absolutely beyond human thought; and therefore, as prerequisite to that order, there must come a crisis that denies all human thought." Barth, *The Word of God and the Word of Man,* 473 (emphasis omitted).

28. "The 'historical Jesus' reconstructed from the records is not identical to revelation, to the active God, which cannot be *directly* perceived in history. Yet the connection between God and history is not severed; the relationship is dialectical, which means that the action of God in the event of Jesus Christ must be understood in the terms that *God has established* and not in our turning it into premature identity of time and eternity, history and the Absolute. The tension and mystery inherent in holding together the sovereignty of God and the human requires that all human testimony be understood dialectically as both 'no' and 'yes'—for revelatory truth never can be pronounced directly or as the last word." H. Martin Rumscheidt, *Religion and Theology: an Analysis of Barth-Harnack Correspondence of 1923,* 46, in Livingston and Fiorenza, *Modern Christian Thought: The Twentieth Century,* 70-71(emphasis in original), 104-05.

29. Zahrnt, *The Question of God,* 31 (emphasis in original).

30. Livingston and Fiorenza, *Modern Christian Thought: The Twentieth Century,* 75-76.

31. Ibid., 109. According to Livingston and Fiorenza, Barth "had a wider and more enduring influence on theology in the twentieth century than any other thinker." Zahrnt concurs. Zahrnt, *The Question of God,* 59.

32. Livingston and Fiorenza, *Modern Christian Thought: The Twentieth Century,* 99-100. On January 20, 1933, when Hitler became German Chancellor, Barth, then a professor at the University of Bonn, promptly determined to resist National Socialism because he considered the Nazi policy designed to eliminate the expression of Christian faith. In April 1933, the Nazis required all the German churches to assimilate under the "Evan-

gelical Church of the German Nation" and to operate under guiding principles that considered the Jews a grave national danger and forbade intermarriage between Germans and Jews. In June 1933, Barth wrote a pamphlet published in *Theological Existence Today* (banned by the Nazi's in July 1934), attacking the Nazi church program. Barth joined what became known as the Confessing Church, which held a synod of 138 delegates at Barmen in May 1934, and issued the famous Barmen Declaration.

33. Zahrnt, *The Question of God*, 56.

34. Ibid., 96.

35. Livingston and Fiorenza, *Modern Christian Thought: The Twentieth Century*, 108.

36. Ibid.

37. Ibid., 109.

38. Ibid.

39. Ibid., 66; Zahrnt, *The Question of God*, 85-86.

40. Zahrnt, *The Question of God*, 99-107; Livingston and Fiorenza, *Modern Christian Thought: The Twentieth Century*, 107.

41. Mary Lucas and Ellen Lucas, *Teilhard*, (New York: McGraw-Hill, 1981), 46- 48; Thomas M. King, *Teilhard's Mysticism of Knowing* (New York: Seabury Press, 1981), 15.

42. Lucas and Lucas, *Teilhard*, 50. Teilhard posited Cosmic Organizing Energy, similar to Bergson's *élan vital*, which drew subatomic particles together into increasingly complex matter that produced Life and eventually Man, both heading toward an ultimate goal: "Everything that is hard, crusty, or rebellious ... all that is false and reprehensible ... all that is physically or morally evil," Teilhard wrote, "will disappear. ... Matter will be absorbed into Spirit."

43. Ibid., 53, 56

44. Ibid., 69; Ursula King in Introduction to Pierre Teilhard de Chardin and Ursula King, *Pierre Teilhard De Chardin: Writings* (Maryknoll, NY: Orbis Books, 1999), 15. The Muslim soldiers called him *Sidi Marabout*, which is "an acknowledgment of his spiritual power as a man closely bound to God, a saint and ascetic protected from all injuries by divine grace."

45. Pierre Teilhard de Chardin, *Writings in Time of War* (New York: Harper & Rowe, 1968), 219, in Teilhard and King, *Pierre Teilhard De Chardin: Writings*, 15.

46. King, *Teilhard's Mysticism of Knowing*, 120, 124; Ursula King, "Postscript: The Heart of Teilhard's Faith Questioned and Reaffirmed" in *Pierre Teilhard De Chardin: Writings*, 165.

47. Lucas and Lucas, *Teilhard*, 64.

48. Ibid., 69-73.

49. Ibid., 65-67, 74-75. With the death of Pius X at the beginning of World

War I, the Curia's "White Terror" had quieted down. It slowly reemerged after the election of Benedict XV in 1914, when the largely unchanged Curia began cataloging heresies. The Jesuits followed suit in imposing strict censorship under the militaristic control of the Jesuit General Vladimir Ledochowski, who developed the board of censors to oversee the writings and teachings of Jesuits.

50. Ibid., 74.

51. Ibid., 86-88.

52. Remark to Paul Rivet in Ibid., 95; Livingston and Fiorenza, *Modern Christian Thought: The Twentieth Century*, 376.

53. Lucas and Lucas, *Teilhard*, 109.

54. Ibid., 89-90.

55. Ibid., 113.

56. Ibid., 50, 146, 160.

57. Ibid., 50, 168.

58. Ibid., 199.

59. Ibid., 229, 235.

60. Ibid., 269. 274.

61. Ibid., 285. In May 1950, the papal encyclical *Humani Generis* chastised those responsible for the "disagreements and errors" circulating in theology and philosophy and for their acceptance of the "still unproved scientific theory of evolution." In addition, the encyclical insisted on the correctness of the doctrines adopted at the Council of Trent and of the philosophy of Thomas Aquinas.

62. Ibid., 296-98.

63. Ibid., 340-42, 345.

64. Ibid., 167-68. In "My Universe" (March 1924), (Teilhard wrote an essay by the same title in 1918), Teilhard wrote: "It has been my destiny to stand at a privileged cross-roads in the world; there, in my twofold character of priest and scientist, I have felt passing through me, in particularly exhilarating and varied conditions, the double stream of human and divine forces." Pierre Teilhard de Chardin, *Science and Christ* (New York: Harper & Row, 1965), 38. Writing five years after the end of World War I, his only concern was his ability "to show how it is possible, by approaching the vast disorder of things from a certain angle, suddenly to see their obscurity and discord become transformed in a vibration that passes all description, inexhaustible in the richness of its tones and its notes, interminable in the perfection of its unity." Ibid., 38-39.

65. Pierre Teilhard de Chardin, *The Phenomenon of Man* (New York: Harper Torch books, 1965), 180-84.

66. Teilhard's conception of God as the inspiration for cosmic evolution was much like that of Alfred North Whitehead, who viewed God as a cre-

ative lure toward increased novelty and complexity. Whereas Henri Bergson had considered evolution to be a divergent process that multiplied the number of forms, Teilhard considered it a convergent process, setting evolution in a new direction of human socialization made possible by rapid communication and "planetizitation." Livingston and Schuessler. *Modern Christian Thought: The Twentieth Century*, 311-16.

67. Teilhard, *The Phenomenon of Man*, 269-70. By picturing God, the Omega Point, as present with, but independent of, the cosmic evolutionary process, Teilhard seems to distinguish his idea of God from other process theologies, like those of Hegel and Whitehead, which consider God affected by and, to an extent, dependent on the cosmic evolutionary process. Livingston and Fiorenza, *Modern Christian Thought: The Twentieth Century*, 311, 314-15.

68. Lucas and Lucas, *Teilhard*, 167-75. "Life has made us conscious collaborators in a Creation which is still going on in us, in order to lead us, it would appear, to a goal (even on Earth) much more lofty and distant than we imagined. We must, therefore, help God with all our strength, and handle matter as though our salvation depended solely upon our industry." Teilhard, "Science and Christ or Analysis and Synthesis" (February 1921) in Teilhard, *Science and Christ*, 32.

69. Teilhard, "Science and Christ or Analysis and Synthesis" (February 1921) in Teilhard, *Science and Christ*, 22, 35-36.

70. Teilhard, "Research, Work and Worship" (March 1955) in Teilhard, *Science and Christ*, 214. Because the motto of the Society of Jesus is *Ad Majorem Dei Gloriam*, Teilhard was in effect saying that it was his superiors rather than he who were betraying Jesuit principles.

71. Lawrence M. Principe, *Science and Religion* (Chantilly, VA: The Teaching Company, 2006), Course Guidebook, 40.

72. Teilhard defines evil as "disunity" produced through evolution in "My Universe" (March 1924) in Teilhard, *Science and Christ*, 80n15.

73. Zahrnt, *The Question of God*, 103.

74. Teilhard, "Some Reflections on the Conversion of the World" (October 1936) in Teilhard, *Science and Christ*, 118, 120.

75. Ibid., 120-23.

76. Ibid., 125-27.

77. Teilhard, "Catholicism and Science" (August 1946) in Teilhard, *Science and Christ*, 189, 190-91 (emphasis in original).

78. Zahrnt, *The Question of God*, 71-72.

79. Emil Brunner, *Man in Revolt* (Philadelphia: Westminster Press, 1947), 9, in Ibid., 71.

80. Emil Brunner, *Truth As Encounter* (Philadelphia: Westminster Press, 1964), 165, in Ibid., 73.

81. Zahrnt, The Question of God, 67.

82. Livingston and Fiorenza, *Modern Christian Thought: The Twentieth Century*, 79-80.

83. Ibid., 85, 102.

84. Zahrnt, *The Question of God*, 148.

85. Friedrich Gogarten, *The Reality of Faith, the Problem of Subjectivism in Theology*, trans. Carl Michlson (Philadelphia: Westminster Press, 1957), 52-54.

86. Zahrnt, *The Question of God*, 151-52.

87. Gogarten, *The Reality of Faith*, 92.

88. Livingston and Fiorenza,. *Modern Christian Thought: The Twentieth Century*, 88.

89. Gogarten, *The Reality of Faith*, 93-94.

90. Ibid., 94; Livingston and Fiorenza,. *Modern Christian Thought: The Twentieth Century*, 88.

91. Zahrnt, *The Question of God*, 153.

92. Ibid.

93. Livingston and Fiorenza,. *Modern Christian Thought: The Twentieth Century*, 86-88.

94. Catholicism also had its existentialist thinkers, such as Gabriel Marcel (1888-1973). Ibid., 138-39.

95. Ibid., 153-60.

96. Tillich, *The Courage to Be*, 86, 163-81.

97. George M. Marsden, *Fundamentalism and American Culture: The Shaping of Twentieth-Century Evangelicalism: 1870-1925* (New York: Oxford University Press, 1980), 149-52.

98. Statement of Bryan's wife quoted in Ronald L. Numbers, "The Creationists," in *God in Nature: Historical Essays on the Encounter between Christianity and Science*, eds. David C. Lindberg and Ronald L. Numbers (Berkeley: University of California Press, 1986), 395.

99. Numbers, "The Creationists," in *God in Nature,* 393.

100. Marsden, *Fundamentalism and American Culture*, 141.

101. Numbers, "The Creationists," in *God in Nature,* 399; Marsden, *Fundamentalism and American Culture*, 214-15.

102. L. S. K[eyser], "No War against Science—Never!" *Bible Companion* (1925): 413, in Numbers, "The Creationists," in *God in Nature,* 399.

103. Ibid., 398.

104. Marsden, *Fundamentalism and American Culture*, 191.

105. Numbers, "The Creationists," in *God in Nature,* 402.

106. Ibid.; Marsden, *Fundamentalism and American Culture*, 186-87.

107. Numbers, "The Creationists," in *God in Nature,* 403.

108. Ronald L. Numbers, "Aggressors, Victims, and Peacemakers," in *The Religion and Science Debate*, 39-40.

109. Numbers, "The Creationists," in *God in Nature,* 409; Principe, *Science and Religion,* Course Guidebook, 45.

110. Robert T. Pennock, *Tower of Babel: The Evidence against the New Creationism* (Cambridge: MIT Press, 1999), 10-18.

111. Ibid., 26-27. Creationists like law professor Philip Johnson consider Darwinian evolution a scientifically fallacious and atheistic theory, and the biblical account of creation a superior explanation deserving equal time in the science classroom unless Darwinian evolution is banished. John F. Haught, *God after Darwin, A Theology of Evolution* (Boulder, Colorado: Westview Press, 2000), 26-28.

112. *Kitzmiller v. Dover Area School District,* 400 F. Supp. 2d 707 (M.D. Pa. 2005).

113. Livingston and Fiorenza, *Modern Christian Thought: The Twentieth Century,* 316-36. Whitehead's assistant, philosopher Charles Hartshorne (1897-2000), continued the development of process theology from the 1940s through the 1960s, as did the theologian Schubert Ogden (b. 1928) thereafter.

114. Baumer, *Modern European Thought,* 450-51; Stanford Encyclopedia of Philosophy, "Jacques Maritain," http://plato.stanford.edu/entries/maritain/ (accessed May 17, 2012).

Chapter 5. Postwar Western Philosophy

1. Ludwig Wittgenstein, Introduction to *Tractatus Logico-Philosophicus* (n.p.: Seven Treasures Publications, 2009), 3.

2. Martin Heidegger (presumably from Lectures on Nietzsche, 1936-40), quoted in William Barrett, *Irrational Man,* 184.

3. Chambers, Hanawalt, Rabb, Woloch, and Tiersten, *The Western Experience,* 829-30.

4. Baumer, *Modern European Thought,* 460-63.

5. Einstein, *Relativity,* trans. Robert Lawson (New York: Henry Holt, 1921), 65, in Baumer, *Modern European Thought,* 461.

6. Werner Heisenberg, *Physics and Philosophy* (New York: Harper Torch Books, 1962), 60, in Baumer, *Modern European Thought,* 462.

7. Baumer, *Modern European Thought,* 464.

8. Ibid., 463, 471.

9. Whitehead, *Science and the Modern World,* 64-74, 93-94.

10. Baumer, *Modern European Thought,* 463.

11. Morton White, *The Age of Analysis: 20th Century Philosophers* (New York: Mentor Book, 1957), 13-21. "In Husserl, then, we see a heroic effort to re-establish metaphysics according to the canons set up by science." Quentin Lauer, *Phenomenology: Its Genesis and Prospect* (New York: Harper Torchbooks, 1965), 159.

12. Baumer, *Modern European Thought*, 464.

13. Wittgenstein was the youngest of eight children of a wealthy and cultured Viennese family; he was baptized a Roman Catholic and educated at home until age 14. He attended grammar school in Vienna, secondary school in Linz, and technical college in Berlin to develop his early aptitude in engineering. A. C. Grayling, *Wittgenstein: A Very Short Introduction* (Oxford: Oxford University Press, 2001), 1-4; Allan Janik and Stephen Toulmin, *Wittgenstein's Vienna* (Chicago: Elephant Paperback, 1973), 171-73, 200.

14. Grayling, *Wittgenstein*, 6; G. H. Von Wright Biographical Sketch in Norman Malcolm, *Ludwig Wittgenstein: A Memoir* (New York: Oxford University Press, 1972), 6n1.

15. Stumpf, *PHILOSOPHY: History & Problems*, 419. American philosopher William Barrett characterizes the goal of the *Principia Mathematica* as creating "the language of languages," the "technique of techniques," and "the most potent instrument of thought yet devised." William Barrett, *The Illusion of Technique: A Search for Meaning in a Technological Civilization* (Garden City: Anchor Books, 1979), 7-8.

16. Barrett, *The Illusion of Technique*, 10-14.

17. Janik and Toulmin, *Wittgenstein's Vienna*, 209-12.

18. Ibid., 165.

19. Ibid., 121-32.

20. Ibid., 164-65.

21. Arthur Schopenhauer, *The Basis of Morality*, trans. A. B. Bullock, 2nd ed. (London: Allen & Unwin, 1915), 372, in ibid., 156-57. For Schopenhauer, ethics is a compassionate, ethical, even mystical experience, like that described in Hinduism.

22. Søren Kierkegaard, *Philosophical Fragments Johannes Climacus*, ed. and trans. with Introduction and Notes by Howard V. Hong and Edna H. Hong (Princeton: Princeton University Press, 1987), 76, 78n. "Hegel is not right in his attempt to unite logical, metaphysical and historical categories in his system, with the result that he understands historical events as having occurred with necessity." For Kierkegaard, Hegel's dialectical necessity relates to "essence" (Kant's *noumena*), which is beyond human knowledge; scientific knowledge about "being" (*phenomena*) differs from matters of subjective belief; and faith (especially in the Absolute Paradox of Christ's divinity) "does not result simply from a scientific inquiry … [and] does not need [proof]." Søren Kierkegaard, *Concluding Unscientific Postscript*, in Walter Kaufmann, *EXISTENTIALISM From Dostoevsky to Sartre*, revised and expanded, ed. and trans. with Introduction and Prefaces by Walter Kaufmann (New York: New American Library, 1975), 114.

23. Janik and Toulmin, *Wittgenstein's Vienna*, 163.

24. Barrett, *The Illusion of Technique,* 35; Janik and Toulmin, *Wittgenstein's Vienna,* 200-04.

25. Von Wright, "Biographical Sketch," in Malcolm, *Ludwig Wittgenstein: A Memoir,* 8-9.

26. Ibid., 7-10.

27. Wittgenstein, *Tractatus Logico-Philosophicus,* sec. 1; Grayling, *Wittgenstein,* 18-19. "The main point [of the *Tractatus*] is the theory of what can be expressed by propositions—i.e. by language—(and, which comes to the same thing, what can be thought), and what cannot be expressed by propositions, but only shown; which, I believe, is the cardinal problem of philosophy." Letter to Bertrand Russell.

28. Wittgenstein, *Tractatus,* secs. 3, 3.1, 3.2, 3.203.

29. Ibid., secs. 1.1, 2, 2.01, 2.02, 2.021, 3.221.

30. Grayling, *Wittgenstein,* 35. See Grayling's summary, 18-38.

31. Wittgenstein, *Tractatus,* secs. 3, 4.01, 2.04, 4.11, 6.53 ("The correct method in philosophy would really be the following: to say nothing except what can be said, i.e. propositions of natural science—i.e. something that has nothing to do with philosophy—and then, whenever someone else wanted to say something metaphysical, to demonstrate to him that he had failed to give meaning to certain signs in his proposition.").

32. Ibid., secs. 4.111, 4.112.

33. Ibid., sec. 4.114.

34. Barrett, *The Illusion of Technique,* 45-49.

35. Wittgenstein, *Tractatus,* sec. 6.54.

36. Ibid., secs. 6.42, 6.54.

37. Ibid., secs. 6.432, 6.44-45.

38. Ibid., secs., 6.421, 6.522, 6.52.

39. Ibid., sec. 7; Ludwig Wittgenstein, *Briefe an Ludwig von Ficker,* ed. G. H. Von Wright (Salzburg: Otto Müller , 1969), 35, in Janik and Toulmin, *Wittgenstein's Vienna,* 192. In a letter to his German publisher Fricker Wittgenstein wrote that the most important part of the *Tractatus* to be the mystical world of the ethical and life's meaningfulness about which he had been silent, except for his emphasis in the introductory and concluding remarks. Ethics and value, for Wittgenstein, concern the world as a whole and not the facts within the world: "How things are in the world is a matter of complete indifference for what is higher. God does not reveal himself in the world," because it "is not how things are in the world that is mystical, but that it exists." Secs., 6.432, 6.44.

40. Barrett, *The Illusion of Technique,* 49; Grayling, *Wittgenstein,* 70-71; Von Wright, Biographical Sketch in Malcolm, *Ludwig Wittgenstein: A Memoir,* 13. By the early 1930s, Wittgenstein had distanced himself from the Circle's ideas, even though the Circle members associated their ideas with

the *Tractatus*. Janik and Toulmin, *Wittgenstein's Vienna*, 216. Grayling disputes the claim that the *Tractatus* was a major inspiration for the logical positivism of the Vienna Circle, contending that the Circle's views had already solidified before reading the *Tractatus*. Grayling, *Wittgenstein*, 65-68.

41. Janik and Toulmin, *Wittgenstein's Vienna*, 216.

42. "Any one fact can either be the case, or not the case, and everything else remains the same." Wittgenstein, *Tractatus*, sec. 1.21.

43. Barrett, *The Illusion of Technique*, 36-44.

44. Von Wright, Biographical Sketch, in Malcolm, *Ludwig Wittgenstein: A Memoir*, 6-17; Janik and Toulmin, *Wittgenstein's Vienna*, 174-76.

45. Von Wright, Biographical Sketch, in Malcolm, *Ludwig Wittgenstein: A Memoir*, 16.

46. Ludwig Wittgenstein, *Philosophical Investigations*, ed. G. E. Entry Anscombe and R. Rhees (Oxford: Blackwell, 1981), 664, in Grayling, *Wittgenstein*, 80.

47. Dermot Moran, *Edmund Husserl, Founder of Phenomenology* (Cambridge, UK: Polity Press, 2005), 17; Barry Smith and David Woodruff, eds., *The Cambridge Companion to Husserl* (Cambridge: Cambridge University Press, 1996), 4-5.

48. Moran, *Edmund Husserl*, 16-17, 19, 22, 25. He was baptized in the Lutheran Church in Vienna and thereafter read the New Testament daily as a committed, if non-confessional, Christian. Husserl's religious commitment was to a quasi-Hegelian "absolute spirit" in the sense that he aimed to reach "God without God." His academic reputation spread, bringing him brilliant students like Adolph Reinach, who died in the war in 1917, and of whom Husserl wrote several moving obituaries.

49. Edmund Husserl, *Ideas, General Introduction to Pure Phenomenology*, trans. W. R. Boyce Gibson (New York: Collier Books, 1962), 19 (emphasis in original).

50. Quentin Lauer, *Phenomenology, Its Genesis and Prospect* (New York: Harper Torchbooks, 1965), 1-2; Albert B. Hakim, *Historical Introduction to Philosophy*, 2nd ed. (New York: Macmillan, 1992), 728-29. Phenomenology arises from the distinction drawn by Kant between *phenomena* (the appearance of reality in consciousness) and *noumena* (reality in itself). By considering scientific knowledge possible only of phenomena and not noumena, Kant engaged in a kind of phenomenology in order to resist the rationalism of Descartes, who sought knowledge of all reality, and the skepticism of Hume, who accepted no scientific knowledge except in mathematics. Following Kant, Hegel specifically characterized his approach as phenomenology, contending that we can only know phenomena but that phenomena nevertheless provide sufficient basis for understanding reality. For Hegel, reality is revealed in the dialectical process, starting

with consciousness of the self and progressing to reason, then to the unity of reality, and finally to the Absolute Spirit. On the other hand, Husserl remained concerned that the success of the natural sciences would cause the sciences to reduce human consciousness and spirit to physical matter.

51. Edmund Husserl, *Ideen I,* ed. Walter Biemel (The Hague: Martinus Nijhoff, 1950), 154, in Lauer, *Phenomenology,* 8n5. The characterization and terminology is from Lauer, *Phenomenology,* 3-4.

52. Lauer, *Phenomenology,* 5-6.

53. Ibid., 46-64; Stumpf, *PHILOSOPHY: History & Problems,* 455-57; White, *The Age of Analysis,* 103-04.

54. Lauer, *Phenomenology,* 67n5.

55. Ibid., 69. Lauer explains: "Thus, intentional constitution has become a universal explanation of the 'clarification' of being. 'Nothing is, except by a proper *operation* of consciousness, *whether actual or potential.*' If, then, the task of philosophy is to understand being, its method must be to penetrate the subjectivity wherein being has its source. In this way Husserl derives an entire philosophy from what he calls a 'radical consciousness of self.'" An individual consciousness is a "transcendental" subject related to objects, and for Husserl the sum total of subjective relations to the world constitutes "transcendental subjectivity." 79-80 (emphasis in original). Herman Phillipse explains that Kant's thing-in-itself is the ideal consequence of this phenomenological subjectivity, i.e., "an *ideal limit* of the phenomenal thing." Herman Philipse, "Transcendental idealism," in Smith and Smith, eds., *The Cambridge Companion to Husserl,* 274 (emphasis in original).

56. Edmund Husserl, *Formale und transzendentale Logic* (Halle: Niemeyer, 1929), 14, in Lauer, *Phenomenology,* 80.

57. Learning, for Husserl, is not an accumulation but a growth in knowledge that renders the subject capable of ever greater and more complex objectivities. Lauer, *Phenomenology,* 105, 109-10.

58. Ibid., 159. Even though Husserl seeks to avoid metaphysical presuppositions, his phenomenology has metaphysical implications because metaphysics rests on epistemology and Husserl is an ontological idealist. Herman Philipse explains the metaphysical implications of Husserl's phenomenology: "In short, Husserl's theory of perceptions, combined with his new conception of a *Ding an sich* [Kant's thing-in-itself], implies the idealist ontology of the real world which Husserl states in *Ideas* I. The real world is nothing but a 'sense,' constituted by consciousness, because it is the product of a transcending interpretation of really imminent sensations." Herman Philipse, "Transcendental idealism," in Smith and Smith, eds., *The Cambridge Companion to Husserl,* 276.

59. Stumpf, *PHILOSOPHY: History & Problems,* 458.

60. Quoted in Moran, *Edmund Husserl*, 31-32.

61. Moran, *Edmund Husserl*, 32.

62. Ibid., 22, 35.

63. Edmund Husserl, *Husserl, Shorter Works*, trans. and ed. Frederick Elliston and Peter McCormick (Notre Dame, Indiana: University of Notre Dame Press, 1981) 10; 25: 69, in Moran, *Edmund Husserl*, 34.

64. Edmund Husserl, "Fichte's Ideal of Humanity," in *Husserl, Shorter Works*, 25: 279, in Moran, *Edmund Husserl*, 33.

65. Moran, *Edmund Husserl*, 32.

66. Ibid., 35-36.

67. Stumpf, *PHILOSOPHY: History & Problems*, 452-53.

68. Edmund Husserl, *The Crisis of European Sciences*, in Hakim, *Historical Introduction to Philosophy*, 749.

69. Ibid., 749-50; see also Lauer, *Phenomenology*, 161-62.

70. Edmund Husserl, *Philosophy and the Crisis of European Man*, in Stumpf, *PHILOSOPHY: History & Problems*, 454.

71. Husserl, *The Crisis of European Sciences*, in Hakim, *Historical Introduction to Philosophy*, 751.

72. W. Biemle, ed., *Husserliana Edition VI, Die Krisis der europhätschen Wissenschaften und die transcendentale Pharrenomenologie. Eine Einleitung in die phänomenologische Philosophie,* (The Hague: Nijhoff, 1954), Beilage XXVIII, in Smith and Smith, eds., *The Cambridge Companion to Husserl*, 74 (emphasis in original).

73. Moran, *Edmund Husserl*, 39. Considering his friendship and professional support for Heidegger during the 1920s, Husserl found Heidegger's *Being in Time* a shocking departure from his own vision of transcendental phenomenology: "A philosophy that takes its start from human existence falls *back* into that naïveté the overcoming of which has, in our opinion, been the whole meaning of modernity." 37.

74. Ibid., 40.

75. Barry Smith and David Woodruff, *The Cambridge Companion to Husserl*, 8. Husserl wrote *Cartesian Meditations* (1931), *Philosophy and the Crisis of European Man* (1936), and *The Crisis of European Sciences* (1937, unfinished). "And we old people remain here," wrote Husserl, largely forsaken at the end of his career by former friends and students, "a singular turn of the times: it gives the philosopher—if it does not take away his breath— much to think of. But now: *Cogito ergo sum*, i.e., I prove *sub specie aeterni* my right to live. And this, the *aeternitas* in general, cannot be reached by any earthly powers." Marvin Farber, *The Foundation of Phenomenology* (Cambridge: Harvard, 1943), 23, in White, *The Age of Analysis*, 104.

76. Moran, *Edmund Husserl*, 41-42; Smith and Smith, *The Cambridge Companion to Husserl*, 7-8; Hakim, *Historical Introduction To Philosophy*, 728.

77. Barrett, *The Illusion of Technique*, 139-45.

78. He attended school on scholarship, first in Konstanz and later in Freiburg, to prepare for the priesthood. Discharged from his Jesuit novitiate because of his bad heart and lack of vocation, Heidegger entered Freiburg University to study theology and scholastic philosophy. In 1917, Heidegger married Elfriede Petri, a Protestant, and in 1919, upon the birth of the first of their two sons, he renounced his Catholicism for Protestantism. Inwood, Michael. *Heidegger: A Very Small Introduction* (Oxford University Press, 2000), 1-2; Rüdiger Safranski, *Martin Heidegger: Between Good and Evil*, trans. Ewald Osers (Cambridge: Harvard University Press, 1998), 55-57.

79. Barrett, *What is Existentialism?*, 158; Inwood, *Heidegger*, 36.

80. Martin Heidegger, *Being and Time*, in *Basic Writings from Being and Time (1927) to The Task of Thinking (1964)*, ed. with General Introduction and Introductions to each section by David Farrell Krell (New York: Harper & Row, 1977), 54.

81. Ibid., 43, 73, 214. In his later *Letter on Humanism* (1947), Heidegger defines Being as "there is/it gives" since "'gives' names the essence of Being that is giving, granting its truth. The self-giving into the open, along with the open region itself, is Being itself."

82. Inwood, *Heidegger*, 22; Lawrence Cahoone, Lectures and Course Guide on Heidegger, in *The Modern Intellectual Tradition: From Descartes to Derrida* (Chantilly, Virginia: The Teaching Company, 2010).

83. "Being 'is' only in the understanding of those entities to whose Being something like an understanding of Being belongs." Heidegger, *Being and Time*, trans. J. Macquarrie and E. Robinson (Oxford, 1962), 183, in Inwood, *Heidegger*, 60-61.

84. Barrett, *The Illusion of Technique*, 158.

85. Barrett, *Irrational Man*, 200.

86. Heidegger, *Being and Time*, in *Basic Writings*, 69-70.

87. Ibid., 209-10. Heidegger considered philosophy the key to Western development because it laid down general frameworks within which history worked out details. Therefore, philosophical history played a central role in the development of the modern technological era. Technology originated in the West as a product of science, which, for Heidegger, distinguishes East from West more so than any other cultural factor, such as religion or art. In Heidegger's view, science began with the Greeks, rather than the Asians, because the Greeks were philosophically oriented toward detaching objects from Being's enveloping presence and began to focus their research on these objects.

88. Barrett, *What is Existentialism?*, 196-99.

89. Ibid., 166. Heidegger still saw the possibility for man to direct civi-

lization toward an entirely new outlook, not some new philosophical theory, but a new kind of thinking, beyond the metaphysical and technical. To retrieve Being from this oblivion humankind must assume a passivity toward Being and learn to let Being be, instead of trying only to draw answers out of Being through science.

90. Inwood, *Heidegger*, 15.

91. Ibid., 63.

92. Ibid., 61.

93. Ibid., 63.

94. Martin Heidegger, *What Is Metaphysics?*, in *Basic Writings*, 110.

95. Ibid., 111-12.

96. Ibid., 112.

97. Barrett, *The Illusion of Technique*, 262. Early Heidegger considers the correspondence theory of meaning (mental judgment matching a material fact) possible only when judgment and fact meet in the field of Being. In other words, the openness to Being as un-hiddenness makes propositional truth possible. Late Heidegger, by contrast, asserts that truth is only accessible through freedom, the freedom to let-be, by which Heidegger means a characteristic of Being itself rather than of Dasein. In this later view, Being and truth are interchangeable in that Being reveals itself. Heidegger never explains how to achieve this selfless exercise of freedom, this will-less state of letting things be, or how to overcome the human will that leads men into untruth. Indeed, Heidegger neglects the connection between Being and doing because he considers Being to be the product of aesthetic rather than moral action.

98. Ibid., 263.

99. Barrett, *Irrational Man*, 209-10.

100. Inwood, *Heidegger*, 120.

101. Ibid., 123.

102. Ibid., 121.

103. Ibid., 124-25. Art grounds the viewers by featuring their earth, their language, and their customs, beliefs, and traditions, and constitutes an explosion of creativity, a beginning or a leap, from which future generations may benefit. According to Heidegger, this has been the experience of art through the ages: the Greeks conceived of art as presence, the medievalists as created things, and the modernists as objects to be manipulated. Whereas Hegel considered art non-essential to historical existence because truth was already revealed, Heidegger thought of himself as a prophet for a new art and a new era in which art served as a founding of truth.

104. Ibid., 3-7.

105. Martin Heidegger (presumably from Lectures on Nietzsche, 1936-40), in Barrett, *Irrational Man*, 184.

106. Barrett, *What is Existentialism?*, 49.

107. Samir Okasha, *Philosophy of Science: A Very Short Introduction* (Oxford: Oxford University Press, 2002), 78.

108. Stumpf, *PHILOSOPHY: History & Problems*, 424-25.

109. Okasha, *Philosophy of Science*, 78.

110. Rudolf Carnap, *Philosophy and Logical Syntax*, Chapter I, in Stumpf, *PHILOSOPHY: History & Problems*, 425.

111. Stumpf, *PHILOSOPHY: History & Problems*, 425.

112. Ibid., 427-28. Analytic statements are true or false depending upon the meaning of their words or symbols and contribute nothing to knowledge. If true, the statements are tautologies, e.g., all men are mortal, and if false, the statements are contradictions, e.g., all men are not mortal. By contrast, synthetic statements are true or false depending upon their verifiability by empirical observation, e.g., snow is crystallized water. Thus, analytic statements are either tautologies or contradictions, whereas synthetic statements can add to factual knowledge if empirically verified as true. If a statement is neither analytic nor synthetic, it is judged to be emotive or non-cognitive. For the logical positivists, metaphysics, ethics, and aesthetics fall into this latter category.

113. Thomas R. Flynn, *Existentialism: A Very Short Introduction* (Oxford: Oxford University Press, 2006), 17-20.

114. Ibid., 23.

115. Ibid., 51; Barrett, *What Is Existentialism?*, 164.

116. Barrett, *What is Existentialism?*, 146-74. Heidegger describes the structures of human existence only as the point of departure for his fundamental ontological inquiry. By contrast, Kierkegaard urges pursuit of authentic human existence and opposes the use of philosophical systems in this regard because he considers them incompatible with such authenticity. As a speculative philosopher, Heidegger deals with pure possibilities; as a Christian moralist, Kierkegaard deals with the specific ethical and religious choices of actual individuals. In short, Heidegger and Kierkegaard are doing two different things, which reflect the two different types of existentialism.

117. Ibid., 52-53. Existentialism's overriding concern was existing authentically, becoming an individual, making one's actions one's own. One's choices define one's essential being, or, in Sartre's words, "*existence* comes before *essence*." Jean-Paul Sartre, *Existentialism Is a Humanism* (1946), in Walter Kaufmann, *Existentialism from Dostoevsky to Sartre* (New York: New American Library, 1975), 348.

118. Baumer, *Modern European Thought*, 465. Karl Jaspers, *Man in the Modern Age*, trans. Eden and Cedar Paul (New York: Henry Holt, 1933), 153, in Ibid.

119. Flynn, *Existentialism*, 54.

120. Jean-Paul Sartre, *Existentialism Is a Humanism* in Kaufmann, *Existentialism from Dostoevsky to Sartre*, 369.

121. Søren Kierkegaard, *Concluding Unscientific Postscript*, in Kaufmann, *Existentialism from Dostoevsky to Sartre*, 117.

122. Ibid., 349.

123. Barrett, *What Is Existentialism?*, 165. Heidegger distinguishes between the ontological aspects (general structure or laws) and the ontic aspects (actual facts) of human existence to determine the *a priori* structures that pervade human existence as potentialities. Heidegger, *Basic Writings*, 53-54n. In distinguishing between ontological and ontic, Heidegger considers the characteristics of being-in-the-world (care, anxiety, death, guilt, etc.) to be ontological possibilities rather than ontic actualities. Thus, for Heidegger, death pervades human existence as potential not actual mortality. The ever-present possibility of death is the ontological context within which man makes his ontic decisions.

Sartre flip-flops between ontic and ontological viewpoints, attempting a phenomenological description of Being in *Being and Nothingness*, yet periodically exhorting free individual action as the moral leader of the mid-century French generation. Barrett, *What Is Existentialism?*, 164. The distinction between Heidegger and Sartre is set out in bold relief by their disparate views of actions and potentialities. Sartre says you are what you do—a moral viewpoint that the authentic individual cannot evade personal responsibility for what he does or fails to do. Thus, Sartre is fundamentally concerned with the ontic level of individual acts, not the ontological level of human possibilities. For Heidegger, by contrast, Being takes precedence over Doing since man's ontic actions occur within the context of man's ontological possibilities, which is his primary concern. The celebrated will to action or will to power, for Heidegger, inevitably thwarts man's fundamental endeavor to let Being reveal itself.

124. Whitehead, *Science and the Modern World*, 54-55, 142.

125. Ibid., 142.

Chapter 6. Postwar Western Literature

1. Ernest Hemingway, *A Farewell to Arms* (New York: Charles Scribner's Sons, 1957), 239.

2. F. Scott Fitzgerald, *This Side of Paradise* (New York: Simon & Shuster, 2010), 330.

3. Barbusse, *Under Fire*, 138.

4. Remarque, *All Quiet on the Western Front*, 294.

5. Robert Graves, *Good-Bye to All That*, 228, 321 (Prologue to his 1957 revision).

6. Ernest Hemingway, *In Our Time* (1925) in Ernest Hemingway, *The Short Stories* (New York: Scribner Classics, 1997), 138-45.

7. Ezra Pound, *Hugh Selwyn Mauberley (Life and Contacts)* (1920), lines 73-75, 91, in *The Norton Anthology of American Literature, 1914-1945*, 7th ed., Vol. D, eds. Nina Baym and Mary Loeffelholz (New York: W. W. Norton, 2007), 1486-87.

8. Frederic J. Hoffman, *The 20s: American Writing in the Postwar Decade*, rev. ed. (New York: Free Press, 1965), 75.

9. Baumer, *Modern European Thought*, 411.

10. Ibid., 419-424.

11. Ibid., 419-20.

12. Nathalie Sarraute, *The Age of Suspicion: Essays on the Novel* (New York: George Braziller, 1963), 54-55.

13. Ibid., 54, 57, 62.

14. Sigmund Freud, *Introductory Lectures on Psychoanalysis*, trans. and ed. James Strachey (New York: W. W. Norton, 1966), 21.

15. Sigmund Freud, *Civilization and Its Discontents,* trans. and ed. James Strachey (New York: W. W. Norton, 2010), 94.

16. Baumer, *Modern European Thought*, 421.

17. Aldous Huxley, *Brave New World* (New York: Harper & Row, 1969), 4.

18. C. E. M. Joad, *Under the Fifth Rib* (New York: E. P. Dutton, 1933), 18-19, 23; *Guide to Modern Wickedness* (London: Farber & Farber, 1939), 38-57, both in Baumer, *Modern European Thought*, 425.

19. Andre Malraux's term quoted in Baumer, *Modern European Thought*, 424.

20. M. H. Abrams and Jeffrey Gault Harpham, *A Glossary of Literary Terms*, 9th ed. (Boston: Wadsworth Cengage Learning, 2009), 177-78. We commonly think of literature as fictional works of poetry, prose, and drama, but it also can include expressive philosophical, historical, and scientific writing intended for the general audience, and that is the sense in which literature is used in this chapter.

21. Hoffman, *The 20s,* 21.

22. Ibid.

23. Walter Isaacson, *Einstein: His Life and Universe* (New York: Simon & Schuster, 2007), 263-64.

24. Bertrand Russell, *A Free Man's Worship and Other Essays* (London: Unwin Paperbacks, 1976), 11-12. Russell wrote his essay "A Free Man's Worship" in 1902, first published it in 1903, and published it in book form in 1917.

25. Ibid., 18-19.

26. Bertrand Russell, "Causes of the Present Chaos" (1923), in Hoffman, *The 20s,* 279.

27. Bertrand Russell, *What I Believe* (1925), in Hoffman, *The 20s,* 279-80.

28. Joseph Wood Krutch, *The Modern Temper* (New York: Harcourt, Brace, 1929), 9.

29. Ibid., 10.

30. Ibid., 61.

31. Ibid., 97, 101.

32. Ibid., 137, 141.

33. Ibid., 170.

34. Ibid., 205.

35. Ibid., 204, 222, 228, 232.

36. Ibid., 249.

37. Max Eastman, *The Literary Mind: Its Place in an Age of Science* (1931), in Hoffman, *The 20s*, 315.

38. Ibid. in Hoffman, *The 20s*, 316.

39. I. A. Richards, *Science and Poetry* (New York: W.W. Norton, 1926), 33.

40. Ibid., 71.

41. Ibid., 57, 77, 82.

42. Ibid., 95.

43. Hoffman, *The 20s*, 321.

44. Ibid., 319.

45. In *God without Thunder* (1930), Ransom argued for return of the "old God" of the Old Testament to address the problems of evil in the world because God provides a basis for the moral law. For Ransom, science is a truth but not the whole truth because it focuses on abstractions and reduces objects to their measurable aspects, thereby eliminating God and myth, when science and religion should work in partnership. Ransom concludes by challenging modern man: "Let him restore to God the thunder." Hoffman, *The 20s*, 327-29.

46. Kirtley F. Mather, *New Republic* (September 9, 1925) in Hoffman, *The 20s*, 283. Mather stood among Bertrand Russell, J. B. S. Haldane, and others, in rejecting traditional notions and sanctions against sin. All three advocated a scientific approach to ethics, as a corrective to the morality of both fundamentalism and industrialism.

47. Hoffman, *The 20s*, 284. In his article in the *New Republic* (August 6, 1924), William Pepperell Montague staked out a middle ground between science and religion that Hoffman characterized as "a request that God be allowed in the modern Temple on probation, that His attributes and the terms of belief in Him be accepted as hypotheses, presumably hypotheses that might never be pressed for evidence nor embarrassed by the need for verification; unless, of course, the immortality of the soul and the existence of the supernatural beings can eventually be proved as 'highly probable' through some extension either of science or of religion as not yet proposed." 284-85.

48. Ibid., 284. Herbert Croly made these points in successive articles in the *New Republic* (June 9, 1920 and January 27, 1926).

49. Hoffman, *The 20s*, 330.

50. Abrams and Harpham, *A Glossary of Literary Terms*, 201-02.

51. R. B. Kershner, *The Twentieth-Century Novel, An Introduction* (Boston: Bedford Books, 1997), 45.

52. Ibid., 39.

53. Abrams and Harpham, *A Glossary of Literary Terms*, 228.

54. Leonard Tancock, Introduction in Emile Zola, *Germinal*, trans. with Introduction by Leonard Tancock (New York: Penguin Books, 1983), 6. (Emile Zola describing his intentions in writing *Germinal*.)

55. Virginia Woolf, "Mr. Bennett and Mrs. Brown" (1923), *A Bloomsbury Group Reader*, ed. S. P. Rosenbaum (Cambridge: Blackwell, 1993), 235, in Kershner, *The Twentieth-Century Novel*, 35; David Thorburn, *Masterworks of Early 20th-Century Literature* (Chantilly, Virginia: The Teaching Company, 2007), Course Guidebook, Part I, 14.

56. Contrast the all-knowing narrators in Austen and Zola with Conrad's ironic narrator Marlow whose vague, impressionistic language ("the implacable force brooding over an inscrutable intention") proves inadequate to convey the promised enlightenment, "the clue" anticipated from Marlow's long narrative toward Kurtz's final "cry" ("The horror! The horror!"). Joseph Conrad, *Heart of Darkness* A Norton Critical Edition, 4th Ed. (New York: W. W. Norton, 2006), 27. Conrad's linguistic technique conveys the instability of civilization, while simultaneously tainting the reader with knowledge of the mysterious heart of darkness, the "horror." Peter Brooks, "An Unreadable Report: Conrad's *Heart of Darkness*," 384-85.

57. Virginia Woolf, "Modern fiction" (1925) in *The Norton Anthology of English Literature: The Twentieth Century and After*, 2150.

58. Ibid., 2151-52.

59. Kershner, *The Twentieth-Century Novel*, 38. Kershner quotes historian Eric J. Hobsbawm to show that "modernism" had begun by 1914: "cubism; expressionism; futurism; pure abstraction in painting; functionalism and flight from ornament in architecture; the abandonment of tonality in music; the break with tradition in literature."

60. Ibid., 39. Abrams and Harpham, *A Glossary of Literary Terms*, 201-02.

61. Virginia Woolf, *Mrs. Dalloway* (San Diego: Harvest/HBJ Book, 1981), 7.

62. Ibid., 5. "The War was over," Clarissa thinks, but not for "Mrs. Foxcroft at the Embassy last night eating her heart out because that nice boy was killed" or "Lady Bexborough who opened the bizarre, they said, with the telegram in her hand, John, her favorite killed." Doris Kilman still holds a "violent grudge against the world" because she lost her teaching job during the war due to her German origin; uniformed boys march

toward Whitehall to lay a wreath at the tomb of the Unknown Warrior; and Dr. Bradshaw discloses the suicide of a shell-shocked soldier—"in the middle of my party, here's death, she thought." 129, 183.

63. Ibid., 86-88. Septimus Warren Smith is self-loathing and tormented because of his inability to feel following the death of his lover and fellow officer Evans. Nancy Topping Bazin and Jane Hamovit Lauler draw the many parallels between Clarissa Dalloway and Septimus Smith in "Virginia Woolf's Keen Sensitivity to War, Its Roots and Its Impact on Her Novels" in *Virginia Woolf and War, Fiction, Reality, and Myth*, ed. Mark Hussey (Syracuse: Syracuse University Press, 1991).

64. As Karen L Levenback notes, "Septimus does not remember the war; unlike the civilian characters, he daily lives with its reality, that is, the war has become his *actuality*. For him, the postwar world has duplicated the war in the trenches—without the trenches." Karen L. Levenback, *Virginia Woolf and the Great War* (Syracuse: Syracuse University Press, 1999), 50-51.

65. Woolf, *Mrs. Dalloway*, 151.

66. Quoted in Levenback, *Virginia Woolf and the Great War*, 72, 76, 78. ("What causes his death is Smith's recognition of individual powerlessness in an indifferent postwar world.")

67. Roger Poole, "'WE ALL PUT UP WITH YOU VIRGINIA,' Irreceivable Wisdom about War" in *Virginia Woolf and War, Fiction, Reality, and Myth*, ed. Mark Hussey, (Syracuse: Syracuse University Press, 1991), 79-80.

68. Wilfred Owen, "Mental Cases," lines 10-12, in *The Penguin Book of First World War Poetry*, 218.

69. Woolf, *Mrs. Dalloway*, 92.

70. Poole, "'WE ALL PUT UP WITH YOU VIRGINIA,' Irreceivable Wisdom about War" in Hussey, *Virginia Woolf and War*, 82.

71. Woolf, *Mrs. Dalloway*, 88.

72. *Some Do Not ...* (1924), *No More Parades* (1925), *A Man Could Stand Up* (1926), and *The Last Post* (1928).

73. Ford Madox Ford, *Some Do Not...* (1924), in *Parade's End* (New York: Penguin Books, 1982), 3-5, 13, 151.

74. Ibid., 20, 32, 39-41. While having an affair herself, his wife Sylvia slanders him, alleging that he has a mistress and child out of wedlock; she causes him credit problem with his bank; and she claims (outrageously) he could restore their marriage by calling her a whore and a bitch. Sylvia hates her husband because of his "dull display of the English gentleman" and his being "the soul of truth" (Sylvia's mother calls him "the best ever"), and Sylvia equates his fundamental goodness with "immorality," for which she intends to "torment that man." Tietjens's friend McMaster

upholds Edwardian attitudes and worldview, rising in the Imperial Department of Statistics essentially by stealing Tietjens's statistical analysis that earns McMaster a knighthood.

75. Ibid., 3.

76. Ibid., 155.

77. As Ford wrote in a dedicatory letter to *No More Parades*: "We were oppressed, ordered, counter-ordered, commanded, countermanded, harassed, strafed, denounced—and, above all, dreadfully worried. The never-ending sense of worry, in fact, far surpassed any of the 'exigencies of troops actually in contact with the enemy forces,' and that applied not merely to the bases, but to the whole field of military operations. Unceasing worry!" Quoted in Robie Macauley, Introduction to *Parade's End*, xiii.

78. Hynes, Samuel. *A War Imagined*, 433.

79. Ford, *No More Parades*, in *Parade's End*, 306-07.

80. Macauley, Introduction to *Parade's End*, xviii-xix.

81.Bernard Bergonzi, *Heroes Twilight* (Manchester: Carcanet Press, 1996), 167-68.

82. Ibid.

83. Hoffman, *The 20s*, 101.

84. John Keegan, *The First World War*, 373, 411.

85. Hoffman, *The 20s*, 71.

86. Ernest Hemingway, *A Farewell to Arms* (New York: Charles Scribner's Sons, 1957), 18.

87.Hoffman, *The 20s*, 72-73; *The Norton Anthology of American Literature, 1914-1945*, 1379, 1807, 1980-81.

88. Hoffman, *The 20s*, 77.

89. Ibid. Hoffman characterizes the feelings conveyed in the 1920s war literature as follows: (1) "a monstrous hoax, and unendurable outrage committed or by the elders, who were brutal, insensitive, and stupid"; (2) "a violent re-education of the soldier in the ugliness and the scatological realities underlying the surface of decorum"; and (3) "a means of testing the true nature of men and of reclassifying them morally."

90. Ibid., 83. In a 1988 letter Brown states that "it was not those dumb, jejune letters of mine that got us into trouble. It was the fact that C and I knew all about the violent mutinies in the French Army a few months before Cummings and I reached the front. We learned all about them from the poilus. The French did everything, naturally, to suppress the news. We two were loaded with dynamite." Quoted in John M. Gill, "'All These Fine People Were Arrested as Espions': Detainees in *The Enormous Room*" (Fall 2006), 81-93, 86, Http://www.gvsu.edu/ english/cummings/Gill14.pdf (accessed May 13, 2011).

91. E. E. Cummings, *The Enormous Room* with the Author's Introduction (New York: Modern Library, 1949), 61-62.

92. Ibid., 64, 167. Cummings particularly admires four inmates, the so-called Delectable Mountains, who convey learning beyond their education. Faithful to their values and wise in their compassion, the four Delectable Mountains exemplify truths that inspire Cummings, bring him "alive," and turn him into a new person. Ibid., 325.

93. Quoted in Claudia Matherly Stolz, "Dos Passos's Three Soldiers: A Case Study," *West Virginia University Philological Papers* 51 (Fall 2004): 77.

94. John Dos Passos, *Three Soldiers* (New York: George H. Doran, 1921). The first soldier and hero of the book is John Andrews, discussed in the text. The second is "Chris" Crisfield, a 20-year-old Indiana farm boy, who becomes murderously angry at his superior, Corporal Anderson, finds Anderson helplessly wounded in France, leaning against a tree with his arm in a sling, and tosses not one but two grenades at Anderson to guarantee his murder. Next, "burst out laughing," Crisfield mercilessly kicks a helpless German prisoner. 188-89. The third is Dan Fuselli, a 19-year-old San Francisco factory worker, who resents being a "slavey" for a lieutenant (62-63) and ultimately is sentenced to a labor battalion at his court-martial for contracting venereal disease.

95. Ibid., 21.

96. Ibid., 421-23.

97. Quoted in Stolz, "Dos Passos's Three Soldiers: A Case Study," 82-83.

98. In an October 18, 1924, letter to Edmund Wilson, Hemingway claimed the book "has a pretty good unity. Michael S. Reynolds, ed., *Critical Essays on Ernest Hemingway's In Our Time* (Boston: GK Hall, 1983), 89. Hemingway takes the book's ironic title from *The Anglican Book of Prayer*, which reads "Give us peace in our time, O Lord." Wendolyn E. Tetlow, *Hemingway's In Our Time, Lyrical Dimensions* (Lewisburg: Bucknell University Press, 1992), 46.

99. Hemingway's final collection has a total of 16 short stories and 16 italicized interchapter prose poems. Tetlow, *Hemingway's In Our Time, Lyrical Dimensions*, 122n2.

100. Robert M. Slabey, "The Structure of *In Our Time*" in *Critical Essays on Ernest Hemingway's In Our Time*, 79, proposed the follows the four-part organization: (1) Nick Adams as a young man, (2) the effects of war, (3) the failure of marriage, and (4) the search for a code.

101. Ernest Hemingway, *A Farewell to Arms* (New York: Charles Scribner's Sons, 1957), 20, 111. Count Greffi also advises Frederick: "Then you are in love. Do not forget that is a religious feeling." 251.

102. Ibid., 54, 62, 284-85.

103. Ibid., 285, 251.

104. Ibid., 239.

105. Ibid., 177-78, 306.

106. Ernest Hemingway, *The Sun Also Rises* (New York: Charles Scribner's Sons, 1954), 34. As Guenter Schmigalle points out, Jake lost his penis on the Italian Front, which means that he has the sex drive without the means for sexual performance and satisfaction. To exacerbate his sexual frustration, Jake is in love with an oversexed woman. Günther Schmigalle, "'How People Go to Hell': Pessimism, Tragedy, and Affinity to Schopenhauer, in *The_Sun_Also_Rises*," *Hemingway Review* 25 (1) (Fall 2005): 7-21.

107. Hemingway, *The Sun Also Rises*, 148.

108. Ibid., 131-32, 167-68, 216-17.

109. Ibid., 10.

110. F. Scott Fitzgerald, *This Side of Paradise* (New York: Simon & Shuster, 2010). After desperately turning to drink and even contemplating suicide, Blaine emerges from four failed love affairs, altruistically jeopardizes his own reputation to rescue his friend Alec from woman trouble with the law, honestly examines his own shortcomings, and finally discovers his calling "to be necessary to people, to be indispensable" —now he can say, "I know myself." 310-12, 330. Much like Amory Blaine, Fitzgerald also was educated at a New Jersey Catholic boarding school (Newman School) and at Princeton University, but he was mobilized into the Army during World War I too late for active service. *The Norton Anthology of American Literature, 1914-1945*, 1822.

111. Although Blaine joins the Army even before his Princeton graduation, the war only covers the novel's brief Interlude (May, 1917-February, 1919) and serves primarily as a backdrop for Amory Blaine's coming-of-age and America's emergence into the Jazz Age.

112. Fitzgerald, *This Side of Paradise*, 324, 249, 194, 307-08, 310, 330.

113. Aldrich, John. *After the Lost Generation: a Critical Study of the Writers of Two Wars* (New York: McGraw-Hill, 1951), excerpted in *This Side of Paradise*, 368; Robert E. Spiller. *The Cycle of American Literature, An Essay in Historical Criticism* (New York: Mentor Book, 1956), 196; Edmund Wilson, "The Delegate from Great Neck," in *F. Scott Fitzgerald: the Man and His Work*, ed. Alfred Kazin (Cleveland: World Publishing, 1951), excerpted in *This Side of Paradise*, 367.

114. F. Scott Fitzgerald, *The Great Gatsby* (New York: Scribner, 2004), 149.

115. Ibid., 47-48, 66, 150, 171.

116. Ibid., 32, 44, 61, 101, 154.

117. Ibid., 179.

118. Ibid., 2.

119. Weinstein, Arnold. *NOBODY'S HOME, Speech, Self, and Place in American Fiction from Hawthorne to DeLillo* (New York: Oxford University Press, 1993), 144.

120. Franz Kafka, *The Metamorphosis* in *Imaginative Literature: Selections*

from the Twentieth Century trans. Willa and Edwin Muir, vol. 60, of *Great Books of the Western World*, ed. Mortimer J. Adler (Chicago: Encyclopaedia Britannica, 2007), 111.

121. Stanley Corngold, *Lambent Traces, Franz Kafka* (Princeton: Princeton University Press, 2006), 43.

122. Baumer, *Modern European Thought*, 441.

123. Barrett, *Irrational Man*, 215.

124. Flynn, *Existentialism*, 58-59.

125. Jean-Paul Sartre, *Nausea*, trans. Lloyd Alexander (New York: New Directions, 1964), 127-29.

126. Ibid., 133.

127. Hayden Carruth, Introduction to *Nausea*, xi.

128. Sartre, *Nausea*, 114, 170.

129. Ibid., 178.

130. Carruth, Introduction to *Nausea*, xiii.

Chapter 7. Postwar Western Art

1. Tristan Tzara, *1918 DadaManifesto,www.mariabuszek.com/.../DadaSurrealism/DadaSurrReadings/TzaraD...* (accessed September 1, 2012).

2 . Hamilton, George H. *Painting and Sculpture in Europe, 1880-1940* (Baltimore: Penguin books, 1972), 15. The 1886 exhibition of the Society of Independent Artists featured two landmarks of modern art, George Seurat's *Sunday Afternoon on the Island of La Grande Jatte* (1884-86) and Henri Rousseau's *An Evening of Carnival* (1886). Roger Shattuck, *The Banquet Years: The Origins of the Avant Garde France, 1855 to World War I* (New York: Vintage Books, 1968), 19; Frederick R. Karl, *Modern and Modernism: The Sovereignty of the Artist, 1885-1925* (New York: Atheneum, 1985), 80; Jonathan Fineberg. *Art Since 1940: Strategies of Being,* 2nd ed. (Prentice-Hall, 2000), 16-17. Fineberg considers that modern art started even earlier, with Gustav Courbet's *Stonebreakers* (1849). Also, David Hopkins, *Dada and Surrealism: A Very Short Introduction* (Oxford: Oxford University Press, 2004), 2 (Hopkins agrees with Fineberg regarding Courbet.)

3. Hamilton, *Painting and Sculpture in Europe, 1880-1940*, 17.

4. Ibid., 15.

5. American Professor of English and cultural critic Frederick R. Karl defined "modern" as an ongoing process of defying authority, escaping historical imperatives, departing from traditional art, and constantly breaking new ground. Karl, *Modern and Modernism*, xii, xvii, 3, 13-15.

6. Robert Rosenblum, *Cubism and Twentieth-Century Art* (New York: Abrams, 1968), 14-16, 25; Amy Dempsey, *Styles, Schools and Movements* (London: Thames & Hudson, 2002), 84.

7. Richard Sheppard, *Modernism—Dada—Postmodernism* (Evanston, IL: Northwestern University Press, 2000), 50, 60. Sheppard attributes this point to Rosalind Krauss.

8. "The world pictured by the modern artist," according to philosopher William Barrett, "is, like the world mediated by the existential philosopher, a world where man is a stranger." Barrett, *Irrational Man*, 43.

9. Dempsey, *Styles, Schools and Movements*, 83-84.

10. Rosenblum dated this work as May 1912 rather than traditional winter date of 1911-12. Rosenblum, *Cubism and Twentieth-Century Art*, 67.

12. Hamilton, *Painting and Sculpture in Europe 1880-1940*, 250

13. F. T. Marinetti, "Manifesto of Futurism," in *The Norton Anthology of American Literature, 1914-1945*, 7th ed., vol. D, ed. Nina Baym and Mary Loeffelholz (New York: W. W. Norton, 2007), 1501.

14. Hamilton, *Painting and Sculpture in Europe, 1880-1940*, 280.

15. "Manifesto of the Futurist Painters," in Dempsey, *Styles, Schools and Movements*, 89. Gino Severini met Picasso and Braque on a Paris trip in 1911, and three other futurist painters followed him there: Umberto Boccioni, Luigi Russo, and Carlo Carrá. The Futurists explained the "lines of force" concept in their 1912 Paris exhibition catalogue. Ibid., 88-89.

16. Ibid., 91.

17. Dempsey, *Styles, Schools and Movements*, 66.

18. Ludwig Meidner, "Ein denkwürdiger Sommer," *Der Monat* 16 (August 1964), 75, in Richard Cork. *A Bitter Truth: Avant-Garde Art and the Great War* (New Haven: Yale University Press in association with Barbican Art Gallery, 1994), 13.

19. Rosenblum, *Cubism and Twentieth-Century Art*, 133; Hamilton, *Painting and Sculpture in Europe, 1880-1940*, 253.

20. Hamilton, *Painting and Sculpture in Europe, 1880-1940*, 253.

21. Cork, *A Bitter Truth*, 86, 164.

22. Quoted and translated by Douglas Cooper in *Fernand Léger et le nouvel espace* (London and Paris, 1949), vii, 74-75, in Hamilton, *Painting and Sculpture in Europe, 1880-1940*, 253-54.

23. Cork, *A Bitter Truth*, 87. This work is a reprise of Léger's earlier painting *The Card Players*, executed on a shell crate in 1915.

24. Ibid., 164. Indeed, Léger later described *The Card Game* as "the first picture in which I deliberately took the subject from my own time."

25. The player on the right looks anonymous beneath his helmet as he puffs clouds of solid smoke that match the formidable balls of the pipe smoke coming from the rival on his right. The open jacket of the large, fierce-looking figure on the left displays his imposing red, triangular vertebrae, as he rests a massive right forearm confidently on the table. He plays his cards with a left forearm that is curiously detached from the rest of his arm, suggesting a prosthesis.

26. Léger evokes the city's complexity and unity, its visually shifting and partially observed makeup, evoking its "order and beauty" rather than "its confusion and ugliness." Rosenblum, *Cubism and Twentieth-Century Art*, 136-153.

27. Cork. *A Bitter Truth*, 70-71; Hamilton, *Painting and Sculpture in Europe, 1880-1940*, 294.

28. Cork, *A Bitter Truth*, 71.

29. Ibid., 72.

30. *The Observer* (Nov. 28, 1915), in Cork, *A Bitter Truth*, 74.

31. Cork, *A Bitter Truth*, 74. In Wyndham Lewis's characterization of the letter, Nevinson asserted "that he no longer shares, that he REPUDIATES, all his (Marinetti's) utterances on the subject of war. ... Marinetti's solitary English disciple has discovered that War is not Magnifique."

32. Guillaume Apollinaire, "Echos et on-Dit des Letteres et des Arts," *L'Europe Nouvelle* (July 20, 1918), in Cork, *A Bitter Truth*, 74.

33. Christopher Nevinson, *Paint and Prejudice* (London, 1937), 95-96, in Cork, *A Bitter Truth*, 72.

34. Ibid., 96-97, in Cork, *A Bitter Truth*, 131.

35. Cork, *A Bitter Truth*, 169.

36. Ibid., 24; Hamilton, *Painting and sculpture in Europe, 1880-1940*, 199. They derived the name "Bridge" from the prologue to Nietzsche's *Thus Spoke Zarathustra*. Felix Kramer, "In Contradiction: Ernst Ludwig Kirchner," in *Ernst Ludwig Kirchner: Retrospective*, ed. Felix Kramer (Frankfurt: Stadel Museum, 2010), 14.

37. Kramer, "In Contradiction: Ernst Ludwig Kirchner," in *Ernst Ludwig Kirchner: Retrospective*, 14-17.

38. Ibid., 17-19; Hamilton, *Painting and Sculpture in Europe, 1880-1940*, 18-20.

39. Nicole Brandmueller, "The Expressionist in Berlin," in Kramer, *Ernst Ludwig Kirchner: Retrospective*, 102-03.

40. "What is harder to bear than anything else is the burden of the war and the prevalence of superficiality. I constantly have the impression of a bloody carnival. Where will it all end?" Ernst Ludwig Kirchner to Gustaf Schiefler, November 12, 1916, in Wolfgang Henze, ed., *Ernst Ludwig Kirschner-Gustaf Schiefler: Briefweichesel, 1910-1935/1938* (Stuttgart and Zürich, 1990), 83, in Felix Kramer, "In Contradiction: Ernst Ludwig Kirchner," in *Ernst Ludwig Kirchner: Retrospective*, 18-19.

41. Javier Arnaldo, "War and Breakdown," in Kramer, *Ernst Ludwig Kirchner: Retrospective*, 151.

42. Cork, *A Bitter Truth*, 107.

43. "I feel half dead with mental and physical torment." Ernst Ludwig Kirchner to Karl Ernst Osthaus, quoted by Wieland Schmied, "Points of Departure and Transformations in German Art, 1905-1985," in Ibid., 109.

44. Arnaldo, "War and Breakdown," in Kramer, *Ernst Ludwig Kirchner: Retrospective*, 152.

45. Sandra Oppmann, "The 'New Style'" in Kramer, *Ernst Ludwig Kirchner: Retrospective*, 199-201.

46. Kramer, "In Contradiction: Ernst Ludwig Kirchner," in Kramer, *Ernst Ludwig Kirchner: Retrospective*, 22.

47. Sabine T. Kriebel, "Otto Dix" in Leah Dickerman, ed. *Dada: Zürich, Berlin, Hanover, Cologne, New York, Paris* (Washington: National Gallery of Art, 2006), 466.

48. Ibid. Upon invitation from George Grosz, Dix exhibited at the 1920 Berlin Dada Fair, affiliating himself with the outspokenly antiwar and antimilitary Berlin Dadaists.

49. Ibid.

50. "The war was a horrible thing," Dix declared, but he volunteered out of a compelling "need to experience all the depths of life for myself." Otto Dix, interview, December 1963, quoted by Dieter Schmidt, *Otto Dix im Selbstbildnis* (East Berlin, 1978), 237, in Cork. *A Bitter Truth*, 93.

51. Cork. *A Bitter Truth*, 95.

52. Kriebel, "Otto Dix" in Dickerman, *Dada: Zürich, Berlin, Hanover, Cologne, New York, Paris*, 466.

53. His *Signal Flare* (1917) is a shocking image of nighttime death in No Man's Land, and his *Setting Sun (Ypres)* (1918) is an apocalyptic image of an explosive sunset radiating over the pockmarked battlefield at Ypres, perhaps reflecting Dix's realization that the war would end disastrously for Germany. Cork, *A Bitter Truth*, 204.

54. Hamilton, *Painting and Sculpture in Europe, 1880*-1940, 477.

55. Ibid., 478; Cork, *A Bitter Truth*, 272-73, 305.

56. David Hopkins. *Dada and Surrealism: A Very Short Introduction* (Oxford University Press, 2004), 1-2; Sheppard, *Modernism — Dada — Postmodernism*, 173.

57. Hopkins, *Dada and Surrealism*, 6-7, 9-10; Dickerman, Introduction to *Dada: Zürich, Berlin, Hanover, Cologne, New York, Paris*, 6-7.

58. Hopkins, *Dada and Surrealism*, 8-9.

59. Ibid., 9.

60. Sheppard, *Modernism — Dada — Postmodernism*, 178-79, 183.

61. Quoted in Hopkins, *Dada and Surrealism*, 8.

62. Hopkins, *Dada and Surrealism*, 3-4; Sheppard, *Modernism — Dada — Postmodernism*, 201.

63. Hopkins, *Dada and Surrealism*, 2.

64. Ibid., 3.

65. Dickerman, Introduction to *Dada: Zürich, Berlin, Hanover, Cologne, New York, Paris*, 1-2.

66. Ibid.

67. Amanda L. Hockensmith, "Hans (Jean) Arp," in Dickerman, *Dada: Zürich, Berlin, Hanover, Cologne, New York, Paris*, 460-61.

68. Quoted in ibid.

69. Hans (Jean) Arp, "And so the Circle Closed," *Arp on Arp: Poems, Essays, Memories*, ed. Marcel Jean, trans. Joachim Neugroschel (New York, 1972), 246, in Dickerman, *Dada: Zürich, Berlin, Hanover, Cologne, New York, Paris*, 37.

70. Quoted in Hopkins, *Dada and Surrealism*, 71.

71. Sheppard, *Modernism—Dada—Postmodernism*, 275, 287.

72. Ibid., 286-87.

73. Ibid., 196; Dickerman, *Dada: Zürich, Berlin, Hanover, Cologne, New York, Paris*, 38.

74. Hans Arp, "I became More and More Removed from Aesthetics," in *Arp on Arp: Poems, Essays, Memories*, ed. Marcel Jean, trans. Joachim Neugroschel (New York, 1972), 238, in Dickerman, "Zürich" in *Dada: Zürich, Berlin, Hanover, Cologne, New York, Paris*, 38.

75. Sheppard, *Modernism—Dada—Postmodernism*, 268; Hopkins, *Dada and Surrealism*, 110.

76. Amanda L. Hockensmith, "Marcel Duchamp," in Dickerman, *Dada: Zürich, Berlin, Hanover, Cologne, New York, Paris*, 467-68; Sheppard, *Modernism—Dada—Postmodernism*, 173.

77. Michael R. Taylor, "New York" in Dickerman, *Dada: Zürich, Berlin, Hanover, Cologne, New York, Paris*, 278.

78. William Seitz, "What's Happened to Art? An Interview with Marcel Duchamp on Present Consequences of New York's 1913 Armory Show," *Vogue*, February 15, 1963, 113; Pierre Cabanne, *Dialogues with Marcel Duchamp*, trans. Ron Padgett (New York, 1971), 39; and James Johnson Sweeney, interview with Marcel Duchamp, February 23, 1945, in Sweeney, "Eleven Europeans in America," *Museum of Modern Art Bulletin* 13, nos. 4-5 (1946), 20 — all three citations in Taylor, "New York" in Dickerman, *Dada: Zürich, Berlin, Hanover, Cologne, New York, Paris*, 280-81.

79. Hopkins, *Dada and Surrealism*, 86-7.

80. Taylor, "New York," in Dickerman, *Dada: Zürich, Berlin, Hanover, Cologne, New York, Paris*, 287; Hopkins, *Dada and Surrealism*, 44-45.

81.Marcel Duchamp interview, "The New-Descending-a-Staircase Man Surveys Us," *New York Tribune*, Special Features Section (September 12, 1915), 2, in Taylor, "New York," in Dickerman, *Dada: Zürich, Berlin, Hanover, Cologne, New York, Paris*, 290. Richard Sheppard speculates that Duchamp's use of R. Mutt on his *Fountain* was a pun on the German word for poverty (*Armut*) since he wrote it shortly after America, which was his refuge from war, had gone to war. Sheppard, *Modernism—Dada—Postmodernism*, 202-03.

82. Quoted in Hopkins, *Dada and Surrealism*, 130.

83. Ibid., 103-04. Similarly, *Rrose Selavy* (his feminine pseudonym and nominal pun, pronounced "Eros, c'est la vie") ironically conflates male and female—a female impersonator impugning the authenticity of American mass media and commercial culture. Taylor, "New York," in Dickerman, *Dada: Zürich, Berlin, Hanover, Cologne, New York, Paris*, 293-96.

84. Amanda L. Hockensmith, "Kurt Schwitters," in Dickerman, *Dada: Zürich, Berlin, Hanover, Cologne, New York, Paris*, 485.

85. Ibid.

86. Ibid.; Letter to Alfred Barr, November 23, 1936, Archives of the Museum of Modern Art, New York, cited by John Elderfield, *Kurt Schwitters* (New York, 1985), 156, in Dietrich, "Hanover," in Dickerman, *Dada: Zürich, Berlin, Hanover, Cologne, New York, Paris*, 177.

87. Kurt Schwitters, "Merz" (1920), in Schwitters, *Das literarishe Werk*, vol. 5, in Werner Schmalenbach, *Kurt Schwitters* (New York, 1967), 76, 406, in Dietrich, "Hanover," in Dickerman, *Dada: Zürich, Berlin, Hanover, Cologne, New York, Paris*, 159.

88. Kurt Schwitters, *Sturm-Bilderbuch IV* (Berlin, 1921), 2, in Dietrich, "Hanover," in Dickerman, *Dada: Zürich, Berlin, Hanover, Cologne, New York, Paris,*158.

89. Ibid., 157.

90. Kurt Schwitters, "Die Bedeutung des Merzgedankens in der Welt" (1923), *Merz 1*, in Schwitters, *Das literarishe Werk*, vol. 5, 133, in Dietrich, "Hanover," in Dickerman, *Dada: Zürich, Berlin, Hanover, Cologne, New York, Paris,*169; Hopkins, *Dada and Surrealism*, 13.

91. Hamilton, *Painting and Sculpture in Europe 1880-1940*, 476.

92. Sabine T. Kriebel, "George Grosz," in Dickerman, *Dada: Zürich, Berlin, Hanover, Cologne, New York, Paris*, 471-72.

93. Hopkins, *Dada and Surrealism*, 139-40.

94. Richard Huelsenbeck, *Berlin Dada Manifesto* (1920), in Hopkins, *Dada and Surrealism*, 12, 35.

95. Ibid., 57. Helmut Herzfelde anglicized his name to John Heartfield, who is Wieland Herzfeld's brother, Grosz's friend, and a fellow Dadaist known for his collages and photomontages.

96. Quoted in Ibid., 103.

97. Sheppard, *Modernism—Dada—Postmodernism*, 193.

98. Timothy O. Benson, "Mysticism, Materialism, and the Machine in Berlin Dada," *Art Journal* (Spring 1987)/1:46-47.

99. Ibid., 49-50.

100. Sheppard, *Modernism—Dada—Postmodernism*, 278-79.

101. Sabine T. Kriebel, "Max Ernst," in Dickerman, *Dada: Zürich, Berlin, Hanover, Cologne, New York, Paris*, 470.

102. Hopkins, *Dada and Surrealism*, 14.

103. Ibid., 76.

104. Charlotte Stokes, "Rage and Liberation: Cologne Dada," in Charlotte Stokes and Stephen C. Forster, eds. *Dada, Cologne, Hannover* (New York, 1997), 21, in Sabine T. Kriebel, "Cologne," in Dickerman, *Dada: Zürich, Berlin, Hanover, Cologne, New York, Paris*, 236.

105. Hopkins, *Dada and Surrealism*, 18, 76.

106. Hamilton, *Painting and Sculpture in Europe, 1880-1940*, 399.

107. Ibid.

108. Hopkins, *Dada and Surrealism*, 12, 77.

109. Ibid., 101.

110. Ibid., 100-03.

111. Tristan Tzara, *1918 Dada Manifesto*, in Marc Dachy, *Dada: The Revolt of Art* (New York: Abrams, 2006), 98.

112. Quoted in Hopkins, *Dada and Surrealism*, 46.

113. Ibid., 16; Janine Mileaf and Matthew S. Witkovsky, "Paris," in Dickerman, *Dada: Zürich, Berlin, Hanover, Cologne, New York, Paris*, 375.

114. Dickerman, Introduction to *Dada: Zürich, Berlin, Hanover, Cologne, New York, Paris*, 11.

115. Ibid.

116. Hopkins, *Dada and Surrealism*, 16.

117. Quoted in Ibid., 17.

118. Ibid.

119. Ibid., 78-80.

120. bid., 80. Citing the critic Max Morise, Hopkins also refers to the inability of Surrealist painting to render dreams as they unfold.

121. Ibid., 84.

122. Maurice Nadeau, *The History of Surrealism*, trans. Richard Howard (Cambridge, MA: Belknap Press, 1989), 43-44, 4.

123. Ibid., 48.

124. Ibid., 227.

125. Ibid.

126. Walter Benjamin, "The Work of Art in the Age of Mechanical Reproduction," (1936) in *Art in Modern Culture: An Anthology of Critical Texts*, eds. Francis Francina and Jonathan Harris (New York: Harper Collins, 1992), 304.

127. Tristan Tzara, *1918 Dada Manifesto*, in Dickerman, Introduction to *Dada : Zürich, Berlin, Hanover, Cologne, New York, Paris*, 13, fig. 9; Sheppard, *Modernism—Dada—Postmodernism*, 176.

128. Raoul Huelsenbeck, *En avant Dada*, 36, in Sheppard, *Modernism—Dada—Postmodernism*, 180-81.

129. Ibid., 196.

130. Hopkins, *Dada and Surrealism*, 99.

131. Ibid., 104-05. For Berlin Dadaist Raoul Hausmann, "Dada is the full absence of what is called Geist (Spirit). Why have Geist in the world that runs on mechanically?" Yet, Hausmann evolved a secular view of spirit underlying his monist materialism. Benson, "Mysticism, Materialism, and the Machine in Berlin Dada," 47, 52.

Chapter 8. Materialism from World War I to the Present

1. Darwin to W. Graham, July 3, 1881, in *The Life and Letters of Charles Darwin*, ed. Francis Darwin (New York: Basic Books, 1959), 285, in John F. Haught, *Is Nature Enough? Meaning and Truth in the Age of Science* (Cambridge: Cambridge University Press, 2006), 32.

2. Livingston and Fiorenza,. *Modern Christian Thought: The 20th Century*, 35, 388.

3. Whitehead, *Science and the Modern World*, 189.

4. Barrett, *Irrational Man*, 19.

5. Flynn, *Existentialism*, 104-05.

6. Okasha, *Philosophy of Science*, 78.

7. Flynn, *Existentialism*, 104-10. According to Thomas R. Flynn, structuralism "tends to neglect the existential and historical in favor of ahistorical structures."

8. Ibid., 125.

9. Arnold Weinstein, *Classics of American Literature* (Chantilly, VA: The Teaching Company, 1997), Course Guidebook, Part V, 37 (Weinstein takes this position on Hemingway).

10. Robert E. Spiller, *The Cycle of American Literature, An Essay in Historical Criticism* (New York: Mentor Book, 1960), 207.

11. Ernest Hemingway, *The Old Man and the Sea* (New York: Charles Scribner's Sons, 1980), 92.

12. Abrams and Harpham, *A Glossary of Literary Terms*, 203.

13. Ibid., 203-04.

14. Jean-François Lyotard, *The Postmodern Condition: a Report on Knowledge*, trans. Geoff Bennington and Brian Masumi (Minneapolis: University of Minnesota Press, 1984), xxiii-iv, 51.

15. Stuart Sim, "Postmodernism and Philosophy," *The Routledge Companion to Postmodernism*, ed. Stuart Sim, 2d ed. (London and New York: Routledge, 2005), 12, 289-90.

16. Colin Trodd, "Postmodernism and Art," *The Routledge Companion to Postmodernism*, 82.

17. Dempsey, *Styles, Schools and Movements*, 201-06, 188-91.

18. Ibid., 263-64.

19. Trodd, "Postmodernism and Art," 92. Lyotard also sees modernism as a constant, latent aspect of postmodernism. Jean-François Lyotard,

"Answering the Question: What Is Postmodernism?" in *The Postmodern Condition*, 79.

20. Whitehead, *Science and the Modern World*, 17. Whitehead's book, with slight expansion, reprints his Lowell Lectures as delivered. Ibid., viii.

21. Ibid., 54-55.

22. Isaacson, *Einstein*, 384-85.

23. Baumer, *Modern European Thought*, 470-72. Baumer cites the 1934 interviews by the mathematician J. W. N. Sullivan purportedly finding unanimity among European scientist-philosophers on mind-matter and on anti-materialism. 470. Max Planck thought matter derived from consciousness, and James Jeans thought that Heisenberg's indeterminacy principle made room for mind in the universe. 471. The physicist-astronomer A. S. Eddington did not know the extent to which scientists accepted materialism in 1929, but he considered materialism inconsistent with physical principles. 471-72. The zoologist Lloyd Morgan considered mind an emergent rather than a resultant phenomenon, both novel and qualitatively new. 472. In response to C. P. Snow's essay on the two cultures many scientists, like Julian Huxley and Jacob Bronowski, defended science as humanistic and man's emergence as no longer blindly deterministic biology. 474. Bertrand Russell's view on materialism seems to have evolved into a neutral monism, which he considers the source of both mind and matter. 470. A. C. Grayling, *Russell: a Very Short Introduction* (Oxford: Oxford University Press, 2002), 72-74.

24. Baumer, *Modern European Thought*, 467-69.

25. F. Sherwood Taylor, "The Scientific World-Outlook," *Philosophy*, XXII, no. 83 (November, 1947), 203, in Baumer, *Modern European Thought*, 469n28; Chapter 1, note 8.

26. Stace, "Man against the Darkness," 54.

27. Ibid., 57.

28. Ibid., 53; Monod, *Chance and Necessity*, 170.

29. Hawking and Mlodinow, *The Grand Design*, 8, 181, 117-18.

30. Ibid. 181 (emphasis in original).

31. Ibid., 8.

32. Ibid., 180.

33. Ibid., 127-30, 32.

34. Ibid., 30, 32-33.

35. Ibid., 32, 33.

36. Ibid., 5.

37. Ibid., 5, 10 (emphasis omitted).

38. I am indebted to Oxford Professor of Mathematics John C. Lennox for this line of argument. John C. Lennox, *God and Stephen Hawking: Whose Design Is It Anyway?* (Oxford: Lion Book, 2011), 30-49. By referring

to "nothing," Hawking presumably means a quantum vacuum. Hawking and Mlodinow, *The Grand Design,* 139. But as Lennox points out, a quantum vacuum is not nothing. Lennox, *God and Stephen Hawking,* 30. Furthermore, it is "logically impossible for a cause to bring about some effect without already being in existence." Keith Ward, *God, Chance and Necessity* (Oxford: One World Publications, 1996), 49, quoted in Ibid.

39. Lennox, *God and Stephen Hawking,* 40. Hawking also challenges the theism of scientific pioneers like Descartes and Newton who believed that the laws of nature are God's handiwork. Hawking has just done the converse, turned a law of nature into God. Hawking and Mlodinow, *The Grand Design,* 29.

40. Hawking and Mlodinow, *The Grand Design,* 161.

41. John Polkinghorne, *One World* (London: SPCK, 1986), 92-93, in Lennox, *God and Stephen Hawking,* 74-75.

42. Monod, *Chance and Necessity,* 13, 102.

43. Ibid., 104, 9.

44. Ibid., 10, 24.

45. Ibid., 23-24.

46. Ibid., 118.

47. Ibid., 95, 98.

48. Ibid., 113 (emphasis in original).

49. Ibid., 39.

50. Ibid., 169, 172 (emphasis in original).

51. Ibid., 179-80.

52. Ibid., 21-22.

53. W. T. Stace, "Man against Darkness," *The Atlantic Monthly* (Sept. 1948): 54.

54. Monod, *Chance and Necessity,* 45-46 (emphasis in original).

55. Ibid., 148.

56. Ibid., 159.

57. Whitehead, *Science and the Modern World,* 17.

58. Monod, *Chance and Necessity,* 21.

59. Whitehead, *Science and the Modern World,* 51.

60. Monod, *Chance and Necessity,* 21; Whitehead, *Science and the Modern World,* 44.

61. Whitehead, *Science and the Modern World,* 3-4 (emphasis in original).

62. David Hume, *An Enquiry concerning Human Understanding* Sec. I, *Of the Different Species of Philosophy* in *Hume Selections,* ed. Charles W. Hendel, Jr. (New York: Charles Scribner's Sons, 1955), 107-22; Samir Okasha, *Philosophy of Science: A Very Short Introduction* (Oxford: Oxford University Press, 2002), 27.

63. Whitehead, *Science and the Modern World,* 18.

64. Monod, *Chance and Necessity*, 21.

65. Ibid., 111, 45.

66. Whitehead, *Science and the Modern World,* 55

67. John F. Haught, *Science and Religion: From Conflict to Conversation* (New York: Paulist Press, 1995), 80.

68. Michael Polanyi, *The Tacit Dimension* (Garden City, NY: Doubleday Anchor Books, 1967), 29-52, in Haught, *Nature and Purpose*, 44-57.

69. Monod, *Chance and Necessity*, 28-29 (emphasis omitted).

70. Ibid., 170 ff.

71. Ibid., 80.

72. John F. Haught, *Nature and Purpose* (Washington, D.C.: University Press of America, 1980), 54.

73. Whitehead, *Science and the Modern World*, 55.

74. Monod, *Chance and Necessity*, 138, 172, 167, 40.

75. Ibid., 116, 159.

76. Ibid., xi.

77. Whitehead, *Science and the Modern World,* 142.

78. Ibid., 87.

79. Richard Dawkins, *The Blind Watchmaker: Why the Evidence of Evolution Reveals a Universe without Design* (New York: W. W. Norton, 1996), x-xi.

80. Ibid., xvi-xvii.

81. Sherman, *Biology*, 511-12.

82. Ibid., 456-57, 511; Haught, *Making Sense of Evolution*, 3.

83. Sherman, *Biology*, 456-57, 511.

84. Haught, *Making Sense of Evolution*, xiii-xiv; John F. Haught, *Deeper Than Darwin, The Prospect for Religion in the Age of Evolution* (Boulder: Westview Press, 2003), 103. In 1999, *Scientific American* reported that 90% of the 1,800 members of the National Academy of Sciences consider themselves atheists or agnostics. In addition, only 40% of all US scientists believe in a personal God. Haught, *Deeper Than Darwin*, 15.

85. Dawkins, *The Blind Watchmaker*, 9 (emphasis in original).

86. Ibid., 10.

87. Ibid., 21 (emphasis in original)

88. Ibid., 21-22.

89. Ibid., 22.

90. Ibid., 61.

91. Ibid., 24, 29.

92. Ibid., 30, 157-95, 164, citing his book *The Selfish Gene* (Oxford: Oxford University Press, 1989). See also, Richard Dawkins, *The God Delusion* (Boston: Houghton Mifflin, 2008), 246-47.

93. Dawkins, *The Blind Watchmaker*, 207.

94. Ibid., 200.

95. Ibid., 212-237.

96. Ibid., 234, 236-377.

97. Dawkins, *The God Delusion,* 24, 137-90.

98. Ibid., 147.

99. Ibid., 202, 205, 208-09. For Dawkins, therefore, religion is the "psychological byproduct of the misfiring of several of these modules [collections of brain organs], for example the modules for forming theories of other minds, for forming coalitions, and for discriminating in favor of in-group members and against others." 209, 218, 221, 233. Dawkins also considers memes "units of cultural inheritance," analogues of genes, and part of his ultimate explanation for religion. This interplay of genes and memes, for Dawkins, is responsible for human morality. 222-23, 231-33.

100. Dawkins, *The God Delusion,* 209-10.

101. Ibid.

102. Ibid., 251.

103. Dennett, *Darwin's Dangerous Idea,* 21.

104. Ibid., 50.

105. Ibid., 18 (emphasis in original).

106. Ibid., 25, 68.

107. Ibid., 82-83.

108. Ibid., 83 (emphasis omitted).

109. Ibid., 365-66, 20.

110. Ibid., 145, 310-11.

111. *Edwards v. Aguillard,* 482 U.S. 578 (1987). In 1987, the US Supreme Court ruled decisively that the teaching of creation science in public schools violates the First Amendment prohibition against establishment of religion.

112. Haught, *Science and Religion,* 53-54.

113. Michael J. Behe, "Irreducible Complexity, Obstacle to Darwinian Evolution" in *Debating Design: From Darwin to DNA,* eds., William A. Dembski and Michael Ruse (New York: Cambridge University Press, 2004), 354.

114. Ibid., 355, 367.

115. William A. Dembski, "The Logical Underpinnings of Intelligent Design," in *Debating Design,* 319-23, 323.

116. Stephen C. Meyer, "The Cambrian Information Explosion, Evidence for Intelligent Design," in *Debating Design,* 372-74, 378-89.

117. Francisco J. Ayala, "Designed without Designer, Darwin's Greatest Discovery" in Dembski and Ruse, *Debating Design,* 58-64, 69, 71-72; Haught, *Deeper Than Darwin,* 89-90.

118. E. O. Wilson, *The Creation: An Appeal to Save Life on Earth* (New York: W. W. Norton, 2006), 166.

119. *Kitzmiller v. Dover Area School District*, 400 F. Supp. 2d 707, 720 (M.D. Pa. 2005).

120. Ibid., 400 F. Supp. 2d at 718.

121. Ibid., 400 F. Supp. 2d at 721-22.

122. Ibid., 400 F. Supp. 2d at 745.

123. Ibid., 400 F. Supp. 2d at 735, 737.

124. Ibid., 400 F. Supp. 2d at 737.

125. Ibid., 400 F. Supp. 2d at 740-41.

126. Ibid., 400 F. Supp. 2d at 745.

127. Kenneth R. Miller, "Darwin, God, and Dover, What the Collapse of 'Intelligent Design' Means for Science and Faith in America," in *The Religion and Science Debate: Why Does It Continue?*, ed. Harold W. Attridge (New Haven: Yale University Press, 2009), 81 (emphasis in original).

128. International Theological Commission, "Communion and Stewardship: Human Persons Created in the Image of God," *Report of the International Theological Commission*, 2004, para. 64, in Ibid., 91.

129. Haught, *Making Sense of Evolution*, 58-63.

130. Ibid., 63.

131. Alfred North Whitehead, *Adventures of Ideas* (New York: Free Press, 1933), 265; Alfred North Whitehead, *Process and Reality*, corr. ed., eds. David Ray Griffin and Donald W Sherburne (New York: Free Press, 1978), 105.

132. Whitehead, *Process and Reality*, 111.

133. In 1996, Pope John Paul II agreed that "the theory of evolution is no longer a mere hypothesis. It is... accepted by researchers, following a series of discoveries in various fields of knowledge." Quoted in Ayala, "Designed without Designer, Darwin's Greatest Discovery" in Dembski and Ruse, *Debating Design*, 58-59.

134. Keith Ward, *Why There Almost Certainly Is a God: Doubting Dawkins* (Oxford: Lion, 2008), 20, 145.

135. Ibid., 12.

136. Dawkins, *The God Delusion*, 159.

137. Ward, *Why There Almost Certainly Is a God*, 61, 66.

138. Bernard Lonergan, S.J., *Insight: a Study of Human Understanding*, 3rd ed. (New York: Philosophical Library, 1970), xvii-xxx, in Haught, *Is Nature Enough?*, 125.

139. Thomas Nagel, *Mind and Cosmos, Why the Materialist Neo-Darwinian Conception of Nature Is Almost Certainly False* (Oxford: Oxford University Press, 2012), 128.

140. Ibid., 121, 123. Nagel's idea that scientific reasoning can uncover nature's inherent teleology is itself a misperception of the epistemological limits of science.

141. Ibid., 127-28 and book title.

Chapter 9. Conclusion

1. Alfred North Whitehead, *The Concept of Nature* (London: Cambridge University Press, 1964), 163. The Tanner Lectures delivered in Trinity College, November, 1919.

2. Rainer Maria Rilke, *Letters to a Young Poet* (letter of July 16, 1903) in Frances J. Ambrosio, *Philosophy, Religion, and the Meaning of Life* (Chantilly, VA: The Teaching Company, 2009), Course Guidebook, 1.

3. Friedrich Nietzsche, *The Gay Science* (1882) in *The Portable Nietzsche*, 95.

4. Baumer, *Modern European Thought*, 415.

5. Ferguson, *The War of the World*, xxxiv.

6. Barrett, *Irrational Man*, 68.

7. Richard J. Bernstein, *Beyond Objectivism and Relativism: Science, Hermeneutics, and Praxis* (Philadelphia: University of Pennsylvania Press, 1983), 86-93.

8. Stumpf, *PHILOSOPHY: History & Problems*, 24-27.

9. Stephen Greenblatt, *The Swerve* (New York: W. W. Norton, 2011).

10. Stumpf, *PHILOSOPHY: History & Problems*, 105-10.

11. Greenblatt, *The Swerve*, 253.

12. Ibid., 253-55. In 1551, the Council of Trent formally decreed the doctrine of transubstantiation during the Counter-Reformation following the Protestant revolt.

13. Hawking and Mlodinow, *The Grand Design*, 100.

14. Bernstein, *Beyond Objectivism and Relativism*, 46.

15. Ibid., 18.

16. Ibid., 19, 48.

17. Whitehead, *The Concept of Nature*, 163.

18. Whitehead, *Science and the Modern World*, 142.

19. Bernstein, *Beyond Objectivism and Relativism*, 133.

20. Dennett, *Darwin's Dangerous Idea*, 63.

21. Heidegger, *Basic Writings*, 58, 112; Bernstein, *Beyond Objectivism and Relativism*, 113.

22. Whitehead, *Science and the Modern World*, 91; Bernstein, *Beyond Objectivism and Relativism*, 126.

23. Bernstein, *Beyond Objectivism and Relativism*, 138-39.

24. Haught, *Is Nature Enough?*, 120.

25. Ibid., 121-25.

26. John F. Haught, *God after Darwin: A Theology of Evolution* (Boulder, CO: Westview Press, 2000), 33.

27. Haught, *God After Darwin* (Revised Edition, 2008), Chapter 11.

28. Read Carter Phipps, *Evolutionaries, Unlocking the Spiritual and Cultural Potential of Science's Greatest Idea* (New York: Harper Perennial, 2012).

29. As Haught explains, genuine theology seeks "levels of depth to

which science cannot reach," "assumes that there is more than one level of explanation for everything," "endorses the idea of a plurality of explanations, perhaps hierarchically arranged, such that no discipline can give an exhaustive account of anything whatsoever," and recognizes that the Darwinian explanation "is inevitably an abstraction and needs to be complemented by a luxuriant explanatory pluralism." John F. Haught, "Darwin, Design, and the Divine Providence," in *Debating Design*, 237.

30. See the discussion of Creation and Original Sin from the perspective of evolutionary theology in Haught, *God after Darwin*, 36-44, 137-44.

31. "The notion of an originally and instantaneously completed creation is theologically unthinkable," since it would be a mere "appendage of God, and not a world unto itself; nor could God conceivably transcend such a world." Ibid., 37.

32. Whitehead, *Science and the Modern World*, 190-92; also, Alfred North Whitehead, *Adventures of Ideas* (New York: Free Press, 1993), 273-83. Evolutionary thought also might envision God, as "letting the world be itself," by lovingly withdrawing and "allowing the world to emerge on its own so as to attain a possible status of being capable of the deep relationship with God." Haught, *God after Darwin*, 40.

33. Haught, *God after Darwin*, 36.

34. Bernstein, *Beyond Objectivism and Relativism*, 165-69.

35. As Bernstein rightfully stresses, however, "techne [technical knowledge] without phronesis [practical wisdom] is blind, while phronesis without techne is empty." Ibid., 161.

36. Jurgen Habermas, "What Is Universal Pragmatics?" and "Historical Materialism and the Development of Normative Structures," in his *Communication and the Evolution of Society*, trans. Thomas McCarthy (Boston: Beacon Press, 1979), 3, 119-20, in Bernstein, *Beyond Objectivism and Relativism*, 185-86, 188.

37. Richard Rorty , "Pragmatism, Relativism, and a Rationalism," *Proceedings and Addresses of the American Philosophical Association* 53 (1980): 354, in Bernstein, *Beyond Objectivism and Relativism*, 201, 203-04.

38. E. O. Wilson, *Consilience* (New York: Alfred A. Knopf, 1998), 4-6.

39. Pierre Teilhard de Chardin, *The Future of Man* (New York: Harper & Row, 1964), 11, 13, 16-17 ("A Note on Progress," August 10, 1920).

Bibliography

Cultural, Intellectual, and Military History

Arnold, Matthew. *Culture and Anarchy and Other Writings.* Edited by Stefan Collini. Cambridge: Cambridge University Press, 1993.

Aschheim, Steven E. *The Nietzsche Legacy in Germany, 1890-1990.* Berkeley: University of California Press, 1992.

Barzun, Jacques. *Classic, Romantic and Modern.* Chicago: University Of Chicago Press, 1961.

Baumer, Franklin L. *Modern European Thought: Continuity and Change in Ideas, 1600-1950.* New York: McMillan Publishing, 1977.

Bond, Brian. *The Unquiet Western Front: Britain's Role in Literature and History.* Cambridge: Cambridge University Press, 2002.

Chambers, Mortimer, Barbara Hanawalt, Theodore K. Rabb, Isser Woloch, and Lisa Tiersten. *The Western Experience.* 10th ed. New York: McGraw-Hill, 2010.

Clark, Christopher. *The Sleepwalkers: How Europe Went to War in 1914.* New York: HarperCollins, 2012.

Clark, Kenneth. *Civilisation: A Personal View.* New York: Harper & Row, 1969.

Eksteins, Modris. *Rites of Spring: The Great War and the Birth of the Modern Age.* Boston: Houghton Mifflin Company, 1989.

Ferguson, Niall. *The War of the World: Twentieth-Century Conflict and the Descent of the West.* New York: Penguin Books, 2006.

_____. *The Pity of* War. Great Britain: Penguin Press, 1998.

Freud, Sigmund. *Civilization and Its Discontents.* Translated and edited by James Strachey. New York: W. W. Norton, 2010.

_____. *Introductory Lectures on Psychoanalysis.* Translated and edited by James Strachey. New York: W. W. Norton, 1966.

Fussell, Paul. *The Great War and Modern Memory.* Oxford: Oxford University Press, 1975.

Goebel, Stefan. *The Great War and Medieval Memory: War, Remembrance and Medievalism in Britain and Germany, 1914-1940.* Cambridge: Cambridge University Press, 2007.

Greenberg, Robert. *Great Masters: Mahler — His Life & Music.* Course Guidebook. Chantilly: The Teaching Company, 2001.

Hoffman, Frederic J. *The 20s: American Writing in the Postwar Decade.* Revised edition. New York: Free Press, 1965.

Howard, Michael. *The First World War: A Very Short Introduction.* Oxford: Oxford University Press, 2007.

Hynes, Samuel. *A War Imagined: The First World War and English Culture.* New York: Atheneum, 1991.

Keegan, John. *The First World War.* New York: Vintage Books, 1999.

Kitto, H. D. F. *The Greeks.* London: Penguin Books, 1991.

Kramer, Lloyd. *European Thought and Culture in the 20th Century.* Chantilly, VA: The Teaching Company, 2002.

Leuchtenburg, William E. *The Perils of Prosperity, 1914-32.* Chicago: University of Chicago Press, 1958.

Liulevicius, Vejas Gabriel. *World War I: The "Great War."* Course Guidebook (Parts 1, 3). Chantilly, VA: The Teaching Company, 2006.

Phipps, Carter. *Evolutionaries: Unlocking the Spiritual and Cultural Potential of Science's Greatest Idea.* New York: Harper Perennial, 2012.

Rubenstein, Richard L. *The Cunning of History: The Holocaust and the American Future.* New York: Harper Colophon Books, 1978.

Sherman, Irwin W. and Vilia G. Sherman. *Biology: A Human Approach.* 2nd ed. New York: Oxford University Press, 1979.

Stromberg, Roland N. *Redemption by War: The Intellectuals and 1914.* Lawrence: The Regents Press of Kansas, 1982.

Taylor, A. J. P. *The First World War: An Illustrated History.* New York: Perigee Books, 1980.

Tuchman, Barbara W. *The Guns of August.* New York: Ballantine Books, 1962.

_____. *The Proud Tower: A Portrait of the World before the War, 1890-1914.* New York: Ballantine Books, 1962.

Wohl, Robert. *The Generation of 1914.* Cambridge: Harvard University Press, 1979.

Theology

Ayala, Francisco J. "Design without Designer, Darwin's Greatest Discovery" in Dembski and Ruse, *Debating Design, From Darwin to DNA*, 55-80.

Barth, Karl. *The Word of God and the Word of Man* (1924) in vol. 55 of *Great Books of the Western World, Philosophy and Religion: Selections from the Twentieth Century.* Edited by Mortimer J. Adler. Chicago: Encyclopaedia Britannica, 2007.

Crites, Stephen D. "The Gospel According to Hegel," *The Journal of Religion* 46 (1966).

Gogarten, Friedrich. *The Reality of Faith: The Problem of Subjectivism in Theology.* Translated by Carl Michlson. Philadelphia: Westminster Press, 1957.

Harnack, Adolph von. *What Is Christianity?* Translated by Thomas Bailey Saunders. New York: Harper & Row, 1957.

Haught, John F. *Deeper Than Darwin: The Prospect for Religion in the Age of Evolution.* Boulder: Westview Press, 2003.

_____. *God After Darwin: A Theology of Evolution.* Boulder: Westview Press, 2000.

_____. *Is Nature Enough? Meaning and Truth in the Age of Science.* Cambridge: Cambridge University Press, 2007.

_____. *Making Sense of Evolution: Darwin, God, and the Drama of Life.* Louisville: Westminster John Knox Press, 2010.

_____. *Nature and Purpose.* Washington, DC: University Press of America, 1980.

_____. *Science and Religion: From Conflict to Conversation.* New York: Paulist Press, 1995.

_____. *What Is Religion? An Introduction.* New York and New Jersey: Paulist Press, 1990.

Kierkegaard, Søren. *Concluding Unscientific Postscript* in Walter Kaufmann, *Existentialism from Dostoyevsky to Sartre.* New York: New American Library,1975.

_____. *FEAR AND TREMBLING* and *THE SICKNESS UNTO DEATH.* Translated with introductions and notes by Walter Lowrie. New York: Doubleday Anchor Books, 1954.

_____. *Philosophical Fragments, Johannes Climacus.* Edited and translated with an introduction and notes by Howard V. Hong and Edna H. Hong. Princeton: Princeton University Press, 1987.

King, Thomas M. *Teilhard's Mysticism of Knowing.* New York: Seabury Press, 1981.

King, Ursula. Introduction to *Pierre Teilhard De Chardin: Writings.* Maryknoll, NY: Orbis Books, 1999.

_____. "Postscript: The Heart of Teilhard's Faith Questioned and Reaffirmed" in *Pierre Teilhard De Chardin: Writings,* 165-73.

Livingston, James C. *Modern Christian Thought: The Enlightenment and the Nineteenth Century.* Minneapolis: Fortress Press, 2006.

Livingston, James C. and Francis Schuessler Fiorenza. *Modern Christian Thought: The Twentieth Century.* Minneapolis: Fortress Press, 2006.

Lucas, Mary and Ellen Lucas. *Teilhard.* New York: McGraw-Hill, 1981.

Maritain, Jacques. *Bergsonian Philosophy and Thomism.* Translated by Mabel L. Andison and J. Gordon Andison. New York: Philosophical Library, 1955.

_____. *The Peasant of the Garonne; An Old Layman Questions Himself about the Present Time.* Translated by Michael Cuddihy and Elizabeth Hughes. New York: Holt, Rinehart and Winston, 1968.

Marsden, George M. *Fundamentalism and American Culture: The Shaping of Twentieth-Century Evangelicalism, 1870-1925.* New York: Oxford University Press, 1980.

Numbers, Ronald L. "Aggressors, Victims, and Peacemakers: Historical Actors in the Drama of Science and Religion" in *The Religion and Science Debate: Why Does It Continue?* Edited by Harold W. Attridge. New Haven: Yale University Press, 2009.

_____. "The Creationists," in *God in Nature: Historical Essays on the Encounter between Christianity and Science.* Edited by David C. Lindberg and Ronald L. Numbers. Berkeley: University of California Press, 1986.

Pennock, Robert T. *Tower of Babel: The Evidence against the New Creationism.* Cambridge: MIT Press, 1999.

Principe, Lawrence M. *Science and Religion.* Chantilly, VA: The Teaching Company, 2006. Course Guidebook.

Schleiermacher, Friedrich. *Second Speech: The Nature of Religion* in *Friedrich Schleiermacher on Religion: Speeches to Its Cultured Despisers.* New York: Harper & Row, 1958.

Stanford Encyclopedia of Philosophy. "Jacques Maritain." http://plato.stanford.edu/entries/maritain/ (accessed May 17, 2012).

Teilhard de Chardin, Pierre. *The Future of Man.* New York: Harper & Row, 1964.

_____. *The Phenomenon of Man.* New York: Harper Torch Books,1965.

_____. *Science and Christ.* New York: Harper & Row, 1965. See esp. chap. XII, "Catholicism and Science"; chap. VI "Christianity in the World"; chap. IV, "My Universe"; chap. XIX "Research, Work and Worship"; chap. III, "Science and Christ or Analysis and Synthesis"; and chap. VIII, "Some Reflections on the Conversion of the World."

_____ and Ursula King. *Pierre Teilhard De Chardin: Writings.* Maryknoll, NY: Orbis Books, 2011.

Ward, Keith. *Why There Almost Certainly Is a God: Doubting Dawkins.* Oxford: Lion, 2008.

Zahrnt, Heinz. *The Question of God: Protestant Theology in the Twentieth Century.* Translated by R. A. Wilson. New York: Harvest Book, 1966.

Philosophy

Ambrosio, Francis J. *Philosophy, Religion, and the Meaning of Life.* Chantilly, VA: The Teaching Company, 2009.

Ayala, Francisco J. "Design without Designer: Darwin's Greatest Discovery" in Dembski and Ruse, *Debating Design: From Darwin to DNA,* 55-80.

Barrett, William. *Death of the Soul: From Descartes to the Computer.* New York: Anchor Books, 1986.

_____. *The Illusion of Technique: A Search for Meaning in a Technological Civilization.* Garden City: Anchor Books, 1979.

_____. *Irrational Man*. Garden City: Doubleday Anchor Books, 1958.

Behe, Michael J. "Irreducible Complexity, Obstacle to Darwinian Evolution" in Dembski and Ruse, *Debating Design: From Darwin to DNA*, 352-70.

Bergson, Henri. *Creative Evolution* (1907) in Hakim, *Historical Introduction To Philosophy*, 692-700.

_____. *The Two Sources of Morality and Religion*. New York: Henry Holt, 1935.

Bernstein, Richard J. *Beyond Objectivism and Relativism: Science, Hermeneutics, and Praxis*. Philadelphia: University of Pennsylvania Press, 1983.

Burtt, Edwin Arthur. *The Metaphysical Foundations of Modern Physical Science: A Historical and Critical Essay*. Rev. ed. London: Routledge & Kegan Paul, 1950.

Cahoone, Lawrence. *The Modern Intellectual Tradition: From Decartes to Derrida*. Chantilly, VA: The Teaching Company, 2010. Lectures and Course Guide on Heidegger.

Dawkins, Richard. *The Blind Watchmaker: Why the Evidence of Evolution Reveals a Universe without Design*. New York: W. W. Norton, 1986.

_____. *The God Delusion*. Boston: Houghton Mifflin, 2008.

Dembski, William A. and Michael Ruse, eds. *Debating Design: From Darwin to DNA*. New York: Cambridge University Press, 2004.

Dembski, William A. "The Logical Underpinnings of Intelligent Design," in Dembski and Ruse, *Debating Design: From Darwin to DNA,* 311-30.

Dennett, Daniel C. *Darwin's Dangerous Idea: Evolution and the Meanings of Life*. New York: Simon & Schuster, 1995.

Descartes, René. *Meditations on the First Philosophy in Which the Existence of God and the Distinction between Mind and Body Are Demonstrated*, Meditation III, *Of God: That He Exists* in Vol. 28 of *Great Books of the Western World: Bacon, Descartes, Spinoza*. Edited by Mortimer J. Adler. Chicago: Encyclopaedia Britannica, 2007.

Desmond, Adrian and James Moore. *Darwin*. New York: Warner Books, 1991.

Grayling, A. C. *Russell: A Very Short Introduction*. Oxford: Oxford University Press, 2002.

_____. *Wittgenstein: A Very Short Introduction*. Oxford: Oxford University Press, 2001.

Greene, Theodore M. Introduction to *Kant Selections*. Edited by Theodore M. Greene. New York: Charles Scribner's Sons, 1957.

Hakim, Albert B. *Historical Introduction To Philosophy*. 2nd ed. New York: Macmillan Publishing, 1992.

Hawking, Stephen, and Leonard Mlodinow, *The Grand Design*. New York: Bantam Books, 2012.

Heidegger, Martin. *Basic Writings from Being and Time (1927) to The Task of Thinking (1964)*. Edited, with general introduction and introductions to each section, by David Farrell Krell. New York: Harper & Row, 1977.

Hume, David. *An Inquiry Concerning Human Understanding*. Edited by Charles W. Hendel, Jr. New York: Liberal Arts Press, 1955.

_____. *An Inquiry Concerning Human Understanding*, Section IV, Part I, in *The Philosophy of David Hume*. Edited, with introduction by V. C. Chappell. New York: Modern Library, 1963.

Husserl, Edmund. *The Crisis of European Sciences* (1937) in Hakim, *Historical Introduction To Philosophy*, 748-53.

_____. *Ideas, General Introduction to Pure Phenomenology*. Translated by W. R. Boyce Gibson. New York: Collier Books, 1962.

Inwood, Michael. *Heidegger: A Very Short Introduction*. Oxford: Oxford University Press, 2000.

Isaacson, Walter. *Einstein: His Life and Universe*. New York: Simon & Schuster, 2007.

Kant, Immanuel. *Critique of Pure Reason* in *Kant Selections*. Edited by Theodore M. Greene. New York: Charles Scribner's Sons, 1957.

_____. *Theory of Ethics* in *Kant Selections*. Edited by Theodore M. Greene. New York: Charles Scribner's Sons, 1957.

Kaufmann, Walter. *Existentialism from Dostoevsky to Sartre*. New York: New American Library, 1975.

Lauer, Quentin. *Phenomenology, Its Genesis and Prospect*. New York: Harper Torchbooks, 1965.

Locke, John. *An Essay Concerning Human Understanding* (1690) in Vol. 33 of *Great Books of the Western World: Locke, Berkeley, Hume*. Edited by Mortimer J. Adler. Chicago: Encyclopaedia Britannica, 2007.

Lennox, John C. *God and Stephen Hawking: Whose Design Is It Anyway?* Oxford: Lion Book, 2011.

Lyotard, Jean-François. *The Postmodern Condition: A Report on Knowledge*. Translated by Geoff Bennington and Brian Masumi. Minneapolis: University of Minnesota Press, 1984.

Meyer, Stephen C. "The Cambrian Information Explosion: Evidence for Intelligent Design," in Dembski and Ruse, *Debating Design: From Darwin to DNA*, 371-92.

Miller, Kenneth R. "Darwin, God, and Dover: What the Collapse of 'Intelligent Design' Means for Science and Faith in America," in *The Religion and Science Debate: Why Does It Continue?*. Edited by Harold W. Attridge. New Haven: Yale University Press, 2009.

Monod, Jacques. *Chance and Necessity*. Translated by Austryn Wainhouse. New York: Vantage Books, 1972.

Moran, Dermot. *Edmund Husserl, Founder of Phenomenology.* Malden, MA: Polity Press, 2005.

Moyal-Sharrock, Danièle. *Understanding Wittgenstein's On Certainty.* New York: Palgrave Macmillan, 2004.

Nagel, Thomas. *Mind and Cosmos: Why the Materialist Neo-Darwinian Conception of Nature Is Almost Certainly False.* Oxford: Oxford University Press, 2012.

Nietzsche, Friedrich. *The Gay Science* (1882) in *The Portable Nietzsche.* Translated by Walter Kaufmann. New York: Vintage Books, 1967.

_____. *The Will to Power* (1895) in *Existentialist Philosophy, An Introduction,* 2d ed. Edited with text by L. Nathan Oaklander. Upper Saddle River, NJ: Prentice Hall, 1996.

Okasha, Samir. *Philosophy of Science: A Very Short Introduction.* Oxford: Oxford University Press, 2002.

Russell, Bertrand. *A Free Man's Worship and Other Essays.* London: Unwin Paperbacks, 1976.

_____. *Religion and Science.* New York: Oxford University Press, 1961.

Russell, John. *Science and Metaphysics.* New York: Sheed and Ward, 1958.

Sorell, Tom. *SCIENTISM: Philosophy and the Infatuation with Science,* London: Routledge, 1991.

Safranski, Rüdiger. *Martin Heidegger: Between Good and Evil.* Translated by Ewald Osers. Cambridge: Harvard University Press, 1998.

Stace, W.T. "Man against the Darkness." *The Atlantic Monthly* (September 1948): 53-58.

Stumpf, Samuel Enoch. *PHILOSOPHY: History & Problems.* 2nd ed. New York: McGraw-Hill, 1983.

Thilly, Frank. *A History of Philosophy.* 3rd ed. Revised by Ledger Wood. New York: Holt, Rinehart and Winston, 1957.

Wellmuth, John. *The Nature and Origins of Scientism.* Milwaukee: Marquette University Press, 1944.

White, Morton. *The Age of Analysis: 20th Century Philosophers.* New York: Mentor Books, 1957.

Whitehead, Alfred North. *Adventures of Ideas.* New York: Free Press, 1993

_____. *The Concept of Nature.* London: Cambridge University Press, 1964.

_____. *Process and Reality.* Corr. ed. Edited by David Ray Griffin and Donald W Sherburne. New York: Free Press, 1978.

_____. *Science and the Modern World.* New York: Free Press, 1967.

Wilson, E. O. *Consilience.* New York: Alfred A. Knopf, 1998.

_____. *The Creation: An Appeal to Save Life on Earth.* New York: W. W. Norton, 2006.

Wittgenstein, Ludwig. *Tractatus Logico-Philosophicus.* n.p.: Seven Treasures Publications, 2009.

Literature

Aldington, Richard. Introduction to *Women in Love*. New York: Viking Press, 1950.

Arnold, Matthew. "Dover Beach"(1851) in *The Norton Anthology of English Literature*, 1492-93.

_____. *Stanzas from the Grande Chartreuse* (1852) in *The Norton Anthology of English Literature*. 1493-98.

Barbusse, Henri. *Under Fire: The Story of a Squad*. Translated by Fitzwater Wray. n.p.: Digireads.com Book, 2010.

Bazin, Nancy Topping, and Jane Hamovit Lauler "Virginia Woolf's Keen Sensitivity to War, Its Roots and Its Impact on Her Novels" in Hussey, *Virginia Woolf and War: Fiction, Reality, and Myth*.

Bergonzi, Bernard. *Heroes' Twilight*. Manchester, UK: Carcanet Press, 1996.

Blake, William. "Auguries of Innocence" in *The Complete Poems*. Edited by Alicia Ostriker, 506-10. London: Penguin Books, 1977.

_____. *Jerusalem* in *The Complete Poems*, 635-796.

Bloom's Modern Critical Interpretations, Erich Maria Remarque's All Quiet on the Western Front. New edition. New York: Bloom's Literary Criticism, 2009.

Brooke, Rupert. "Peace" in Walter, *The Penguin Book of First World War Poetry*, 11.

_____."The Soldier" in Walter, *The Penguin Book of First World War Poetry*, 108.

Brooks, Peter. "An Unreadable Report: Conrad's *Heart of Darkness*," in *Heart of Darkness*. Norton Critical Edition, 4th edition. New York: W. W. Norton, 2006.

Carruth, Hayden. Introduction to *Nausea*. Translated by Lloyd Alexander. New York: New Directions, 1964.

Conrad, Joseph. *Heart of Darkness*. Norton Critical Edition, 4th edition. New York: W. W. Norton, 2006.

_____. *Lord Jim*. New York: Signet Classic, 1961.

Corngold, Stanley. *Lambent Traces: Franz Kafka*. Princeton: Princeton University Press, 2006.

Cummings, E.E. *The Enormous Room*. New York: Modern Library, 1949.

Dos Passos, John. *Three Soldiers*. New York: George H. Doran, 1921.

Eksteins, Modris. "Memory" in *Bloom's Modern Critical Interpretations, Erich Maria Remarque's All Quiet on the Western Front*, 57-79.

Eliot, T.S. *The Love Song of J. Alfred Prufrock* in *The Norton Anthology of English Literature: The Twentieth Century and After*, 2289-93.

_____. *The Waste Land* in *The Norton Anthology of English Literature: The Twentieth Century and After*, 2295-2308.

_____. "*Ulysses*, Order, and Myth" (1923) in *The Norton Anthology of English Literature: The Twentieth Century and After*, 2294.

Gill, John M. "'All These Fine People Were Arrested as Espions': Detainees in *The Enormous Room.*" (Fall 2006). Http://www.gvsu.edu/ english/ cummings/Gill14.pdf (accessed May 13, 2011).

Graves, Robert. *Good-Bye to All That.* New York: Anchor Books, 1998.

Greenblatt, Stephen. *The Swerve.* New York: W. W. Norton, 2011.

Hardy, Thomas. "'And there was a great calm' (On the Signing of the Armistice, Nov. 11, 1918)" in Hynes, *A War Imagined*, 256.

_____. "Channel Firing" (1914) in *The Norton Anthology of English Literature: The Twentieth Century and After*, 1877-78.

_____. "The Darkling Thrush" (1900) in *The Norton Anthology of English Literature: The Twentieth Century and After*, 1871.

_____. "Hap" (1866) in *The Norton Anthology of English Literature: The Twentieth Century and After*, 1851-52.

Hemingway, Ernest. *A Farewell to Arms.* New York: Charles Scribner's Sons, 1957.

_____. *The Old Man and the Sea.* New York: Charles Scribner's Sons, 1980.

_____. *The Short Stories.* New York: Scribner Classics, 1997.

_____. *The Sun Also Rises.* New York: Charles Scribner's Sons, 1954.

Hopkins, Gerard Manley. "Felix Randal" (1880, 1918) in *The Norton Anthology of English Literature*, 1655.

_____. "God's Grandeur" (1877, 1918) in *The Norton Anthology of English Literature*, 1651.

_____. "I Wake and Feel the Fell of Dark, Not Day" (1885, 1918) in *The Norton Anthology of English Literature*, 1657.

_____. "The Windhover" (1877, 1918) in *The Norton Anthology of English Literature*, 1652-53.

Hussey, Mark., ed. *Virginia Woolf and War: Fiction, Reality, and Myth.* Syracuse: Syracuse University Press, 1991.

Huxley, Aldous. *Brave New World.* New York: Harper & Row, 1969.

Kafka, Franz. *The Metamorphosis* in Vol. 60, of *Great Books of the Western World: Imaginative Literature: Selections from the Twentieth Century.* Translated by Willa and Edwin Muir. Edited by Mortimer J. Adler. Chicago: Encyclopaedia Britannica, 2007.

Kershner, R. B. *The Twentieth-Century Novel: An Introduction.* Boston: Bedford Books, 1997.

Krutch, Joseph Wood. *The Modern Temper.* New York: Harcourt, Brace, 1929.

Lawrence, D.H. *Women in Love*, New York: Viking Press, 1950.

Levenback, Karen L. *Virginia Woolf and the Great War.* Syracuse: Syracuse University Press, 1999.

Lewis, Pericles. "The Waste Land." *The Modernism Lab at Yale University*. http://modernism.research.yale.edu/wiki/index.php/The_Waste_Land (accessed October 26, 2010).

Macauley, Robie. Introduction to *Parade's End*. New York: Penguin Books, 1982.

Owen, Wilfred. "Dulce et Decorum Est" (1917-18) in *The Norton Anthology of English Literature: The Twentieth Century and After*, 1974.

_____. "Futility" (1918, 1920) in *The Norton Anthology of English Literature: The Twentieth Century and After*, 1976.

_____. "Mental Cases," in Walter, *The Penguin Book of First World War Poetry*, 218.

_____. "Strange Meeting" (1918) *The Norton Anthology of English Literature: The Twentieth Century and After*, 1975-76.

Poole, Roger. "'WE ALL PUT UP WITH YOU VIRGINIA,' Irreceivable Wisdom about War" in Hussey, *Virginia Woolf and War: Fiction, Reality, and Myth*.

Pound, Ezra. "Hugh Selwyn Mauberley (Life and Contacts)" in Walter, *The Penguin Book of First World War Poetry*. 248.

Remarque, Erich Maria. *All Quiet on the Western Front*. New York: Ballantine Books, 1982.

Reynolds, Michael S., ed. *Critical Essays on Ernest Hemingway's In Our Time*. Boston: GK Hall, 1983.

Richards, I. A. *Science and Poetry*. New York: W. W. Norton, 1926.

Sartre, Jean-Paul. *Nausea*. Translated by Lloyd Alexander. New York: New Directions, 1964.

Sassoon, Siegfried. "The General" (1918) in *The Norton Anthology of English Literature: The Twentieth Century and After*, 1961-62.

_____. "Blighters" (1917) in Walter, *The Penguin Book of First World War Poetry*, 181.

_____. "Glory of Women" (1918) in *The Norton Anthology of English Literature: The Twentieth Century and After*, 1962.

_____. "On Passing the New Menin Gate" (1928) in *The Norton Anthology of English Literature: The Twentieth Century and After*, 1963.

_____. "They" (1917) in *The Norton Anthology of English Literature: The Twentieth Century and After*, 1960-61.

Sarraute, Nathalie. *The Age of Suspicion: Essays on the Novel*. New York: George Braziller, 1963.

Schmigalle, Günther. "'How People Go to Hell': Pessimism, Tragedy, and Affinity to Schopenhauer in *The Sun Also Rises*." *Hemingway Review* 25 (1) (Fall 2005): 7-21.

Shaw, George Bernard. *Heartbreak House*. New York: Classic Books International, 2009.

_____. Introduction to *Heartbreak House*. New York: Classic Books International, 2009.

Shelley, Percy Bysshe. *Mont Blanc, Lines Written in the Veil of Chamouni* (1817) in *The Norton Anthology of English Literature*, 720.

_____. "Ode to the West Wind" (1820) in *The Norton Anthology of English Literature*, 730-32.

Slabey, Robert M. "The Structure of *In Our Time*" in Reynolds, *Critical Essays on Ernest Hemingway's In Our Time*.

Spiller, Robert E. *The Cycle of American Literature: An Essay in Historical Criticism*. New York: Mentor Book, 1960.

Stolz, Claudia Matherly. "Dos Passos's Three Soldiers: A Case Study." *West Virginia University Philological Papers* 51 (Fall 2004): 77.

Tancock, Leonard. Introduction to Emile Zola, *Germinal*. Translated with Introduction by Leonard Tancock. New York: Penguin Books, 1983.

Tennyson, Alfred, Lord. *In Memoriam A. H. H.* (1950) in *The Norton Anthology of English Literature*, 1231-1279.

Tetlow, Wendolyn E. *Hemingway's In Our Time, Lyrical Dimensions*. Lewisburg: Bucknell University Press, 1992.

The Norton Anthology of English Literature. 7th ed., Vol. 2. Edited by M. H. Abrams and Stephen Greenblatt. New York: W. W. Norton, 2000.

The Norton Anthology of English Literature: The Twentieth Century and After. 8th ed., Vol. F. Edited by Stephen Greenblatt, M. H. Abrams, John Stallworthy, and Jahan Ramazani. New York: W. W. Norton, 2006.

The Norton Anthology of American Literature: 1914-1945, 7th ed., Vol. D. Edited by Mary Loeffelholz. New York: W. W. Norton, 2007.

Thorburn, David. *Masterworks of Early 20th-Century Literature*. Chantilly, VA: The Teaching Company, 2007.

Walter, George. ed. *The Penguin Book of First World War Poetry*. London: Penguin Books, 2006.

_____. Introduction to *The Penguin Book of First World War Poetry*, viii-1.

Weinstein, Arnold. *Classics of American Literature*. Chantilly, VA: The Teaching Company, 1997.

_____. *NOBODY'S HOME: Speech, Self, and Place in American Fiction from Hawthorne to DeLillo*. New York: Oxford University Press, 1993.

Woolf, Virginia. *Mrs. Dalloway*. San Diego: Harvest/HBJ Book, 1981.

_____. "Modern fiction" (1925) in *The Norton Anthology of English Literature: The Twentieth Century and After*, 2087-92.

Wordsworth, William. *Lines Composed A Few Miles above Tintern Abbey, on Revisiting the Banks of the Wye during a Tour, July 13, 1798* in *The Norton Anthology of English Literature*, 239-51.

_____. Preface to *Lyrical Ballads, with Pastoral and Other Poems* (1802) in *The Norton Anthology of English Literature*, 239-51.

_____. "The Tables Turned, An Evening Scene on the Same Subject" (1798) in *The Norton Anthology of English Literature*, 228.

Art

Arnoldo, Javier. "War and Breakdown," in Kramer, *Ernst Ludwig Kirchner: Retrospective*, 151-73.

Benjamin, Walter. "The Work of Art in the Age of Mechanical Reproduction," (1936) in *Art in Modern Culture: An Anthology of Critical Texts*. Edited by Francis Francina and Jonathan Harris. New York: Phaidon Press, 1992.

Benson, Timothy O. "Mysticism, Materialism, and the Machine in Berlin Dada." *Art Journal* (Spring 1987) 1: 46-47.

Brandmueller, Nicole "The Expressionist in Berlin," in Kramer, *Ernst Ludwig Kirchner: Retrospective*, 55-69.

Cork, Richard. *A Bitter Truth: Avant-Garde Art and the Great* War. New Haven: Yale University Press in association with Barbican Art Gallery, 1994.

Dachy, Marc. *Dada: The Revolt of Art*. New York: Abrams, 2006.

Dempsey, Amy. *Styles, Schools and Movements*. London: Thames & Hudson, 2002.

Dietrich, Dorothea. "Hanover," in Dickerman, *Dada: Zürich, Berlin, Hanover, Cologne, New York, Paris*, 154-179.

Dickerman, Leah, ed. *Dada: Zürich, Berlin, Hanover, Cologne, New York, Paris*. Washington: National Gallery of Art, 2006.

_____. Introduction to Dickerman, *Dada: Zürich, Berlin, Hanover, Cologne, New York, Paris*, 1-15.

Fineberg, Jonathan. *Art Since 1940: Strategies of Being*, 2nd ed. Upper Saddle River, NJ: Prentice-Hall, 2000.

Hamilton, George H. *Painting and Sculpture in Europe, 1880-1940*. Baltimore: Penguin Books, 1972.

Hockensmith, Amanda L. "Hans (Jean) Arp," in Dickerman, *Dada: Zürich, Berlin, Hanover, Cologne, New York, Paris*, 460-61.

_____. "Kurt Schwitters," in Dickerman, *Dada: Zürich, Berlin, Hanover, Cologne, New York, Paris*, 485.

Hopkins, David. *Dada and Surrealism: A Very Short Introduction*. Oxford: Oxford University Press, 2004.

Karl, Frederick R. *Modern and Modernism: The Sovereignty of the Artist, 1885-1925*. New York: Atheneum, 1985.

Kramer, Felix, ed. *Ernst Ludwig Kirchner: Retrospective*. Frankfurt: Stadel Museum, 2010.

_____. "In Contradiction: Ernst Ludwig Kirchner," in Kramer, *Ernst Ludwig Kirchner: Retrospective*, 13-31.

Kriebel, Sabine T. "Cologne," in Dickerman, *Dada: Zürich, Berlin, Hanover, Cologne, New York, Paris*, 214-37.

_____. "George Grosz," in Dickerman, *Dada: Zürich, Berlin, Hanover, Cologne, New York, Paris*, 471-72.

_____. "Max Ernst," in Dickerman, *Dada: Zürich, Berlin, Hanover, Cologne, New York, Paris*, 470.

_____. "Otto Dix," in Dickerman, *Dada: Zürich, Berlin, Hanover, Cologne, New York, Paris*, 466.

Marinetti, F. T. "Manifesto of Futurism" in *The Norton Anthology of American Literature: 1914-1945*, 1501.

Mileaf, Janine and Matthew S. Witkovsky. "Paris," in Dickerman, *Dada: Zürich, Berlin, Hanover, Cologne, New York, Paris*, 346-72.

Nadeau, Maurice. *The History of Surrealism*. Translated by Richard Howard. Cambridge, MA: Belknap Press, 1989.

Oppmann, Sandra. "The 'New Style'" in Kramer, *Ernst Ludwig Kirchner: Retrospective*, 199-219.

Rosenblum, Robert. *Cubism and Twentieth-Century Art*. New York: Abrams, 1968.

Shattuck, Roger. *The Banquet Years: The Origins of the Avant-Garde France, 1855 to World War I*. New York: Vintage Books, 1968.

Sheppard, Richard. *Modernism—Dada—Postmodernism*. Evanston, IL: Northwestern University Press, 2000.

Sim, Stuart. "Postmodernism and Philosophy," in *The Routledge Companion to Postmodernism*. 2d ed. Edited by Stuart Sim. London and New York: Routledge, 2005.

Taylor, Michael R. "New York" in Dickerman, *Dada: Zürich, Berlin, Hanover, Cologne, New York, Paris*, 274-98.

Trodd, Colin. "Postmodernism and Art," in *The Routledge Companion to Postmodernism*, 2d ed. Edited by Stuart Sim. London and New York: Routledge, 2005.

Tzara, Tristan. "1918 Dada Manifesto," in *Dada: The Revolt of Art*. New York: Abrams, 2006.

Index